THE ART OF REVITALIZATION

D0140038

CONTEMPORARY URBAN AFFAIRS
VOLUME 12
GARLAND REFERENCE LIBRARY OF SOCIAL SCIENCE
VOLUME 1470

CONTEMPORARY URBAN AFFAIRS

RICHARD D. BINGHAM, *Series Editor*

THE ART OF REVITALIZATION
IMPROVING CONDITIONS IN DISTRESSED INNER-CITY NEIGHBORHOODS

SEAN ZIELENBACH

The Maxine
Goodman Levin
College of
Urban Affairs at
Cleveland State
University

THE URBAN CENTER

GARLAND PUBLISHING, INC.
A MEMBER OF THE TAYLOR & FRANCIS GROUP
NEW YORK & LONDON
2000

Published in 2000 by
Garland Publishing, Inc.
A member of the Taylor & Francis Group
29 West 35th Street
New York, NY 10001

10   9   8   7   6   5   4   3   2   1

Library of Congress Cataloging-in-Publication Data
Zielenbach, Sean
    The art of revitalization : improving conditions in distressed inner-city
neighborhoods / Sean Zielenbach.
        p. cm.—(Garland reference library of social science; v. 1470.
    Contemporary urban affairs ; v. 12)
    Includes bibliographical references and index.
    ISBN 0-8153-3597-0 (hardcover: alk. paper)—ISBN 0-8153-3598-9
    (pbk. : alk. paper)
    1. Urban renewal—Illinois—Chicago.   2. Community development,
Urban—Illinois—Chicago.   3. Inner cities—Illinois—Chicago.   I. Title.

HT177.C5 Z54 2000
307.3'416'0977311 21—dc21

                                                                99-043812

Printed on acid-free, 250-year-life paper.
Manufactured in the United States of America

The work that provided the basis for this publication was supported by funding under a grant from the U.S. Department of Housing and Urban Development. The substance and findings of that work are dedicated to the public. The author and publisher are solely responsible for the accuracy of the statements and interpretations contained in this publication. Such interpretations do not necessarily reflect the views of the U.S. Government.

This study was also supported in part by a grant from the Steans Family Foundation. The Local Initiatives Support Corporation/Chicago and the Woodstock Institute provided invaluable in-kind assistance.

Many thanks to all of those who helped with the project, including staff members at community organizations and at other local and city-wide institutions throughout Chicago; my colleagues at Northwestern University and at the CDFI Fund; and my family and friends. Your support has been tremendously appreciated.

Contents

List of Tables

Series Editor's Foreword

Sean Zielenbach's *The Art of Revitalization: Improving Conditions in Distressed Inner-City Neighborhoods* is a study of the kinds and causes of economic revitalization in 36 low- and moderate-income neighborhoods in Chicago. Zielenbach defines revitalization of low-income areas as "both the reintegration of the neighborhood into the market and the improvement of economic conditions for existing residents." His approach combines traditional physical redevelopment and private investment activities with an anti-poverty component and allows for the economic, political and social changes that have affected Chicago over the past several decades.

Zielenbach's quantitative analysis of these neighborhoods found no single factor which explained economic revitalization. Rather it was the interplay of numerous local individual, institutional, and organizational decisions interacting with geographic, economic, and social forces that had the most impact. Other important characteristics Zielenbach associates with redevelopment are physical amenities, community organizations, local leadership, and social capital. Quantitative analysis is supplemented by two detailed ethnographic case studies of demographically similar neighborhoods—North Lawndale on the city's west side and Englewood on the south side. The book concludes with a discussion concerning the role of government in neighborhood redevelopment.

Richard D. Bingham

THE ART OF REVITALIZATION

CHAPTER 1

Introduction

The litany of inner-city ills has become all too well-known. Local newscasts regularly chronicle murders, drug raids, and other social catastrophes in poor urban neighborhoods. Journalists and commentators routinely use terms such as "war zones" and adjectives such as "bombed out" to describe such communities. Policy makers decry the abject failure of public housing high-rises to provide safe shelter for the country's urban poor. All cite the neighborhoods' high rates of poverty, crime, and unemployment; their large percentages of high school dropouts, teenage mothers, and single-parent families; and their dearth of mainstream commercial, retail, and financial institutions. Scholars such as Elijah Anderson have even identified a violent "code of the street" unique to youths in these urban ghettos.[1]

The widespread urban rioting of the 1960s raised the problems of inner-city neighborhoods in the national consciousness. Assessing the riots, the Presidentially-appointed Kerner Commission concluded in 1968 that they had stemmed from urban economic and social distress. The Commission warned that the country was "moving toward two societies, one black, one white—separate and unequal."[2]

Although few publicly conclude that the Kerner Commission's prophecy has come true, conditions in urban America have worsened considerably in the past 30 years. Poverty rates in almost all of the country's major cities increased between 1970 and 1990. Baltimore, Cleveland, Chicago, Detroit, and Philadelphia had poverty rates between 20 and 32 percent in 1990, compared to 18 percent or less in 1970. The bulk of the increase has occurred in predominantly minority neighborhoods within these cities. Only three of Chicago's 77 designated community areas had poverty rates of 30 percent or more in 1970. Twenty years later, the city had 19 such community areas, all but one of which had a minority population of at least 53 percent.[3] During the same period the number of census tracts with poverty rates of 40 percent or more increased by roughly 400 percent in New York and 500 percent in Detroit. The total number of people living in high-poverty tracts throughout the country nearly doubled, from 4.1 million to 8 million.[4]

Once-stable middle-class urban communities have become socially and economically devastated areas. Consider the Chicago community of Washington Park. In the years following World War II, the neighborhood housed numerous members of the city's black middle class. A majority of residents held steady jobs, and numerous local institutions created a vibrant community. Yet between 1970 and 1990 the neighborhood lost almost 60 percent of its population. By 1990 the area's per capita income was only $4,994, its poverty rate exceeded 58 percent, and roughly half of its residents received public welfare assistance. A series of dilapidated, drug-infested public housing high-rises towered over the neighborhood. By 1994, dropout rates in the local high schools exceeded 57 percent and the median eleventh-grade reading score ranked in the bottom 15 percent nationally. The community had few retail establishments and received little in the way of conventional bank financing. Indicative of historical patterns of racial and economic segregation, roughly 99 percent of Washington Park's residents were black.[5]

Despite the widespread problems in inner-city neighborhoods, some of these communities have begun to show improvement. The South Bronx, cited by both Jimmy Carter and Ronald Reagan as an example of inner-city devastation, has attracted considerable private investment in the past few years. Single- and multi-family houses now sit on once-vacant lots. Retailers have opened a few stores in the area, and crime rates have declined. The Woodlawn neighborhood in Chicago saw its poverty rate fall in 1990 after years of increases. Developers recently broke ground for a shopping center in Chicago's North Kenwood/Oakland community, an area that had been largely devoid of private investment since the 1960s. Even Washington Park has experienced some revitalization. Thanks to the efforts of a local nonprofit, the community has a re-opened parochial school and some rehabilitated apartment buildings.

What distinguishes the revitalizing communities from those that continue to decline? Why do some poor urban neighborhoods seem to improve, stabilize, or decline at a relatively slow rate, while others experience an economic free fall? What can local leaders do to promote revitalization, and what factors are beyond their control? What conditions are necessary for the development of distressed inner-city neighborhoods? How can these communities attract private investment and improve conditions for their current residents?

This book addresses these questions through an analysis of low- and moderate-income neighborhoods in Chicago. Unlike previous revitalization studies, which have tended to focus on neighborhoods located close to a central business district, this one concentrates on improvements in severely economically distressed communities elsewhere in the city. It illustrates both the broader forces that affect urban development as well as the particular characteristics that enable conditions in some low-income neighborhoods to improve.

The remainder of this chapter outlines some of the factors inhibiting neighborhood revitalization as well as explanations for positive local change. It emphasizes the need to consider local neighborhood factors in the context of more macro-level economic, social, and political trends. Chapter 2 assesses different definitions of revitalization to develop a single, measurable way of viewing neighborhood improvement. It quantifies the extent of revitalization and decline that has occurred in Chicago in the past 20 years. Chapter 3 explains these changes by describing the impact of macro-level forces on Chicago since the end of World War II. It examines the decline of the city's neighborhoods and outlines both the opportunities and constraints with which revitalization efforts must deal. Chapter 4 quantitatively analyzes revitalization since 1979, using the indicators developed in Chapter 2, and presents a rationale for selecting two neighborhoods for more detailed case studies.

Qualitative, ethnographic analyses of two Chicago neighborhoods provide the basis for the second part of the study. Chapter 5 presents a comparative history of the revitalizing North Lawndale neighborhood and the stagnating Englewood community. Chapter 6 identifies and examines the causes of Lawndale's revitalization in light of Englewood's continuing struggles. It illustrates how various community-level factors interact to promote social and economic change. Chapter 7 draws upon the two neighborhood studies, as well as literature and examples from Chicago and other cities, to assess the role that major institutional and organizational actors play in revitalization.

Chapter 8 pulls together the quantitative, historical, and ethnographic components of the study to explain why certain economically distressed inner-city neighborhoods revitalize. It illustrates the interactions necessary for such improvement to take place and the factors that determine when (or if) it will occur. It also offers suggestions as to how to promote and how to evaluate the process.

FACTORS INHIBITING NEIGHBORHOOD REVITALIZATION

Neighborhood revitalization has emerged as a way of addressing the social and economic problems of cities. The strategy consists of multiple components, all concentrated in a particular geographic area experiencing economic distress. Revitalization involves the eradication of blight. It promotes increased economic activity in the form of business development and other private investment. It also serves as part of a broader poverty reduction effort. Because an individual's development depends in large part on the quality of his or her interaction with the surrounding environment, improving the condition of that environment can only improve the life chances for that particular individual. Effective neighborhood revitalization strategies cannot by themselves alleviate the poverty of low-income residents, nor can they eliminate the social and economic inequalities present in society. They can, however, increase the safety of an area, enhance its appearance, and make it a more livable place for its residents. Revitalization strategies can attract businesses that create additional jobs, some of which may be filled by individuals living within the community. In concert with more individually-targeted programs such as income transfers and improved health care, they can help improve the economic opportunities for low-income city residents. (Chapter 2 provides a more detailed discussion of these and other components of neighborhood revitalization.)

Despite the acknowledged need for inner-city development, a number of broader national trends have hampered the process. Perhaps most importantly, urban development efforts have taken place in the context of increasing suburbanization. Since the early 1800s individuals have sought to distance themselves from the congestion and grime of central cities. Millions of people have moved out of cities to quieter, more expansive outlying areas in search of the "American dream" of owning a home and having a yard. Determined to leave the hustle and bustle behind, they have incorporated their new locations as separate political entities. They no longer vote or pay taxes in the city and consequently have little responsibility for its condition.

Spurred by federal and state policies and programs that have encouraged suburbanization (the construction of interstate highways, tax breaks given to homeowners and relocating businesses, and the like), the out-migration of individuals and businesses from the central cities has accelerated considerably in the last few decades. More people now live in suburbs than in central cities, and most of the economy's new jobs are created in the suburbs. New "edge cities" such as Schaumburg, Illinois, and the intersection of Interstates 278 and 78 in New Jersey have emerged as retail and commercial nodes, pulling economic activity away from traditional centers such as Chicago, Newark, and New York.[6] The changing demographics have altered the political makeup of state and federal legislatures, with suburban representatives outnumbering their city counterparts. As a result, public policies tend to focus more on the needs of the suburban majority than on the concerns of the central cities. Representatives of city constituencies now tend to have much more difficulty enacting urban-specific programs than they did a few decades ago.

Suburbanization has hindered the ability of city officials to address the needs of their low-income neighborhoods. City governments must provide basic public services such as police and fire protection, street cleaning, and infrastructure maintenance for not just residents but also commuters and tourists who come to the cities for work and recreation. They often have responsibility for public education, recreation, and various social welfare services. Because many of the more affluent city residents have left for the suburbs, cities now contain a higher proportion of poor residents, whose material needs place additional demands on city treasuries. These various obligations, coupled with a declining revenue base, have created fundamental resource constraints for most city governments.[7] Cities' taxing powers are generally determined by their individual state legislatures and rarely extend beyond their geographical boundaries. In most cases cities can only extract property and income tax revenue from individuals and corporations who list the city as their primary place of residence or business.

Since many individuals and corporations are relatively mobile, they can choose the municipality in which they want to locate. Political economist Paul Peterson has argued that issues such as taxes, the quality of the local school system, and the quality of the labor force largely determine these location decisions. Cities therefore have to compete with each other and with suburbs to attract and retain people and businesses that will generate revenue. Officials try to improve their municipalities' economic and social attractiveness by creating a high-quality infrastructure, building a skilled workforce, ensuring public safety, and otherwise developing local amenities, all at a cost that maximizes the benefit/tax ratio for the average taxpayer. Because of their limited resources, local governments focus their energies on developmental policies that increase the city's economic competitiveness. They are not inclined to pursue redistributive programs such as affordable housing, remedial education, job training, and health care because such efforts increase the city's attractiveness to poor, low revenue-generating individuals. Cities that pursue such "redistributive" policies risk severe financial distress and possible bankruptcy, as occurred in New York City in the early 1970s.[8]

Public officials lavish particular attention on businesses because the jobs they can create have numerous "multiplier effects." A company and its employees pay taxes and consume local goods and services, which can lead to the hiring of more local residents, who would pay more taxes and consume more goods, and so forth. City officials therefore try to satisfy potential corporate investors' wishes by packaging desired land parcels and selling them at a reduced price, assisting with the cleanup of *brownfield* sites (former industrial zones that are presumed environmentally contaminated), offering breaks on local property and/or sales taxes, and committing to specific improvements in the local infrastructure. They justify the granting of these benefits by arguing that the public expenditures will be more than offset by the increased economic activity that the corporations will generate and (less publicly) that the non-provision of benefits would cause the companies to go elsewhere and thus deprive the city of their economic resources.

The typical pro-business, pro-growth approach to urban policy results from a number of economic and political factors. The nation's strong commitment to privatism encourages policies that promote business-oriented solutions to problems affecting the populace. Many public officials have come from the private sector and support corporate interests. Mayors are often predisposed to large-scale physical projects because of their visibility. The construction of a highway or a skyscraper indicates to voters that the officials are able to get things done. Focusing on downtown projects maximizes the number of people who will see them while showing potential corporate investors that the city is serious about creating a strong business climate. Satisfying the corporate community—the chief job generator in almost every major city—becomes crucial to maintaining and enhancing the city's economic prospects. Political economist Clarence Stone argues that the importance of the private sector to the city's well-being has effectively created governing regimes of corporate leaders and public officials.[9]

Pro-growth policies may well stimulate economic activity and generate tax revenues and job opportunities that benefit low-income residents. At the same time, they often tie up a significant portion of a city's more discretionary funds and have adverse effects on certain parts of the city. Efforts to redevelop downtown Atlanta, Boston, and Chicago have resulted in the demolition of some surrounding low-income neighborhoods and the displacement of their residents.[10] Citing these instances of "Negro removal" as well as his case studies of four small northeastern cities, political economist Ross Gittell concludes that the "trickle down aspects of development cannot be assumed; it often requires an engaged citizenry to ensure that the benefits from development are more evenly distributed" across the city.[11] Yet there are few countervailing interests strong enough to reshape development policies. Residents of poor neighborhoods may push for greater allocations of public resources for their communities (instead of for the central business district), but they usually lack the influence to alter allocational policies significantly. The residents are often resource-poor and relatively unsophisticated about the development process, and the groups that they form suffer from similar limitations. For the most part, they lack the money to devote to research, public education, and voter mobilization, and they therefore cannot force public officials to respond consistently to their needs. In contrast, the business community has reserves of financial and human resources that it can more easily use for desired political and economic ends. Corporations and their executives comprise some of the principal funders of public officials' campaigns, a position which bestows considerable political influence. A unified group of pro-growth businesses can often "buy off" potentially influential opponents. For example, Atlanta's corporate community won the support of the city's black middle class for certain downtown development projects by agreeing to support their affirmative action demands.[12] Mayors who have publicly challenged the political primacy of the corporate community and chosen to allocate scarce resources to neighborhood interests instead of business development projects have encountered private sector retrenchment and strong electoral opposition.[13]

Attaining widespread public support for inner-city revitalization programs also proves problematic because of the country's mixed feelings toward governmentally-sponsored anti-poverty efforts. Americans desire to help the less fortunate members of society, yet they also hold strong beliefs in the primacy of the private sector and the importance of individual autonomy and responsibility. Public opinion surveys continually illustrate a widespread belief in hard work as a predictor of success and unyielding faith in the free market as the best means for promoting economic gain. Regardless of race or income level, most citizens believe that people should be free to make whatever they can and are entitled to what they earn. They feel that individuals should take primary responsibility for their own material well-being. They believe government should ensure that individuals have a fair opportunity to make a living and attain their goals, but it should not guarantee people jobs or give certain individuals preferential treatment.[14] A majority of citizens feel that the public sector should do more to expand employment—by stimulating private sector activities.[15]

Policies to improve conditions for the poor inevitably confront what David Elwood, one of the individuals charged with reforming welfare in the Clinton Administration, has dubbed the "helping conundrums." The public believes that people should have enough money to support themselves adequately, but it does not favor providing direct income transfers. Instead, most Americans feel that individuals should earn money by working, even if their jobs do not pay enough to support them. Many suspect that income support programs decrease individuals' incentive to work. Furthermore, programs that target specific needy constituencies run the risk of stigmatizing that population and thus violating the principles of individual autonomy and governmental non-interference.[16]

A principal way that society has attempted to resolve these conundrums has been to distinguish between the "deserving" and the "undeserving" poor.[17] The former group encompasses people who have fallen on hard times primarily because of old age, bad luck, sickness, or other forces perceived to be outside of their control. These individuals (widows, orphans, the elderly, and veterans, among others) have either worked for a number of years and contributed to the community, served the country militarily, or simply experienced a debilitating illness or injury. Public opinion polls have consistently indicated strong support for programs to help those individuals who cannot help themselves, and policies to assist these "deserving" poor have generally been warmly received and successfully implemented. For example, between 1880 and 1910 the federal government devoted over one-fourth of its total expenditures to citizen pensions, including over 500,000 Civil War veterans.[18] The federal social security program has engendered widespread support in large part because it helps individuals perceived as truly needy and rewards recipients for their previous work.

The country has been much more reluctant to support programs that benefit the "undeserving" poor: able-bodied individuals who are economically disadvantaged. Sociologist Michael Katz argues that "the culture of capitalism measures persons, as well as everything else, by their ability to produce wealth and by their success in earning it; it therefore leads naturally to the moral condemnation of those who, for whatever reason, fail to contribute or prosper."[19] Assuming that there are ample opportunities for healthy people to profit from the system, many citizens perceive the able-bodied poor to be lazy, undisciplined, or morally weak. The alleged personal defects make them undeserving of public aid. In this view, denying public benefits to able-bodied citizens should force them to work and become mainstream members of the society.

Racial prejudice has also affected attitudes toward efforts to improve conditions for inner-city minorities. The prospect of integration has historically sparked violent responses among whites directly affected by the process. Boston experienced months of rioting in the early 1970s after Judge Arthur Garrity ordered the busing of children across the city to achieve racial integration in the public schools. Similarly, blacks attempting to move into predominantly white Chicago neighborhoods in the 1950s and 1960s often encountered hostility from the existing residents. Although racial violence has decreased considerably in the past 20 years, residential segregation persists at all income levels. Polls indicate widespread black support for integration as well as white support for the right of blacks to live where they want. Yet at the same time, whites consistently exhibit a preference not to live with a large number of blacks, under the belief that the presence of blacks decreases property values.[20] Such prejudice carries over into the workplace. Employers have perceived blacks and Latinos who reside in low-income urban neighborhoods to be illiterate, dishonest, unmotivated, involved with drugs, and the like. They have used residence to screen out potential employees and have employed race and class as proxies for residence.[21]

These attitudes have contributed to a national ambivalence about inner-city revitalization efforts. Public opinion polls taken over the past several decades indicate that roughly half of those surveyed support additional public spending on the problems of the cities. Numerous federal and state programs—including urban renewal, Model Cities and other Great Society initiatives, and enterprise zones—have attempted to improve inner-city conditions. Yet the continued decay of urban neighborhoods, coupled with the increased concentration of urban poverty, has convinced many citizens and policy-makers that such programs are inherently ineffective. Ronald Reagan expressed the sentiments of millions of Americans in 1982 when he characterized the federal War on Poverty of the 1960s as an "abysmal failure." He emphasized that $7 billion had been spent on urban renewal efforts between 1965 and 1974, yet more housing units had been destroyed in that time than had been created.[22] The antigovernment sentiment of many Republicans now in Congress, coupled with the Clinton Administration's concern with reducing the federal budget deficit, has precluded extensive federal support of inner-city revitalization efforts.[23] Although most individuals associated with neighborhood development have decried the government's retrench-ment, a few have publicly questioned the effectiveness of the entire place-based approach. John Foster-Bey, then a program officer at the MacArthur Foundation, argued in 1992 that antipoverty strategies should focus principally on helping low-income individuals and devote rela-tively little attention to the improvement of their surroundings.[24] Nicholas Lemann, a respected author who has written about the plight of the nation's cities, contended in 1994 that targeted community economic development strategies were destined to fail because the majority of resi-dents and potential investors had no interest in distressed neighbor-hoods.[25]

THE CASE FOR INNER-CITY REVITALIZATION

The sentiments and actions of certain policy makers notwithstanding, the improvement of inner-city neighborhoods is crucial to the well-being of not only those cities but also the nation. Cities continue to play a central role in the country's social and economic life. They have historically been the cradles of civilization, the primary meeting places where people come to exchange goods, services, and ideas. The concentration of people within a city promotes the interplay of ideas necessary for the de-velopment of culture and technology. Most of the symphonies, operas, theaters, and nightclubs in a metropolitan area are located in its central city. The diversity of people and lifestyles within a city creates a level of activity that challenges and stimulates people. The exposure to different people and ideas breeds a level of tolerance necessary for the develop-ment of civil society.[26]

The density of population within cities creates the economies of scale necessary for the development of business and industry. Many businesses depend on easy access to goods and services, access that can only be provided within a central city area. Despite the increased use of telecommuting and electronic interaction, companies that provide financial, informational, and legal services still require the extensive face-to-face contact that cities permit.[27] The concentration of population and business within central cities has led to the development of transportation, communication, and other infrastructures that are not always present in outlying areas. Taken together, these advantages make cities the primary economic engines driving the national economy. Despite the growth of its suburbs, Chicago continues to be the single largest job hub in its metropolitan area. More than half a million people work in the downtown Loop, a larger number than the other six largest employment hubs in the region. Three of those other job centers are located within the Chicago city limits.[28]

The economic and social health of cities depends on the quality of their neighborhoods. Areas with high concentrations of poorly educated workers are unattractive to companies requiring a skilled workforce. Since such businesses often base their location decisions on the presence of a talented labor force, cities with troubled neighborhoods can find their future economic prospects limited. Individuals and investors tend to shy away from blighted areas with high levels of crime and poverty, thereby reducing the level of social and economic interaction in those neighborhoods (and by extension, in the city as a whole). The financial burdens that these troubled communities impose negatively affect the entire region. Public officials need to devote additional resources to public safety in those areas and to programs that help meet the basic subsistence needs of the poor. Governments consequently have fewer monies available to spend on infrastructure improvements which are necessary for the continued growth of the metropolitan (and national) economy. Similarly, public agencies have fewer resources available for the many cultural and recreational facilities and activities that increase the quality of life in an area. Individuals and companies may well choose to go to areas that offer more amenities and fewer problems.

Healthy, dynamic city neighborhoods tend to provide a number of economic, social, and political benefits to the society. Stable neighborhoods can promote the development and maintenance of sound markets by lowering the cost of doing business. Because merchants trust that others will not steal from them and will pay their bills (trust that has developed through interpersonal relationships), they can keep prices lower and may extend informal lines of credit. With greater levels of trust, there is less need for formal regulations to guide behavior, which lowers the transaction costs of doing business.[29] For example, the lower security costs in such communities attract additional companies, which provide local residents with additional goods, services, and job opportunities. Even inner-city neighborhoods characterized by lower levels of trust and higher security costs often have distinct economic advantages. Many of these neighborhoods have transportation and communication infrastructures not available in more vibrant outlying areas. Using existing assets may well prove less costly than building from scratch in a community with rising land values.[30]

Neighborhoods provide venues for social interaction among individuals. These interactions help shape people's lives. The quality of individual educational and interpersonal skills depends on environmental factors such as the opportunities to which someone is exposed, the amount of positive reinforcement he or she receives, and the level of trust the person builds with others. Teenagers living in communities where many adults have high-status occupations are less likely to drop out of high school and/or become teen parents.[31] In contrast, children living in neighborhoods with high poverty rates, large percentages of female-headed families, and high population turnover are at greatest risk of maltreatment.[32] Interpersonal interactions create social networks that can help people find jobs. Not surprisingly, individuals living in communities with a high percentage of steady wage-earners typically have easier times finding gainful employment because their neighbors are more aware of available job opportunities.[33]

The social relationships within a healthy neighborhood help build a sense of trust and interdependence among local residents. People in these communities are often more likely to watch each other's children, help dig each other's cars out of snowdrifts, and provide emotional, moral, and even financial support to neighbors in times of need. These relationships create a shared sense of responsibility that translates into a type of self-governance. Acting together, residents create and maintain public meeting places such as parks, playgrounds, and streets. Equally importantly, they help ensure a level of safety and respect for others within the community.[34]

EXPLAINING NEIGHBORHOOD REVITALIZATION

An appreciation of the importance of inner-city revitalization has not translated into a widely accepted blueprint for its implementation. The inability of federal programs to turn around distressed urban communities has convinced the majority of policy makers that revitalization requires significant activity independent of the public sector. Yet there is relatively little consensus about the conditions and activities necessary for alleviating the problems of these communities. Researchers, policymakers, and practitioners have offered six different explanations for positive neighborhood change.

Neighborhood Location

Proximity to highly desirable locales makes certain communities appealing to both individuals and businesses. Individuals are attracted to neighborhoods that abut mountains, lakes, and other topographically defining features. Many people choose to live in neighborhoods close to their place of work; as central business districts continue to be major employment hubs, the communities surrounding downtown have an intrinsic appeal. Access to transportation lines (commuter trains, subways, highways, and the like) constitutes a distinct advantage for neighborhoods, as their residents can more easily commute to and from work, shopping, and cultural/recreational activities. Similarly, many neighborhoods have competitive locational advantages for particular corporations. Situated near major business centers and transportation and communication nodes, they are appealing to companies that benefit from proximity to downtown and to other businesses. Access to navigable rivers and lakes, seaports, rail lines, highways, and airports reduces the cost of obtaining raw materials and shipping finished products. Companies whose business depends on networks with wholesalers and/or financial and other professional service firms benefit from locating in areas in which these firms are clustered (generally close to the central business district). They can take advantage of existing economies of scale to lower their costs and increase their profits. The fact that many central-city neighborhoods have a large proportion of low-income residents makes them even more attractive to business, as many residents would presumably be willing to take moderate-wage positions.[35]

Although economists such as Michael Porter and countless realtors extol the value of location, it alone cannot explain revitalization. Many neighborhoods lie adjacent to central business districts, lakes, and transportation nodes yet have continued to experience severe economic decline. A static factor such as location cannot adequately explain why a community improved at a particular time. Chicago's Near West Side suffered from widespread economic and social decay for years despite being located directly to the west of the downtown Loop. Many of the neighborhoods that Porter lauds for their locational advantages are areas that corporations previously abandoned in favor of other areas within and outside the central city.

Local Physical Amenities

In addition to topographical features and transportation infrastructures, other physical characteristics can increase the attractiveness of a neighborhood and thus its potential for revitalization. Philip Clay and Dennis Gale, among others, have emphasized the importance of a neighborhood's housing stock in encouraging investment. Many people relish the opportunity to live in older, architecturally pleasing brownstones, for instance. They are willing to move into declining communities and renovate deteriorating housing, provided that the housing is cheap and physically sound enough to warrant the investment.[36] Neighborhoods with greater proportions of owner-occupants—generally those communities with larger numbers of detached single-family homes—also tend to be more likely to revitalize.[37]

At the same time, certain types of housing and land use minimize locational advantages and deter revitalization. The presence of dilapidated public housing high-rises often casts a pall over local economic and social conditions. Once seen as desirable residences by many low- and moderate-income families, many high-rises have become concentrated centers of crime, drug activity, and debilitating poverty. Median incomes of families living in public housing are less than one-fifth of the national average, and roughly 20 percent of public housing residents make less than a tenth of the local median income.[38] Environmentally contaminated brownfield sites also tend to dissuade investment, as developers and corporations hesitate to assume the risks associated with toxic waste left by previous industrial occupants. Again, the presence of such sites can counteract other advantages a neighborhood might have.

Local Institutions

Although an economically distressed neighborhood may enjoy locational, infrastructure, and housing amenities, its revitalization results from individual decision-making. Corporations and potential residents choose to invest in a community if they believe that the economic and social benefits outweigh the costs. They must feel that the neighborhood's future prospects warrant commitments of financial and emotional resources. Sociologists Richard Taub, Garth Taylor, and Jan Dunham have contended that individuals have a certain threshold at which they decide to invest, and that the threshold rises or falls based on the actions of other investors. Because of their size and resources (relative to individual investors or small businesses), large local corporations and nonprofit institutions such as hospitals can have a considerable influence on a neighborhood's future. By publicly affirming their own commitment to the community, they can effectively lower the investment threshold of other individuals and businesses. They can help stabilize the neighborhood's real estate market by purchasing properties, rehabilitating their existing holdings, publicizing the community's virtues, organizing crime prevention efforts, and generally encouraging interpersonal tolerance and interaction.[39] The decisions of a few individuals within an influential local institution can therefore have extensive ramifications for a neighborhood.

Institutions can play a critical role in spurring reinvestment, but their involvement in the process cannot be assumed. Many private and nonprofit institutions have left economically distressed urban neighborhoods for less troubled suburban regions. Of those that have remained, only a fraction have taken an active role in trying to improve local conditions. Local institutions often do not have obvious incentives for promoting revitalization, especially if conditions in the surrounding area do not directly affect them. Such institutions may be unwilling to lead the process, particularly if their stakeholders are ambivalent or opposed to extensive community activity.

Community Organizations

Like institutions, community organizations tend to have access to more resources than individual investors. These groups can effectively mobilize people, promote face-to-face interaction, define collective political and economic interests, and access larger pools of financial, technical, and informational resources.[40] Because of their nonprofit status, these organizations can better address issues of the public good than can many for-profit institutions. Since they are not constrained by the need to make money and satisfy their shareholders, the groups can undertake riskier, less cost-effective projects in communities with little market activity and private sector interest. They can draw on the resources of philanthropists to improve local conditions without having to worry as much about a direct economic return on the project. One of the more active types of local organizations in promoting inner-city revitalization has been the community development corporation, or CDC. CDCs typically strive to rejuvenate

their communities through real estate projects, especially the development of affordable housing and/or commercial/retail centers. Individuals
within and outside of the community development field have praised
them as catalysts of revitalization, able not only to improve conditions in
local real estate markets but also to promote community safety and increased local job opportunities.[41]

Despite their accomplishments, CDCs and other locally based organizations have not single-handedly revitalized distressed inner-city
neighborhoods. Their annual budgets, the vast majority of which are less
than $1 million, limit their ability to effect significant change. Their con-
tributions remain relatively unpublicized, and many individuals outside
of the CDCs' neighborhoods do not even know that such groups exist. Individuals associated with these community organizations readily acknowledge that the groups need the support of public and private sector
actors to implement specific projects, let alone to change entire neighborhoods. The success of the organizations' endeavors also depends on
the social characteristics of their neighborhoods. A CDC-sponsored retail center is more likely to become profitable in an area of greater social
stability than in one plagued by high levels of drug, gang, and criminal
activity.

Social Capital

As mentioned earlier, the type and extent of interpersonal relationships
within a neighborhood tend to have considerable economic, political, and
social effects on the community's residents. Communities with stronger
interpersonal networks, more wide-reaching social ties, and greater levels
of trust typically have higher levels of employment, lower high school
dropout rates, and greater appeal to individuals within and outside of the
neighborhoods. In effect, these relationships constitute a capital asset for
members of the community. People can draw upon others to help them
obtain jobs, carry out particular short-term or long-term projects, and otherwise achieve goals that they could not accomplish by themselves. These
mutually beneficial, reciprocal interactions generate intangible goods for
the community as a whole, a form of social capital.[42]

Francis Fukuyama has argued that modern economics places too
much emphasis on individuals' attempts to maximize their own personal
good through rational, profit-focused decision making. Economics ignores the aspect of human behavior that encourages people to assist other
individuals in need. Some of this "irrational" behavior may stem from ra-

tional calculations of future benefit (if I help someone now, he will owe me in the future), but much results from social and cultural norms promoting honesty, tolerance, and cooperation. These shared ethical values create more trusting communities, societies with greater respect and concern for individuals and their needs. Fukuyama contends that nations with higher levels of communal action produce higher levels of social trust, which facilitates greater economic stability and productivity.[43] Similarly, Robert Putnam contends that the greater presence of stronger civic communities—societies with higher levels of interpersonal interaction, trust, and participation in social organizations—explains the greater efficiency, legitimacy, and effectiveness of regional governments in northern Italy.[44]

Fukuyama's and Putnam's arguments apply to inner-city neighborhoods as well. Individuals who are more trusting of each other are more willing to join organizations that seek to improve local conditions. Because they believe that others will do their share, they are less likely to shun their responsibilities for projects requiring collective action; neighborhoods with greater amounts of social capital are better able to govern themselves. Trust breeds confidence and a sense of efficacy within the community, creating a friendlier investment climate and helping to attract the resources necessary for successful revitalization. The non-monetary nature of social capital enables it to exist in areas regardless of the level of financial wealth.[45] "Like conventional capital for conventional borrowers, social capital serves as a kind of collateral for men and women who are excluded from ordinary credit or labor markets. In effect, the participants pledge their social connections, leveraging social capital to improve the efficiency with which markets operate."[46]

Social capital does not develop by itself, however. It results from repeated decisions by community members to interact with each other to promote both their own goods and those of the broader society. In inner-city communities racked by fear of crime and distrust of one's neighbors, its development often requires the concerted leadership of certain individuals, organizations, and institutions determined to foster greater tolerance and interpersonal interaction.

Local Leadership

Revitalization results ultimately from the decisions of individual and corporate investors to commit time, money, and energy to the improvement of a neighborhood. The economic, social, and political disarray of many inner-city communities militates against investment, however. Concerted action generally requires some catalyst, usually an individual or group of individuals so determined to effect change that they are willing to risk failure. These individuals must be able to engage others in the process, convincing members throughout the society of the importance and viability of the redevelopment enterprise. Like leaders of any social movement, such individuals typically have visions of change, charismatic personalities, well-developed communication skills, and an ability to engender respect and support among potential participants.

Any explanation of social change necessarily involves a discussion of the role of the relevant leaders. While such individuals are crucial to the process, they operate within a broader community context. Certain people are more successful leaders than others, partly because of their innate talents and partly because of the socialization and support that they have received from their surroundings. The fact that some neighborhoods have stronger leaders than others results in part from chance, but in part because of characteristics within the individual neighborhoods. The odds suggest that two communities of similar size and demographics would produce a similar number of potential leaders. The extent to which that leadership materializes depends on a variety of community factors such as the extent of social capital, the strength and capacity of local organizations and institutions, and the availability of resources to implement the leaders' vision. Leadership is therefore intertwined with the other five components of revitalization previously outlined.

THE ART OF REVITALIZATION

Whether revitalization occurs depends principally on factors particular to an individual neighborhood. When it occurs is determined more by economic, political, and social factors largely outside of the neighborhood's control. Communities respond to and are shaped by public policies, regional and national economic trends, and racial and demographic shifts. Such forces have precipitated the decline of many inner-city neighborhoods. Other city-wide, regional, and national forces have created opportunities for revitalization; community-level characteristics determine the extent to which neighborhoods are able to take advantage of these changes.

The neighborhood-specific factors outlined in the previous section all play an important part in enabling revitalization to take place, yet none of these factors can solely account for change. Simply put, there is no clear-cut, overarching explanation for inner-city revitalization. The process is highly nuanced and at times downright messy, more of an art than a science. Instead of a single "magic bullet," revitalization requires a series of factors working in concert. A neighborhood's location and physical amenities determine its potential for revitalization. Local leaders associated with and supported by stable institutions and community organizations take advantage of those physical attributes to design and implement revitalization strategies. The extent to which the leaders and their strategies can succeed ultimately depends on the level of social capital present in the community.

NOTES

[1]Elijah Anderson, "The Code of the Streets," *Atlantic Monthly* (May 1994): 81–94.

[2]*Report of the National Advisory Commission on Civil Disorders,* by Otto Kerner, Chairman (New York: Bantam Books, 1968), p. 1.

[3]Rebecca London and Deborah Puntenney, *A Profile of Chicago's Poverty and Related Conditions* (Evanston: Northwestern Univ. Center for Urban Affairs, 1993), pp. 20–21, 32.

[4]Paul A. Jargowsky, *Poverty and Place* (New York: Russell Sage Foundation, 1997), pp. 30, 46.

[5]Socio-economic and demographic data from London and Puntenney and from the 1990 U.S. Census; education data from the Chicago Board of Education.

[6]See Joel Garreau, *Edge City* (New York: Doubleday, 1991). Edge cities are newer retail, commercial, and residential nodes located on the outskirts of older metropolitan areas, generally near modern transportation centers such as airports and/or interstate highway intersections.

[7]David Rusk outlines the problem in *Cities without Suburbs,* 2d ed. (Washington, DC: Woodrow Wilson Center Press, 1995). He argues that "inelastic" central cities, those that cannot expand their boundaries through annexation and similar policies, are particularly prone to high levels of economic and residential segregation, low central city bond ratings, high income gaps between the central city and the suburb, and low rates of economic growth.

[8]See Paul E. Peterson, *City Limits* (Chicago: University of Chicago Press, 1981).

[9]Clarence N. Stone, *Regime Politics* (Lawrence: University Press of Kansas, 1989).

[10]See, for instance, Stone, *Economic Growth and Neighborhood Discontent* (Chapel Hill: University of North Carolina Press, 1976) for a discussion of Atlanta;

John Mollenkopf, *The Contested City* (Princeton: Princeton University Press, 1983) for an examination of redevelopment politics in Boston and San Francisco; and Arnold R. Hirsch, *Making the Second Ghetto* (New York: Cambridge University Press, 1983) for an analysis of urban renewal in Chicago.

[11]Ross J. Gittell, *Renewing Cities* (Princeton: Princeton University Press, 1992), p. 92.

[12]Stone, *Regime Politics,* Chapter 5.

[13]For example, Dennis Kucinich's elimination of tax abatements to businesses and his refusal to sell the publicly owned Municipal Light System to the private Cleveland Electric Illuminating Company in the late 1970s prompted members of the local banking community to cut off Cleveland's credit and force the city into default. Kucinich was defeated in the subsequent mayoral election. See Todd Swanstrom, *The Crisis of Growth Politics* (Philadelphia: Temple University Press, 1985). Adolph Reed, Jr., contends that black mayors with electoral bases in poor neighborhoods are particularly likely to court business interests in order to allay the corporate community's fear that public resources will be allocated along racial lines and thus away from the predominantly white private sector. See "The Black Urban Regime: Structural Origins and Constraints," *Comparative Urban and Community Research* 1 (1988): 138–189.

[14]See Everett Carll Ladd, *The American Ideology* (Storrs, CT: Roper Center for Public Opinion Research, 1994), especially Appendix 2.

[15]Benjamin I. Page and Robert Y. Shapiro, *The Rational Public* (Chicago: University of Chicago Press, 1992), pp. 122–123.

[16]Elwood, *Poor Support* (New York: Basic Books, 1988), Chapter 2.

[17]See Michael Katz, *The Undeserving Poor* (New York: Pantheon Books, 1989).

[18]Theda Skocpol, *Social Policy in the United States* (Princeton: Princeton University Press, 1995), p. 37.

[19]Katz, p. 7.

[20]See Douglas S. Massey and Nancy A. Denton, *American Apartheid* (Cambridge: Harvard University Press, 1993).

[21]See Joleen Kirshenman and Kathryn Neckerman, " 'We'd Love to Hire Them, But . . .': The Meaning of Race for Employers," in *The Urban Underclass,* ed. Christopher Jencks and Paul E. Peterson (Washington, DC: Brookings Institution, 1991), pp. 203–232.

[22]Remarks at the National Black Republican Council Dinner (Washington), July 15, 1982.

[23]Many federal programs that directly or indirectly target inner-city communities have either been eliminated, reduced, or maintained at non-inflation-adjusted levels. Few, if any, monies have been made available for individuals or

communities not currently served. Jason De Parle expounds on the effects of these new federal policies on the affordable housing problem in "The Year That Housing Died," *New York Times Magazine* (October 20, 1996): 52–105.

[24]Foster-Bey, "Removing the Barriers: An Approach to Increasing Economic Opportunity and Reducing Poverty," paper prepared for the John D. and Catherine T. MacArthur Foundation, Chicago, 1992. One solution has been to focus on moving low-income inner-city residents to the more job-rich suburbs. Proponents cite the success of the Gautreaux program in metropolitan Chicago, in which eligible inner-city families have been placed in publicly supported suburban housing. These new suburbanites have consistently been better able to access jobs than have their counterparts who remained in Chicago. See James Rosenbaum and Susan Popkin, "Employment and Earnings of Low-Income Blacks Who Move to Middle-Class Suburbs," in *The Urban Underclass,* pp. 342–356.

[25]Lemann, "The Myth of Community Development," *New York Times Magazine* (January 9, 1994): 26–60.

[26]See Jane Jacobs, *The Death and Life of Great American Cities* (New York: Random House, 1961), especially Chapters 6 and 15, and *The Economy of Cities* (New York: Random House, 1969), Chapters 1 and 3.

[27]Keith Ihlanfeldt, "The Importance of the Central City to the Regional and National Economy," *Cityscape* 1 (June 1995): 125–150.

[28]See Siim Sööt and Ashish Sen, *Analysis of Employment Hubs and Work Trip Patterns in the Chicago Metropolitan Region* (Chicago: University of Illinois–Chicago Transportation Center, 1994).

[29]See Francis Fukuyama, *Trust* (New York: Free Press, 1995). He also contends that companies with a high level of trust between managers and workers may be more productive because of greater autonomy given workers.

[30]See Roger Bolton, " 'Place Prosperity vs. People Prosperity' Revisited: An Old Issue with a New Angle," *Urban Studies* 29 (1992): 185–203.

[31]Jonathan Crane, "Effects of Neighborhoods in Dropping Out of School and Teenage Childbearing," in *The Urban Underclass,* pp. 299–320.

[32]Claudia Coulton, Jill Korbin et al., "Community Level Factors and Child Maltreatment Rates" (Cleveland: Case Western Reserve University, 1994).

[33]See William Julius Wilson, *The Truly Disadvantaged* (Chicago: University of Chicago Press, 1987).

[34]See Matthew A. Crenson, *Neighborhood Politics* (Cambridge: Harvard University Press, 1983).

[35]Michael E. Porter, "The Competitive Advantage of the Inner City," *Harvard Business Review* 75 (May–June 1995): 55–71.

[36]See Phillip L. Clay, *Neighborhood Renewal* (Lexington, MA: D.C. Heath & Co., 1979) and Dennis E. Gale, *Neighborhood Revitalization and the Postindustrial*

City (Lexington, MA: D.C. Heath, 1984). The renovation of some of these desirable neighborhoods has involved the displacement of existing low-income residents, an issue that will be discussed in more detail in Chapter 2.

[37]Anthony Downs, *Neighborhoods and Urban Development* (Washington, DC: Brookings Institution, 1981), p. 76.

[38]Rob Gurwitt, "The Projects Come Down," *Governing* (August 1995): 18.

[39]Taub, Taylor, and Dunham, *Paths of Neighborhood Change* (Chicago: University of Chicago Press, 1984).

[40]See, for example, Susan Bennett, "Community Organizations and Crime," *Annals of American Association of Political and Social Science* 539 (May 1995): 72–84, and Peter Medoff and Holly Sklar, *Streets of Hope* (Boston: South End Press, 1994).

[41]See Avis Vidal, *Rebuilding Communities: A National Study of Urban Community Development Corporations* (New York: Community Development Research Center, 1992); Mercer Sullivan, *More than Housing: How Community Development Corporations Go About Changing Lives and Neighborhoods* (New York: Community Development Research Center, 1993); and Bennett Harrison, "Building Bridges: Community Development Corporations and the World of Employment Training," report prepared for the Ford Foundation, New York, September 1994.

[42]James S. Coleman, *Foundations of Social Theory* (Cambridge, MA: Belknap Press, 1990), pp. 300–321.

[43]See Fukuyama.

[44]Robert D. Putnam, *Making Democracy Work* (Princeton: Princeton University Press, 1993).

[45]Because of its nonmonetary quality, social capital is difficult to measure. Its value to a community consequently tends to be under-appreciated by investors and others associated with revitalization. Chapter 4 deals more directly with the issue of quantifying social capital.

[46]Putnam, "The Prosperous Community," *The American Prospect* (Spring 1993): 40.

CHAPTER 2

Conceptualizing and Operationalizing Revitalization

In order to determine the factors that enable certain inner-city neighborhoods to improve, we first must have a clear understanding of what constitutes revitalization. In common use, "inner-city revitalization" is a slippery concept. Some people equate it with gentrification, while others associate it with the alleviation of poverty. Revitalization can mean the physical redevelopment of blighted areas, the creation of additional jobs, the improvement of local infrastructure, and/or the elimination of "undesirable" individuals and businesses.

This chapter first examines the different approaches to inner-city revitalization. It analyzes both the conceptual and operational approaches of each perspective. Drawing from these blueprints, I offer a new framework for thinking about and measuring revitalization. The second part of the chapter develops a revitalization index that gauges economic conditions in a neighborhood in a given year and quantifies changes in those conditions over time. This index provides a means for analyzing the revitalization of low-income neighborhoods in Chicago.

DEFINING REVITALIZATION

The lack of a widely accepted definition of neighborhood revitalization results in large part from the complexity of the term "neighborhood." On one level, neighborhoods are places of residence. People choose to live in a particular area because of the social amenities that area offers. They build friendships with those living around them, attend local schools and churches, participate in various communal activities, and so forth.

Residents assess the neighborhood's wealth in social, psychological, and economic terms. The amount of interpersonal interaction, the strength of those relationships, the general feeling of inclusion, and the availability of social and economic opportunities all contribute to better-off neighborhoods. In short, the neighborhood-as-residence view implicitly considers revitalization as a process of improving conditions for people in the area.

An alternative view considers neighborhoods as economic entities. Places within a city have "exchange values" that determine the type and extent of development that takes place within them. Developers, investors, and others assess neighborhoods in terms of their potential for generating economic rewards, potential that manifests itself in the value of neighborhood land. The profitable uses of that land (and hence its value) may well change with variations in market demand. For example, property that is profitable today as a factory site may be more desirable in the future as the site of luxury condominiums, depending on broader economic and residential trends. From this perspective, neighborhood revitalization focuses more on the physical development (or redevelopment) of an area and the maximization of its economic value for property owners.[1]

Efforts to revitalize neighborhoods generally fall under one of these two categories. The first, which I loosely describe as individual-based approaches, focuses on improving conditions for the residents of a particular area. Ensuring the long-term viability of the neighborhood as a geographic place takes on secondary importance; a reasonable goal of many programs may be to enable individuals to leave the community for better opportunities elsewhere. In effect, these initiatives are variations on anti-poverty programs. The second category, place-based approaches, contains those revitalization strategies that emphasize the development of a neighborhood as a more economically viable entity. Improving property values is a primary goal, and bettering conditions for existing residents may be viewed as a less important outcome.

Individual-Based Approaches

1. Social Development

One of the most widespread approaches to neighborhood revitalization has been the improvement of local institutional capacity. Beginning in the early 1960s, foundations and public agencies have funded organizations and programs to build and enhance local public schools, community colleges, job training centers, day care facilities, health clinics, and police departments. By strengthening these institutions, policy makers have sought to develop the skills of individuals within a particular neighborhood while simultaneously improving the community's overall sense of livability. Indicators such as improved test scores; lower dropout rates, crime rates, and infant mortality rates; higher numbers of job placements; and higher levels of resident satisfaction all signify the social revitalization of a neighborhood.

2. Program-Driven Economic Development

Other people equate neighborhood revitalization with economic development, more specifically the generation and circulation of additional money in the community. Increasing the number and availability of jobs for local residents is a primary goal and generally features two reinforcing approaches. The first typically focuses on attracting companies to the neighborhood and/or keeping them there. Governmental and nonprofit agencies will often work with businesses to improve the mechanisms by which they buy, produce, and sell goods and services. They may offer technical and financial assistance to purchase land for expansion, modernize their plants, and so forth. The efforts seek to lower the costs of doing business in the area and thus make the neighborhood a more economically desirable place. The presence of more companies theoretically translates into additional job opportunities for local residents. The second job development approach involves preparing residents to be more productive workers. Businesses tend to locate in areas in which workers' skill levels are commensurate with the needs of the company. With the decrease in the number of well-paying jobs requiring low skill levels, individuals increasingly need to have advanced technical, communicative, and problem-solving skills to succeed in the workplace. Various education and job training programs, ranging from the federal Comprehensive Employment Training Act (CETA) and Job Training Partnership Act (JTPA) initiatives to local school-to-work efforts, have attempted to improve the employability of low-income individuals. Measures of revitalization in these approaches include the number of jobs created and/or retained and the local employment rate.

Neighborhood economic development also involves improving local access to goods and services. Generating more retail activity in an area provides residents with a greater variety of items from which to choose, makes the neighborhood more appealing to individuals both within and outside it, and creates additional job opportunities. A number of organizations consequently work to develop shopping centers and other retail outlets in order to spark such economic growth. Such groups measure success (revitalization) in terms of the number of retail establishments in the area, the amount of sales such stores generate, and the amount of commercial space that is developed.

3. Trickle-Down Economic Growth

In addition to the more locally driven processes of social and economic development, policy makers have consistently promoted regional and national economic growth as a solution for many of the problems affecting distressed inner-city neighborhoods. By adjusting interest rates and providing financial and regulatory incentives to business, the policy makers have sought to spur greater consumption and production. They assume that macro-level economic growth will ultimately improve conditions throughout the nation/region, including those in distressed inner-city communities. If large corporations such as General Motors and Motorola can increase their sales and profits, they will presumably hire more individuals and generate more money for their shareholders. People will use their additional wealth to buy more goods, which creates a higher demand for labor. In this cycle of consumption, companies will hire more workers, who will spend more money and create more of a demand for labor, and so forth. Ultimately the benefits of the expanding economy will "trickle down" to the residents of distressed inner-city neighborhoods, since cities themselves are integral components of the national and regional economies. Again, indicators of revitalization primarily include reduced poverty and unemployment rates.

Pursued in some form on a national level since the early 1930s, the trickle-down approach has not proven to be a panacea for inner-city residents. Central-city poverty has often increased with economic declines (such as in the early 1980s) and decreased during boom times (the 1960s). For example, the strong Massachusetts economy of the late 1980s helped cause the unemployment rate for all of Boston's racial and socioeconomic groups to fall markedly.[2] At the same time, the economic growth of the late 1980s and mid-1990s has had surprisingly little effect nationally on many of the lowest income individuals. Chicago, Cleveland, Detroit, and Milwaukee all had more census tracts with poverty rates of 40 percent or more in 1990 than they did in 1980.[3]

Place-Based Approaches

1. Gentrification

One of the most widely accepted definitions of revitalization is *gentrification,* the physical restoration of central-city neighborhoods by and for middle- and upper-income professionals. The roots of gentrification lie in the growth of industries that require relatively high levels of education and that are located in or near the downtown business district. The bulk of these positions have been filled by relatively young, well-educated professionals.[4] Unlike many older workers with families, a large proportion of these individuals have preferred to live amid the hustle, bustle, and diversity of the city, ideally in areas convenient to their place of work.

When viewed in these ways, many of the older neighborhoods surrounding the central business district held distinct advantages. They were close to downtown and often benefited from topographical amenities such as lakeside or riverside locations. Much of their housing stock had architectural and historical appeal. The downside was the communities' general decline. Much of the housing stock needed considerable renovation. The areas often had pockets of considerable poverty and relatively high rates of crime and social disorder, which had dissuaded investment. Yet for adventurous individuals, the attractions outweighed the drawbacks. Beginning in the 1970s, some of these younger professionals began purchasing the relatively inexpensive properties in neighborhoods such as Boston's South End, Philadelphia's Society Hill, San Francisco's Western Addition, and Washington's Capitol Hill. They gradually restored the housing stock and encouraged the establishment of restaurants and businesses that catered to their tastes and needs. As the neighborhoods improved and their appeal increased, property values rose. More members of the middle class moved in, which created more economic activity and increased attention to local social issues. Taken together, the changes helped reduce urban blight and expanded the cities' tax base.

For many policy makers, gentrification represented a boon for the inner cities. The increased economic activity created jobs. The influx of well-educated individuals generated increased concern about adequate policing of the area and the condition of the local school system. The renovation of decaying properties reversed trends of decline and reduced the threat of the areas becoming urban wastelands. The House Subcommittee on the City claimed in 1977 that "gentrification is in fact the only realistic cure for abandonment. . . . The displacement it causes (if any) is trivial. Therefore a policy of encouraging gentrification, through tax benefits, zone changes, or whatever other means are available, should be pursued."[5]

Despite the House's contentions, displacement of a gentrified neighborhood's existing residents has remained controversial. Many landlords have raised rents to take advantage of the increased demand for housing, effectively pricing lower-income tenants out of the market. Others have converted multifamily apartments into condominiums, substituting middle-class owners for poor renters. Single-room occupancy hotels have often been replaced by apartment buildings or office space. Longtime home-owners with fixed incomes have suddenly found themselves unable to meet the higher property tax burdens that have resulted from the appreci-ated value of their homes. In addition to these financial pressures, lower-income residents have often experienced strained relationships with the gentrifiers. The gentrifiers have tended to be white, while the existing residents have often been black and/or Latino; the combination of differ-ent socioeconomic statuses and different cultures has generated tension. For example, some gentrifiers have viewed the presence of homeless in-dividuals, street vendors, and other poor minority residents as jeopardiz-ing the value of their newly refurbished homes and have consequently sought antiloitering ordinances. These various pressures have caused many of the original residents to move out of the communities.[6]

The extent to which displacement has taken place remains unclear. Advocates for low-income residents claim that the process has been widespread, although there are few evaluations that conclusively support such assertions. Undoubtedly some residents have had to move, yet it is hard to know whether they have stayed within the neighborhood or left it entirely.[7] The important point is that most individuals who are displaced are done so involuntarily. People in general often prefer to pay more in rent and/or taxes than to leave an area where they have developed strong emotional, psychological, and social ties. Individuals with lower in-comes may have even greater motivation to stay in a familiar neighbor-hood. For example, finding adequate day care in a new community may prove financially troublesome if it had previously been provided by local neighbors. Informal credit arrangements built up with local merchants (as well as lending relationships with local banks) may well disappear, at least in the short run until they can be reestablished. Small, break-even businesses may find it difficult to build a new market for their goods in their new locales.[8]

Among the indicators of a gentrifying community are increases in property values, per capita incomes, and residential loans. The neighbor-hood's racial and socioeconomic composition often changes, with the community gaining a larger percentage of white, college-educated, mid-dle- to upper-income individuals. The proportion of individuals who have recently moved into the neighborhood also tends to be higher than that in other communities.

2. Incumbent Upgrading

Like gentrification, incumbent upgrading involves the rehabilitation of a declining neighborhood's housing stock. The difference lies in the renovators: gentrification tends to be sparked by outsiders revitalizing the community, whereas incumbent upgrading involves the improvement of communities by their existing residents. Gentrification typically starts in the neighborhoods located closest to downtown (and/or having the most amenities). To the extent that demand for city housing remains strong, these development pressures may then spread out to the next ring of communities. These "second-ring" neighborhoods are often more socially and economically stable than their first-ring counterparts, with a higher proportion of employed, moderate- to middle income homeowners. They tend to be more ethnically and racially homogenous, and their housing tends to be in at least slightly better physical condition than that of the first-ring communities.[9]

When gentrification takes place in first-ring communities, moderate-income residents of second-ring communities may decide to renovate their homes. Such renovation is largely a defensive move to protect the current character of the neighborhood. Renovation typically increases local property values, which makes the area less appealing to potential gentrifiers. Higher prices also dissuade poorer individuals, who often look to second-ring communities after being displaced by the gentrification of their first-ring neighborhoods.

Incumbent upgraders often mobilize behind a community organization expressly designed to preserve the stability of the neighborhood. The organization, acting in concert with existing local institutions such as hospitals, universities, and large industries, works to improve the area's housing stock, attract middle-income (preferably white) home buyers, and generally strengthen the local real estate market. When successful (as in the Beverly and Hyde Park/Kenwood communities in Chicago), such incumbent upgrading efforts result in additional investment within the neighborhood. Banks make more home improvement and other residential loans, property values increase, the amount of local commercial activity often increases, and the neighborhood's racial composition remains relatively constant.[10]

3. Adaptive Re-Use

In addition to increasing demand for property located close to downtown, the growth of the high-technology and service industries has led to the abandonment of many once-prosperous urban industrial plants. Although some are in out-of-the-way, environmentally contaminated areas, others are located along rivers, near downtown, and/or near fashionable residential neighborhoods—in short, in areas of high residential demand. Developers have increasingly sought to convert old factories and warehouses into residential lofts, retail stores, and office space, particularly if the style of the buildings lends itself to such renovation. Chief indicators of adaptive re-use are increased numbers of building permits and construction loans.

As with gentrification, the process brings in new residents and commercial tenants, generates additional economic activity, and results in either renovation or development of the surrounding infrastructure. The conversion of abandoned properties into functional ones increases the city's tax base and may spur additional investment in the area. Since the process focuses on industrial sites, it does not directly affect existing residents. Yet rarely does the redevelopment include housing or stores catering to a lower-income clientele.[11]

Toward a New Approach to Revitalization

The individual-based approaches previously outlined tend to focus on the needs of low-income inner-city residents without adequately addressing the economic development of the neighborhood as a whole. The place-based approaches focus more on the economic development and marketing of the neighborhood, but largely ignore the needs of the low-income residents currently living there. What is needed is an approach to revitalization that addresses both of these characteristics of neighborhoods.

As places of residence, neighborhoods ideally provide nurturing environments. The physical layout of the neighborhood promotes social interaction and a sense of safety. As outlined in Chapter 1, the community of people that live in a particular area offers social, cultural, and psychological guidance, support, and strength for its members. With such support, individuals can develop their goals, talents, and personalities. They build the academic, emotional, and interpersonal skills necessary to succeed in the workplace and in the broader society. They develop a sense of confidence and control over their lives.

Although they may not contain many jobs (because zoning regulations generally separate residential and commercial areas), neighborhoods play important roles in the broader economic marketplace. Their property has value for developers and investors. Their residents constitute a potential labor source for businesses throughout the metropolitan area. As consumers of goods and services, the residents also create a market for certain commodities.

The extent to which neighborhoods are connected to the broader marketplace largely determines their economic and social health. In neighborhoods with high unemployment rates, residents are bringing lower amounts of capital back to the community. The presence of fewer financial resources limits the community's ability to address the concerns and desires of local individuals. Local institutions such as churches, schools, recreation centers, and social service agencies may not acquire the resources they need to carry out effective skill-building programs. Individuals may not have the money they need to maintain their homes; the deterioration of housing, coupled with the lower skill levels of area residents, causes outside investors such as banks, retailers, and other businesses to look elsewhere for profits. The negative cycle gradually accelerates: low skill levels translate into few jobs, which generate few resources, which create few social opportunities and reduced confidence in the area, which leads to greater disinvestment, which creates fewer opportunities, and so forth. The individuals in the community often feel trapped, constrained in their ability to realize their dreams, talents, and capacities.

Recognizing the inherent interplay between investment in a neighborhood and improved conditions for local residents, I offer a two-pronged definition of revitalization: *the improvement of economic conditions for existing residents and the re-integration of the neighborhood into the market system.* Revitalization is not simply about rehabilitating an area to make it more attractive for more affluent residents, because that process fails to take into account the less affluent individuals currently living there. By focusing on the residents currently in the community, my definition implicitly addresses the poverty reduction goal of neighborhood development. Successful revitalization does not create a static community: the nature of social mobility is such that individuals often move to "better" areas once they attain a certain level of affluence. Instead, successful revitalization creates a neighborhood whose conditions help enable all of the residents to succeed economically and socially. Reintegrating a distressed neighborhood into the market generates additional economic activity and thus more material resources. These improved economic conditions typically lead to improved social conditions, as evidenced by numerous studies showing high correlations among poverty, crime, low educational achievement, poor nutrition, teen parenting, child maltreatment, and so forth. At the same time, market reintegration enables the broader society (and market) to benefit from the community's various economic and human resources.

MEASURING REVITALIZATION

There is no single measurement tool that adequately captures the complex, multifaceted nature of neighborhood revitalization. Part of the difficulty in developing such a tool lies in the competing conceptions of revitalization itself. Part results from the absence of easily obtainable data on a neighborhood level; neighborhoods often are not clearly defined, and information tends to be aggregated on at least a city-wide level. Quantifying local change has nevertheless become a chief concern of those involved in inner-city development. The Urban Institute, the Development Leadership Network, and the Local Initiatives Support Corporation, to name only a few organizations, have recently embarked on projects to measure and assess neighborhood revitalization.

Recognizing the inherent limitations of such a tool, I offer in the remainder of this chapter an index for evaluating economic change in a neighborhood. The index emerges from the two-pronged definition of revitalization previously outlined. It takes into account both increased private investment and improved conditions for local residents, using individual neighborhoods as the units of analysis. It does not measure improvements or declines in a community's education level, physical health, or political participation. It similarly ignores changes in local social conditions. Improvements in a neighborhood's economic well-being generally translate into improvements in its social conditions; this study measures only the economic aspect of that process. The index of revitalization is far from perfect—each of its components essentially serves as a proxy for less quantifiable factors—but it provides a useful way of quantifying local change.

Level of Analysis

This book addresses why certain low-income neighborhoods in a city are able to revitalize, not why certain cities fare better than others. It therefore focuses exclusively on neighborhoods within the city of Chicago. Concentrating on a single city controls for differences in regional economic conditions, municipal political structures and leadership, federal resource allocations, and the presence of corporations and foundations. Chicago has historically had widely acknowledged characteristic neighborhoods. Although the city's racial and demographic changes have altered them in many ways, the communities still vary enough to allow for comparative analysis. More broadly, Chicago as a whole has a number of resources upon which the neighborhoods can conceivably draw. The city continues to be a national center of trade and is rapidly becoming a major actor in global financial markets. It has traditionally been a hotbed of community activism, having served as a training ground for organizers such as Saul Alinsky.[12] It has a well-developed transportation and communication infrastructure, and the Chicago region boasts some of the nation's best universities.

In the late 1920s, sociologists at the University of Chicago divided the city into 75 community areas. Roughly representative of the city's neighborhoods (and/or groups of neighborhoods), the community area boundaries were arranged when possible in a manner consistent with physical boundaries such as rivers and railroad tracks. The initial community area map served as the basis for census tracts: tract boundaries are contiguous with community area boundaries. The boundaries have remained constant ever since—save for the bisection of Uptown (community area 3) to create Edgewater (area 77) and the addition of O'Hare (area 76) following the 1970 census—and have become an official level of analysis for many of the city's reports. I am therefore using them as units of analysis in this study, collecting and analyzing all of the data on the community area level. (A map of the community areas follows.)

Chicago's well-defined communities set it apart from many other cities and make it an excellent place in which to conduct neighborhood-level research. At the same time, its community areas have certain limitations for research. The community areas may no longer represent commonly held views of neighborhoods. In some cases, both the boundaries and even the community's name differ greatly from those put forth by local residents and public officials.[13] Local housing markets often span community areas. Although relatively small, a community area may nevertheless still be too large a unit of analysis to capture instances of local revitalization.

The majority of Chicago's community areas are between two and four square miles in size and contain both residential and commercial sections. The biggest is O'Hare (13.7 square miles), which consists primarily of the city's international airport. The smallest is Burnside (area 47), containing 0.53 square miles. The community areas vary considerably in population. The largest (Austin—area 25) had 114,079 residents in 1990, while the smallest (Burnside) had only 3,314. The average for the 77 areas was 36,152 residents. Both O'Hare and the Loop (area 32, encompassing the central business district) have fewer than 12,000 residents

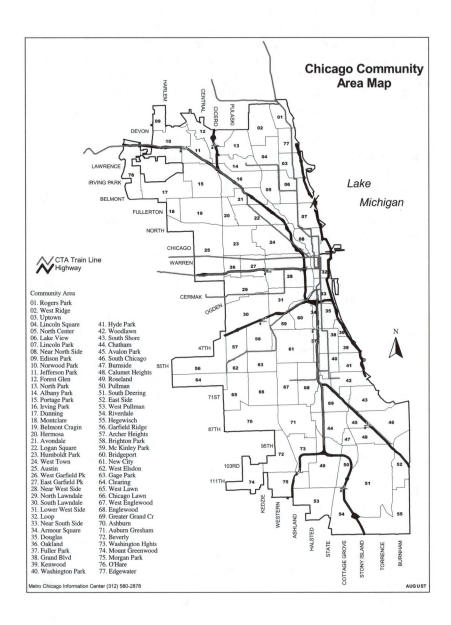

Chicago Community Area Map

Lake Michigan

CTA Train Line
Highway

Community Area
01. Rogers Park
02. West Ridge
03. Uptown
04. Lincoln Square
05. North Center
06. Lake View
07. Lincoln Park
08. Near North Side
09. Edison Park
10. Norwood Park
11. Jefferson Park
12. Forest Glen
13. North Park
14. Albany Park
15. Portage Park
16. Irving Park
17. Dunning
18. Montclare
19. Belmont Cragin
20. Hermosa
21. Avondale
22. Logan Square
23. Humboldt Park
24. West Town
25. Austin
26. West Garfield Pk
27. East Garfield Pk
28. Near West Side
29. North Lawndale
30. South Lawndale
31. Lower West Side
32. Loop
33. Near South Side
34. Armour Square
35. Douglas
36. Oakland
37. Fuller Park
38. Grand Blvd
39. Kenwood
40. Washington Park

41. Hyde Park
42. Woodlawn
43. South Shore
44. Chatham
45. Avalon Park
46. South Chicago
47. Burnside
48. Calumet Heights
49. Roseland
50. Pullman
51. South Deering
52. East Side
53. West Pullman
54. Riverdale
55. Hegewisch
56. Garfield Ridge
57. Archer Heights
58. Brighton Park
59. Mc Kinley Park
60. Bridgeport
61. New City
62. West Elsdon
63. Gage Park
64. Clearing
65. West Lawn
66. Chicago Lawn
67. West Englewood
68. Englewood
69. Greater Grand Cr
70. Ashburn
71. Auburn Gresham
72. Beverly
73. Washington Hghts
74. Mount Greenwood
75. Morgan Park
76. O'Hare
77. Edgewater

Metro Chicago Information Center (312) 580-2878   AUGUST and are often excluded from statistical analyses because their concentrations of commercial activity skew the data.

Prior to its bisection, Uptown had a population of over 130,000; it was divided partly because of its size and partly because its northern section (now Edgewater) was widely believed to constitute a separate community. Since the change did not go into effect until the 1980 census, much of the previous data was collected only for the overarching Uptown area. When necessary, I have allocated this Uptown data to Edgewater, either by breaking it down by individual census tracts or by estimating it based on the ratio between the two community areas in 1980.

Time Period

Measuring revitalization requires an assessment of conditions at multiple times. By definition, revitalization involves change. Do neighborhood indicators improve, worsen, or stay the same from one time period to the next? How do they compare to similar communities at the same point? This study focuses principally on changes that have occurred in the past 18 years, beginning in 1979. The year 1979 is the first for which the majority of the data is consistently available by community area. The city as a whole, and thus many of its neighborhoods, has experienced considerable economic change in the past two decades.

Measures

As defined in this study, revitalization has two central outcomes: improved social and economic conditions for the neighborhood's existing residents and increased market activity within the community. Assessing the nature and extent of revitalization therefore requires a focus on both individual economic opportunity and private investment. Within these categories I have used three specific indicators of economic change. Per capita income estimates the material opportunities available to individual residents of a community. The number of residential loans per housing unit and median property values show the level of private investment in an area. The following sections describe the conceptual and empirical rationale behind the revitalization measures.

1. Individual Opportunity

The chief measure of an individual's material well-being is the amount of income he or she has. Although money does not necessarily translate into happiness and emotional security, it does enable people to obtain goods and services. Having more money allows people to purchase more consumables and better housing. It makes travel more feasible, and generally opens the door to a wider range of educational, cultural, and recreational opportunities.

A primary indicator of revitalization is therefore an *increase in a neighborhood's real per capita income.* (For simplicity's sake, the income measure does not include in-kind transfers.) An alternative approach would be to use area poverty rates, but the income measure offers more useful information. First, the poverty line is artificially set and generally lags below what is commonly considered to be a minimally acceptable level of income.[14] Second, poverty rates only illustrate economic conditions for a certain subset of the community's population. Per capita income provides a better sense of the entire community's material well-being. The fact that it deals with all individuals makes it more comprehensive than either median household or median family income, since the organization of both households and families varies a great deal across the city's neighborhoods.[15] Third, increases in per capita income generally indicate reductions in poverty, and there is a strong correlation between the two measures.

Per capita income serves as a better indicator of individual well-being than measures of employment. Considering the number of jobs present in a neighborhood has limited usefulness because many people do not work in the same community where they live. A community's unemployment rate provides a rough indicator of the job opportunities available to its residents, but it has limited usefulness in illustrating individual economic conditions. It considers only those people actively looking for work, not those who have voluntarily left the labor force, become disabled, or become too discouraged to continue looking. It also ignores individuals who support themselves through a variety of temporary jobs; someone could live comfortably from the income generated by numerous part-time jobs, yet still be officially unemployed. The jobless rate does not account for individuals who are *underemployed,* able and willing to work more yet unable to find a suitable job. Furthermore, unemployment data for community areas is unavailable after 1990, while estimates of per capita income are available for each year through 1995.

The federal census provides tract-level data on per capita income for 1979 and 1989; the Chicago Community Area Fact Book has aggregated this tract-level data to community areas.[16] The Center for Urban Economic Development (CUED) at the University of Illinois at Chicago has projected per capita income levels for each of the city's community areas for both 1993 and 1998, using data collected by Claritas/NPDC.[17] Prior to 1979, the census provided information only about median family income. I assumed that the ratio of per capita income to median family income remained constant over time and used the 1979 relationship to determine the 1969 per capita income values.

One difficulty in using per capita income (and any other individual-level census indicator) is that there is no way of determining the level of residential turnover between surveys. Simply put, the census does not capture the extent of displacement in a neighborhood. An area's per capita income may have risen considerably in ten years because higher-income individuals replaced the previous poor residents. The census provides information about whether individuals have lived in their current residence for the past five years and, if not, whether the previous place of residence was within or outside of the county. There is no way, however, of determining if recent intra-county movers previously lived within the neighborhood, within the city, or in another town. It is possible to determine only a base proportion of residents who remained in the area (at least 26 percent, for example), not how much higher the actual percentage was. Discerning the extent of displacement requires detailed, longitudinal surveys of either specific individuals or specific addresses, tracking their residence or inhabitants over time.[18]

All neighborhoods experience a certain extent of population turnover, and urban neighborhoods with large proportions of renters typically have the highest turnover rates. The key issue concerns the people who replace the emigrants. If the newcomers are of the same racial and socioeconomic status as their predecessors, the neighborhood is considered stable: it essentially reproduces itself. If the newcomers are of a "higher" status, the neighborhood is seen as gentrifying, whereas if they are of a "lower" status, the area is viewed as declining. Gentrifying neighborhoods often experience a change in their racial composition, with the percentage of white residents increasing. The extent of racial change can therefore help determine the type of neighborhood change taking place. Yet racial and ethnic indicators cannot capture the movement of more affluent blacks into already predominantly black neighborhoods. Such indicators also have limited usefulness in cities such as Chicago, where long-established patterns of racial and ethnic segregation continue to shape the demographics of gentrification and revitalization. Thus in addition to indicators of racial change, I have relied on interviews and conversations with realtors and others associated with neighborhood development to distinguish between gentrification and revitalization.

2. Private Investment

The other indicators of revitalization concern the extent of private investment in a community. Private investors focus on areas of potential profit; if they see an opportunity to make money in the long term, they will commit resources to a particular location. In effect, they develop a material interest in the community's long-term health. If they do not see economic potential, they commit their resources elsewhere. Thus the market's perception of a neighborhood's future economic prospects determines the allocation of private resources.

There are essentially two types of investment: necessary maintenance and *anticipatory investment*, resources committed in expectation of future economic return. Both types are driven by a series of individual decisions. Local residents, bankers, and other potential investors commit monies to a neighborhood based on their beliefs about the neighborhood's future prospects. Each of these individuals has a certain threshold above which he or she will invest, the point at which the rewards outweigh the risks. The thresholds vary for different people and often depend on a person's response to local factors such as crime, racial transition, and the decisions of other investors.[19]

Increased confidence in an area breeds increased investment. More residents repair and improve their properties. Developers may decide to rehabilitate buildings and/or build new homes in the community. Bankers reconsider the neighborhood as a potentially profitable lending area and may well increase the number of conventional mortgages, construction loans, and home improvement loans they make there. Business owners may feel that the increased attention to the neighborhood will generate enough demand for their goods and services so as to warrant keeping open, expanding, and/or opening stores in the community. In short, neighborhoods with more investment capital can better maintain their physical character and their social amenities. They create more potential rewards and fewer risks for potential investors and consequently become more likely to retain local residents and attract outside individuals and businesses.

This study uses two private investment measures of revitalization. The first, the *number of residential loans per housing unit*,[20] provides an indicator of economic activity in a neighborhood. Bankers and representatives of other financial institutions lend money in areas where they feel a certain level of comfort: they believe that the community will be stable enough that they will be able to make a profitable return (or in the case of a third-party mortgage broker, pocket a fee). Such loans are essential for a community's economic health, in that they enable people to purchase and refurbish homes. With residential stability comes social improvement. People who make a long-term financial commitment to an area are more likely to try to ensure a higher quality of life for themselves and their families.

The passage of the Home Mortgage Disclosure Act (HMDA) in 1975 compelled banks and savings and loans to report to federal regulators the number and amount of loans they made in each census tract for the previous year. Since the early 1980s, the state of Illinois has also required mortgage companies to report their neighborhood lending activity. The Woodstock Institute has collected HMDA data for each of Chicago's community areas since 1980 and has produced annual reports since 1983.[21] (It has included the mortgage company data in the reports when possible.) A 1986 Woodstock study detailed the total number of loans made in each community from 1980 to 1983; I subtracted the 1983 figures and then averaged the remainder over 1980–1982 to obtain data for those years.[22] I determined the number of loans made in 1979 by taking one-third of the three-year (1977–1979) HMDA totals gathered by Melaniphy and Associates in a 1982 assessment of the city's community areas.[23] In each year the loan figure represents the sum of conventional mortgages for 1–4 unit properties, FHA/VA loans for 1–4 unit properties, home-improvement loans, and multifamily loans.[24]

The second private investment component addresses the economic impact of investment on a neighborhood. As conditions in a community improve, there is an increased interest on the part of individuals and businesses to locate within the area. Heightened demand leads to higher land prices. *Median property values* reflect the market's assessment of the neighborhood's economic worth, which implicitly includes an evaluation of its future prospects.

For this study I have used the median sale prices of detached single-family homes (not including sales of townhouses, condominiums, or cooperatives). Property sale data are available for each year beginning in 1979. The information from 1979–1989 comes from data collected by CUED for the Woodstock Institute; the information for 1990–1995 comes from data collected by the Chicago Association of Realtors.[25] (Data for 1990–1991 are only available for community areas 1 through 27 and 77.)[26]

Using median sale prices presents a few difficulties, however. The data include only those properties that were actually sold. Including estimates of the market value of properties that failed to sell and either remained on the market or were taken off by their owners would presumably lower the median value. The type of housing varies considerably across neighborhoods; some areas have mostly single-family homes, while others have primarily multi-family dwellings. There is a large discrepancy in the number of home sales across neighborhoods, partly as a result of the different types of housing and partly as a result of the wide variations in market conditions. Some areas have hundreds of sales in a given year, while others (generally the poorest areas) have as few as one or two.[27] To increase the validity of the median price in low-sale areas, I have averaged the medians for two years in community areas with fewer than 10 single-family sales in a given year. For example, East Garfield Park's 1979 median property value is actually an average of its 1979 and 1980 medians. In communities in which there were no sales in a given year, I relied solely on the other "partner" year's figures.[28]

A third potential indicator of private investment would be either the number of retail establishments and/or the amount of retail sales per square mile, which would help quantify the extent of commercial economic opportunities. Improving neighborhoods attract new residents who generate additional demand for goods and services. Retailers see an opportunity to make a profit in the area and consequently locate or expand stores in the community.

I have not used a retail measure as a primary dependent variable, however. Although all of Chicago's community areas have a certain amount of retail activity, the number of establishments varies widely across neighborhoods for reasons only partially associated with local economic conditions. The nature of a community's housing stock largely determines the population density of an area and thus indirectly affects the level of demand for goods and services. Zoning regulations and housing density affect the amount of retail development. For example, Edison Park and Norwood Park are two reasonably affluent, overwhelmingly single-family residential neighborhoods on the northwest side with far fewer retail establishments than the less affluent South Shore and Lower West Side communities. It is therefore difficult to compare retail conditions across communities. Retail activity may well move independently of other private investment indicators. Furthermore, the federal Census of Retail Trade breaks down retail establishments by zip code, not census tract, making it problematic to obtain accurate numbers for community areas.[29]

Developing an Index of Revitalization

As mentioned earlier, quantifying revitalization has typically proven problematic. The lack of a clearly understood, widely accepted measure of neighborhood economic change has resulted in analyses of community improvement that tend to be largely subjective. This study offers a more objective approach by using a single index of local economic conditions. It focuses on Chicago's low- and moderate-income neighborhoods: the 36 community areas whose per capita incomes were below the city average in 1979.

To create the index, I first compared the community areas to the city average (set at 100) on each of the three indicators. The individual neighborhood scores indicate the community area's position as a proportion of that average (or median, in the case of property values). For example, West Town's per capita income was 67.92 percent of the city average in 1979. It had 32.69 percent as many loans per housing unit as Chicago as a whole, and its median property value was 36.96 percent of the city median. I then took a weighted average of these three proportional values to create an index measure of the community's overall economic position relative to the city. Based on the two-pronged definition of revitalization outlined earlier, I weighted individual economic opportunity and private investment equally. Per capita income constitutes 50 percent of the index, and loans and property values each comprise 25 percent.[30] West Town's 1979 index score of 51.37 shows that the neighborhood's economic condition was roughly half as good as the city average. I computed the index score for 1979 (the first year for which data is available), 1989 (ten years later), and 1995 (the last year for which data is available). Changes in a neighborhood's index score indicate the extent of revitalization (or decline) that occurred during a particular period. Between 1979 and 1995, West Town's economic condition improved by over 35 percentage points relative to the city average. In comparison, New City's relative position declined by over 10 percentage points during the same period. A breakdown of all of the index scores and their components is found in Table 2-1 (on the following pages).

Creating a single index of revitalization is possible because of the moderate, positive correlations among the various components. The three indicators were closely related in 1979: areas with high per capita

Table 2-1. Index Scores for Low- and Moderate-Income Chicago Community Areas

CA	Name	Per Capita Income '79	Loan Rate '79	Property Value '79	Index 1979
0	City of Chicago	100	100	100	**100.00**
3	Uptown	95.30	109.00	125.98	**106.39**
14	Albany Park	98.81	103.02	130.43	**107.77**
20	Hermosa	96.36	144.20	89.13	**106.51**
21	Avondale	99.20	89.49	80.43	**92.08**
22	Logan Square	81.38	77.99	56.52	**74.32**
23	Humboldt Park	65.60	77.64	52.17	**65.25**
24	West Town	67.92	32.69	36.96	**51.37**
25	Austin	75.05	112.94	80.05	**85.78**
26	W. Garfield Park	54.05	24.63	29.84	**40.65**
27	E. Garfield Park	51.54	18.46	22.15	**35.92**
28	Near West Side	52.35	18.84	19.57	**35.78**
29	N. Lawndale	50.52	20.09	27.23	**37.09**
30	S. Lawndale	62.86	100.40	56.52	**70.66**
31	Lower West Side	63.61	31.47	41.30	**50.00**
33	Near South Side	50.01	28.54	0.00	**39.27**
34	Armour Square	75.64	21.78	94.24	**66.83**
35	Douglas	76.57	6.21	20.58	**44.98**
36	Oakland	33.79	4.40	19.50	**22.87**
37	Fuller Park	53.20	35.95	26.18	**42.13**
38	Grand Blvd.	42.79	7.52	32.46	**31.39**
40	Washington Park	49.33	8.14	29.35	**34.04**
42	Woodlawn	64.04	14.51	34.78	**44.34**
46	South Chicago	87.21	114.34	60.87	**87.41**
47	Burnside	75.72	180.61	65.22	**99.32**
49	Roseland	85.52	150.43	76.09	**99.39**
50	Pullman	97.98	109.76	61.96	**91.92**
51	S. Deering	90.61	161.57	71.20	**103.50**
53	W. Pullman	80.21	167.37	70.11	**99.48**
54	Riverdale	45.46	14.45	50.26	**38.91**
60	Bridgeport	93.90	46.97	58.70	**73.37**
61	New City	69.63	81.55	45.65	**66.61**
67	W. Englewood	58.91	105.38	54.13	**69.33**
68	Englewood	54.60	31.45	50.00	**47.66**
69	Gr. Grand Crossing	81.63	51.12	60.22	**68.65**
71	Auburn Gresham	88.84	104.24	76.09	**89.50**
73	Washington Heights	95.22	155.46	79.35	**106.31**

Per Capita Income '89	Loan Rate '89	Property Value '89	Index 1989	Index Change '79–'89	Income Change. '79–'89
100	100	100	**100.00**	0.00	0.00
96.05	56.51	135.62	**96.06**	−10.34	0.75
79.64	119.01	132.81	**102.78**	−4.99	−19.17
72.00	161.78	96.25	**100.51**	−6.00	−24.36
87.05	112.01	105.62	**97.93**	5.85	−12.16
68.58	111.00	81.25	**82.35**	8.03	−12.80
53.53	100.49	65.16	**68.18**	2.93	−12.07
64.02	94.66	73.75	**74.11**	22.74	−3.90
67.90	87.06	83.75	**76.65**	−9.12	−7.15
47.86	48.20	39.96	**45.97**	5.32	−6.19
45.37	27.23	35.97	**38.48**	2.56	−6.17
64.39	46.71	18.75	**48.56**	12.78	12.04
43.03	45.99	41.20	**43.31**	6.22	−7.49
48.90	117.36	55.00	**67.54**	−3.12	−13.96
50.14	70.61	53.75	**56.16**	6.16	−13.48
46.45	42.38	0.00	**44.41**	5.14	−3.56
72.77	62.37	102.99	**77.72**	10.90	−2.87
71.50	9.79	65.73	**54.63**	9.65	−5.07
28.20	6.23	25.51	**22.04**	−0.83	−5.58
47.55	53.73	30.58	**44.85**	2.72	−5.65
36.54	17.58	30.00	**30.16**	−1.23	−6.25
38.72	21.25	27.44	**31.53**	−2.51	−10.61
58.21	25.63	21.25	**40.83**	−3.51	−5.83
68.88	60.15	57.12	**63.76**	−23.65	−18.33
69.97	99.17	63.75	**75.71**	−23.61	−5.76
79.21	95.40	66.25	**80.02**	−19.37	−6.31
83.55	92.17	67.50	**81.69**	−10.23	−14.43
77.82	111.23	66.25	**83.28**	−20.22	−12.79
73.32	112.91	67.00	**81.63**	−17.84	−6.90
30.64	26.59	43.59	**32.86**	−6.05	−14.83
83.07	106.49	85.94	**89.64**	16.27	−10.83
51.22	88.72	38.12	**57.32**	−9.29	−18.40
54.08	79.81	47.81	**58.95**	−10.39	−4.83
45.85	40.33	31.25	**40.82**	−6.84	−8.75
71.35	56.73	63.12	**65.64**	−3.01	−10.28
77.04	89.23	73.12	**79.11**	−10.39	−11.80
89.53	123.17	76.81	**94.76**	−11.55	−5.70

**Table 2-1. Index Scores for Low- and
Moderate-Income Chicago Community Areas (*cont.*)**

CA	Name	Loan Rate Change '79–'89	Property Value Change '79–'89	Per Capita Income '95	Loan Rate '95
0	City of Chicago	0.00	0.00	100	100
3	Uptown	−52.49	9.65	103.41	58.10
14	Albany Park	15.99	2.38	73.40	84.83
20	Hermosa	17.58	7.12	64.16	127.05
21	Avondale	22.52	25.19	82.60	102.46
22	Logan Square	33.01	24.73	65.35	90.45
23	Humboldt Park	22.85	12.98	50.45	111.33
24	West Town	61.97	36.79	60.74	104.74
25	Austin	−25.88	3.70	64.90	126.66
26	W. Garfield Park	23.56	10.12	43.04	68.47
27	E. Garfield Park	8.77	13.82	43.34	56.56
28	Near West Side	27.86	−0.82	67.05	31.24
29	N. Lawndale	25.90	13.98	40.22	59.55
30	S. Lawndale	16.96	−1.52	44.67	103.22
31	Lower West Side	39.14	12.45	47.08	65.25
33	Near South Side	13.84	0.00	45.34	114.15
34	Armour Square	40.59	8.75	71.27	39.30
35	Douglas	3.58	45.15	60.91	13.59
36	Oakland	1.83	6.01	27.91	12.49
37	Fuller Park	17.78	4.40	48.63	59.04
38	Grand Blvd.	10.06	−2.46	37.99	19.14
40	Washington Park	13.10	−1.91	39.91	18.64
42	Woodlawn	11.13	−13.53	55.97	43.90
46	South Chicago	−54.19	−3.74	63.30	82.31
47	Burnside	−81.44	−1.47	65.72	174.55
49	Roseland	−55.02	−9.84	77.78	133.06
50	Pullman	−17.59	5.54	79.63	90.12
51	S. Deering	−50.34	−4.95	71.30	136.80
53	W. Pullman	−54.46	−3.11	70.71	165.41
54	Riverdale	12.13	−6.67	28.13	35.08
60	Bridgeport	59.53	27.24	77.93	79.52
61	New City	7.17	−7.53	47.90	85.61
67	W. Englewood	−25.57	−6.32	51.45	109.60
68	Englewood	8.88	−18.75	43.35	58.79
69	Gr. Grand Crossing	5.61	2.91	70.58	70.85
71	Auburn Gresham	−15.00	−2.96	72.67	121.89
73	Washington Heights	−32.29	−2.54	85.91	161.46

Property Value '95	Index 1995	Index Change '89–'95	Income Change '89–'95	Loan Rate Change '89–'95	Property Value Change '89–'95
100	**100.00**	0.00	0.00	0.00	0.00
160.10	**106.35**	10.29	7.37	1.58	24.86
112.08	**85.93**	−16.85	−6.25	−34.18	−20.73
90.60	**86.49**	−14.02	−7.84	−34.73	−5.65
94.91	**90.64**	−7.29	−4.44	−9.54	−10.72
99.87	**80.25**	−2.10	−3.23	−20.55	18.62
60.31	**68.14**	−0.04	−3.08	10.84	−4.85
119.93	**86.54**	12.43	−3.28	10.09	46.18
75.93	**83.10**	6.44	−3.00	39.60	−7.82
51.64	**51.55**	5.58	−4.82	20.28	11.68
69.32	**53.14**	14.66	−2.03	29.33	33.35
103.49	**67.21**	18.65	2.66	−15.47	84.74
51.75	**47.93**	4.62	−2.81	13.56	10.54
69.03	**65.40**	−2.14	−4.22	−14.14	14.03
60.40	**54.95**	−1.20	−3.06	−5.35	6.65
285.68	**122.63**	78.21	−1.12	71.77	285.68
81.07	**65.72**	−12.00	−1.50	−23.07	−21.92
100.47	**58.97**	4.34	−10.59	3.80	34.75
34.88	**25.80**	3.76	−0.29	6.26	9.37
45.69	**50.50**	5.65	1.09	5.32	15.11
56.08	**37.80**	7.64	1.45	1.56	26.08
61.23	**39.92**	8.39	1.19	−2.61	33.80
48.47	**51.08**	10.25	−2.25	18.27	27.22
50.91	**64.95**	1.19	−5.59	22.15	−6.22
45.64	**87.91**	12.20	−4.24	75.38	−18.11
59.53	**87.04**	7.02	−1.43	37.66	−6.72
55.22	**76.15**	−5.55	−3.92	−2.06	−12.28
54.36	**83.44**	0.16	−6.52	25.57	−11.89
53.49	**90.08**	8.44	−2.61	52.50	−13.51
50.04	**35.35**	2.48	−2.51	8.50	6.45
75.06	**77.61**	−12.03	−5.14	−26.98	−10.87
43.14	**56.14**	−1.18	−3.32	−3.11	5.02
34.51	**61.75**	2.81	−2.63	29.79	−13.30
25.88	**42.84**	2.02	−2.50	18.46	−5.37
47.45	**64.87**	−0.77	−0.78	14.12	−15.67
60.40	**81.91**	2.80	−4.37	32.65	−12.73
62.12	**98.85**	4.09	−3.62	38.29	−14.69

incomes tended to have high loan rates and high property values.[31] In addition, the changes in each of the components from 1979 to 1995 were all positively correlated (between .13 and .36). Each of the indicators moved in the same direction, which suggests that they were measuring the same basic concept.

The use of this revitalization index as the principal dependent variable has a number of advantages. Comparing neighborhoods to the city average controls for the economic, political, and social changes that have affected Chicago as a whole during the past 20 years: the city's population has dropped considerably, its poverty and unemployment rates have increased, and its number of businesses and jobs have declined. Very few of its neighborhoods have experienced real growth in per capita incomes. In fact, most Chicago communities have seen their economic conditions worsen. In this context, merely maintaining existing conditions represents a real accomplishment.[32] This study asks if some neighborhoods have fared better in this environment than others and, if some have, seeks to determine why. By allowing for these relative comparisons, the index approach is sensitive to local policy interventions and differential decision making within the city. At the same time, the comparison to the city average provides a benchmark of economic prosperity; communities at or above the average are assumed to be stable middle-class neighborhoods. Changes in the indices indicate not only whether a particular community improved or declined but also the extent of its change.

Using the city average as a benchmark controls for inflation in property values and per capita incomes. All of the community areas have experienced nominal growth in these indicators since 1979. Comparing the communities to each other and to the city as a whole eliminates having to determine an appropriate deflator rate and convert the monetary values into constant dollars.[33]

Using the city average also alleviates the need for elaborate transformations of the data. Many of the absolute indicators examined in the study generated highly skewed results when analyzed in more customary ways. For example, the small initial number of loans in some neighborhoods contributed to astronomical percentage increases. A number of the absolute changes are negative, making the use of logarithms, square roots, and other conventional statistical tools impractical. Above all, the index offers an easily understood, parsimonious measure of revitalization. A single score can provide a good sense of a community area's overall economic health relative to the city as a whole.

The quantitative analysis focuses on the community areas whose per capita incomes were at or below the city average in 1979, 36 of the 77 areas within Chicago. I chose this subset because of my principal concern with factors promoting revitalization in poor neighborhoods. Why already stable or affluent communities remain that way and/or improve is an important question, but one that lies outside the scope of this book. There are also statistical benefits of focusing on just low- and moderate-income areas. The correlations among the changes in the individual components of the revitalization index are much weaker (and even negative) when one takes into account all of the city neighborhoods.[34] Since an index requires positive correlations among its individual components, it cannot constitute a reliable measure of change for this larger set of neighborhoods.

Focusing on low- and moderate-income neighborhoods also accounts for statistical outliers. For example, Chicago's two most affluent neighborhoods (Lincoln Park and the Near North Side) are significant positive outliers. Compared to the city average, their per capita incomes and median property values rose by between 100 and 400 percent during the period under consideration, resulting in improvements in their index scores of more than 95 percentage points between 1979 and 1995. (The vast majority of Chicago's neighborhoods fall in the $+30$ to -30 percentage point range.) Including the extremely affluent areas in a statistical analysis distorts the correlations upward.

Table 2-2 shows the change in the overall index scores from 1979–1995 as well as the changes in each of the index components for the low- and moderate-income areas. Again, these changes represent improvements and/or declines relative to the city average.

Per capita incomes in all but two of the city's low- and moderate-income neighborhoods have declined relative to the city average. At the same time, incomes have increased in the city's most affluent neighborhoods, providing local evidence of the widening income disparities noted on the national level.[35] Fully 61 percent of the areas have experienced a relative decline in their overall economic condition. Yet 14 community areas have shown overall improvements, including 11 of the 12 worst-off neighborhoods in the late 1970s (see Table 2-1). In particular, these improving areas have experienced increased private investment, which may be a harbinger of better future opportunities for the local residents. Three-fourths of the communities have had a relative increase in the number of residential loans per housing unit. The increase may result from the relative saturation of the lending market in the city's more affluent communities and the efforts by banks to tap into less well-developed

Table 2-2. Changes in Index Scores, 1979–1995

CA	Name	Change in Index Score	Change in Per Capita Income	Change in Loan Rate	Change in Median Property Value
3	Uptown	−0.04	8.11	−50.90	34.50
14	Albany Park	−21.84	−25.42	−18.19	−18.36
20	Hermosa	−20.02	−32.20	−17.15	1.46
21	Avondale	−1.44	−16.60	12.97	14.47
22	Logan Square	5.93	−16.03	12.46	43.35
23	Humboldt Park	2.88	−15.15	33.69	8.14
24	West Town	35.17	−7.18	72.06	82.97
25	Austin	−2.68	−10.15	13.72	−4.13
26	West Garfield Park	10.90	−11.01	43.84	21.80
27	East Garfield Park	17.22	−8.20	38.10	47.17
28	Near West Side	31.43	14.70	12.39	83.93
29	North Lawndale	10.84	−10.30	39.46	24.52
30	South Lawndale	−5.26	−18.19	−2.82	12.50
31	Lower West Side	4.95	−16.53	33.78	19.09
33	Near South Side	83.35	−4.67	85.61	285.68
34	Armour Square	−1.10	−4.37	17.52	−13.17
35	Douglas	13.99	−15.66	7.38	79.90
36	Oakland	2.93	−5.88	8.08	15.38
37	Fuller Park	8.37	−4.56	23.10	19.51
38	Grand Boulevard	6.41	−4.80	11.62	23.62
40	Washington Park	5.88	−9.42	10.49	31.89
42	Woodlawn	6.73	−8.07	29.40	13.69
46	South Chicago	−22.46	−23.92	−32.03	−9.96
47	Burnside	−11.41	−10.00	−6.06	−19.57
49	Roseland	−12.35	−7.74	−17.36	−16.55
50	Pullman	−15.77	−18.35	−19.64	−6.74
51	South Deering	−20.05	−19.30	−24.77	−16.84
53	West Pullman	−9.40	−9.51	−1.96	−16.61
54	Riverdale	−3.56	−17.33	20.63	−0.22
60	Bridgeport	4.24	−15.97	32.55	16.37
61	New City	−10.48	−21.73	4.06	−2.51
67	West Englewood	−7.58	−7.46	4.22	−19.62
68	Englewood	−4.82	−11.25	27.34	−24.12
69	Gr. Grand Crossing	−3.78	−11.06	19.74	−12.76
71	Auburn Gresham	−7.59	−16.17	17.65	−15.69
73	Washington Heights	−7.47	−9.32	6.00	−17.23

areas. It also may stem from intensified enforcement of the federal Community Reinvestment Act, which compels banks to make a certain percentage of their loans in low-income neighborhoods.

Explaining the changes requires a more in-depth analysis of factors operating on multiple levels: the neighborhood, the city, the metropolitan Chicago region, and the nation as a whole. Community-specific characteristics help determine why some neighborhoods fare better than others; we will take a more detailed look at local determinants of change beginning in Chapter 4. Neighborhoods do not exist in a vacuum, however. Embedded within cities and regions, they respond to and are shaped by broader economic, social, and political forces. The general decline in per capita income across Chicago's low- and moderate-income neighborhoods mirrors the national trend of stagnating or declining real wages for middle- and lower-class workers. The growth of the suburbs has affected the economic conditions of the inner cities. Understanding neighborhood decline and revitalization therefore requires an appreciation of the changing urban landscape, a topic to which we now turn.

NOTES

[1]See, for instance, John R. Logan and Harvey L. Molotch, *Urban Fortunes* (Berkeley: University of California Press, 1987). Exchange values often differ sharply from the "use values" held by existing neighborhood residents.

[2]See, among others, Richard Freeman, "Employment and Earnings of Disadvantaged Young Men in a Labor Shortage Economy," in *The Urban Underclass,* ed. Christopher Jencks and Paul E. Peterson (Washington, DC: Brookings Institution, 1991), pp. 103–121, and Paul Osterman, "Gains from Growth? The Impact of Full Employment on Poverty in Boston," in *The Urban Underclass,* pp. 122–134.

[3]Jargowsky, p. 46. See also James Robin, "Poverty in Relation to Macroeconomic Trends, Cycles, and Policies, in *Confronting Poverty,* ed. Sheldon H. Danziger, Gary D. Sandefur, and Daniel H. Weinberg (Cambridge: Harvard University Press, 1994), pp. 147–167.

[4]John D. Kasarda, "Urban Industrial Transition and the Underclass" *Annals of the American Association of Political and Social Sciences* 501 (January 1989): 31–32.

[5]Cited in Peter Marcuse, "Abandonment, Gentrification, and Displacement: The Linkages in New York City," in *Gentrification of the City,* ed. Neil Smith and Peter Williams (Boston: Allen & Unwin, 1986), p. 153.

[6]See Richard T. LeGates and Chester Hartman, "The Anatomy of Displacement in the United States," in *Gentrification of the City,* pp. 178–200.

[7]For the most part, displacement occurs in areas in which high demand for scarce land raises the economic value of property above its use value. The cost of land increases to a point at which it is affordable only to more affluent individuals. Lower-income people can no longer afford the cost of living in the area and have to move elsewhere. Displacement pressures are most acute in highly dense, highly desirable areas such as those located either close to a major employment center or an appealing geographic amenity. In Chicago, displacement has occurred principally in communities such as Uptown, Lincoln Park, West Town, and parts of the Near West Side, all of which either adjoin Lake Michigan and/or are near the downtown Loop. Displacement is a non-issue, however, in many other low-income neighborhoods throughout the city. The exodus of residents from Chicago as a whole, but especially from distressed minority neighborhoods, has created numerous low-density communities with considerable amounts of vacant land. Communities such as North Lawndale, the Garfield Parks, Grand Boulevard, and Woodlawn had roughly half the population density in 1990 that they had in 1970. Because of the low density in these areas, tremendous amounts of development can take place without exerting any displacement pressures on the existing residents and businesses.

A number of other factors make displacement less of an issue than it was in the past. The growth and sophistication of the nonprofit community development industry has changed the dynamics of revitalization. These organizations, typically created as a means of improving conditions for low-income individuals, play integral roles in the redevelopment of economically distressed inner-city neighborhoods. Either they develop an area largely by themselves or they work in conjunction with for-profit developers. The nonprofits' involvement in the process ensures greater benefits for the existing residents.

The anti-displacement protests of the 1970s and early 1980s made the issue more salient in public legislatures. Ordinances in cities such as Boston and San Francisco mandate that private developers either set aside a proportion of their units for low-income residents and/or contribute to an affordable housing trust fund. Legislatures have also blessed the creation and use of land trusts and other preservation mechanisms to ensure the continued affordability of properties for low-income residents. Taken together, these factors have significantly reduced the contention (and thus the concern) surrounding displacement as a byproduct of revitalization.

[8]Gale, p. 92.

[9]Phillip Clay devotes much of *Neighborhood Renewal* to a comparison of gentrification and incumbent upgrading. Ernest W. Burgess first outlined the con-

cept of concentric residential zones emanating from downtown in "The Growth of the City: An Introduction to a Research Project," in *The City,* ed. Robert E. Park, Burgess, and Roderick D. McKenzie (Chicago: University of Chicago Press, 1925).

[10]See Chapter 5 of Taub, Taylor, and Dunham for a discussion of incumbent upgrading in Beverly and Hyde Park/Kenwood. David P. Varady's *Neighborhood Upgrading* (Albany: SUNY Press, 1986) also discusses the process of neighborhood racial transition and analyzes the limited effects of an urban homesteading program in managing the change.

[11]The Near South Side, the Clybourn Street Corridor, and the Fulton Street warehouse district in Chicago are examples of areas undergoing adaptive re-use. See "Lookin' Up Down South" *Chicago Tribune* (April 13, 1996), Sec. 4, pp. 1–4 for a discussion of some of the issues associated with the process.

[12]Alinsky is viewed by many as the father of modern grass-roots organizing efforts. His theories and tactics have strongly influenced groups such as the Industrial Areas Foundation and the National Training and Information Center.

[13]Albert Hunter's *Symbolic Communities* (Chicago: University of Chicago Press, 1974) offers a sociological analysis of Chicago's neighborhoods and remaps the city based on views of community boundaries in 1974. Hunter and other sociologists have focused on the question of what constitutes a "community." (See Peter H. Rossi, "Community Social Indicators," in *The Human Meaning of Social Change,* ed. Angus Campbell and Phillip E. Converse (New York: Russell Sage Foundation, 1972), pp. 87–126, among others.) Their research has generally dealt with the extent of social interaction among area residents, the degree to which residents could identify the name of the area, and so forth. While recognizing the rich nuances of the term "community," I am nevertheless using it interchangeably with "neighborhood" and "community area" to represent a clearly demarcated geographical space.

[14]At the same time, calculations of the poverty rate do not account for benefits such as health care or housing subsidies, which effectively raise an individual's material condition.

[15]For example, a household may consist of a single person, unrelated individuals sharing the same apartment or house, or a family. A family may be defined as two parents and their children, a single parent with children, or a married couple. Median individual income might well be a better measure than per capita income, in that it indicates how most people are doing and eliminates potential skewing caused by someone unusually wealthy such as Bill Gates. Unfortunately, median individual income measures are unavailable.

[16]Chicago Fact Book Consortium, *Local Community Fact Book—Chicago Metropolitan Area* (Chicago: Chicago Review Press, 1984).

[17]Claritas/NPDC estimates per capita income for census tracts using data from federal revenue sharing files, which contain income data for census-defined place levels. Projections are created using the historical (1989 to current estimated year) ratio of per capita income growth rates for individual census tracts to the larger geographic area in which it is located (Claritas/NPDC methodology description). To obtain 1995 data, I assumed a linear progression from 1993 to 1998 and interpolated accordingly. The 1995 per capita measures are inherently less reliable than the 1979 and 1989 figures, but they are the best ones available.

[18]See Richard P. Taub, *Nuance and Meaning in Community Development: Finding Community and Development* (New York: Community Development Research Center, 1989), particularly pp. 9–21, for a discussion of these issues.

[19]See Taub, Taylor, and Dunham, Chapter 6.

[20]The number of loans made in an area provides a better indication of market activity than the total dollar value of those loans. More loans suggests more widespread interest on the part of bankers and other financial institutions. Higher total values may be driven by a single large loan made to a project on the edge of a community area. The project might well be an anomaly, having little spillover value for the rest of the neighborhood. Because Chicago's community areas vary considerably in size, all of the indicators have been converted into rates to allow for meaningful comparisons.

[21]See the following Woodstock Institute (Chicago) publications: Daniel Immergluck, *Focusing In: Indicators of Economic Change in Chicago's Neighborhoods* (1994); *1993 Community Lending Fact Book* (1995); *1994 Community Lending Fact Book* (1996); *1995 Community Lending Fact Book* (1997).

[22]Jean Pogge, Josh Hoyt, and Elspeth Revere, *Partners in Need: A Four-year Analysis of Residential Lending in Chicago and Its Suburbs* (Chicago: Woodstock Institute, 1986).

[23]*Chicago Comprehensive Neighborhood Needs Assessment,* vol II (Chicago: Melaniphy & Associates, 1982).

[24]Such a measure is not perfect, although it does effectively get at an important component of investment. Theoretically banks could make a large number of federally-guaranteed (higher-risk) FHA loans in a neighborhood and have a large percentage of them default. The loan measure would indicate improvement in the neighborhood, even though the community was hemorrhaging economically. The use of an index (to be described in the next section), with individual components weighted separately, helps to address this potential problem.

[25]Immergluck, pp. 46–51. The 1990–1995 data came directly from the realtors' database.

[26]The August 1992 merger of the North Side and South Side Real Estate Boards established the Chicago Association of Realtors. CAR has computerized

single-family sales information by community area for the entire city since August of 1992 and for areas north of I-290 (the Eisenhower Expressway and southern boundary of the North Side Board) since the beginning of 1990. It does not have any of the old South Side Real Estate Board's sale data broken out by community area, making it unrealistic to gather information south of the Expressway for 1990 and 1991. For 1992, I assumed that the median price for post-July sales in south-side communities was representative of those areas for the year. I then doubled the total number of post-July sales to obtain the number for the entire year.

[27]The numbers may under-represent the actual sale volume in low-income areas, as people in those communities tend to be less likely to use a realtor to sell their home. The database only includes home sales involving a real estate agent.

[28]An alternative approach would be to include median sale prices of small multifamily properties and average the two medians. Unfortunately, the CUED and CAR data is broken into different categories. CUED has information on 2–6 unit properties, while CAR has data on 2–4 unit buildings. Rather than compare different measures, I decided to accept the limitations of single-family data.

[29]While retail indicators are not specific dependent variables, they do provide valuable information about neighborhood change. Using the Census data from 1982, 1987, and 1992, I developed a rough measure of community area retail activity by allocating establishments to community areas based on the percentage of the areas' territory that is located within the zip code boundaries. The 1982–1992 change in the number of retail establishments was correlated .30 with the change in the index score, .26 with the change in per capita income, .01 with the change in loan rate, and .37 with the change in property value.

[30]This formula applies for all neighborhoods except for the Near South Side, which remained primarily non-residential until the early 1990s. (The area had no recorded single-family home sales until 1993.) For the Near South Side's 1979 and 1989 indices, I weighted per capita income and residential loans equally.

[31]The 1979 correlations among the variables ranged from .63 to .75, with all being statistically significant at the .001 level.

[32]Very few neighborhoods within the city have improved on all three indicators; many have experienced increased private investment while still witnessing a drop in their per capita incomes. "Revitalization" may in essence describe a relative lack of decline in certain communities.

[33]The federal Department of Commerce determines annual inflation rates for different metropolitan areas (including Chicago), yet there is some question as to whether the rate is the same for all parts of a region. Chicago's inflation rate

may be slightly different from Schaumburg's, and individual communities within the central city may also differ depending on their consumption patterns.

[34]More specifically, changes in loans and income are negatively correlated, as are changes in loans and property values. A possible explanation is that more affluent communities within Chicago tend to be both more developed and more stable (having less population turnover) than poorer neighborhoods. The greater saturation of the lending market in these areas would suggest a lower rate of increase in the number of loans made. Less developed and less stable neighborhoods have greater potential growth opportunities and thus would likely have faster rates of loan increases

[35]See, for instance, Kevin Phillips, *The Politics of Rich and Poor* (New York: Random House, 1990).

CHAPTER 3

The Context for Neighborhood Decline and Revitalization

The character of urban life has changed radically in the past 50 years. Once the nation's unquestioned centers of cultural, residential, and economic life, cities no longer hold as many attractions as they once did. Central cities now house fewer residents than their surrounding suburbs in virtually every metropolitan area throughout the country, and the suburbs continue to gain population at a faster rate than the cities. Suburbs also continue to experience the highest rates of employment growth, even though cities contain the highest number of jobs in the metropolitan regions.

The suburbanization of residents and jobs has negatively affected economic conditions in central cities, but it alone has not caused the well-publicized decline of urban America. Broad national changes, particularly the movement away from a manufacturing-dominated economy to one predicated more on service delivery, have created a more bifurcated labor market. Lower-skilled workers, many of whom reside in inner-city neighborhoods, have fewer opportunities to find and retain stable, well-paying jobs. The exodus of residents and businesses from the cities, coupled with reductions in state and federal aid, has reduced resources available to city governments for the provision of social and economic services.

These broader economic and political forces have affected central cities as entire entities. In concert with local social and political factors, they have had devastating consequences for many inner-city neighborhoods. This chapter illustrates how the interplay of national and regional economic changes, national social policies, local racial and ethnic tensions, and local political considerations has affected Chicago's low-income communities. In describing the historical factors and context for neighborhood decline, the chapter also outlines some of the forces that provide opportunities for revitalization.

RESIDENTIAL SEGREGATION (1940–1960)

One of the country's leading manufacturing centers, Chicago historically attracted job seekers from all over the world. Throughout the 1800s and early 1900s the city welcomed immigrants from Ireland, Sweden, Poland, Germany, and other parts of Europe, enticing them with the prospect of steady, well-paying factory work. The city's economic opportunities also attracted thousands of individuals from within the United States in the 1930s and 1940s, especially from Appalachia and the South. Poor blacks found the city's industrial opportunities particularly appealing, as they required relatively little education and paid far more than the cotton-picking jobs prevalent in the South. With the emergence of the mechanical cotton-picker and the consequent reduction in Southern jobs, Chicago became an even more appealing destination. The city's black population grew by over 550,000, to 812,637, between 1940 and 1960.[1]

The many ethnic groups within the city had traditionally carved out their own distinct neighborhoods. Chicago's Italian residents lived in separate areas from the city's Irish residents. Poles had their own communities, as did Germans and Swedes. To a large extent the residential segregation was self-imposed: immigrants and second-generation Americans often desired to live among people with similar cultures and backgrounds. Many of the incoming blacks shared such mind-sets and clustered in an area extending south of the downtown Loop. Yet blacks encountered more than the normal amount of segregation. In 1917, the Chicago Real Estate Board (CREB) had specifically endorsed a policy to preserve the existing racial character of the city's communities (and thus its public schools). CREB regulations mandated that realtors confine black housing opportunities to predominantly black city blocks. When a block filled, realtors were to move on to the next adjacent block. The practice of enforced segregation gained widespread popularity following a 1919 race riot precipitated by a black swimmer accidentally coming ashore on a white-dominated south side beach. By 1960, blacks comprised one-fourth of Chicago's population yet were crowded into only about 10 percent of the city's geographical area.

Federal housing policies reinforced these local patterns of segregation. The Federal Housing Authority's 1938 manual listed the presence of "incompatible racial and social groups" as one criterion lenders could use in writing residential mortgages. The FHA observed that "if a neighborhood is to remain stable, it is necessary that properties . . . continue to be occupied by the same social and racial classes."[2] The Authority's guidelines seemingly justified the CREB's use of restrictive covenants, written agreements that prevented white home owners from selling their properties to blacks.

The restrictions on black residential mobility had predictable consequences. The south side "black belt" had a severe housing shortage for most of the 1940s. In April of 1942 the vacancy rate was a microscopic 0.9 percent, and in 1950 nearly one-fourth of Chicago's non-white residents were living in overcrowded conditions. Landlords subdivided already small units to exploit the overwhelming demand for housing, finding it more profitable to pay court-mandated fines than to abide by the city's housing codes.[3]

In 1948 the Supreme Court invalidated the use of restrictive covenants in *Shelley v. Kramer,* a decision that eliminated a major legal barrier to residential integration. Although the decision resulted in a somewhat expanded housing market for Chicago's black residents, it did not alleviate the city's segregation. Fearing that blacks would move into their neighborhoods and depress the value of their properties, many residents of predominantly white areas near the "black belt" scrambled to sell their homes and maximize the financial return on their investment. The process encouraged widespread speculation and panic peddling, as realtors scared otherwise contented residents into selling their properties. Racial transition constituted a boon for realtors. The overcrowded conditions in the black belt created considerable demand for housing among blacks willing and able to move. Blacks were thus willing to pay higher prices than whites for homes in racially changing areas; there was often a considerable gap between the price at which panicked whites sold a house (often to a realtor) and the price at which blacks bought the same property. Realtors could and did make substantial commissions on the sales, in addition to whatever profits they might accrue by serving as short-term owners of various properties. The decades-old process of concentrating blacks in particular blocks continued.

The elimination of restrictive covenants added to the growing movement of white Chicago residents to the suburbs. Advances in transportation, continued post-war economic growth, and availability of cheap land outside the city made moving out of Chicago affordable for an increasing number of individuals. The availability of low-interest federal loans for veterans encouraged greater home ownership and created a need for more residential loans. Since FHA lending guidelines emphasized the desirability of stable, racially homogeneous areas, places with more land and fewer minorities (i.e., suburbs) became more favorable locations for loan guarantees.[4] This greater availability of land, coupled with the growing minority presence in the city, led thousands of Chicagoans to leave the city for the surrounding suburbs.

As individuals moved to the suburbs and the "black belt" south of the Loop became increasingly overcrowded and run-down, sales in the downtown shopping center declined. To reverse the trend, the chief executives at Marshall Field's and the Chicago Title and Trust Company spearheaded a lobbying effort that resulted in the passage of state legislation encouraging slum redevelopment: the Blighted Areas Redevelopment Act of 1947 and the Urban Community Conservation Act of 1953.[5] These measures, along with the federal Housing Act of 1949, justified the use of eminent domain powers and public resources for the clearance and redevelopment of decaying central-city areas. Chicago obtained public funds to eradicate blighted areas and to build replacement housing for those individuals displaced by the process.

These Acts sought to improve conditions both for low-income residents and for central city businesses, yet the benefits disproportionately favored influential downtown businessmen. The definition of a slum area became increasingly flexible—in many cases only 20 percent of the area's housing had to be classified as blighted for the area to be eligible for clearance and redevelopment funds—and was often determined principally by the desirability of the property for economic uses.[6]

Many Republican legislators opposed increased governmental activity in social welfare and feared that creating housing for low-income individuals would interfere with the operations of the private real estate market. They therefore made the dispersal of public funds for urban renewal programs conditional on chief priority being given to land redevelopment. Chicago redevelopment ordinances mandated that no more than 15 percent of the targeted land could be used for replacement housing and that any new housing had to be built by private developers.[7] Although the federal Housing Act called for each demolished housing unit to be replaced by a new structure, the actual number of new homes lagged far behind the number razed. By 1965, nearly one-fourth of the housing that had existed in Chicago's black belt fifteen years earlier had been demolished.[8]

Within Chicago, the task of relocating displaced slum residents fell to the Chicago Housing Authority. The CHA had been established in the mid-1930s as part of federal legislation designed to address the shelter needs of low-income workers affected by the Depression. It had initially pursued a racial policy endorsed by then-Secretary of the Interior Harold Ickes: public housing tenants should not alter a neighborhood's existing racial composition. The overwhelming need for housing among Chicago's low-income blacks gradually forced the CHA to change its policies, however. The Authority pursued a clear policy of non-discrimination for black veterans after World War II, trying to place them in public housing facilities throughout the city. Such actions provoked denunciation of the CHA in many of the city's lower-income white neighborhoods, as residents charged the Authority with being out of touch with the majority's view on race relations.[9]

The CHA increasingly had to take public opinion into account when addressing local housing needs, as integration had little legal support. Beginning in 1948 the Chicago City Council had the power to approve public housing sites. The United States Senate defeated a proposed amendment to the 1949 Housing Act that would have mandated the integration of public housing; opponents threatened to kill the entire bill if the non-discrimination provision were accepted. The CHA had no strong local political support, as it was formally independent of both the City Council and the Mayor. In many cases, the Authority's non-partisan stances engendered considerable opposition among the city's more patronage-oriented aldermen. Attempts on the part of CHA officials to relocate displaced black families into the communities of Englewood, Gage Park, and Cicero sparked local riots and furthered antipathy toward the "social engineers" within the Authority.[10]

The continued overcrowding within the "black belt" ensured that a significant proportion of the new public housing tenants would be black, and a vocal (and increasingly violent) segment of Chicago's white population insisted that such housing would not be built in their neighborhoods. One option was to build on vacant land in outlying areas of the city, yet Chicago's aldermen generally opposed such plans in favor of protecting the land for other future uses. Alderman Michael Duffy explained that "public housing should not be placed where it will stymie the growth of a community. . . . Wherever there is a project there is a deterioration of the surrounding neighborhood. No one will invest in a

$15,000 or $18,000 house near one of those projects."[11] Of the 9,000 public housing units approved by the City Council in 1950, only 2,000 were to be constructed on vacant property.[12] With aldermen rejecting almost all of the developments CHA officials proposed for white areas of the city, the Authority had little alternative but to concentrate the new housing within the "black belt."

By 1962 the CHA had built four separate public housing complexes on the south and near west sides, developments consisting of 75 buildings of at least seven stories each. CHA employees received instructions to maintain the racial composition of the neighborhoods when they assigned applicants to the buildings. These mandates resulted in the steering of black applicants to black projects, a process which avoided ugly racial conflicts but effectively legitimized and institutionalized segregation. By 1968 the CHA managed 64 projects throughout the city. In 60 of those projects (containing 29,000 units), blacks comprised 95 percent of the tenants. The other 4 projects had 1,700 units and were 95 percent white.[13] The two-mile stretch of high-rises on the south side (Stateway Gardens and the Robert Taylor Homes) housed nearly 40,000 poor blacks.[14]

The discriminatory site selection process provoked relatively little organized opposition within the black community, however. Many of the public housing residents found their new homes to be markedly better than their previous ones. Concentrating voters in high-rises within their wards suited the needs of many black aldermen. The manager of the Robert Taylor Homes contended that "we had to build [the housing] here because Negro aldermen wanted those extra votes; when you build straight up like this, you inflate a constituency."[15] The aldermen and others justified the resulting segregation as actually benefiting the city's black residents. For example, the Chicago Commission on Human Relations asserted in 1951 that racially closed communities would help protect indigenous businesses and therefore benefit struggling black entrepreneurs.[16]

Reluctance to invest in all black and/or racially changing areas, coupled with the overcrowded conditions of the ghettos, caused banks and insurance companies to shy away from the "black belt." In 1960, 285 of the state's 310 casualty and fire insurance companies refused to write policies in the predominantly black areas of the south and west sides. Obtaining mortgage financing remained problematic for many aspiring black homeowners. Taking their cue from FHA lending guidelines, the majority of banks deemed blacks unacceptable credit risks and simply refused to make loans to them. Blacks therefore had to work out payment plans with individual sellers or realtors, some of whom charged rates double or triple those of conventional banks. The banks that did lend to blacks also discriminated in their lending rates. Whereas whites typically received five percent interest rates and one percent surcharges, blacks usually received loans with six percent interest rates and ten percent surcharges.[17]

THE CIVIL RIGHTS MOVEMENT AND
THE WAR ON POVERTY (1960–1968)

The increasingly powerful Civil Rights Movement, in concert with increased attention to urban social and economic inequalities on the part of academics and philanthropists,[18] gradually moved urban redevelopment to the national policy agenda. John Kennedy's establishment of the Presidential Committee on Juvenile Delinquency in 1962 presaged the passage of the Economic Opportunity Act in 1964. The Act, the centerpiece of Lyndon Johnson's War on Poverty, sought to expand opportunity for poor urban residents through a series of education and job training programs. Head Start offered additional educational resources for disadvantaged preschoolers, Upward Bound provided similar services for poor school-aged children, and the Job Corps established vocational skill-building programs for troubled teenagers and young adults. The Act also created the Community Action Program (CAP), which encouraged the "maximum feasible participation" of the poor in designing and implementing programs to address the wide range of needs in low-income neighborhoods. The CAP's framers contended that the poor needed a "real voice in their institutions" to become full participants in the country's economic and social system.[19]

Many of the Act's components—particularly the CAP—funneled federal resources directly to local, non-governmental agencies. In addition to solidifying the Democrats' grass-roots urban constituencies, these programs sought to bypass traditionally intransigent city bureaucracies and catalyze significant local changes. The CAP's framers naively believed that mayors would wholeheartedly support such attempts at reducing bureaucratic influence; in reality, many mayors viewed the independent community action agencies as threats to their power. San Francisco Mayor John Shelley lambasted the federal policy-makers for "undermining the integrity of local government."[20] In Chicago, Mayor Richard J. Daley complained that the CAP jeopardized his ability to allocate services appropriately and sought to co-opt much of the program within the city.

Elected as mayor in 1955, Daley retained his post as chairman of the Cook County Democratic Party's Central Committee. The dual positions gave him unprecedented control over the Chicago Democratic Machine, one of the country's most efficient (and most ruthless) political apparatuses, and over thousands of patronage jobs within the city. The Party's intricate system of aldermen, ward committeemen, and precinct captains worked to turn out votes for its candidates of choice. In exchange for their votes, constituents received jobs in city government, attention to their material needs, government contracts for their businesses, and so forth. The extent to which Machine operatives could bestow such favors depended on their ability to generate votes. Those who consistently demonstrated loyalty and political efficiency received more power. Similarly, loyal constituents were more likely to obtain special consideration.

The Machine's strength lay among lower- and lower middle-class city residents, who relied on it for material benefits and viewed it as an indispensable intermediary between them and the formal institutions of government. Its local orientation—embodied in the local residents who served as precinct captains—gave the Machine a personal, comforting quality.[21] Its influence crossed racial lines: the south side black wards represented by Congressman William Dawson regularly turned out some of the highest percentages of votes for Daley. Yet these and other votes throughout the city did not translate into significant policy changes. The Machine's effectiveness depended on its ability to control political power, particularly the allocation of resources throughout the city. Anything that weakened the Machine's ability to obtain votes and wield that power could not be tolerated. Attempts at social reform (such as locating public housing in white neighborhoods) were guaranteed to generate controversy and threaten the Party's base of support in certain communities. Furthermore, Daley himself had little interest in effecting significant social and economic change. Born and bred in the south-side, staunchly Irish Catholic neighborhood of Bridgeport, Daley believed in the primacy of the family, the Church, the local schools, and the ward organization (all status quo-oriented groups) as guiding social institutions. He felt that every man had an obligation to lift himself up by his own bootstraps and had little patience with those who became unwarranted burdens on the larger society.[22] How he personally viewed blacks is unclear; Bridgeport, however, had a reputation as one of the most parochial, racially prejudiced neighborhoods in the city.

The political mobilization of the poor inherent in many of the federal War on Poverty programs posed a threat to the Machine's power in Chicago. In the early 1960s, individuals associated with a federal juvenile delinquency program publicly criticized the Chicago public schools, promoted a number of independent community organizations, and sponsored rallies in which Daley himself was roundly booed. Determined to prevent further attacks on the Machine, Daley ensured that City Hall-controlled agencies administered Chicago's Community Action Program. In addition to controlling the allocation of the program's material benefits, the move precluded the political and social mobilization of disaffected poor minorities. "Many depressed urban citizens are ready for sub-leadership roles," Daley argued, but he contended that they would be better off in salaried subprofessional positions than in "mere advisory roles in action committees that lead also to nonproductive protest activities." In short, he refused to allow the maximum feasible participation of the poor in programmatic decision-making, a central component of the CAP. The city's community action agency personnel (appointed by the Mayor) repeatedly stated that their mission did not include strengthening neighborhood political resources.[23]

Not surprisingly, Daley's stance provoked conflict with the Johnson Administration. Officials within the Office of Economic Opportunity (OEO), the agency charged with implementing many of the federal anti-poverty programs, reported that Daley and his aides "do not permit any type of community organization. The problems of the Chicago program are sins not of commission, but of omission. We sensed a general hostility . . . to programs involving community organization or social action."[24] Reformers within OEO blasted the Community Action Program in Chicago as a blatantly Machine-dominated operation. On the other side, Daley could not understand the federal government's bypassing of elected officials. He screamed at Johnson aide Bill Moyers, "What in the hell are you people doing? Does the President know he's putting MONEY in the hands of subversives? To poor people that aren't a part of the organization?"[25] Yet Daley's influence within the national Democratic Party—a result of his ability to produce hundreds of thousands of Chicago votes for the Party's Presidential candidates—prevented the Administration from cutting the federal money earmarked for the city.

OEO's frustration with the Machine's implementation of various War on Poverty programs mirrored that of an increasing number of black inner-city residents. The CAP and other federal initiatives had raised the hopes of thousands of poor minorities with its promise of involving local residents in comprehensive efforts to improve conditions in low-income areas. OEO Director Sargent Shriver had described the initiative as the "corps of a new social revolution," one that would eliminate poverty by the two-hundredth anniversary of the Declaration of Independence.[26] Yet the programs' results did not match their lofty rhetoric. In 1965 the unemployment rate for Chicago's black residents stood at 17 percent.[27]

With the passage of the Voting Rights Act in 1965, the Civil Rights Movement had succeeded in eliminating much of the legal segregation in the country. Yet the Movement's success had only heightened the economic and social expectations and aspirations of minorities. The August 1965 riot in the Watts section of Los Angeles highlighted the growing disaffection and unrest among blacks living in high-poverty urban neighborhoods. To Martin Luther King, Jr. and other civil rights leaders, Watts demonstrated the urgent need to address the problems of the inner cities.

As in other cities throughout the country, conditions in Chicago reduced the opportunities available to black residents. Most of the black neighborhoods remained dangerously overcrowded, with deteriorating housing and relatively little private sector investment. Blacks had little political influence. They held only five percent of the policy-making positions within the Cook County Machine, even though they constituted 20 percent of the county population and overwhelmingly voted Democratic. Blacks headed none of the city's agencies.[28] Perhaps the most glaring deficiencies lay in the city's public schools. Public officials in the city had long pursued a neighborhood school policy that effectively created schools as ethnically and racially homogeneous as their surrounding communities. By the late 1950s, schools in many black neighborhoods had become dangerously overcrowded, while many predominantly white schools remained far short of capacity: the National Association for the Advancement of Colored People issued a report in 1958 that found that predominantly white schools had an average of 669 pupils, while predominantly black schools had an average of 1,275 students.[29] The federally commissioned Hauser study group reported in 1964 that 90 percent of the city's black students were in schools at least 90 percent black, and that more money was spent per pupil in white schools than in black ones. It concluded that "quality education is not available in Chicago to the children who are in greatest need of it."[30] In 1965, the federal Department of Health, Education, and Welfare (HEW) found the Chicago Board of Education in noncompliance with the 1964 Civil Rights Act and withheld $30 million in educational aid.

Such conditions had caused a number of community groups to organize collective protests against School Superintendent Benjamin Willis, who steadfastly refused to acknowledge the existence of any segregation. Unwilling to consider transferring black students to white schools, Willis instead ordered the use of trailers and mobile homes (derided as "Willis wagons" by civil rights activists) as auxiliary classrooms outside the crowded schools. Although their efforts galvanized considerable local support—as evidenced by a school boycott involving nearly 225,000 black students in October of 1963—the community groups never succeeded in winning concessions or markedly improving conditions. For example, Willis remained in his post until 1966.

Chicago civil rights activists had repeatedly pleaded with King and other members of the Southern Christian Leadership Conference (SCLC) to focus their efforts on the city, to little avail. Yet the activists' continued mobilization, the seemingly entrenched nature of poverty in the city, and the growing black furor epitomized by the Watts riots convinced SCLC to commit to a Chicago campaign in 1966. SCLC's leaders envisioned a wide-ranging movement to eradicate the poverty of the slums and eliminate "the total pattern of economic exploitation under which Negroes suffer in Chicago and other northern cities."[31] Staff member Jim Bevel sought to combat the "four major forces which keep the ghetto in place: a) lack of economic power, b) political disenfranchisement, c) lack of knowledge and information, [and] d) lack of dignity and self-respect among the people of the ghetto."[32] In addition to orchestrating the movement's moral crusade, he and other staffers established a number of tangible anti-poverty organizations throughout the city. Operation Breadbasket worked to combat discrimination in the workplace. The Kenwood-Oakland Community Organization mobilized residents in two of the south side's poorest communities. The Union to End Slums served as an umbrella group for west-side tenant organizations seeking improved living conditions in their buildings.

The key to SCLC's success in the South had been its ability to identify well-known individuals and organizations who perpetuated segregationist policies and mobilize against them, ultimately provoking a public confrontation that generated media and political support for the protesters' position. Success therefore also required a reasonably focused approach, one that targeted a specific, easily understood problem (such as the right to vote). Although activists such as Bevel denounced the "plantation politics" practiced by Daley and the Machine, their multi-faceted approach struggled to generate the necessary negative reaction to a popular, powerful local political institution.

Frustrated by their other attempts to provoke conflict and achieve change, movement leaders eventually concentrated on the problem of fair housing. Most of the city's predominantly white neighborhoods remained effectively off-limits to black home buyers despite the communities' low housing prices and the illegality of restrictive covenants. Chicago realtors continued to steer blacks to predominantly black neighborhoods, defending their actions by asserting that they were merely mirroring popular sentiments and were not "in the business of solving social problems."[33] Civil rights leaders were not satisfied. Bevel contended that "the real estate dealers in Chicago are the equivalent to [Alabama Governor George]Wallace and [Selma, Alabama police chief] Jim Clark in the South."[34] SCLC staffers consequently organized fair housing marches in the overwhelmingly white communities of Gage Park and Marquette Park in the summer of 1966. The marches provoked violent responses on the part of local residents. Mobs of angry whites pummeled the marchers (including priests and nuns) with rocks, cherry bombs, and bottles. King confessed that he had "never seen as much hatred and hostility on the part of so many people."[35] The riots generated indignation both within Chicago and throughout the nation. Citizens were shocked that such virulent racism existed outside of the South and blamed Daley for allowing the protests to get out of hand. Fearing that future marches could provoke a city-wide race riot, Daley and members of the city's business community agreed to negotiate with King and the other civil rights leaders.

The ensuing Summit Conference involved representatives from all parties involved in and affected by the movement: civil rights leaders (representing potential black home buyers), the Mayor and other city administrators, CREB members, religious leaders, and influential members of the business community. After considerable acrimony, the participants agreed to a series of steps. The Chicago Commission on Human Relations promised to enforce the city's fair housing ordinance. Daley committed to working with the Chicago Housing Authority to desegregate the city's public housing. Representatives of the city's major banks vowed to offer mortgages irrespective of the applicant's race. CREB promised to educate its members about open housing and drop its formal opposition to the city's fair housing ordinance and Illinois's proposed open housing law. Business and religious leaders agreed to establish a new fair housing organization (the Leadership Council for Metropolitan Open Communities) that would promote and coordinate programs of education and direct action. Amid much internal contention, the movement leaders consented to cancel their planned march in suburban Cicero and suspend other marches in Chicago.

Although King characterized the campaign a success, it actually did little to improve conditions in Chicago's economically distressed communities. The only tangible outcome of the summit conference was the establishment of the Leadership Council. The majority of the other agreements, reached on principle with no specific guarantees of enforcement, never translated into programs of local improvement. Chicago remained one of the nation's most residentially segregated cities. A number of local civil rights activists accused King of selling out the city's poor blacks.

SUBURBANIZATION, ECONOMIC RESTRUCTURING, AND URBAN DECLINE (1968–1983)

The failure of King's nonviolent campaign to improve economic and social conditions in Chicago's low-income black neighborhoods added fuel to the growing militancy within the Civil Rights Movement. Growing frustration about seemingly unchanging ghetto conditions, as well as the endorsement of violence on the part of some "black power" proponents, contributed to widespread urban rioting in the summers of 1966 and 1967. The Governor of Michigan had to call in the National Guard to restore order in Detroit, a process which took nearly a week and led to the devastation of a large section of the city. From the relative sanctity of Chicago, a city largely spared of violence through 1967, Richard J. Daley criticized what he perceived to be ineffective responses on the part of his mayoral counterparts. When asked by reporters how he would respond to such riots, Daley replied, "I can assure you there won't be any blank ammunition [in National Guard firearms]. The ammunition will be live."[36]

Daley's turn came a year later. Chicago's black neighborhoods had a shortage of 50,000 low-income housing units. Infant mortality rates in the communities had gone up 25 percent or more in the previous ten years. Only three of the 150 discrimination complaints registered with the Chicago Commission on Human Relations in 1967 had led to the suspension of a realtor's license.[37] Eventually local frustrations came to a boil. Following the assassination of Martin Luther King, Jr. on April 4, 1968, a number of black teenagers walked out of their high schools, massed in Garfield Park, and then fanned out along the major thoroughfares on Chicago's west side. What ensued was the most devastating riot in the city's history. Nine people were killed, over 500 were injured, 162 buildings were destroyed, and nearly 270 buildings and homes were looted, almost all in already poor minority areas.[38] Unwilling to believe that such an uprising could occur in his city, an incensed Daley ordered the police to shoot to kill arsonists and to maim looters.[39]

The riots in Chicago, Detroit, Washington, and other cities increased public opposition to the existing federal approach to urban development. Claiming that it was "time that good, decent people stopped letting themselves be bulldozed by anybody who presumes to be the self-righteous judge of our society," Richard Nixon moved to reduce the federal government's specific targeting of low-income minority neighborhoods.[40] By illustrating the increasingly violent tensions present in the central cities, the riots also accelerated the process of suburbanization. Roughly 500,000 white Chicagoans left the city between 1970 and 1975.

Suburbanization further exacerbated the racial polarization within Chicago. The fair housing campaign of 1966 had generated criticism of Daley among some of his white ethnic constituents. Stung by these criticisms and struggling to stem the migration to the suburbs, Richard Daley and his advisers pursued policies designed to keep whites in the city. For example, the Chicago Board of Education operated from the premise that "the immediate short range goal must be to anchor the whites that still remain in the city. To do this requires that school authorities quickly achieve and maintain stable racial attendance proportions in changing fringe areas."[41] Such policies, coupled with the resentment toward Daley stemming from King's campaign, increased anti-Machine sentiment within the city's black community. Although Daley's 1967 re-election represented his largest margin of victory, it also marked the emergence of nascent anti-Machine sentiment in the city's black wards. Three of the five black anti-Machine aldermanic candidates won election to City Council.[42] Recognizing the growing racial fissures, the city's Democratic establishment focused increasingly on solidifying the white vote and demobilizing the black one. By 1977, black voter turnout had fallen to 27 percent, down from 65 percent in 1964.[43]

By 1970, blacks comprised more than 90 percent of the residents in 12 of Chicago's 77 community areas. Ten of the 12 had poverty rates of 22 percent or greater, well above the city average of 14.5 percent.[44] Machine officials did little to alleviate the city's residential segregation. In *Gautreaux v. Chicago Housing Authority* (1969), federal District Judge Richard Austin found the CHA guilty of discrimination in its selection of sites and housing of applicants. Austin mandated that any additional public housing units had to be built in areas of the city that did not have a majority of black and/or Hispanic residents. Reflecting the sentiments of many of the city's white residents, Daley denounced the ruling and vowed to fight it. City officials prevented the CHA from building any new units from 1969 through 1974 while City lawyers appealed the ruling. Between 1974 and 1979 city officials targeted $2.9 billion of federal apartment rehabilitation monies to blighted black neighborhoods, and nearly five times that amount to high-income communities along Lake Michigan.[45]

Residential segregation persisted despite passage of the federal Fair Housing Act in 1968. Local realtors risked social ostracism and lost business if they showed homes in white neighborhoods to black families. Individuals who felt that they were victims of segregation had to take individual realtors to court, a process which often took months or even years. In 1972 HUD suspended allocation of neighborhood development funds to Chicago because of continued discrimination in CHA buildings. Yet two years later the agency essentially rubber-stamped Chicago's CDBG application (despite continued segregation), in part because of the Nixon Administration's reduction of federal oversight regulations.[46] Eventually the federal regulators gave up trying to address racial problems in the city. An assistant secretary in the Department of Health, Education, and Welfare explained in the early 1970s, "In Chicago, the people at HEW told me it's impossible. . . . Sometimes there's a case where you just throw up your hands, and Chicago was it."[47]

The Machine's various efforts did not stop the growing exodus of Chicago residents to the suburbs. The prospect of more land in cheaper, safer localities—a centerpiece of the American dream—proved too appealing to thousands of middle- and upper-class residents. People viewed the city as dirty, dangerous, noisy, and chaotic. Insurance costs were high, and the poor condition of many of the city's public schools forced many families to send their children to private educational institutions. Not only did the suburbs and their better public school systems offer a cheaper alternative, but the communities tended to be more homogeneous and thus less prone to race- and class-based conflict. By 1979 Chicago had 37 percent fewer upper-income and 35 percent fewer middle-income families than it had 20 years earlier. The suburbanization involved both whites and blacks. The population of the city's predominantly black West Garfield Park, East Garfield Park, Near West Side, North Lawndale, Grand Boulevard, and Washington Park community areas all dropped by at least 25 percent between 1970 and 1980.[48]

The individuals remaining in the city tended to be poorer than those moving to the suburbs. Poverty rates in many of Chicago's inner-city neighborhoods consequently increased. Eight of the city's community areas had poverty rates of 30 percent or higher in 1970, and none had unemployment rates of as high as 20 percent. Ten years later, 14 community areas had poverty rates of at least 30 percent, and 10 had at least one-fifth of their eligible workers unemployed. The absolute number of poor households had remained essentially constant, yet the number of more affluent residents had decreased considerably. The loss of the economically better-off individuals had debilitating effects on the communities. Most of these individuals had jobs, which gave them (and by extension, those with whom they interacted in the community) greater access to employment networks. With weakened networks, the remaining residents had less knowledge of and access to available jobs. The loss of more affluent residents also affected local social institutions such as churches and YMCAs. Many of these organizations depended on local individuals for financial support and found themselves no longer able to maintain their previous level of services.[49]

The loss of population in inner-city neighborhoods coincided with the deterioration of public housing. Policies lowering the income ceiling for public housing recipients ensured that residents of CHA properties would be among the poorest members of the society. CHA officials were urged to house as many people as quickly as they could, a mandate that limited the time they could spend screening tenants. Whereas the CHA projects had initially been designed to provide temporary shelter for displaced individuals, by the mid-1960s they had become "ghettoized repositories" for Chicago's poorest and most troubled black families.[50] Tenants often could not afford to pay the rent asked of them, so the CHA routinely had to write off thousands of dollars in uncollectibles. Graft and mismanagement within the Authority further worsened conditions. HUD evaluators concluded in 1982 that the CHA's maintenance costs were more than twice as high as those of any other public housing authority in the "rust belt."[51] Lacking the money to maintain the buildings—a condition made worse by cutbacks in federal public housing monies—the CHA saw its buildings deteriorate badly. Gangs took advantage of vacancies and lax security to establish headquarters in some of the high-rise complexes. By the early 1980s projects such as Stateway Gardens and the Robert Taylor Homes had become synonymous with poverty, social disorder, and urban decay.

The concentration of poverty in the public housing complexes and their surrounding neighborhoods had devastating economic and social consequences. Poor residents often did not have the income necessary to support the existing neighborhood rental market. Faced with declining revenues, landlords spent less on maintenance, which helped accelerate the deterioration of the communities' housing stock. The need for money led people to engage in and tolerate more illegal activity such as drug dealing. Youths in the communities had fewer positive role models, as fewer residents were employed full-time. Public school teachers noted that the increased poverty of the student body generated a widespread sense of despair in the classroom: students seemingly had no real desire to do better.[52] Insurance companies either refused to write policies in the neighborhoods or charged exorbitant rates. The three largest property insurance companies in Illinois charged an average of $157 for $50,000 worth of coverage for a house in a white Chicago neighborhood and an average of $213 for the same amount of coverage for a house in a black community.[53]

The pull of the suburbs and the push of inner-city decline affected businesses as well as residents. Chicago lost 88,660 jobs in the 1970s while its suburbs gained 630,040.[54] The south-side black community of Woodlawn lost over 85 percent of its commercial and industrial establishments between 1950 and 1995.[55]

The city's loss of jobs resulted only in part from businesses following workers to the suburbs. The increased globalization of the economy introduced a number of foreign competitors to industries previously dominated by United States firms. For example, steelmakers in Chicago, Cleveland, and Pittsburgh found that their products could be purchased more cheaply from overseas producers.

In their quest to be more competitive, companies restructured their plants to take advantage of technological improvements in electronics, robotics, and the like. Another solution involved lowering their costs of labor, taxes, security, and raw materials. Neither approach encouraged remaining in aging northern cities such as Chicago. Building new factories often proved cheaper than retrofitting existing ones, and Chicago had relatively little open space on which to build. The city's grid-like streets and decaying transportation infrastructure paled in comparison to industrial parks built for easy access to highways and airports. Chicago's strong labor unions required higher wages and benefits for their members, and the city's northern location guaranteed high energy costs. Furthermore, the high poverty and crime in many city neighborhoods imposed greater security costs. Firms had to pay more to protect their plants, inventories, and employees.

Federal policies also promoted economic changes, particularly in the steel industry. The high exchange rate of the early 1980s, coupled with the United States's continued international trade deficit, encouraged the consumption of foreign-produced steel. The Reagan Administration's increased spending on weapons and warships failed to compensate for its reductions in such steel-intensive areas as mass transit, urban development, and housing. Much of its increased defense spending focused on high-technology industries such as electronics, computers, and scientific instruments, sectors that use almost no steel. Taken together, these factors contributed to the closing of both Wisconsin Steel and U.S. Steel's South Works between 1979 and 1984, closings which eliminated 13,000 jobs from Chicago's south side. These shutdowns were a major cause of the city's losing 40 percent of its steel-related jobs between 1980 and 1983.[56]

The closing of the steel mills represented only part of the major economic restructuring affecting Chicago. In the 1970s, Western Electric and International Harvester, two of the major employers on the city's west side, closed their factories. By the end of the 1980s, a number of other corporations had followed suit. Campbell's Soup, Johnson & Johnson, and Schwinn Bicycle Company (among others) shut down their major Chicago production facilities.[57] Some companies moved to the suburbs, where land was cheaper and buildings could be expanded (and where the commute was easier for the chief executives). Between 1947 and 1982 Chicago lost over 400,000 factory-based jobs while suburban Cook County gained almost 160,000 and its adjacent counties gained 125,000.[58] Other corporations moved a large portion of their operations to developing nations such as Thailand and Peru, where lower labor costs and fewer governmental regulations sharply increased profitability. Many moved to the southern and western United States. The "sun belt" offered more temperate winters, summers made tolerable by air conditioning, generally lower energy costs, lower taxes, fewer regulations on business, and relatively weak labor unions. As the Chicagos, Clevelands, and Pittsburghs of the country lost people and jobs, the Dallases, Atlantas, and Los Angeleses experienced an economic boom. Between 1945 and 1980 Fort Lauderdale's population increased from 18,000 to 153,000. Phoenix grew from 65,000 to 790,000, and Houston more than quadrupled in size, from 385,000 to 1,595,000.[59]

The economic changes had particularly devastating effects for already poor inner-city neighborhoods. The unemployment caused by the closing of the Western Electric and International Harvester plants drastically reduced consumption on Chicago's west side, forcing many small businesses to move and/or shut down. What once had been stable, lower-middle class neighborhoods with decent schools, thousands of blue-collar jobs, and active shopping strips became urban ghost towns marked by boarded-up buildings and vacant lots. Between 1963 and 1977 the "black belt" areas of the west and south sides lost roughly 45 percent of their jobs.[60]

Like other old industrial cities, Chicago experienced an increase in service-sector jobs, particularly in finance, insurance, and real estate. These new jobs generally required higher levels of education, however: fully 112,500 of the jobs created in the 1970s demanded a college degree.[61] Less well-educated individuals—including many of the residents of the city's low-income neighborhoods—found themselves without the skills necessary to obtain new positions. Whereas two-thirds of Chicago's males between the ages of 22 and 58 who lacked a high school diploma had jobs in 1970, only half were employed in the 1980s.[62] Chicago had 211,000 fewer jobs in 1980 that required only a high school education than it had had a decade earlier, and only 44.7 percent of Chicago's black males had high school diplomas.[63] Not surprisingly, less than 40 percent of the eligible workers in Chicago's poorest black neighborhoods had jobs in 1980, a decline of roughly 12 percent since 1970.[64] Those who did find work often earned considerably less than they had previously. In 1987, the average earnings for males between the ages of 20 and 29 who worked in retail or service jobs were 25 to 30 percent lower than the earnings of similar individuals working in manufacturing.[65]

The federal government took an essentially laissez-faire response to the growing poverty of inner-city areas. Ronald Reagan asserted that individuals were "voting with their feet" and leaving the cities for more desirable regions. He and his advisors contended that the federal anti-poverty programs of the previous few decades had actually worsened conditions for the poor, a sentiment shared by the majority of voters. In 1980, only 35 percent of surveyed citizens felt that the social programs of the 1960s had made things better for the poor, and roughly 60 percent felt that the nation spent too much on welfare.[66]

The Reagan Administration therefore eliminated or sharply reduced many of the federal agencies and programs that worked to alleviate inner-city poverty. It eliminated the remnants of the Office of Economic Opportunity, cut HUD's funding by $29 billion, and reduced the Urban Development Action Grant budget by $450 million. The Administration replaced the Comprehensive Employment and Training Act with the Job Training Partnership Act, cutting $7 billion from job training programs. The cuts generated widespread opposition among liberals and urban mayors, who rightly feared that they would further reduce the flow of resources into already disinvested neighborhoods.[67]

THE SEEDS OF REVITALIZATION (1983–PRESENT)

Conditions in low-income neighborhoods in Chicago and other cities throughout the country continued to worsen in the 1980s. Chicago's population dropped by over 221,000 (7.4 percent) between 1980 and 1990, and a number of city businesses closed or reduced their operations. The city lost $1 billion in federal funds between 1981 and 1987 as a result of the Reagan Administration's cutbacks. The Chicago Housing Authority needed $750 million to fix its buildings in 1986, yet only received $8.9 million in federal rehabilitation funds.[68] The deterioration of the projects accelerated, with negative consequences for their residents and for the surrounding neighborhoods. By the end of the decade, ten of the city's community areas had poverty rates of 48 percent or more, up from four in 1980. Oakland, a south side community with a particularly high concentration of public housing, had a poverty rate of 72 percent. Unemployment rates in many low-income neighborhoods exceeded 25 percent.[69]

Poverty bred numerous other social ills, most notably increases in drugs and violent crime. The emergence of crack in the late 1980s triggered an unprecedented growth in gang-related homicides. In 1966, a year of heated conflict between the People and the Folks on the city's south side, Chicago had 14 gang-related deaths. The annual total remained under 100 until 1990. With the introduction of semiautomatic weapons to the streets the following year, the death total skyrocketed. Homicides in the city increased 30 percent between 1992 and 1993 and an additional 45 percent the next year, topping out at 240 in 1994.[70]

In short, the 1980s were not good to Chicago. The mix of suburbanization, the changing national and regional economy, and reduced federal urban expenditures had devastating effects on many of the city's low-income neighborhoods. Chicago continued to rank as one of the nation's most racially segregated cities and metropolitan areas.[71] Journalists routinely described some of the city's neighborhoods, particularly those in the south side's "black belt," as urban wastelands, and policy makers questioned whether anything could realistically be done to im-

Table 3-1. Population and Poverty, Selected Neighborhoods

	Population 1970	Poverty 1970	Population 1990	Poverty 1990
West Garfield Park	48,464	23.3%	24,095	40.8%
East Garfield Park	52,185	29.7%	24,030	48.1%
Near West Side	78,703	29.3%	46,197	54.5%
North Lawndale	94,772	28.2%	47,296	48.4%
Oakland	18,291	37.4%	8,197	72.3%
Grand Boulevard	80,150	32.0%	35,897	64.7%
Washington Park	46,024	25.9%	19,425	58.4%
Woodlawn	53,814	22.8%	27,473	37.0%
Englewood	89,713	22.4%	48,434	43.2%
City of Chicago	3,369,357	14.5%	2,783,726	21.6%

Source: Data taken from London and Puntenney

prove conditions in the areas. Yet in the midst of this despair, a number of events and trends offered some hope for revitalization. The changes have not resulted in phenomenal improvements in inner-city communities, but they have created a context for potential neighborhood improvement.

The Election of Harold Washington

As mentioned earlier, black disenchantment with Chicago's Democratic Machine had grown since the mid-1960s. Many residents of the city's "black belt" wards believed that the Machine took advantage of their continued political support without providing any real benefits in return. Political opposition gradually mobilized. The 1967 elections witnessed the defeat of three Machine-backed candidates in black wards. In 1972, strong black opposition doomed the candidacy of Edward Hanrahan for State's Attorney General. In 1976, Ralph Metcalfe won a seat in the U.S. House of Representatives by mobilizing grass-roots support against the Machine-endorsed candidate.

Richard J. Daley's death in 1976 did little to change blacks' perception of the Machine. Michael Bilandic took over as Mayor and continued most of his predecessor's policies. Little of significance occurred until January 1979, when a heavy snowstorm paralyzed the city. Bilandic's failure to get the streets plowed in a timely manner generated widespread resentment among all Chicagoans; his decision to have the Chicago Transit Authority's elevated lines bypass certain stops in low-income neighborhoods particularly angered the city's black community. An above-normal 53 percent of eligible black voters turned out later in the year to elect Jane Byrne as the city's new mayor.[72]

Byrne campaigned as a pro-neighborhood reformer, one who sought to overturn the long-standing patronage politics of the Machine. Early in her term she took a number of steps to try to satisfy minority constituents and address the needs of the city's poorest residents. She appointed blacks to 47 percent of City offices in 1980–1981, and she moved into the notorious Cabrini Green development for a few weeks as a way of calling attention to the problems in the city's public housing facilities. Her support among minorities waned considerably in the last two years of her term, however. Byrne antagonized many low-income voters with her hard-line approach to the strikes by Chicago Transit Authority workers, public school teachers, and city garbage collectors. She continued to support Charles Swibel, the head of the Chicago Housing Authority, despite the presence of well-publicized graft and mismanagement within the CHA and the continuing deterioration of its properties. Only 28 percent of Byrne's 1982 appointees were black, a sharp decline from the previous years.[73] The announced 1983 candidacy of Richard M. Daley (the former mayor's son) certainly affected Byrne's political considerations. She sought to neutralize the strong support Daley enjoyed in the city's white ethnic neighborhoods.

The building resentment of the Machine (and Byrne's seeming reversion to Machine politics) among the black community contributed to Harold Washington's decision to run for mayor in 1983. His campaign, in conjunction with opposition to the policies of the Reagan Administration, resulted in unprecedented political mobilization within Chicago's black community. Local churches and community organizations sponsored extensive voter registration campaigns: between 1979 and 1983 registration in the city's 17 predominantly black wards increased by nearly 30 percent, so that by 1983 over 89 percent of eligible blacks in the city were registered to vote.[74] With Byrne and Daley splitting the city's white vote, the high (73 percent) turnout and almost unanimous (99 percent in 10 wards) support of the black community gave Washington a surprise victory in the mayoral primary. The resulting general election showcased the city's continuing racial rift. Washington's campaign, one that used the slogan "it's our turn" in many of the black wards, split the city's Democratic party. Numerous white voters and aldermen flocked to the campaign of Republican Bernie Epton. Washington won the 1983 general election, but garnered only 23 percent of the vote in the predominantly white northwest and southwest sides.[75]

As with the election of any black mayor after years of white-dominated political leadership, Washington's victory generated tremendous anticipation of change within Chicago's minority community. He had run on an anti-Machine platform, had promoted greater equality of resource allocation, and had promised to open City Hall to interests and concerns that had rarely gotten a significant voice in political decision-making. He also sought to address the declining economic conditions in many of the city's low-income neighborhoods. Political and economic realities tempered what he could accomplish, however.

Washington and his advisors had to contend with a declining revenue base. The reduced tax revenues resulting from the suburbanization of residents and businesses, coupled with a 26 percent cut in federal assistance, increased the fiscal strain on the city.[76] Suspicious of the city's ability to meet its financial obligations, Moody's lowered the city's bond rating from A to Baa1 in March 1984. The need to satisfy the bond market, coupled with a court decree limiting the number of public service jobs a mayor could fill, constrained Washington in his ability to alter the city's political structure. He spent much of his first term working to pare costs by cutting services and eliminating city jobs. In trying to rebuild the city's tax base, he often had to support pro-business initiatives having questionable benefits for the city as a whole. He had to continue devoting considerable public monies to the redevelopment of the North Loop area. He steadfastly emphasized the need for enterprise zones and their tax breaks for business, despite studies showing that the zones provided few gains for the disadvantaged residents they were ostensibly trying to help.

Washington's election had signaled an end to the Machine's control of the mayor's office, but it did not represent an end to the Machine's influence. Many of the incumbent aldermen had grown used to the traditional workings of City Hall. They and their constituents were relatively content with the existing allocation of resources; like many politicians, they wanted more for their wards. Washington's proposed reordering of the city's fiscal priorities so as to provide more resources to needier areas therefore generated considerable opposition, as did many of his desired political appointments. Alderman Ed Burke, a longtime stalwart within the Machine, stated that numerous members of City Council simply refused "to put [Washington's] buddies and pals and cronies in positions presently held by buddies and pals and cronies of the City Council."[77] The opposition of these aldermen within the Council (dubbed the "Vrdolyak 29" after their leader) for much of his first few years in office often limited Washington's power to that of the veto.

In spite of these limitations, Washington's administration succeeded in calling greater attention to the needs of the city's low-income communities. The administration transferred about $13 million in CDBG monies away from central administrative costs to specific neighborhood projects. Washington established an "early warning system" on the Near West Side that provided the city with information about potential plant closings and helped design intervention strategies. The City provided loans and development funds to convince Sears to keep a store open on the southwest side. The administration used city funds for the rehabilitation of low-income housing and, in concert with Peoples Gas, it developed a low-interest energy conversion loan program administered by community organizations.[78]

Washington granted community organizations far more involvement in the policy-making process, often deferring to them on issues affecting particular neighborhoods. Reformers applauded the increased number of public hearings and the additional built-in opportunities for citizen participation. On a city-wide level, the power of these groups became evident in the administration's decision to buck corporate leaders and remove Chicago from contention for the 1992 World's Fair. Community activists had claimed (among other arguments) that the Fair would divert scarce city resources away from high-need neighborhoods such as Lawndale, Grand Boulevard, and Woodlawn.

The racial and demographic composition of Washington's electoral constituency, coupled with the increased participation of community groups in the policy-making process, created a greater awareness among city officials about the needs of low-income neighborhoods. Much more so than previous mayoral administrations, the Washington administration began to embrace housing, economic development, and neighborhood revitalization as important city-wide concerns. The city's current mayor, Richard M. Daley, continues to embrace the strategic value of such approaches.

Increased Inner-City Lending

Improving neighborhood economic conditions requires the financial support of the private sector, particularly the banking industry. Yet many banks have historically shied away from lending in inner-city areas because of the perceived high risk. Congress has enacted a series of laws designed to abolish redlining, the practice of systematically denying loans to residents of particular geographic areas.[79] The Fair Housing Act of 1968 prohibited discrimination in any real estate transaction, and the Equal Credit Opportunity Act of 1974 outlawed discrimination in any credit transaction. These laws, although not always actively enforced, addressed the legal issue of unequal treatment of individuals. It took an extensive campaign on the part of the Chicago-based National People's Action to address the preferential treatment given to geographic areas.

NPA director Gail Cincotta and others argued that banks had a responsibility to lend in the neighborhoods in which they operated branches and otherwise did business; it was fundamentally unjust for individuals in a community to be able to deposit money in a bank but be unable to borrow from that same institution. The organization's efforts gained popularity both locally and nationally. Chicago passed the country's first lending disclosure ordinance in 1974, a law compelling local banks to report the location and amount of their loans to public regulators. Congress passed the national Home Mortgage Disclosure Act (HMDA) in 1975, forcing almost all of the country's large financial institutions to report loans by census tract.

The disclosure laws provided reformers with access to information, but they did not force banks to change their neighborhood lending patterns. The breakthrough for community activists came in 1977 with the passage of the federal Community Reinvestment Act. The CRA asserted that banks "have a continuing and affirmative obligation to help meet the credit needs of the local communities in which they are chartered . . . consistent with the safe and sound operation of such institutions."[80] Subsequent amendments gave the Act more teeth by establishing an HMDA database, giving the federal Department of Justice more responsibility for enforcing the regulations, and establishing fair lending guidelines for the banks themselves. Banks were initially rated in five categories: ascertainment of community credit needs, marketing and types of credit offered, geographic distribution and opening and closing of offices, discrimination, and community development. Banks received a score for their performance in each of the categories. The process was streamlined in 1995, with banks being rated in only three areas: lending, investment, and service. Community lending efforts now receive twice as much weight (50 percent) as each of the other two (25 percent apiece).

Although banks have rarely been denied acquisitions because of poor performances in community lending, the CRA has been used as a tool by numerous community groups to force investment on the part of major banks.[81] In Chicago in the early 1980s, the Reinvestment Alliance used HMDA data to illustrate lending discrepancies for members of the local media. In the late 1970s and early 1980s, most of the major downtown banks' lending had taken place in suburban markets. Loans within the city constituted only 24 percent of banks' metropolitan lending activity between 1980 and 1983, and lending within the city generally focused on only a few select neighborhoods. Banks lent $2,000 or less per housing unit in 60 percent of Chicago's community areas, compared to their lending $5,000 or more per housing unit in over half of the region's suburbs. Over 28 percent of the city's neighborhoods—including all of the low-income black communities—received so little loan money as to be classified as "credit starved."[82] The First National Bank of Chicago had concentrated its loans almost exclusively along the lakefront and in other high-income neighborhoods of the city. Predominantly black communities got 60 cents back in loans for every $100 they deposited, while largely Hispanic neighborhoods received only 40 cents on their $100.[83]

In addition to publishing these data, the Alliance used a variety of direct action tactics to force additional lending activity. Alliance organizers mobilized local residents to open and close $1 accounts at offending banks, effectively preventing bank staffers from carrying out their other tasks. Protesters picketed both the banks and the homes of the bank executives, occasionally covering the houses with red paper to highlight the bankers' redlining policies. Confronted with increasingly negative public opinion, the banks relented. In 1984, First Chicago, The Northern Trust, and Harris Bank committed to lend a total of $153 million over five years to housing projects, mixed-use developments, and small businesses in Chicago's low-income neighborhoods. They also agreed to provide $3 million in grants to build the capacity of organizations in those communities. The five-year neighborhood lending programs ultimately poured $117.5 million in loans and over $3 million in grants into the targeted neighborhoods, directly leading to the creation of nearly 5,000 units of housing. Perhaps more importantly, the efforts encouraged the banks to commit an additional $200 million beginning in 1989 and well over $1 billion starting in 1994.[84]

The presence of CRA has contributed in large part to the increased lending in low-income, predominantly minority communities in the 1990s. Then Secretary of the Treasury Robert Rubin claimed that, through mid-1996, urban neighborhoods had received $96 billion in loan commitments through CRA.[85] Ten of Chicago's low- and moderate-income communities experienced at least an 80 percent increase in the number of home purchase loans made between 1990 and 1994.[86] From 1983–1985 to 1991–1993, twenty-one such neighborhoods had a more than 250 percent increase in the amount of loan dollars committed for multi-family housing projects. The number of conventional mortgages increased by at least 120 percent in each of the city's five poorest neighborhoods during that time.[87] The impact of CRA is discussed further in Chapter 7.

School Reform

Along with the difficulty in obtaining loans, the poor quality of Chicago's public schools has driven many individuals out of the city. While Chicago has some nationally renowned public schools such as Whitney Young and Lane Technical High Schools, it has many others that qualify as among the worst in the nation. Nearly half of the city's high school students drop out before graduation, the city's median scores on standardized tests have consistently ranked in the lower third nationally, and a number of schools have become centers of gang activity. Chicago's community colleges have also not proven effective in providing individuals with quality educations.

As mentioned earlier, the city's public schools have historically been neighborhood-based. A school's student population typically mirrors the surrounding community's ethnic, racial, and socioeconomic demographics. As conditions in Chicago's low-income neighborhoods worsened in the 1960s, 1970s, and 1980s, the quality of the schools in those areas also declined. Parents who could afford to do so either sent their children to private or parochial schools and/or moved to suburbs with better school systems.

The plight of the schools, coupled with the desire to keep middle-class individuals and families in the city, sparked action on both the local and mayoral levels. In the late 1980s the City implemented a system of local school councils, in which residents within an individual school's "catchment" area elected representatives to approve the curriculum, supervise the principal, and so forth. More recently, Mayor Daley has made school reform the centerpiece of his efforts to revitalize Chicago. He successfully appealed to the state legislature for the power to oversee the Board of Education, he negotiated a long-term contract with the teachers union, and he appointed a "school czar" to address the schools' financial crisis. Although many schools remain troubled, there is a sense that the quality of education is beginning to improve.

Community Policing

In 1993, the *Chicago Tribune* ran a front-page series titled "Moving Out" that chronicled the ongoing exodus of residents from the city. Those who left the city listed fear of crime as the primary cause of their move. (The need for better schools ranked third, behind a desire for a cleaner community.)[88] In response, city officials instituted a community policing program. Initially tested in a few communities before being implemented city-wide, the new approach focuses on preventing crimes instead of simply reacting to incidents after they have occurred. The approach has emphasized community problem-solving, encouraging greater interaction between police officers and local residents through the implementation of foot patrols and regular neighborhood beat meetings. Officers have necessarily become more attuned to and concerned with the factors in particular communities that promote crime: loitering groups of youths, unrepaired buildings, abandoned cars, and a general sense of disorder, among others. As a result, they have become more active in working with local residents, nonprofit organizations, and public agencies to address these other social issues in order to increase public safety.

The community policing program has increased the visibility of police officers in Chicago's communities. It has contributed to reductions in street-level drug dealing, graffiti, abandoned buildings, and trash-ridden vacant lots, most notably in some of the city's historically troubled communities.[90] The program has also been linked to reductions in both the overall crime rate and the violent crime rate in Chicago. The number of index crimes in the city declined by over 47,000 between 1991 and 1995; again, even the poorest and most crime-ridden neighborhoods have benefited. The number of index crimes in Grand Boulevard fell by over 1,400 during the period, and Woodlawn's dropped by over 45 percent. City residents generally feel safer than they have in the past. A 1996 survey found that 60 percent of Chicagoans felt that their local park was safe during the day (up 17 percent from 1992), and only 19 percent felt that there was a lot of crime in their immediate neighborhood (down 12 percent from 1992).[90]

A Strong Economy

These local changes have joined with a strong regional economy to increase confidence in Chicago's future. The steady economic growth throughout much of the 1990s has resulted in the lowest national unemployment rate in a quarter of a century, and the midwest (especially the greater Chicago area) has been the leading economic engine. With more jobs have come lower unemployment, increased consumption, expanded business opportunities, and additional local revenue. A majority of city officials throughout the country believe that traditionally problematic issues such as violent crime, unemployment, fiscal conditions, neighborhood vitality, and police-community relations are all improving.[91] Such optimism extends to city residents. Thirty-eight percent of Chicagoans currently believe that their neighborhood will improve in the next five years (up 6 percent from 1991), and only 39 percent are thinking of moving within the next two years (down 7 percent from 1991).[92]

CONCLUSION

This chapter has outlined the broad social, economic, and political forces that have affected inner-city neighborhoods in general, and Chicago's low-income communities in particular. The change from an economy largely driven by manufacturing to one focused more on service provision has reduced the number of jobs requiring lower levels of education and thus disproportionately harmed less-skilled residents. The suburbanization of population and jobs has weakened city markets, lowered city tax bases, and made it difficult for many city residents without cars to find and retain employment. The nation's frustration with the continuing high levels of inner-city poverty and the seeming inability of social programs to address the problem has limited the amount of public sector resources devoted to urban revitalization efforts. Taken together, these factors have had devastating effects on many low-income urban communities, as evidenced by the high levels of poverty and unemployment in some of Chicago's neighborhoods.

Although essential for understanding the context of neighborhood decline and revitalization, these broader factors do not adequately explain the differences between communities. For the most part, they affect cities as entire entities: the loss of over 600,000 residents since 1970 has reduced the tax base for all of Chicago. Nevertheless, certain communities in the city have continued to attract investment, while others have experienced an economic free fall. Historical patterns of racial discrimination constitute one explanation for the different economic trends across communities. In Chicago as in other cities, predominantly black neighborhoods have generally fared much worse than their white counterparts.

Yet race cannot explain the differences among black neighborhoods. Understanding the causes of neighborhood change requires consideration of more local factors, a task undertaken in the next chapter.

NOTES

[1]Hirsch, p. 17.

[2]Cited in Alexander Polikoff, *Housing the Poor: The Case for Heroism* (Cambridge, MA: Ballinger Publishing Company, 1978), pp. 10–15.

[3]Hirsch, pp. 20, 24.

[4]Kenneth T. Jackson, *Crabgrass Frontier* (New York: Oxford University Press, 1985), pp. 207–210.

[5]Hirsch, p. 100.

[6]Robert Halpern, *Rebuilding the Inner City* (New York: Columbia University Press, 1995), p. 67. See also Mollenkopf, p. 80.

[7]Hirsch, pp. 110–112.

[8]Harold M. Baron, *Building Babylon: A Case of Racial Controls in Public Housing* (Evanston, IL: Northwestern Univ. Center for Urban Affairs, 1971), p. 58. Other cities experienced similar trends. For example, Boston's urban renewal efforts resulted in the demolition of 9,718 low-rent units and the replacement of only 3,504 (Mollenkopf, p. 166).

[9]Ibid., pp. 17–30.

[10]See Martin Meyerson and Edward C. Banfield, *Politics, Planning, and the Public Interest* (New York: Free Press, 1955) for a discussion of the politics surrounding public housing in Chicago.

[11]Irving Welfeld, "The Courts and Desegregated Housing: The Meaning (if any) of the Gautreaux Case." *Public Interest* 45 (fall 1976): 126–127.

[12]Baron, p. 53.

[13]Polikoff, p. 150. See also Paul Kleppner, *Chicago Divided: The Making of a Black Mayor* (DeKalb, IL: Northern Illinois University Press, 1985), p. 127.

[14]Nicholas Lemann, *The Promised Land* (New York: Vintage Books, 1991), p. 90.

[15]Cited in Baron, p. 72.

[16]Alan B. Anderson and George W. Pickering, *Confronting the Color Line* (Athens, GA: University of Georgia Press, 1986), p. 65.

[17]Dempsey J. Travis, *An Autobiography of Black Chicago* (Chicago: Urban Research Institute, 1981), pp. 128–140.

[18]Michael Harrington's publication of *The Other America* in 1960 detailed the abject poverty present in many inner cities and in Appalachia, areas essentially forgotten by most citizens, politicians, and members of the media. Richard

Cloward and Lloyd Ohlin, studying the increasing role of New York gangs in the late 1950s, concluded that the gang members' anti-social behavior resulted not from individual deficiencies, but primarily from a lack of adequate educational, recreational, employment, and cultural opportunities (see *Delinquency and Opportunity* (New York: Free Press, 1960)). The New York-based Ford Foundation drew upon Cloward and Ohlin's work to guide its "Gray Areas" program, an initiative which sought to alleviate urban poverty by operating a variety of social programs through local school systems.

[19]Cited in Daniel Patrick Moynihan, *Maximum Feasible Misunderstanding* (New York: Free Press, 1969), p. 91.

[20]Cited in John Donovan, *The Politics of Poverty,* 2d ed. (Indianapolis: Bobbs-Merrill Company, 1973), p. 55.

[21]See Meyerson and Banfield, p. 284.

[22]Milton Rakove, *Don't Make No Waves . . . Don't Back No Losers* (Bloomington: Indiana University Press, 1975), p. 62. For more discussion of the Chicago Machine, see (among others) Len O'Connor, *Clout* (New York: Avon Books, 1975); Roger Biles, *Richard J. Daley: Politics, Race, and the Governing of Chicago* (DeKalb, IL: Northern Illinois University Press, 1995); and Mike Royko, *Boss* (New York: Signet Books, 1971).

[23]J. David Greenstone and Paul E. Peterson, *Race and Authority in Urban Politics* (New York: Russell Sage Foundation, 1973), pp. 20, 179, 205.

[24]Cited in Lemann, *Promised Land,* p. 245.

[25]Cited in Biles, p. 106.

[26]Cited in Moynihan, p. 3.

[27]O'Connor, p. 191.

[28]Paul E. Peterson, *School Politics Chicago Style* (Chicago: University of Chicago Press, 1976), p. 30.

[29]Cited in Biles, p. 97.

[30]Gregory D. Squires, Larry Bennett, et al, *Chicago: Race, Class, and the Response to Urban Decline* (Philadelphia: Temple University Press, 1987), p. 130. See also Kleppner, p. 153 and O'Connor, p. 184.

[31]Cited in Anderson and Pickering, p. 189.

[32]Cited in David J. Garrow, *Bearing the Cross* (New York: Vintage Books, 1986), p. 81.

[33]James R. Ralph, Jr., *Northern Protest* (Cambridge: Harvard University Press, 1993), p. 154.

[34]Cited in Garrow, p. 432.

[35]Cited in Ralph, p. 123.

[36]Cited in Biles, p. 138.

[37]Ibid., p. 141.

[38]Kleppner, p. 6.

[39]Daley's comment remains controversial. He and his supporters steadfastly denied his ever making the comment, while many reporters and historians contend that he did. Whatever the case, Daley's reaction caused liberals within and outside of Chicago to denounce his insensitivity.

[40]Cited in Dennis R. Judd, *The Politics of American Cities* (Glenview, IL: Scott, Foresman, & Co., 1988), p. 332. The Community Development Block Grant (CDBG) program, established in 1974, gave elected local officials greater leeway in the allocation of federal dollars. Not surprisingly, the officials often allocated monies in ways that benefited influential local interests. The proportion of monies going to very low-income neighborhoods dropped from their levels in the Johnson Administration's Model Cities program. See Michael J. Rich, *Federal Policymaking and the Poor* (Princeton: Princeton University Press, 1993).

[41]Cited in Biles, pp. 229–230.

[42]William Grimshaw, *Bitter Fruit: Black Politics and the Chicago Machine, 1931–1991* (Chicago: University of Chicago Press, 1992), p. 120. In 1972, the city's black wards gave liberal Republican Bernard Carey a plurality in his successful campaign for State's Attorney against Machine-endorsed Edward Hanrahan. Hanrahan had ordered the deadly 1969 raid on the west-side headquarters of the Illinois Black Panthers.

[43]Michael B. Preston, "The Resurgence of Black Voting in Chicago: 1955–1983," in *The Making of the Mayor: Chicago 1983,* ed. Melvin G. Holli and Paul M. Green (Grand Rapids, MI: William B. Eerdmans Publishing Co., 1984), p. 41.

[44]London and Puntenney, pp. 32–34.

[45]Wilma Lee, "Taxing Minority Communities," *The Neighborhood Works* 3 (Aug. 15, 1980), p. 4. The *Gautreaux* case made its way to the Supreme Court, where in 1976 the Court unanimously found both the Chicago Housing Authority and HUD guilty of racial discrimination in the selection of sites for public housing facilities (*Gautreaux v. HUD*). The Court ruled that remedying the problem required potential tenants to be placed in subsidized housing throughout the Chicago metropolitan area. It argued that restricting placement to the city of Chicago would ensure continued residential segregation because of the racial makeup and distribution of the city's population. Although considerable segregation remains, the ruling has alleviated it somewhat.

[46]Rich, pp. 163–166.

[47]Cited in Lemann, *Promised Land,* p. 252.

[48]See Squires, Bennett, et al., p. 42 and Immergluck, especially pp. 25–28.

[49]See Wilson, *The Truly Disadvantaged* (Chicago: University of Chicago Press, 1987), particularly pp. 50–54. Others have argued that members of the

black middle class largely ignored the communities in which they grew up; once they left the neighborhoods, they simply did not look back and help those who remained.

[50]Polikoff, pp. 14–15.

[51]Gary Rivlin, *Fire on the Prairie* (New York: Henry Holt & Co., 1992), p. 387.

[52]Travis, p. 186. William Julius Wilson describes the social implications of poverty in both *The Truly Disadvantaged* and *When Work Disappears* (New York: Alfred A. Knopf, 1996).

[53]Lee, p. 5.

[54]Kasarda, p. 29.

[55]Wilson, *When Work Disappears,* p. 5.

[56]Ann Markusen, "National Policies Cause Local Steel Decline," *The Neighborhood Works* 9 (March 1986): 3–4. See also Robert Giloth, "National Trends Shatter Local Economy," *The Neighborhood Works* 10 (June 1987): 16.

[57]Squires, Bennett, et al., p. 29.

[58]Ibid., p. 27.

[59]Clarence N. Stone, Robert K. Whelan, and William J. Morin, *Urban Policy and Politics in a Bureaucratic Age,* 2d ed. (Englewood Cliffs, NJ: Prentice-Hall, 1986), p. 9.

[60]Squires, Bennett, et al., p. 30.

[61]Kasarda, p. 30.

[62]Wilson, *When Work Disappears,* p. 26.

[63]Kasarda, p. 30.

[64]London and Puntenney, pp. 29–34 and Immergluck, pp. 29–36.

[65]Wilson, *When Work Disappears,* p. 31.

[66]Page and Shapiro, pp. 125–126.

[67]Not all of the mayors blamed the cuts entirely on Reagan. Chicago Mayor Harold Washington opined in the mid-1980s that "the excesses were not in the programs, the excesses were in the way they were being dispersed and abused. And the problem with the progressives and the liberals was that they didn't recognize it. And they didn't change it. So they were easy ducks for Reagan to come along and knock them over" (cited in Chicago Tribune, *The American Millstone* (Chicago: Contemporary Books, 1986), p. 281).

[68]Rivlin, p. 394.

[69]London and Puntenney, pp. 21–28.

[70]"The Violence of Street Gangs," *The Compiler* (Illinois Criminal Justice Information Authority) Fall 1996: 4–6.

[71]Massey and Denton, p. 222. The Chicago metropolitan area's segregation index was 85.8 in 1990, meaning that nearly 86 percent of blacks would have to

move in order for individual neighborhoods to mirror the racial composition of the region as a whole.

[72]Preston, p. 41.

[73]Rivlin, p. 71.

[74]Preston, p. 47.

[75]For a discussion of the election, see (among others) Kleppner, *Chicago Divided* and Don Rose, "How the 1983 Election Was Won: Reform, Racism, and Rebellion," in Holli and Green, pp. 101–124.

[76]Ester R. Fuchs, *Mayors and Money* (Chicago: University of Chicago Press, 1992), p. 159.

[77]Cited in Rivlin, p. 264.

[78]Squires, Bennett, et al., p. 52 and Doug Gills, "Chicago Politics and Community Development: A Social Movement Perspective," in *Harold Washington and the Neighborhoods,* ed. Pierre Clavel and Wim Wiewel (New Brunswick: Rutgers University Press, 1991), pp. 54–55.

[79]The term "redlining" came about as a result of many bankers using red pens to draw lines around certain neighborhoods on a map. The bankers then refused to consider loan requests from individuals or businesses located within the red boundaries.

[80]Cited in Gregory D. Squires, "Community Reinvestment: An Emerging Social Movement," in *From Redlining to Reinvestment,* ed. Squires (Philadelphia: Temple University Press, 1992), p. 11.

[81]The first time the Federal Reserve denied a bank acquisition because of a poor CRA rating was in 1989. Enforcement has increased in the 1990s, but denials have remained scarce.

[82]Pogge, Hoyt, and Revere, pp. 7–17.

[83]*Partnerships for Reinvestment* (Chicago: National Training and Information Center, 1990), pp. 13–29.

[84]Ibid. Community groups had similar successes in cities such as Boston, Detroit, and Pittsburgh; by 1992, over $18 billion in reinvestment agreements had been negotiated with banks throughout the country (Ibid, p. 12). Squires's *From Redlining to Reinvestment* contains a series of case studies of successful reinvestment campaigns.

[85]Remarks made at a discussion concerning the future of American cities, Chicago, Aug. 27, 1996.

[86]Woodstock Institute, "Expanding the American Dream: Home Lending Surges in Modest-Income Neighborhoods," Reinvestment Alert #9 (May 1996), p. 5.

[87]Woodstock Institute, "CRA Boosts Multifamily Housing Loans in Chicago," Reinvestment Alert #8 (May 1995), p. 4.

[88]See sec. 1, p. 1 of the *Chicago Tribune,* Nov. 28, 1993–Dec. 7, 1993.

[89]See Wesley G. Skogan and Susan M. Hartnett, *Community Policing, Chicago Style* (New York: Oxford University Press, 1997), especially pp. 220–223.

[90]Garth Taylor, *Trends for the Nineties: Changes in Quality of Life Indicators in the Chicago Region* (Chicago: Metro Chicago Information Center, 1996).

[91]U.S. Department of Housing and Urban Development, *The State of the Cities* (Washington, DC: HUD, 1997), p. 20.

[92]See Taylor.

CHAPTER 4

A Quantitative Look at Revitalization

In Chapter 2 I presented a definition of neighborhood revitalization, one that focused both on improved conditions for local residents and increased private investment. I also outlined a way of measuring such local economic change, using an index score comprised of per capita income, residential loan rates, and median property values. The changes in these scores indicate the amount of revitalization or decline within a particular community (see Tables 2-1 and 2-2).

Chapter 3 analyzed the broad social, economic, and political factors that have affected low- and moderate-income communities in the past several decades. The historical approach helps explain some of the trends in the data. The declining per capita incomes relative to the Chicago average have resulted from the general exodus of jobs and middle-class individuals from the city, as well as from the loss of jobs requiring low skill levels. As the bulk of the city's job and population loss occurred before 1990, the decline in per capita incomes is steeper from 1979 to 1989 than from 1989 to 1995. Similarly, the increase in loan rates in the majority of these neighborhoods can be attributed in large part to increased enforcement of the Community Reinvestment Act. The potentially negative regulatory and public relations consequences of ignoring low-income areas has increased banks' motivation and willingness to consider lending in these communities.

Although the broad trends provide a useful context for neighborhood decline and revitalization, they cannot explain the variances among individual communities. Why did the neighborhoods on Chicago's far south side decline, while those closer to the Loop improved? What explains the marked improvement of West Town, the Near West Side, and the Near South Side relative to the other low- and moderate-income communities in the city? This chapter takes a first cut at answering these and other similar questions. It analyzes neighborhood-level factors that can be easily measured and quantified, and correlates them with the changes in index scores developed in Chapter 2. The approach helps to identify some of the components of local economic change, but it has limited usefulness in describing the mechanics of the process.

POTENTIAL EXPLANATORY VARIABLES

I have considered six different, easily measurable factors that are generally associated with neighborhood change: the neighborhood's demographic composition, physical amenities, housing characteristics, educational opportunities, crime, and social organizations. The following sections briefly define the specific variables and outline their expected effects.

Demographics

The distinct patterns of ethnic and racial segregation within Chicago, coupled with research indicating a strong correlation between minority populations and poverty, suggests the important role demographics play in revitalization. Communities with a majority of black and/or Hispanic residents generally have lower per capita incomes and lower property values than areas with a majority of white residents. This analysis considers the percentage of black residents in a neighborhood as of 1979 (%BL79), the percentage of self-described Hispanic residents in the same year (%HIS79), and the percentage of Asian residents in a neighborhood in 1980 (%ASIAN80). As neighborhood change has often followed and/or been driven by demographic change, I have included variables to measure these dynamics. CHBLACK and CHHIS measure the respective changes in the percentages of black and Hispanic residents between 1979 and 1995, and CHASIAN indicates the change in the percentage of Asian residents from 1980 to 1990. The CHPOP variable shows the percent change in the overall community area population between 1979 and 1995. The data came from the decennial U.S. Census and from estimates generated by Claritas/NPDC. I interpolated the data to generate values for the intervening years.[1]

Using the racial composition at the beginning of the period provides a context for revitalization. It enables us to see whether positive change has been more likely in a certain type of racial or ethnic area. Considering racial change also provides one way of discerning between internal revitalization and gentrification. Neighborhoods that experience improved economic conditions as well as a decrease in their proportion of black residents tend to be gentrifying.

I have also included the change in the percentage of young (under 25) and elderly (65 and over) residents of each neighborhood between 1980 and 1990. Both of these groups consist primarily of people who are outside of the labor force. Simultaneous increases in both categories imply a reduction in the proportion of working-age adults and an accompanying reduction in per capita income, and vice-versa. The CHYOUNG and CHOLD variables indicate the extent of these changes.

Physical Amenities

As outlined in Chapter 1, economists such as Michael Porter have emphasized the importance of geographic location for business. Companies either move to or choose to remain in areas in large part because of the amenities such areas offer: access to transportation, the presence of other corporations with which they do business, and so forth. Similarly, realtors have long espoused the importance of location in the buying and selling of property. Areas with desirable topographical features such as lakes, mountains, rivers, and forests are more appealing to potential home buyers. Individuals in the workforce often choose to locate in neighborhoods close to their place of business.

This study measures location in two ways. The LAKE variable accounts for whether or not a neighborhood abuts Lake Michigan, Chicago's only major topographical feature. Communities located on the lakefront would presumably be more likely to revitalize. The DISTANCE variable measures the distance from the center of the community area to the center of the Loop, the largest economic hub in the metropolitan region with over 550,000 jobs.[2] Assuming that businesses and workers desire to locate near the area of greatest economic activity, we would expect the likelihood of revitalization to be highest in neighborhoods near the Loop. The DISTANCE variable provides useful information, but it is far from perfect. There are other employment centers within the city and the metropolitan area; many individuals commute to work from the city to the suburbs each morning. The availability of good transportation also affects the degree to which location matters. It might well be easier to get downtown from an outlying area than from an inner one because of an expressway or a commuter rail line.

One way of addressing the transportation issue is to consider the number of bus lines (BUS) and subway/elevated train stops (ELSTOP) in a community. Using maps provided by the Chicago Transit Authority, I counted the number of bus lines in each community area in 1993 and the number of el stops serving each neighborhood in 1996, dividing them by the population of the community area in 1993.[3] The BUS variable provides a rough estimate of transportation access, since the number and routing of bus lines has changed with the population of certain areas. The ELSTOP variable offers a more concrete measure, as the vast majority of stations have remained in use for the past 20 years. The el measure includes both the west side-south side green line, which was closed for repairs from 1993–1996, and the Loop-southwest side orange line, which opened in late 1993. I have included these two lines because of the potential interrelationship between transportation and revitalization: the promise of future transportation may conceivably spark additional market activity as individuals plan to take advantage of the coming amenity, and/or the need for enhanced transportation may be a response to increased market demand in a particular area.

Parks constitute another potential amenity for a neighborhood. The mixture of open space, greenery, and opportunity for recreation may increase demand for the surrounding property. At the same time, the open space can be a neighborhood liability. Parks can serve as hang-outs for gangs, drug dealers, and other miscreants. They can be a primary site of muggings and assaults, especially at night. The PARKS variable represents the number of parks by community area as identified in the 1980 *Local Community Area Fact Book*.[4]

As neighborhoods have certain assets, they also may possess certain liabilities for revitalization. One major drawback is the presence of *brownfields,* former industrial sites with presumed environmental contamination. Such sites usually dissuade potential investors because of the threat of expensive cleanup and liability issues. The BROWN variable indicates the number of such sites in a community area, based on data from the Chicago Department of Planning and Development. Again, this information has inherent limitations. Many sites are contaminated but either have not yet been identified and/or have not been designated as "brownfields." The process usually requires some sort of demand for the site, as designation carries with it access to a certain pool of monies for environmental cleanup; the City presumably allocates its limited resources to areas of greater demand.

Housing

In addition to its geographic location, the nature of a community's housing may affect the possibilities of revitalization. Areas with a high percentage of single-family homes generally have a high percentage of homeowners and families.[5] These people have made a material investment in the neighborhood and therefore have a stake in its economic and social well-being. One would expect these communities to remain relatively stable; agencies that concentrate on revitalizing urban areas have continually stressed the importance of creating home ownership opportunities in troubled neighborhoods. In contrast, areas with a higher percentage of multi-family apartment buildings tend to have more transient, less stable populations. They tend to have more renters, individuals who are much more likely than homeowners to move out of the area within a few years. Many renters, particularly those in an area for a short time, develop relatively few "roots" in a neighborhood. They do not have a material investment in the area, and their social interactions with other residents are generally not as well established. In short, their stake in the area's future tends to be smaller relative to that of owners. Communities with high proportions of renters would presumably be much more volatile. The AHSGOWN variable represents the average rate of home ownership in a neighborhood from 1979 to 1990, based on federal census data.

The presence of significant concentrations of public housing has often had a strong negative effect on a neighborhood's economic condition, as illustrated in Chapter 3. Stringent income eligibility guidelines have ensured that only the poorest individuals reside in public housing. As a result, public housing projects have become centers of widespread unemployment and intense poverty. Cutbacks in federal housing monies, along with vandalism, shoddy construction, normal wear and tear, and mismanagement on the part of local housing authorities have led to the physical deterioration of many of the projects. Taken together, these factors have promoted extensive drug, gang, and violent criminal activity in areas surrounding public housing buildings. In Chicago, the highest crime rates are invariably in the police beats encompassing projects such as the Robert Taylor Homes, the Henry Horner Homes, and Cabrini Green.

The PUBHSG variable represents the number of public housing units as a percentage of a neighborhood's total housing units. The public housing units consist of projects operated and managed by the Chicago Housing

Authority as of 1996 as well as scattered-site units managed by the Habitat Company, the federally-designated receiver for the CHA. I have assumed that the number of public housing units remained constant in the city's low- and moderate-income neighborhoods from 1979 to 1995. The CHA did not really begin to demolish projects until early 1996, and, as a result of the *Gautreaux* decision, most of Habitat's construction has thus far occurred outside the community areas in the study.

Education

Social factors within neighborhoods may also affect prospects for revitalization. The level of education among neighborhood residents should help determine the community's potential for economic development. More educated individuals tend to have better jobs and therefore have better employment networks. Their greater income potential should generate stronger market activity. Individuals with college educations tend to invest more in the maintenance of their homes.[6] In addition, they typically place a higher value on quality schooling and may implicitly establish a higher standard of achievement for other members of the community. As a measure of the community's level of education, I have used the percentage of residents in 1979 aged 25 and over with a high school diploma. The higher the percentage, the more likely the neighborhood would be to experience economic improvement. HSDIP79 represents an interpolation of data generated by the U.S. Census and aggregated by community level in the *Local Community Area Fact Book*. The CHED variable signifies the change in the percentage of residents with high school diplomas between 1979 and 1990. Again, a large change would suggest greater revitalization.[7]

As emphasized in Chapter 3, many members of Chicago's middle class left the city because of the declining quality of the city's public schools. An improved local school system would therefore seem to be an important component of revitalization. The quality of a school is a product of numerous factors, including its teachers, the strength of students' families, the students' socioeconomic status, and so forth. Since this study focuses not on education, but rather on the effect of education on revitalization, I have developed two rough estimates of school quality and educational achievement for individuals under age 25. MEDREA82 represents the median public school eleventh grade reading score on standardized tests as a percentage of the national average in 1982. DROP86 represents the percentage of public high school students entering in the freshman class who dropped out of school before their expected graduation in 1986.[8] CHREA represents the change in a community's median reading score from 1982 to 1995, and CHDROP shows the change in the dropout rate from 1986 to 1995. I obtained data on dropout rates and median reading scores for each public high school from the Chicago Board of Education. The Board does not keep any data by community area level, and school boundaries are not coterminous with community area boundaries. (Many schools have city-wide enrollments and thus city-wide boundaries.) I mapped the boundaries of the "neighborhood" schools, mapped the (often overlapping) local school council electoral boundaries of the other schools, and compared them to community area boundaries. I assumed that dropout rates and reading scores were constant throughout the individual school's catchment area and allocated those scores to the appropriate community areas. I then took a weighted average of the various scores (based on the percentage of the catchment area within the community area) to determine the overall score for the neighborhood. Lower median reading scores and/or high dropout rates indicate lower levels of education among community teenagers, suggesting lower public school quality and thus less future income-earning potential. Both would presumably reduce the neighborhood's likelihood of revitalizing.

Crime

Like education, public safety seems to contribute to healthy neighborhoods. As outlined in Chapter 1, neighborhoods with greater levels of interpersonal trust tend to be more attractive for businesses and residents. The lower likelihood of theft reduces the cost of doing business and reduces the fear of physical harm. In contrast, areas of high crime can make neighborhoods socially and economically unstable. Greater levels of fear may cause residents to curtail their social interactions and potentially leave the neighborhood altogether. Retailers may suffer a drop in sales and/or an increase in thefts, possibly causing them to close their stores or relocate elsewhere. Outside investors may shun the area as dangerous and unprofitable. Yet the relationship between crime and investment is complex, as crime may also be more of a response to neighborhood decline than a cause. In some cases, economic growth might occur despite high crime rates. A neighborhood's amenities could be desirable enough to outweigh the risks associated with significant levels of crime.[9] Nevertheless, higher crime rates are generally associated with higher rates of poverty, since raised levels of need, frustration, and social isolation tend to breed criminal behavior.[10]

As a way of measuring the amount of crime in a neighborhood, I have used the number of index crimes reported to the Chicago Police Department (CPD). Index crimes are defined as the sum of homicides, sexual assaults, serious assaults, robberies, burglaries, auto thefts, and the "theft index" (a mix of other property crimes). The CPD has kept records of index crimes by police beat since 1987. Since beats are not coterminous with community area boundaries, I determined the percentage of the community area in each beat and then allocated the crimes accordingly. The ACRIME variable represents the neighborhood's average annual crime rate (index crimes per 1,000 residents) from 1987 to 1995, and CHCRIME the change in the crime rate between the two years. Similarly, the AHOM variable indicates the average number of homicides per 100,000 residents between 1979 and 1994, while CHHOM represents the change in the homicide rate between those two years. Homicide data came from the Chicago Department of Public Health, which provided average rates from 1979–1981 and 1992–1994.[11] In each case I assumed that the respective averages applied equally to the three included years and used them as the 1979 and 1994 values.

Liquor stores, particularly those that are poorly managed, are major contributors to crime in low-income neighborhoods. In many of these areas, alcohol is sold principally through liquor stores and not through multi-purpose establishments, which effectively concentrates alcoholics and other troubled individuals around the premises and dissuades other businesses from locating in the area. In short, a preponderance of liquor stores may well hamper a community's ability to revitalize.[12] In this analysis, ALIQ represents the average number of liquor stores per person in a neighborhood between 1982 and 1992, as categorized in the U.S. Census of Retail Trade.

Social Organizations

Local not-for-profit associations have long generated considerable enthusiasm among researchers and policy-makers for their ability to mobilize people, facilitate interpersonal relationships, and otherwise promote social capital. Alexis de Tocqueville noted the seemingly ubiquitous nature of the groups in his study of the United States in the 1830s, and numerous analyses have subsequently elucidated the role that such groups can play in promoting neighborhood stability.[13] This study examines a few different types of these local institutions.

Researchers most often consider community organizations (or neighborhood associations) when studying neighborhood change or stability. Such organizations seek primarily either to mobilize local residents around a particular issue and/or to promote the physical development of a neighborhood. These groups generally focus on catalyzing change or maintaining local conditions. One type of community organization, the community development corporation (CDC), often aims to revitalize a neighborhood through the rehabilitation of the neighborhood's housing and/or through the development of commercial real estate; both efforts seek to attract outside private investment to the area. In Chicago, where the legacy of Saul Alinsky remains strong, local groups have also often taken a more overtly political approach. Organizers have worked to mobilize residents to confront city government, corporations, and absentee landlords. While these groups can increase social capital and achieve change by altering power relationships, their willingness to use confrontational strategies may also cause potential investors to shy away from the community.

I have grouped CDCs and other community groups (defined as not-for-profit, neighborhood-based, multi-purpose organizations with a membership, office, and staff) together into a single COMORG variable. The breakdown of CDCs came from lists generated by the Chicago Association of Neighborhood Development Organizations (CANDO) and the Local Initiatives Support Corporation (LISC) for the 1996 Chicago Neighborhood Development Awards. For community organizations, I used the directory published by the Community Renewal Society in 1987 and updated by the Institute of Urban Life in 1992 and 1996.[14] I eliminated CDCs, determined the average number of organizations in each neighborhood during the period, and per capitized the number. The lack of reliable earlier information limits the ability to assess change in these organizations over time.

Many community organizations have emerged from the outreach efforts of local churches. Religious institutions have often served as both the spiritual and social focal points of their neighborhoods, particularly in ethnic and African-American communities. Many of the more established churches provide a regular meeting place for local residents and may offer various social service and/or human development programs such as emergency food and shelter assistance, after-school recreation, and adult remedial education. While some churches have actively worked to promote stability and social organization in their neighborhoods, others have consciously resisted becoming engaged in community revitalization, choosing instead to concentrate solely on the spiritual needs of their members.

Quantifying the effect of churches on local economic conditions is problematic, as there is no comprehensive listing of Chicago religious institutions, let alone their activities and budgets. As a rough proxy, I have used the number of religious institutions per 10,000 people in each community area, based on the listing of churches, mosques, and synagogues in the 1996 Chicago yellow pages and 1995 population figures. The CHURCH variable has limited validity over time, however, because the number of churches varies considerably with changes in population and local religious affiliation.[15]

Churches have historically played a major role in providing social services to disadvantaged individuals, as evidenced by their operating food pantries, orphanages, and emergency shelters. Many churches continue to perform such tasks, but the bulk of these services now fall to nonprofit agencies. Some of these groups specifically work to alleviate human suffering by providing free meals, shelter for homeless individuals, and/or emotional counseling. Others promote human development through education and employment and training programs. Still others exist as recreational or fraternal organizations, providing a place for people to meet, compete, and socialize. Because they provide a type of safety net for local individuals, such organizations can constitute important community assets.[16]

The human service organizations are classified into three categories. The first (EDORG) consists of educational, cultural, and arts groups and includes after-school programs and day care centers. The second (HLTHORG) is comprised of health-related organizations, including hospitals, clinics, and counseling centers. The third group (SSORG) consists of all other groups, except those that focus principally on research, advocacy, community mobilization, technical assistance provision, and/or real estate development. All government agencies that did not have a direct social service function as well as all public housing agencies were also excluded. These are admittedly rough and somewhat arbitrary categorizations, as a number of agencies provide multiple functions; if a group did not have a clearly predominant activity, it was lumped into the SSORG category.

Every few years the United Way of Metropolitan Chicago publishes a listing of human service agencies in the region.[17] Included agencies are those not-for-profit, proprietary groups providing a unique, specialized, and much needed community service. I gathered lists from each directory since 1977, categorized the groups, and then averaged the number of agencies located in each community area. The directories break down agencies either by zip code or community area; in the former case, I allocated agencies to community areas based on the percentage of the area within the zip code boundary. I per capitized the average to allow for comparisons across communities.

These organizational measures provide some indication of local social activity, but they cannot fully capture the extent of social capital in a neighborhood. Simply put, quantifying social capital is extremely difficult: there is no good measure of the extent and/or strength of interpersonal networks and community trust. Longitudinal surveys would certainly help, but they are presently not available by community area. Similarly, data on other social organizations—Little Leagues, bowling leagues, parent-teacher associations, gangs, and the like—are not collected by community area.

IDENTIFYING TRENDS AND PATTERNS

In an ideal scenario, correlating each of the previously discussed independent variables with changes in the index scores would produce clearly identifiable relationships. This ideal statistical analysis would provide some evidence of revitalization being associated with particular factors such as local social service organizations or the extent of home ownership. These relationships would hold across low- and moderate-income neighborhoods and would provide a framework for subsequent, more detailed analysis. Unfortunately, reality is not so pretty.

Neighborhoods with a high percentage of black residents at the outset of the study experienced more revitalization than those areas with a high proportion of Hispanic residents. The real difference lay in per capita incomes. Hispanic neighborhoods experienced a drop in incomes relative to the city average, while black areas experienced an increase. Communities in which the proportion of minorities increased between 1979 and 1995 tended to decline, a finding that lends credence to the assumption that racially changing areas tend to be economically unstable. While areas that became more heavily black showed the greatest overall decline, areas with an increase in their proportion of Latino residents had the most noticeable drop in per capita incomes (as indicated by the correlation of $-.50$). The differing income trends result largely from the continuing immigration of Mexicans, Central Americans, and other individuals of Hispanic descent to Chicago. Many of these individuals have relatively little education as well as language barriers, making it difficult for them to obtain steady, well-paying jobs.

Table 4-1. Correlations in Low- and Moderate-Income Neighborhoods[a]

Variable	Index Score Change 79–95	Change in Per Capita Income	Change in Residential Loan Rate	Change in Median Property Value	Variable Description
%BL79	.23	.38	.23	.09	% of black residents 1979
%HIS79	–.05	–.33	.00	.04	% of Hispanic residents 1979
%ASIAN80	–.06	.14	–.12	–.07	% of Asian residents 1980
CHBLACK	–.34	–.34	–.35	–.20	% change black residents 79–95
CHHIS	–.14	–.50*	–.11	.02	% change Hispanic residents 79–95
CHASIAN	–.06	.04	–.03	–.08	% change Asian residents 80–90
CHPOP	–.16	–.41	–.18	.04	% change population 79–95
LAKE	.29	.18	–.08	.44*	neigh. adjacent to Lake Michigan
DISTANCE	–.65**	–.31	–.53**	–.58**	neigh. distance from Loop
BUS	.29	.30	.14	.29	bus lines in neighborhood
ELSTOP	.41	.45*	.32	.28	"el" stops in neighborhood
BROWN	–.12	–.07	–.01	–.15	brownfield sites in neighborhood
PARKS	.25	.32	.20	.12	parks in neighborhood
AHSGOWN	–.65***	–.35	–.43*	–.61**	home ownership rate
PUBHSG	.37	.24	.18	.38	% public housing units

HSDIP79	−.34	−.11	−.42	−.22	% w/ high school diploma
CHED	.23	.42	.00	.19	change in % w/ diploma, 79–90
MEDREA82	−.04	−.14	−.14	.06	median reading score, 1982
CHREA	−.28	.07	−.16	−.36	change in reading score, 82–95
DROP86	.29	.13	.32	.21	dropout rate, 1986
CHDROP	.10	.19	−.05	.11	change in dropout rate, 86–95
ACRIME	.70**	.45*	.51*	.65**	average crime rate, 87–95
CHCRIME	−.22	−.24	−.06	−.23	change in crime rate, 87–95
AHOM	.35	.54**	.26	.20	average homicide rate, 79–94
CHHOM	−.62**	−.17	−.47*	−.65**	change in homicide rate, 79–94
ALIQ	.43*	.24	.28	.46*	average # of liquor stores, 82–92
COMORG	.52*	.28	.31	.55**	CDCs + community organizations
CHURCH	−.01	.25	.19	−.22	churches
EDORG	.36	.55**	.05	.29	educational organizations
HLTHORG	.39	.62**	.00	.35	health organizations
SSORG	.38	.60**	.01	.33	other social service organizations

[a] Correlations can have values ranging from −1 to 1. Positive values indicate a positive relationship between variables; for example, being adjacent to the lake is associated with a .29 increase in a community's index score. The higher the value, the stronger the correlation. Similarly, negative values indicate an inverse relationship; as the distance from the Loop increases, the neighborhood's index score tends to decrease.

* Significant at t = .01.

** Significant at t = .001.

As expected, location was positively correlated with revitalization. Neighborhoods along Lake Michigan generally experienced positive economic change, particularly in terms of rising property values. Areas with greater numbers of parks also tended to improve. Together, these findings emphasize the tendency of topographical amenities to increase the desirability (and thus the cost) of an area.

One of the strongest correlations in the study is that of the distance from the Loop to the center of a community area $(-.65)$. The closer a neighborhood to downtown (the smaller the distance variable), the greater the extent of positive economic change. Such a finding, in conjunction with the positive correlations between changes in index scores and the public transportation measures, indicates that proximity and access to major employment centers increases the attractiveness of a neighborhood.

Certain indicators of social capital were correlated with revitalization. Although the presence of churches statistically had little effect on the process, the presence of other nonprofit organizations was positively associated with economic improvement. Areas with larger numbers of educational, health, and other social service organizations experienced greater increases in their index scores. The most significant correlation (between .55 and .62) was with per capita incomes, suggesting that these groups may help enhance the earning capacity of neighborhood residents. Such a trend suggests that the groups have achieved some success in improving individuals' skills, health, and coping mechanisms, all of which would help increase their earning potential. Community organizations were also reasonably strongly correlated (.52) with revitalization. In particular, they were associated with growing property values (.55). Again, the correlation suggests that their traditional emphasis on real estate maintenance and development has borne fruit.

Not surprisingly, changes in certain social indicators tended to be associated with improved economic conditions. Areas with falling crime rates tended to revitalize. Property values and loan rates noticeably increased in areas in which the murder rate dropped, reinforcing the belief that a greater sense of safety promotes additional private investment. Increasing levels of education were also positively correlated with local economic gains, primarily in terms of increased per capita incomes.

Although changes in social indicators were predictably correlated with revitalization, some of the more static measures defied expectations. Conventional wisdom suggests that high crime rates should cause investors to shy away from an area. Yet neighborhoods with higher average crime rates, homicide rates, and numbers of liquor stores experienced more revitalization. The crime rate-index score correlation was especially strong (.70) and statistically significant. Researchers and practitioners consistently promote home ownership as an integral piece of a stable neighborhood. Within Chicago's low- and moderate-income communities, however, higher rates of home ownership were strongly associated with economic decline (a statistically significant correlation of −.65 with changes in the index score). The presence of large amounts of public housing has often contributed to neighborhood decline, yet it was positively correlated (.37) with revitalization. Although not statistically significant, the observed relationships between the educational measures and economic change also defied expectations. Areas whose residents had higher average levels of education in the late 1970s tended to decline, while areas with higher dropout rates tended to improve. Neighborhoods with increases in their median high school reading scores tended to decline: property values, which are often tied to local school quality, actually fell relative to the city median. Furthermore, an increase in population was associated with economic decline, precisely the opposite condition from that described in Chapter 3.

What accounts for these odd observations? One potential explanation lies in the use of a simple correlational model as opposed to a multiple regression framework (which controls for the effect of certain variables on others). For example, the observed relationship of crime on revitalization could be affected by a neighborhood's racial composition, level of education, degree of poverty, proximity to downtown, and so forth. Therefore multiple regressions were performed, using the change in the index score as the dependent variable and both the "logical" indicators (distance from the Loop, the presence of community organizations, and the change in the homicide rate) and the confounding ones (the average numbers of liquor stores—strongly associated with average crime rates—as well as home ownership rates and the percentage of public housing) as independent variables. The following table shows the results of the regression.

Using regression clarified some of the relationships. Revitalization was no longer strongly associated with high numbers of liquor stores or larger amounts of public housing. The positive statistical effect of declining homicide rates and community organizations also decreased considerably. The only variables that remained significant (at p < .10) were the neighborhood's distance from the Loop and its percentage of homeowners, which both remained negatively correlated with changes in the index score. The continuing strength of the distance variable (between two and

Table 4-2. Indicators v. Neighborhood Revitalization[a]

Variable	Beta	T Value
DISTANCE	−.38	.06 *
COMORG	−.13	.39
CHHOM	−.14	.33
ALIQ	.17	.22
AHSGOWN	−.45	.09 *
PUBHSG95	−.12	.52
Multiple R .76; R Square .57		

[a] Beta is a standardized regression coeffient whose absolute value indicates the impact of variables relative to each other. In this table, AHSGOWN has the largest (negative) correlation with a change in the index score. Its effect on the change is nearly four times that of PUBHSG. The standard error of B measures how far a typical measure was from the mean value. Sig. T indicates the extent to which the coefficient is statistically significant; the lower the Sig. T score, the more significant the finding. Statisticians generally consider anything over .10 to be insignificant and prefer findings to be at a level of .05 or lower.
Note: For a description of the variables, see Table 4-1.

three times as great as all but the homeownership variable) further illustrates the importance of location in revitalization. The negative relationship between economic change and home ownership remains baffling. Part of the explanation may lie in the relationship between distance and home ownership, which were more strongly correlated with each other than with the change in the neighborhood index score.[18] Yet the small number of cases (36) limits the ability of regression to identify significant relationships among variables and thus provide further insight into the process.

The presence of significant statistical outliers provides another explanation for the counter-intuitive relationships. In particular, the Near South Side's gain of 83 points in its index score—more than 50 points than the next-highest gainer—skewed the data. Taking the Near South Side out of the data moderated the size of the correlations, but did not affect their general direction.

The independent variables were essentially valid indicators of local physical and social factors. Correlating indicators for a given year with neighborhood index scores for that year produced the expected relationships. For example, higher levels of education in 1979 were associated with higher levels of per capita income, loan rates, property values, and overall index scores in that year. Higher 1989 crime rates were associated with lower 1989 neighborhood per capita incomes, and so forth. The strange observations therefore could have been a by-product of correlating changing dependent variables with static independent ones. While correlating changes with changes helped reduce the size of the contradictory relationships, the process often offered relatively little useful information. Many of the independent variables have values for only a single year (such as the number of churches), or are essentially constant (the percentage of homeowners, for example). These variables seem more useful in providing a context in which change can occur, not necessarily in causing that change directly.

The multiple components of revitalization may also reduce the effectiveness of the statistical analysis. Some of the independent variables (such as crime rates and education levels) could conceivably be dependent variables, as they capture a different aspect of revitalization. The close relationship among these variables could skew the observed correlations. Furthermore, erroneous estimates of post-1989 per capita incomes would skew the index scores and thus affect the observed correlations.

A closer look at individual neighborhood scores (see Tables 2-1 and 2-2) shows that economically better-off neighborhoods tended to decline between 1979 and 1995, while the poorest communities seemed to improve. The 13 community areas with index scores of 80 or higher in 1979 experienced an average decline of 11.7 points relative to the city average between 1979 and 1995. These neighborhoods generally had the highest levels of education and home ownership, the lowest levels of crime, and the fewest units of public housing, all of which helped explain their initially high ranking. In contrast, the economically worst-off 13 neighborhoods (those with 1979 index scores of 50 or lower) improved by an average of 14 points relative to the city average.[19] In general, the better-off areas in 1979 remained absolutely better off in 1995 and vice-versa: the 1995 average index score was 86.37 for the former group and 52.97 for the latter one.[20]

The nature of these trends suggests a reversion to the mean, with all areas naturally moving toward the center. Yet the mean in this study is the city average (set at 100), which is *above* the vast majority of the low- and moderate-income neighborhoods. Were there a reversion to the mean, there should be relative improvements across all 36 of these community areas. The city's more affluent communities, particularly those with the highest initial index scores, should also show relative decline. Such a pattern does not exist. Communities such as Lincoln Park, Lakeview, and the Near North Side had noticeably higher index scores in 1995 than they had in 1979. Alternatively, the numbers could be illustrating a "bottoming out" effect: conditions in the poorest neighborhoods reached their nadir and have begun to improve. The people and investors who were going to leave the areas did so, and the positive economic and social forces within the Chicago region have sparked gradual improvement. The bottoming out theory cannot explain the decline of the moderate-income neighborhoods in the study, however.

Very few of the neighborhoods experienced consistent change from 1979 to 1995. Some improved from 1979 to 1989 and then declined from 1989 to 1995, while others experienced opposite trends. Those areas that either improved or declined in both periods generally had different rates of change in the 1980s and the 1990s. Consider the previously described group of 13 better-off decliners. Only three experienced decline in both periods. One initially improved and then fell, while ten first declined and then rebounded. The overall correlation between the 1979–1989 change and the 1989–1995 change was only .29, indicating a relatively weak (and statistically insignificant) relationship between the two indicators.

The lack of clearly identifiable trends across the communities suggests that economic conditions in Chicago's neighborhoods have changed in different ways, at different rates, and for different reasons. The small number of communities in the sample, coupled with the considerable variation across the communities, limits the usefulness of regression as an analytic tool. Regression helps to describe processes taking place in relatively stable systems. Yet in different systems, in which variables have different relationships and effects on change, regression is not as useful a tool. While the limitations of the data preclude definitive conclusions, the analysis strongly suggests that there is no single factor that causes revitalization of all neighborhoods within a single city, let alone across multiple cities. What causes change in one community does not necessarily cause change in another. The size and timing of these factors vary across neighborhoods. Community economic conditions may be moving in similar directions but for different reasons. In short, none of the theories of revitalization outlined in Chapter 1 can independently explain local economic change. Understanding revitalization requires a more nuanced approach.

Clustering Neighborhoods

The historical analysis of Chapter 3 and the preceding statistical analysis identified two consistently important factors in Chicago's neighborhood economics: location and ethnicity. Communities situated near the Loop and/or adjacent to Lake Michigan have generally experienced more revitalization than their counterparts elsewhere in the city. More broadly, the city's history of segregation has tied demographics and economic opportunity closely to geographic location. Blacks occupy the areas extending south and west of the Loop. Whites have located on the north, far northwest, and southwest sides. Hispanics have generally lived in the near northwest side and in the area north of Chicago River's South Branch, although they have more recently settled in South Chicago. For the most part, there has been little overlap among these populations. Many of the south side neighborhoods are 99 percent black, and parts of the northwest and southwest sides are almost exclusively white. Hispanics generally comprise an absolute majority in their neighborhoods, with whites and/or other ethnic groups constituting the remainder.

There is no clear correlation between race and revitalization. Economic conditions have improved in some virtually all-black communities and declined in others. Similarly, some predominantly Hispanic areas have gotten better while others have gotten worse. At the same time, there are noticeable differences in the characteristics of black and non-black areas. (Non-black low- and moderate-income areas tend to be predominantly Hispanic; almost all of the city's predominantly white areas are above the city average economically.) For example, the average population loss in non-black areas was 1.4 percent from 1979–1995, while the average loss in black areas was 19.3 percent. Public housing constitutes over 14 percent of the total housing stock in black neighborhoods and less than 4 percent in non-black ones. Black neighborhoods have roughly three times as many churches per capita as non-black ones.

There are also a number of differences within the black and non-black areas. For example, black areas with a high proportion of renters (70 percent or more) lost population between 1979 and 1995 at a rate four times higher than black neighborhoods with a high proportion of homeowners. The former areas tended to be poorer, which helps to explain their having roughly twice as many social service and community organizations per capita as the high-homeowner neighborhoods. The higher rates of poverty also help explain the higher crime rates of the renter areas in 1987. Interestingly, those rates declined between 1987 and 1995 while the crime rates in the high-homeowner areas increased.

Table 4-3. Selected Differences, Black and Non-Black Communities

Variable	Average, Black Neighborhoods	Average, Non-Black Neighborhoods
% change in population, 79–95	−19.3	−1.4
% change in homicide rate, 79–94	8.5	−1.7
% black, 1977	88.0	13.6
% Hispanic, 1977	2.2	31.6
% public housing, 1995	14.2	3.5
churches/10,000 people	186.4	62.9
average crimes/10,000 people, 87–95	135.9	83.7

The neighborhoods with more homeowners tend to be on the far south side of the city (where cheaper land prices allowed the construction of more single-family homes), while the higher-density renter communities are found closer to the Loop.

Examining neighborhood economic conditions in the context of geographic location and ethnic composition offers a potentially more useful way of understanding the general trends associated with revitalization. While not a perfect solution, grouping neighborhoods around these variables (the most telling ones to emerge from factor analysis) sheds more light on the patterns of economic change. Chicago's low- and moderate-income neighborhoods fit roughly into five clusters. Cluster 1, the Gentrifiers, includes five neighborhoods that have experienced significant recent increases in private investment. The proportion of young urban professionals among their residents has increased considerably. All of these communities benefit from either a proximity to downtown or a site on the north side of the city along Lake Michigan. Cluster 2, the Moderate-Income Hispanics, consists of five near northwest side neighborhoods that have experienced economic decline since 1989. Most of the decline stems from decreases in per capita incomes resulting from an influx of poor immigrants. Hispanics now constitute at least 40 percent of the population in each area. Cluster 3, the Moderate-Income Blacks, is comprised of nine declining communities on the far south side. These overwhelmingly black areas have mostly single-family homes and thus high rates of home ownership. Their decline results principally from the exodus of black middle class in the 1980s. Cluster 4, the Struggling Ethnics, consists of five slowly declining areas on the near south and southwest sides of the city. These communities have a high proportion of either Hispanic and/or Asian residents and a majority of renters. Finally, twelve neighborhoods in Chicago's historic Black Belt comprise Cluster 5. These south- and west-side communities are among the poorest in the city, yet have recently begun to show signs of revitalization. Private investment in the areas has increased, even though per capita incomes have continued to fall. A closer statistical look at these clusters can help explain some of the changes taking place.

Cluster 1: The Gentrifiers

The first group of neighborhoods has experienced gentrification. Situated either close to downtown or along the northern shore of Lake Michigan, the communities occupy some of the city's most desirable real estate. They have therefore attracted increasing numbers of young middle-class professionals, who have begun to upgrade the areas' aging housing stock. Property values have gone up significantly with the increased demand, and loan rates have generally followed suit.

Uptown, West Town, the Near West Side, the Near South Side, and Douglas comprise the neighborhoods in Cluster 1. Uptown is located on the north side of the city along Lake Michigan. Much of West Town is within two miles of the center of the Loop. The Near West and Near South Sides border the Loop, and Douglas is situated directly south of the Near South Side along the lake. Befitting their location, these areas are well-served by public transportation. They also have the most number of parks, an average of roughly two more than the next highest cluster.

Each of the neighborhoods sits adjacent to an economically vibrant area. Uptown lies directly north of the affluent Lakeview neighborhood. Particularly in the 1990s, it has attracted young urban professionals seeking to take advantage of its relative proximity to the character and night life of Lakeview and Lincoln Park without having to pay the high rents that those neighborhoods command. The community's per capita income rose by over 8 points relative to the city between 1979 and 1995, with the bulk of the increase taking place in the last six years.[21] Wicker Park and Bucktown, two neighborhoods within the larger West Town community area, offer easy access to jobs in the Loop and the Near North Side. Their low housing prices initially attracted artists and other bargain shoppers; the growth of nightclubs and ethnic restaurants has attracted additional professionals and has sparked extensive renovation of the

Table 4-4. Averages for Each Neighborhood Cluster

Variable	Cluster 1	Cluster 2	Cluster 3	Cluster 4	Cluster 5
INDEX79	55.4	89.2	90.8	66.6	46.6
INDEX89	61.5	90.4	74.8	69.7	45.0
INDEX95	87.2	82.3	78.4	63.9	50.8
CHIN7995	31.8	−6.9	−12.3	−2.6	4.2
CHIN7989	6.1	1.2	−16.0	3.1	−1.6
CHIN8995	25.8	−8.1	3.6	−5.7	5.9
CHRET	12.6	−2.8	−5.3	3.8	−13.2
CHPOP	−7.9%	6.6%	−5.7%	−0.5%	−29.0%
%BL79	55.3	7.5	79.3	11.2	95.5
CHBLACK	4.3%	7.9%	9.4%	4.7%	2.2%
%HIS79	17.9	30.4	8.8	40.8	1.4
CHHIS	8.7%	32.1%	1.8%	14.0%	−0.0%
%ASIAN80	3.8	4.6	0.0	8.4	0.3
CHASIAN	1.0%	1.4%	0.0%	5.2%	−0.1%
CHYOUNG	−3.5%	−2.2%	−9.9%	3.7%	−6.3%
CHOLD	−0.1%	−3.7%	2.0%	−0.6	1.5
DISTANCE	29.0	57.0	110.7	34.6	52.3
BUS	3.9	1.9	3.8	2.7	3.4
ELSTOP	0.8	0.3	0.0	0.5	1.2
PARKS	12.0	9.6	5.0	8.0	9.9
BROWN	0.0	0.2	0.4	0.6	0.2
AHSGOWN	10.7%	36.3%	57.8%	32.9%	24.0%
PUBHSG	22.6%	0.7%	7.6%	5.9%	14.6%
HSDIP79	46.0%	44.3%	57.5%	39.6%	41.6%
CHED	12.7%	10.1%	7.9%	2.7%	10.5%

(cont.)

Variable	Cluster 1	Cluster 2	Cluster 3	Cluster 4	Cluster 5
MEDREA82	28.9	40.0	26.6	19.0	23.8
CHREA	−0.7	−1.6	5.3	1.1	0.6
DROP86	41.5%	34.9%	25.6%	56.5%	45.3%
CHDROP	8.7%	1.2%	9.8%	−0.7%	2.4%
ACRIME	174.2	82.9	94.5	81.4	153.4
CHCRIME	−29.4	5.7	4.3	−1.9	−4.3
AHOM	54.9	30.2	43.2	27.7	76.0
CHHOM	−28.3	−2.4	13.5	−3.8	10.7
ALIQ	25.4	16.3	21.6	12.5	20.5
CHURCH	6.0	6.7	12.9	5.4	23.1
EDORG	24.3	6.7	6.6	9.1	11.8
HLTHORG	11.8	2.0	1.9	3.4	3.8
SSORG	18.4	4.7	3.5	6.6	6.2
COMORG	12.1	4.4	4.4	7.2	5.5

Note: For a description of the variables, see Table 4-1.

area. More residential building permits were issued in West Town than in any other community area in the city between 1993 and 1995.[22] The number of residential loans as a percentage of the city average rose from 37 percent in 1979 to 105 percent in 1995, and the average housing loan rose by 236 percent between 1985 and 1995. Three-bedroom apartments in Wicker Park currently rent for $1,800 per month, and two-bedrooms in Bucktown typically fetch over $1,200 per month.[23]

The Near West Side, located immediately west of the Loop, can trace much of its turnaround to the mid-1980s, when the Chicago Bears proposed to build a new football stadium in the area surrounding the old Chicago Stadium. Although the Bears' plan was defeated, the owners of the Bulls and Blackhawks (tenants at the Stadium) joined forces to build a new arena across the street from the decaying Stadium. The United Center, completed in 1994, served as the site of the 1996 Democratic National

Convention and has sparked considerable redevelopment in the community. The City allocated millions of dollars for street repair and other infrastructure improvement in preparation for the convention. Private developers have converted a number of former warehouses and factories into residential lofts (particularly in the West Loop area) and have begun construction on a series of single-family homes. Middle-class professionals have moved back into the area, raising the per capita income relative to the city average by almost 15 points since 1979.

The Near South Side, situated immediately south of the Loop, for years housed factories, warehouses, and flophouses. It has changed markedly as Chicago has moved from a manufacturing center to more of a service-driven city. The area's prime location has had tremendous appeal for private developers, who have converted warehouses into residential lofts, built condominium complexes and townhouses seemingly overnight, and constructed the area's first detached single-family homes. Residential loan rates have skyrocketed as a percentage of the city average; developments such as Central Station and Dearborn Park helped boost loan rates from less than 29 percent of the Chicago mean to over 114 percent in 16 years.

The Near South Side's development has had some spillover effect on the Douglas community to the south. The redevelopment of the McCormick Place convention center along the lakefront has created numerous local job opportunities and has attracted professionals to both the Near South Side and Douglas. The area between 31st and 35th Streets in Douglas, part of the old "Black Metropolis" region, has a number of historic greystone homes that used to house members of the black upper class. The mixture of increasing job opportunities (downtown, at McCormick Place, and at Michael Reese Hospital and the Illinois Institute of Technology, longtime institutional anchors on Douglas's south side), public subsidies,[24] and local activism has generated considerable redevelopment in the area. Members of the black middle class have begun to move back into the community, and loan rates have slowly increased.[25]

As just outlined, all of these neighborhoods are experiencing noticeable improvement. Their index scores have increased by an average of 31.5 points since 1979. Uptown, the only neighborhood with a negative overall change (-.04), improved by over 10 points after 1989 and had a 1995 index score above the city average. Four of the five neighborhoods have experienced increases in the percentage of loans since 1989; the Near West Side, the lone exception, has experienced an overall increase of 12 percent relative to the city. Both Uptown and the Near West Side have experienced increases in their per capita incomes relative to the city. Yet the primary source of growth has come from increased property values. Single-family homes in the Near South Side have sold for nearly three times the city median. Homes in Uptown cost one and one-half times that median. Similar houses in the other communities now sell for at least the city median, up a minimum of 34 percentage points since 1979.

A number of other indicators illustrate the process of gentrification. Population has declined in every neighborhood except the Near South Side, an anomaly because of its recent transition from an industrial to a residential area. Population loss usually accompanies the conversion of multi-family apartment buildings and single-room occupancy hotels into more profitable condominiums. Four of the neighborhoods witnessed an absolute increase in their number of upper-income households (households making $60,000 or more in 1989) between 1979 and 1989.[26] "Reverse" racial change, in which a neighborhood gains white residents while losing blacks, often illustrates gentrification. Between 1980 and 1990 the Near West Side's black-white ratio fell from 6:1 to 3:1. The number of childless young professionals has increased, as suggested by the decline in the proportion of residents under age 25 and the higher average levels of education among neighborhood residents. Crime rates have declined significantly, and the number of retail establishments has grown. All of this change has occurred despite the areas' high initial levels of crime and public housing. Part of the explanation may lie in the well-publicized plans to redevelop public housing projects in Douglas and the Near West Side, which have involved the demolition of some of the Chicago Housing Authority's worst high-rises; developers and investors have speculated on the expected future improvements. More generally, people have seen the communities' negative characteristics as either temporary or controllable and the areas' amenities as too good to pass up.

Cluster 2: Moderate-Income Hispanics

The neighborhoods in Cluster 2 are among the best-off communities in the sample, but have experienced notable decline in the 1990s. The decline has resulted principally from an influx of low-income Hispanics. Even though the communities' population has increased (often an indication of revitalization), the socioeconomic status of the new residents has had a negative impact on the neighborhoods' overall economic condition.

Albany Park, Hermosa, Avondale, Logan Square, and Humboldt Park are all located on the near northwest side of the city. Whereas Hispanics constituted no more than 42 percent of these areas' population in 1979, they comprised no less than 42 percent in 1995—a significant increase. In Hermosa and Logan Square, Hispanics made up more than 80 percent of the total 1995 population.

These neighborhoods have moderate levels of home ownership (between 28 and 46 percent) and the least amount of public housing of any of the five clusters. Perhaps as a result, the neighborhoods had the lowest average crime and homicide rates of any of the clusters. Every neighborhood but Humboldt Park has a higher rate of retail establishments per capita than the city average.

Economic conditions in these neighborhoods were the second-best among the five clusters in 1979. The average index score was 89.2, and both Albany Park and Hermosa were above the city average. Humboldt Park, the most disadvantaged member of the group with an index score of 65.3, nevertheless was better off than 42 percent of the sampled communities. The neighborhoods remained relatively well off in 1995, with an average index score of 82.3, but experienced decline from 1989 to 1995. All of the neighborhoods did worse in the 1990s than they had in the 1980s. Only Logan Square and Humboldt Park experienced overall improvement, while both Albany Park and Hermosa lost over 20 points relative to the city average.

Declining per capita incomes, more so than declining property values or loan rates, accounted for the bulk of the change. Property values in all areas rose relative to the city median between 1979 and 1989 but subsequently fell in every community but Logan Square, which continued to experience the gentrification pressures from the adjacent Lincoln Park and West Town community areas.[27] Similarly, loan rates rose in the 1980s and fell in the 1990s as a percentage of the city average. Most notably, between 1979 and 1989 incomes in the five communities fell by an average of over 16 points. The downward trend slowed after 1989, with the typical neighborhood falling five more percentage points. Whereas the neighborhoods' incomes measured 88.3 percent of the city average in 1979, they dropped to 67.2 percent of the average in 1995.

The population of these five neighborhoods has increased since 1979, one of the few regions in Chicago that has grown during the last two decades. An increase in population often indicates heightened demand for the neighborhood's amenities and usually translates into higher property values, loan rates, and index scores. Yet Albany Park and Hermosa, the areas with the greatest population increases, have seen their index scores and loan rates fall and their property values either fall or remain essentially constant.

The explanation lies in the economic condition of the immigrants. In general, the people moving into the communities have been poorer than the existing residents. The percentage of low-income households (those making $17,500 or less in 1989) rose in each community area between 1979 and 1989. In addition to individuals from outside Chicago, Hispanics from other areas of the city saw these neighborhoods as offering more opportunities than their existing places of residence, even if the difference was marginal. The increasingly poor population has muted the demand for single-family homes and thus the growth in property values. Unable to afford their own homes, a number of families have doubled or tripled up in single-family units.

While the average index score in these neighborhoods remains second-best among the five clusters, the Cluster 2 neighborhoods are experiencing increasing difficulties. Crime rates are rising, and real incomes are falling. The areas have growing concentrations of poor, under-educated Hispanics, many of whom have distinct language barriers. Joel Bookman, the Executive Director of the Albany Park-based Lawrence Avenue Development Corporation, fears that nobody really knows about the changing conditions. The neighborhoods "aren't poor enough to grab people's attention," and therefore haven't received the targeted resources provided to more impoverished communities on the south and west sides.[28]

Cluster 3: Moderate-Income Blacks

Like the Cluster 2 neighborhoods, the Cluster 3 communities are relatively well-off in comparison to the other groups in the sample. Yet these communities have also declined. Their economic difficulties stem primarily from the exodus of the black middle class in the 1980s, not from the influx of poor immigrants.

South Chicago, Burnside, Roseland, Pullman, South Deering, West Pullman, Riverdale, Auburn Gresham, and Washington Heights all lie south of 75th Street. Throughout the 1960s and early 1970s, these low density residential neighborhoods represented the principal destination for members of the black middle class seeking to escape the increasingly crowded mid-south and west side "black belt." All but Riverdale had high proportions of single-family homes, and the properties offered more space at reasonable prices. In 1977 blacks comprised at least 40 percent of the residents in each neighborhood. By 1995, they constituted an absolute majority in each area.

Excluding Riverdale, the site of a number of public housing developments, these far south side communities were stable middle-class areas in the late 1970s.[29] They had the highest average educational level of any of the low- and moderate-income clusters, the highest rate of home ownership, and the highest average index score (97.1). Yet economic conditions in the neighborhoods dropped by more than 17 points relative to the city average between 1979 and 1989, a greater decline than in any other cluster. The decline spanned all of the index components: per capita incomes, loan rates, and property values all fell relative to the city average. Conditions have stabilized since 1989. Although per capita incomes and property values have continued to decline, loan rates have increased and the average index scores have risen by 3.6 points. The neighborhoods remain relatively well-off in comparison to the other low- and moderate-income communities, with an average index score of 83.8.

All of the Cluster 3 neighborhoods lost population between 1979 and 1989. There were almost nine percent fewer residents under age 25 in these areas in 1990 than there were in 1980, suggesting that many families with children had left the region. Public schools on the far south side offered poor educational opportunities—the median eleventh grade reading score in 1982 ranked in the 26th percentile nationally—while students attending suburban schools had much better records of achievement. With the easing of exclusionary zoning and discriminatory housing policies, suburbs had become an increasingly feasible option for members of the black middle class. Numerous individuals sought to obtain their own piece of the American dream and left the city. Each neighborhood in the cluster had a lower proportion of upper-income and middle-income households in 1990 than in 1980. The people who stayed in these communities tended to be older, less educated homeowners. As they reached retirement age, their incomes declined. Not wishing to move, they held on to their homes as their primary assets. With a weak real estate market, property values and loan rates stagnated.

All of the neighborhoods except South Chicago have gained population since 1989, and their economic conditions have slowly improved. The areas have not attracted previous middle-class emigrants, but have instead appealed to moderate-income individuals looking for housing bargains in the city. These buyers have been able to obtain homes at discounts from elderly residents (or their estates) in need of cash, contributing to the continued decline of property values relative to the city median. The influx of these younger individuals has helped moderate the neighborhoods' overall relative reduction in per capita income while sparking additional lending activity on the part of banks and other financial institutions.[30]

Cluster 4: Struggling Ethnics

The trends for Clusters 4 and 5 are not as clearly defined as those for the previous three clusters. In many ways Cluster 4 consists of the residual moderate-income neighborhoods, areas that simply did not fit neatly into any other grouping. These neighborhoods have experienced either stagnant or slowly declining economic conditions, caused largely by decreasing loan rates. In addition, the high proportion of poorly educated immigrants has resulted in low levels of per capita income.

Each of the Cluster 4 neighborhoods has a high proportion of ethnic residents. South Lawndale and the Lower West Side (also known as Little Village and Pilsen) comprise the city's two major Mexican neighborhoods. Hispanics constitute over 90 percent of the population in each area. Armour Square includes Chinatown, explaining the community area's majority (52 percent) of Asian residents. Bridgeport and New City (also known as Back of the Yards) used to be the home of much of Chicago's Irish community. With the economic and demographic changes of the past few decades, many of those Irish have left and have been replaced by Latinos, Asians (in Bridgeport), and blacks (in New City). Latinos now comprise almost 50 percent of New City's residents and over 33 percent of Bridgeport's.

While these neighborhoods have the lowest levels of crime of all the clusters, they nevertheless have experienced little revitalization. All five communities saw their index scores fall between 1989 and 1995. Armour Square and Bridgeport, two of the three areas that improved during the 1980s, fell by more than 10 points in the early 1990s. As a result, the cluster's average 1995 index score was only 63.94, the second worst of the five groups.

The slow decline of the Cluster 4 neighborhoods resembles that of the northwest side Hispanic communities of Cluster 2. All of the areas have attracted a considerable number of poor immigrants, individuals whose low levels of education and difficulty with English have relegated them to low-paying jobs. The Cluster 4 neighborhoods had the lowest percentage of individuals with high school diplomas, the lowest median reading scores, and the highest dropout rates of any of the clusters studied. These areas were the only ones that experienced an increase in the percentage of residents under the age of 25. With more children and students, these communities had a smaller percentage of potential wage-earners and thus lower per capita incomes. More than half of the areas' students have left high school before graduation, often to take a job to help support their families. Yet these jobs typically pay little more than the minimum wage and ensure that the neighborhoods' overall economic condition will remain low.

While per capita incomes have fallen relative to the city average since 1989, the major force behind the declining index scores has been reduced loan rates. All five of the Cluster 4 neighborhoods experienced a decline relative to the city average in the rate of residential loans they received. What makes the trend surprising is that all of the areas' loan rates increased from 1979 to 1989. Each area falls under the purview of the Community Reinvestment Act, which mandates that banks lend in low-income, predominantly minority neighborhoods; since the Act has been more stringently enforced in the 1990s than it was in the 1980s, the rate of loans should presumably have increased. Yet poorly educated ethnic residents tend to be leery of formal financial institutions. A recent study of South Lawndale by the Federal Reserve Bank of Chicago found that the residents primarily used nonbank sources for their financing needs. Only about 21 percent of residents had checking accounts. Most individuals—particularly those with little formal education—relied exclusively on family and friends for financial support.[31] As the percentage of immigrants has increased in South Lawndale, Armour Square, and the other neighborhoods, this trend has become more pronounced.

Cluster 5: The Black Belt

The neighborhoods in Cluster 5 constitute "inner-city Chicago." The poorest communities in the city, the neighborhoods sit within the historical "black belt" extending south and west of the Loop. While remaining the most troubled areas in the city, many of the communities have experienced economic improvement since 1989. Property values and loan rates have increased, even while real per capita incomes have continued to decline.

Austin, West Garfield Park, East Garfield Park, and North Lawndale lie on the west side of the city. Oakland, Fuller Park, Grand Boulevard, Washington Park, and Woodlawn lie directly south of the Loop and contain some of the nation's most notorious public housing projects. West Englewood, Englewood, and Greater Grand Crossing constitute the southwest boundary between the project-pocked communities and the black homeowner neighborhoods of Cluster 3. These 12 community areas had an average index score of only 46.61 in 1979, easily the lowest of any cluster.

Homicide rates in these neighborhoods have traditionally been the highest in the city, and the overall crime rates have been among the worst. Less than 25 percent of the housing units are occupied by their owners, and only about half of the residents have high school diplomas. Grand Boulevard and Oakland have ranked among the most impoverished areas in the country.

Although the neighborhoods still have the lowest index score of any cluster, their economic conditions have improved since 1989. Whereas 4 of the 12 improved during the 1980s, 11 of the 12 have gotten better in the 1990s. Greater Grand Crossing, the only decliner, has fallen by only 0.77 points since 1989. The rate of decline in the communities' per capita income relative to the city average has slowed. Loan rates have continued to increase, and property values in all but the three southwest-side areas have risen relative to the city median. This change has occurred amid considerable population losses in each neighborhood.

Part of the overall improvement stems from additional bank investment. Increased enforcement of the Community Reinvestment Act has compelled bankers to make more loans in these historically redlined areas, leading to a growth in the communities' loan rates relative to the city average. In addition, the strength of the metropolitan economy has had a positive effect on all Chicago neighborhoods. Were the metropolitan region a nation, its gross national product in the past few years would rank among the top ten in the world. According to Bank of America Illinois President William Goodyear, this economic vitality has made every Chicago neighborhood seem viable for investment.[32] Potential home buyers have been willing to reconsider some of the traditionally blighted neighborhoods because of their low housing costs, and bankers have consequently seen greater potential for a return on investment.[33]

These broader factors cannot explain the variation in changes across the neighborhoods, however. Austin, West Englewood, Englewood, and Greater Grand Crossing have all experienced overall decline since 1979. Only West Garfield Park, East Garfield Park, North Lawndale, and Fuller Park have shown increases in their index scores in both the 1980s and the 1990s. Woodlawn has improved by more than 10 points since 1989 after losing over 3 points in the previous 10 years. A significant portion of Woodlawn's recent change can be attributed to the presence and commitment of the University of Chicago to the north, yet other neighborhoods have no such strong local institution. Both of the Garfield Parks have improved noticeably despite the presence of one of the city's strongest drug markets. Grand Boulevard has improved despite the presence of the Robert Taylor Homes, which remains a center of poverty, crime, unemployment, and drug activity.

Since the cluster averages do not provide clear indications of the nature of the change in the black belt neighborhoods, I conducted a more detailed statistical analysis. The following table indicates the correlations between the relevant independent variables and the various change scores.

Although the small number of neighborhoods in the sample precludes the identification of statistically significant relationships, the size of the correlations offers some insight into the characteristics of neighborhood change. Communities with increasing proportions of black residents (and thus decreasing percentages of non-black residents) typically fared worse than their counterparts, as evidenced by the correlation of −.44 between changes in index scores and changes in the percentage of black residents. (The disparity between the 1980s and the 1990s reflects the fact that blacks constituted at least 95 percent of the population in most of the Cluster 5 communities; the areas simply could not get much "blacker.") Such a finding reinforces the trend toward neighborhood decline in overwhelmingly black low-income areas.

Some of the correlations showed the expected relationships. A community's proximity to the Loop continued to be strongly associated with improvement in its economic condition (−.69). A greater number of bus lines was associated with increases in neighborhood per capita income (.61), suggesting the importance of public transportation in being able to access jobs. Declining homicide rates were associated with improving neighborhoods and especially with increasing property values (−.51). Increased education levels were associated with increasing index scores (.46 overall, and .55 in the 1980s); the small correlation (.11) with the 1989–1995 change probably results from the lack of educational attainment data after 1990. The presence of community organizations and health agencies also was associated with neighborhood revitalization, particularly in the 1989–1995 period. The bulk of the change came in the form of higher loan rates. Banks may have seen such organizations as indications of a certain amount of stability within the neighborhood and thus may have felt more comfortable lending in the area. The community groups may also have exerted pressure on the banks to provide capital to local residents.

Table 4-5. Selected Correlations in "Black Belt" Neighborhoods

Variable	Index Score Change 79–95	Index Score Change 79–89	Index Score Change 89–95	Per Capita Income Change 79–95	Loan Rate Change 79–95	Property Value Change 79–95
CHBLACK	−.44	−.57	−.06	−.21	−.29	−.37
CHPOP	−.36	−.44	−.08	−.31	−.01	−.40
DISTANCE	−.69	−.63	−.45	−.48	−.20	−.72
BUS	.30	.36	.07	.61	−.11	.32
ELSTOP	.43	.34	.32	.42	.07	.44
BROWN	.53	.52	.27	−.28	.64	.38
PARKS	−.33	−.38	−.10	−.27	−.02	−.37
AHSGOWN	−.62	−.50	−.44	−.29	−.08	−.70
PUBHSG	.11	.19	−.04	.58	−.42	.27
HSDIP79	−.65	−.66	−.31	−.52	−.24	−.61
CHED	.46	.55	.11	.10	.54	.27
MEDREA82	.21	.00	.35	−.16	.32	.12
CHREA	.03	.03	.02	−.40	.42	−.13
DROP86	.01	.17	−.20	.26	−.16	.05
CHDROP	.45	.29	.45	−.29	.35	.47
ACRIME	.31	.44	−.01	.50	−.15	.39
CHCRIME	−.27	−.18	−.24	−.35	−.27	−.12
AHOM	.65	.51	.49	.57	.06	.70
CHHOM	−.48	−.33	−.41	−.13	−.15	−.51
ALIQ	.23	.06	.32	.27	.02	.23
COMORG	.27	−.05	.52	−.22	.43	.15
CHURCH	.09	.29	−.20	.13	.26	−.06
EDORG	−.19	−.34	.08	−.18	.01	−.22
HLTHORG	.32	.09	.43	−.19	.47	.19
SSORG	−.06	−.23	.18	−.25	.17	−.13

Note: For a description of the variables, see Table 4-1.

Many of the other large correlations suggested the same counter-intuitive relationships found in the overall sample. Areas whose residents had high initial levels of education typically fared worse than their counterparts, although communities with improving education levels fared better. Conceivably the better-educated residents left the neighborhoods during the period in question, depriving the communities of their economic and other resources. Neighborhoods with increasing high school dropout rates generally experienced economic improvement. Areas with higher percentages of homeowners tended to decline, especially with regard to their property values (-.70). One possible explanation for this baffling finding is that the homeowners have been retired individuals who rely principally on the checks from social security and have decided to remain in their homes for the duration. Their incomes have decreased since they retired, and their unwillingness to sell has watered down the real estate market. Neighborhoods with higher average crime rates—and particularly high average homicide rates (.65)—tended to revitalize. These higher rates were mysteriously associated with increases in per capita incomes and property values. (At the same time, decreases in crime and homicide rates were also associated with neighborhood improvement—a more easily understood relationship.)

Neither educational nor social service organizations appear to have a strong and consistent relationship with revitalization. Part of the reason may lie in the fact that these organizations tend to be clustered in the areas of greatest need and (particularly in the case of social service groups such as soup kitchens and homeless shelters) essentially act to mend holes in the social safety net, not to promote economic improvement. The nature of the EDORG and SSORG variables may also contribute to the weak correlation. The variables only take into account the number of organizations and says nothing about their size, capacity, or quality. A single well-managed agency with a $2 million annual budget may well be more effective than five fledgling groups with yearly revenues of $100,000.

Brownfields are positively correlated with revitalization, especially with increasing loan rates (.64). As mentioned earlier, sites designated as brownfields by the City qualify for public clean-up funds. In acknowledging and taking some responsibility for the environmental hazard, the City reduces the liability and the land restoration costs for potential investors. The reduced risk might increase the willingness of banks to lend in the area and raise the value of the surrounding property.

Summing Up the Quantitative Analysis

The aggregate analysis reinforced the importance of location in neighborhood economic development. Communities situated close to downtown and/or along Lake Michigan experienced revitalization to a noticeably greater extent than their counterparts elsewhere in the city. In short, location matters. In addition to physical proximity, areas with good transportation access to major job centers tend to experience more economic improvement. A number of social factors also seem to be associated with revitalization. Reductions in crime and homicide rates are correlated with local economic improvement. Neighborhoods with community organizations tend to fare better, especially with regard to their property values. Although the correlation is not as strong in poor black communities, the presence of various social service organizations tends to be associated with increases in local per capita incomes. Furthermore, increases in an area's average level of education also correlate with revitalization.

The aggregate analysis could not adequately explain some of the more baffling correlations, however, particularly the tendency toward revitalization in neighborhoods with high crime rates, a large number of liquor stores, low percentages of homeowners, and relatively high concentrations of public housing. A more localized look at Chicago's communities helped to account for these odd findings. Considering trends in clusters of neighborhoods indicated that neighborhoods have changed at different rates, at different times, and for different reasons. For example, population growth in some areas could signify revitalization, while in other areas it has been a cause of economic decline. The nature of the population change is also important. The Hispanic areas on the city's northwest side have declined recently in large part because of an influx of immigrants. In contrast, the black neighborhoods on the far south side have experienced decline because of the exodus of the middle class and the aging of the remaining residents.

The quantitative approach identified a number of factors associated with revitalization. It outlined the general economic trends affecting Chicago's poorer communities in the past 20 years and helped create an economic map of the city, one that highlights the distinctions among clusters of geographically concentrated neighborhoods. It suggested that with the exception of location, there are no factors that clearly account for revitalization across all of the city's low- and moderate-income neighborhoods.

The analysis is at best suggestive. Statistical studies are useful primarily in addressing questions of amount and frequency: to what extent did the neighborhoods change, or how prevalent are brownfields, educational organizations, and parks in these areas? A quantitative analysis can indicate relationships between and among variables, but it cannot adequately describe the characteristics and causes of those interactions. Location has been strongly correlated with revitalization in the past 20 years, yet these same revitalizing neighborhoods experienced considerable decline beforehand. The statistical study cannot explain the forces that cause economic turnarounds. It also cannot account for the different importance similar factors have across neighborhoods. It is limited in its ability to distinguish between cause and effect. For example, it cannot determine whether declining crime rates are a product of revitalization, a cause, or a combination. More specifically, consider the black belt neighborhoods in Cluster 5. The statistical survey suggests that educational improvements, reduced crime rates, access to public transportation, and the presence of certain nonprofit organizations help promote revitalization. The presence of brownfields may also have some positive effect, while the effects of home ownership and initial levels of education appear strangely negative. The statistics cannot explain why these factors promote revitalization. They cannot identify which of these elements is most important to the process or determine how many of the components are necessary for positive change.

Part of the limitation results from the small number of neighborhoods in the analysis. Quantitative studies benefit from far more than 36 cases, let alone the 12 in Cluster 5; obtaining statistically significant results from such a small sample is extremely unlikely. The nature of the data makes the approach even more problematic. Relying on estimates of post-1990 population and per capita income figures may distort the neighborhood index scores and thus the correlations. Many of the independent variables are at best rough measures of potentially relevant components of neighborhood revitalization. For example, counting the number of nonprofit social service, educational, community, and health organizations in an area does not take into account the effectiveness or legitimacy of the groups. Dropout rates and median reading scores, used as indicators of school quality, are based on an arbitrary mapping of school boundaries and community areas. Community areas are an official unit of measurement in the city, but the size of the areas may mask changes occurring on an even more local level. One small section of a community area (a census tract, for example) may be experiencing extensive revitalization while the rest of the area is continuing to decline slowly. The improvement may easily skew the overall characteristics of the community area. Furthermore, there are no good measures of political decisions affecting neighborhoods, such as the allocation of public resources.[34] Only by studying the community areas in more qualitative detail can we understand what has actually taken place and why.

TOWARD A MORE DETAILED ANALYSIS— QUALITATIVE CASE STUDIES

A detailed case study approach can effectively identify and assess these micro-level mechanisms of change. Analyzing a community area in depth necessarily involves the use of multiple sources of information, allowing for various (and potentially competing) explanations of particular phenomena. Such a case study focuses on expanding and developing analytical theories, not on enumerating or illustrating statistical frequencies.[35] It identifies the mechanisms by which location and community organizations contribute to revitalization. In short, it augments the aggregate analysis by describing and examining the interactions that are taking place within particular neighborhoods. What are the relationships among individuals, organizations, and agencies that promote or hinder economic change? Why have banks decided to invest (or not invest) in the area? What interventions (if any) have made property values increase? Why has the overall growth in the Chicago economy had different effects on different neighborhoods? Case studies allow for an examination of local leadership and individual decision making. Above all, a case study approach is flexible enough to be able to concentrate on different factors than originally intended should the evidence warrant.

This study is primarily concerned with revitalization in the poorest inner-city neighborhoods. In Chicago, the most economically distressed communities are those in Cluster 5, the historical black belt extending south and west of the Loop. Cluster 5 therefore provides the logical pool from which to select neighborhoods for more in-depth analysis. Virtually all of these neighborhoods still qualify as economically distressed. (Only Austin had a 1995 index score of more than 65.) Yet eight of the community areas have improved since 1979. The remaining four—Austin and the three southwestern neighborhoods (West Englewood, Englewood, and Greater Grand Crossing)—have experienced continued decline. None of the changes has been astronomical, but the positive and negative trends are clear. Selecting one neighborhood from each of the revitalizing and declining groups offers the possibility of comparing differences between the two areas and identifying how those differences led to dissimilar outcomes.

Table 4-6. Change Scores in "Black Belt" Neighborhoods

CA	Name	Index 1979	Index 1995	Change
27	E. Garfield Park	35.92	53.14	17.22
26	W. Garfield Park	40.65	51.55	10.90
29	**N. Lawndale**	**37.09**	**47.93**	**10.84**
37	Fuller Park	42.13	50.50	8.37
42	Woodlawn	44.34	51.08	6.73
38	Grand Boulevard	31.39	37.80	6.41
40	Washington Park	34.04	39.92	5.88
36	Oakland	22.87	25.80	2.93
25	Austin	85.78	83.10	−2.68
69	Gr. Grand Crossing	68.65	64.87	−3.78
68	**Englewood**	**47.66**	**42.84**	**−4.82**
67	W. Englewood	69.33	61.75	−7.58

Studying more than two neighborhoods in depth offers disproportionately little gain for the additional amount of work. The overall economic changes that have taken place in these communities are small and often invisible to casual observers. The changes represent marginal improvements or declines in the context of overall economic distress.

I have chosen to focus on North Lawndale and Englewood. The neighborhoods are similar in a number of respects. Both lie outside the original south side "black belt" area but had almost complete racial turnover in the late 1950s and 1960s. Both experienced considerable rioting, Englewood in response to the black immigration and North Lawndale in response to the assassination of Martin Luther King and the other frustrations of the 1960s. North Lawndale and Englewood each had an active retail strip, and residents in each neighborhood have long had access to the Loop via the Chicago Transit Authority's elevated rail lines. Both have low levels of public housing and experienced considerable economic decline beginning in the late 1960s. Yet conditions in the two communities have more recently diverged, making for a good comparison. North Lawndale improved steadily from 1979 to 1995, increasing its index score by nearly 11 points. Its economic position rose from 37 percent of the city average to 48 percent. In contrast, Englewood fell by almost 5 points relative to the city average, from 48 percent to 43 percent.

The following chapters provide an in-depth analysis of North Lawndale and Englewood. They seek to identify the mechanisms by which location, community organizations, and other local factors contribute to neighborhood economic improvement. In the process, they provide a richer understanding of the nuances of revitalization.

NOTES

[1]Census data were aggregated by community area in the 1980 *Local Community Fact Book* and in the Chicago Department of Planning's 1983 *Chicago Statistical Abstract.* Community area breakdowns for 1990 were generated by London and Puntenney. Hispanics constitute a separate category independent of whites and blacks. Since Claritas/NPDC did not provide estimates of community area Asian populations, I relied on census data.

[2]See Sööt and Sen.

[3]I also set upper limits on the variables in order to reduce the effect of statistical outliers.

[4]A number of parks span multiple community areas, making it difficult to discern the park acreage in each neighborhood.

[5]Home ownership is defined as the percentage of owner-occupied units in a community area, a definition that includes owners of condominiums and cooperatives. The correlation between the percentage of single-family homes and the rate of home ownership is .86 and is statistically significant at the .001 level.

[6]See George Galster, *Homeowners and Neighborhood Reinvestment* (Durham: Duke University Press, 1987).

[7]Education level is a tricky measure: it might well increase as a result of revitalization, not as a cause of economic improvement. This study uses it as a context for revitalization, not as an explicit cause: Are neighborhoods whose residents have higher levels of education more likely to revitalize than those with less-educated individuals?

[8]These years are the first for which data are available.

[9]See Chapters 6 and 8 of Taub, Taylor, and Dunham. They argue that crime plays a role in individuals' investment decisions, but usually is not the determining factor. Certain types of crime (those involving theft of property, for instance) are more likely in more affluent areas simply because there is more of value to steal.

[10]See Elijah Anderson, pp. 81–94, and Chapters 3 and 4 of Wilson, *When Work Disappears,* among other studies.

[11]Chicago Department of Public Health, *Community Area Health Inventory,* Vol. 1 (1984); *Community Area Health Inventory, 1992–1994,* Vol. 1 (1996).

[12]See Ann Maxwell and Dan Immergluck, *Liquorlining: Liquor Store Concentration and Community Development in Lower-Income Cook County*

Neighborhoods (Chicago: Woodstock Institute, 1997). ALIQ is correlated .65 with ACRIME, the average crime rate from 1987 to 1995.

[13]See, among others, Taub, Taylor, Dunham; Clay; and Downs.

[14]See *Chicago Community Organizations Directory* (Chicago: Community Renewal Society, 1990 (reprint)), and *Directory of Community Organizations in Chicago* (Chicago: Loyola Univ. Institute of Urban Life, 1992, updated in 1996).

[15]On one hand, a loss of population tends to decrease the number of churches in an area, as smaller congregations are less able to keep the churches fiscally solvent. On the other hand, the number of churches may increase depending on the religious affiliations of the remaining residents. A predominantly Catholic area will tend to have relatively few churches, while a more Protestant region typically has many more (because of the different Protestant denominations). Neighborhoods that experience considerable ethnic turnover and population loss may actually wind up with more churches than they initially had.

[16]Social service organizations are often clustered in areas of high need (although they were only correlated -.15 with 1979 Chicago community per capita income levels). The presence of such agencies may therefore represent the degree of need in a community, not merely a measure of social capital. On the other hand, high-need neighborhoods tend to be those most in need of enhanced social capital and the potential benefits that these groups can provide. A higher number of organizations in an area would thus suggest a greater potential for local community-building.

[17]*Social Service Directory* (1977–78, 1980), *Human Services Directory* (1981), *United Way Human Care Services Directory* (1986, 1989–90, 1992), and *Human Care Services Directory of Metropolitan Chicago* (1994–95).

[18]The historically lower cost of land further away from the Loop allowed for the construction of larger single-family homes, which have tended to be owner-occupied.

[19]Excluding the Near South Side, where extensive redevelopment increased the index score by over 83 points, these areas still improved by an average of 8.2 points.

[20]The average was 47.16 without the Near South Side.

[21]The increase in the number of affluent individuals has more than compensated for the simultaneous increase in Uptown's number of poor residents.

[22]Chicago Department of Buildings data, 1996.

[23]Linda Lutton, "There Goes the Neighborhood," *The Neighborhood Works* (Jul/Aug 1997), pp. 18–19.

[24]As part of the agreement surrounding the construction of the new Comiskey Park (home of the White Sox), the Illinois Sports Authority built a se-

ries of homes in the area. The city's annual Parade of Homes, a subsidized show-
case of new residential construction, was held in the area in 1992.

[25]See the Goodman Williams Group's "Residential Market Analysis: Mid-
South Area," a report prepared for the Akhenaton/Omnibus Prospective Project
(Chicago, January 1995), for a more detailed breakdown of the Douglas market.
The information was corroborated in a phone interview with Pat Dowell-
Cerasoli, the Executive Director of the Mid-South Planning and Development
Commission, on February 12, 1997.

[26]Immergluck, pp. 19–24. Households in the upper-income category were
making at least $35,000 in 1979.

[27]The average price of a single-family home in Logan Square increased by
14 percent per year between 1985 and 1995 (Chicago Association of Realtors
data).

[28]Phone interview on February 7, 1997.

[29]With a 1979 index score of 38.91 and a 1995 score of 35.35, Riverdale has
consistently ranked as one of the poorest community areas in Chicago. Its
poverty and high proportion of renters set it apart from the other neighborhoods
in Cluster 3. Yet geographically Riverdale belongs with this group, and its demographic and economic trends are similar to the other included areas. The data in
this paragraph do not include Riverdale because of the baseline economic disparities, but the remainder of the paragraphs do include the community in the cluster
averages.

[30]These trends were corroborated in a phone interview with Jim Capraro,
the Executive Director of the Greater Southwest Development Corporation,
Chicago, and a long-time south-side activist, on February 8, 1997, and by the
"Trading Places" series in the *Chicago Sun-Times* (February 7, 9, & 10, 1997).

[31]See Philip Bond and Robert Townsend, "Formal and Informal Financing
in a Chicago Ethnic Neighborhood," *Economic Perspectives* 20 (Jul./Aug. 1996):
3–27.

[32]Keynote address at the Chicago Neighborhood Development Awards, January 28, 1997.

[33]Interview with Peter Levavi, Chicago Association of Realtors, Chicago,
February 2, 1997.

[34]Local political considerations have historically influenced the allocation
of federal Community Development Block Grant funds across neighborhoods,
for example. (See Rich, among other CDBG evaluations.) Yet the City of
Chicago does not break down such expenditures by neighborhood, and various
other organizations have been unable to separate neighborhood-specific projects
from those designed to benefit the city as a whole. While some researchers have

identified positive correlations between the provision of public services and the level of neighborhood need, others (as well as many Chicago neighborhood activists and practitioners) have claimed that resource allocation depends on the characteristics of individual aldermen, city officials, and so forth.

[35]Robert K. Yin, *Case Study Research: Design and Methods* 2d ed. (Thousand Oaks, CA: Sage Publications, 1994), p. 52.

CHAPTER 5

Decline and Revitalization:
A Tale of Two Neighborhoods

As briefly outlined at the end of the last chapter, the Englewood community on Chicago's south side has experienced steady decline over the past 30 years. Once a stable middle-class area, Englewood has become one of the city's poorest and most devastated communities, a neighborhood with high rates of poverty and unemployment, little private investment, and considerable despair. Like Englewood, the west-side neighborhood of North Lawndale declined from a relatively stable mixed-income community to one of the nation's most troubled neighborhoods. In the 1980s, the *Chicago Tribune* used the neighborhood as a case study for its series on the urban underclass, *The American Millstone*. Yet in the last five years North Lawndale has shown considerable improvement. It has attracted numerous private investors and is generally seen as a budding success story by public, private, and nonprofit officials throughout the city.

This chapter provides a comparative history of the two neighborhoods, focusing primarily on the last 30 years. It describes the events and actors that have shaped the communities' development and illustrates the different experiences of the two largely similar neighborhoods. Chapter 6 offers a more detailed analysis of why North Lawndale has improved, both in absolute terms and in relation to Englewood. Chapter 7 draws upon the experiences of these two neighborhoods to examine the roles different institutions play in promoting (or hindering) revitalization. Each chapter illustrates the inherent complexity of revitalization. Neighborhood development is not a clean process, nor does it lend itself to a simple analysis. It can only be described and understood as the highly nuanced interplay of numerous forces, agencies, and individuals.

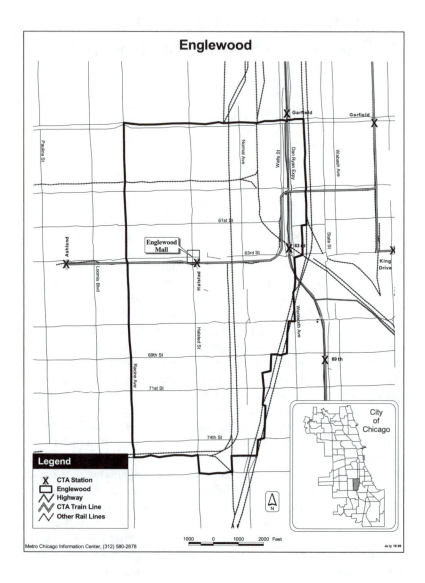

ENGLEWOOD

A Stable Working-Class Area (1930–1950)

German and Irish farmers and railroad workers first settled in Englewood in the mid-1880s. They named the area after Englewood, New Jersey, because of the predominance of forests in each site. The midwestern community became a largely middle-class area with a majority of single-family homes, and the city of Chicago annexed it in 1889. Workers finished construction of an elevated rail line connecting Englewood to downtown in 1907.[1]

Englewood's location attracted retailers. The neighborhood was situated just south of the Chicago stockyards, one of the world's largest meat-processing centers. Unlike other communities, Englewood did not flood or become especially muddy during times of heavy rain. Easily accessible by both the "el" and street-level trolley lines, the 63rd and Halsted intersection became the chief shopping center on Chicago's south side. By the mid-1930s, the shopping center was the largest and most profitable non-downtown retail area in the country. Wieboldt's, a Chicago-based department store, operated its most profitable facility in Englewood (a store that grossed $20 million per year).[2] Piggybacking on Wieboldt's success, Sears, Roebuck, & Co. opened a department store in the shopping center in 1934. The area boasted four movie theaters, one of which (the Southtown Theater) regularly featured films in their first showing outside of downtown.

These retail and cultural amenities continued to attract working-class families. By 1950 the neighborhood had 97,565 residents, many of whom were European immigrants (or children of immigrants) who worked in the stockyards or the south-side rail yards. Since most of the residents were Catholic, the Church became a major local institution. Englewood itself had six Catholic parishes, and the adjacent West Englewood neighborhood had an additional six.

Racial and Economic Transition (1950–1975)

While one of the city's most economically vibrant areas, Englewood remained a somewhat transitory community. Many families considered it to be a "way station," a community where they would live until they could afford to move to a more desirable neighborhood slightly further out in the city. Unlike some of the city's older neighborhoods, Englewood's houses were built primarily of wood. Frame construction requires more maintenance than brick or stone buildings, and parts of the community consequently battled physical deterioration.

More importantly, Englewood was due west of the post World War II "Black Belt" communities on Chicago's south side. Although physically separated from Washington Park by the New York Central railroad and later by the Dan Ryan Expressway, Englewood straddled the city's racial divide. The Supreme Court's nullification of racially restrictive covenants in 1948 began eliminating the legal underpinnings of such segregation and provoked extensive racial transition in neighborhoods such as Englewood. Many of Englewood's residents feared that blacks would be able to move into their community and thus drive down the values of houses they had worked so hard to buy and maintain. They therefore sought to sell their homes quickly to maximize their investment and then move out to neighborhoods further south and west. As whites moved out, blacks moved in. Englewood was less crowded and generally more desirable than neighborhoods such as Grand Boulevard, Woodlawn, and Washington Park. Between 1950 and 1960 nearly two-thirds of Englewood's white residents left the neighborhood. Whereas blacks had comprised only 2 percent of the community's population in 1940, they constituted 69 percent in 1960. By 1970 the racial turnover was complete, as the population was 96 percent black. The speed of the change was mind-boggling. Aurie Pennick, now the President of the Leadership Council for Metropolitan Open Communities, an organization that pushes for fair housing throughout the Chicago area, grew up in Englewood during the transition and remembered a distinct racial line moving across the area. The eastern part of Englewood integrated first, "then the line moved west. Within 18 months, the neighborhood was completely segregated."[3]

The racial change set in motion other forces that accelerated Englewood's decline. A chief exacerbating force was the Federal Housing Authority (FHA).[4] As described in Chapter 3, the FHA historically shied away from guaranteeing mortgages in "unstable" areas. Neighborhoods with high proportions of minorities were almost invariably deemed "unstable," as were communities experiencing racial change. Thus as blacks moved into Englewood and sought to purchase homes, they found themselves unable to secure mortgages. The FHA had essentially defined the neighborhood as one with high risks, a characterization that caused conventional lenders to avoid it almost entirely. Black home buyers consequently had to strike deals with the previous owners and/or the realtors to buy the homes on contract. The lack of other financing available to blacks effectively created a monopoly for the sellers. The sellers consequently tended to charge interest rates that were well above the market rate, inserted no-equity clauses into the agreements, and generally increased the likelihood of foreclosure on the new buyers.

Conditions such as these were not unique to Englewood; a similar problem affected blacks moving into North Lawndale and other previously white urban neighborhoods throughout the country. The need for restructured lending practices became a cause of the national Civil Rights Movement, which successfully pressured Congress into passing the Fair Housing Act in 1968. As part of the Act, the FHA's lending standards were loosened to encourage minority home ownership. The FHA dropped its "stable neighborhood" requirement and established a program in which it provided federally insured mortgages to low-income home buyers. Individuals could buy homes with down payments as low as a few hundred dollars, which suddenly created a new set of opportunities for many urban minorities. At the same time, the program was extremely popular among banks and insurance companies, which could issue loans and be assured no loss because of the federal guarantee.

Englewood experienced the downside of the FHA program. Like realtors, bankers and mortgage companies could only make a profit if homes were sold. They therefore worked closely with the realtors to encourage existing residents to sell their homes to eager black buyers. In their quest to make a sale, some realtors resorted to tactics designed to scare whites into selling: placing for-sale signs in yards throughout the area, emphasizing the influx of blacks in the neighborhood and the schools, raising the unpopular specter of interracial sexual relationships, and so forth. Panicked, many whites chose to sell at prices below the appraised value of the house. The lure of better housing led black buyers to purchase the same houses at prices often well above the appraised value. The realtors pocketed a commission on both ends of the transaction.[5] As this panic peddling spread, whites often became so eager to sell and blacks so eager to buy that badly deteriorating, structurally questionable, essentially unlivable homes readily changed hands.[6]

FHA mortgages constituted the principal financing mechanism for the vast majority of these home sales. While the low down payments enabled low-income people to buy homes, the buyers were often financially hamstrung in their ability to meet the mortgage payments and/or maintain the quality of the structure. Too often the buyers ended up defaulting on their mortgages. From the lenders' perspective, the defaults ironically had distinct financial benefits: the federal guarantee ensured full repayment of the loans, and the defaults enabled the financiers to write new policies on the same property. Likewise, realtors had opportunities for new sales. What resulted was an active campaign to find buyers at high risk of default. Some realtors and bankers resorted to fraud to qualify people for the FHA mortgages, only to have the individuals default within a few months. The continuing defaults, mixed with the already shaky condition of some of the existing housing stock, led to widespread residential abandonment. In 1974 West Englewood had over 200 abandoned homes. The Englewood area lost 6,000 housing units to deterioration and demolition in the 1970s alone.[7]

In addition to the racial turnover, changes in the national and metropolitan economies negatively impacted Englewood. The increased suburbanization of the population and the growing reliance on the automobile reduced the attractiveness of urban shopping centers. Suburban malls, with ample parking and a variety of retailers, appealed far more to an increasingly mobile citizenry. In the 1950s and 1960s, private developers built Evergreen Plaza and the Ford City Mall just across Chicago's southwest border. The appeal of the 63rd and Halsted shopping center—an area with limited parking and increasing residential deterioration—waned considerably.

The restructuring of Chicago's manufacturing base accompanied changes in its retail environment. The closings of the Wisconsin Steel plant in South Chicago (community area 46 on the map of Chicago) and the stockyards in the New City area (community area 61) in the 1970s severely reduced the employment and income base in south-side working class neighborhoods such as Englewood. With fewer jobs available in the surrounding areas, Englewood effectively lost a sizable part of its attractiveness as a residential community. The completion of the Dan Ryan Expressway in the 1960s improved access to the Loop from the southern suburbs and therefore made the outlying areas more attractive. Many members of the skilled, more affluent middle class moved out of Englewood in search of more space elsewhere. Similarly, some displaced workers moved in search of job opportunities elsewhere in the city and/or in the suburbs. Between 1970 and 1990 Englewood's population dropped from 89,713 to 48,434. The neighborhood increasingly became one dominated by low-skilled, low-income individuals. According to Alderwoman Shirley Coleman, Englewood's residents were in one of two extremes: working-age individuals with no money, and seniors with little money.[8]

Private Disinvestment (1965–1990)

Englewood's changing demographic and economic base convinced many of the retailers in the 63rd and Halsted shopping center to reconsider their commitment to the area. After its annual Englewood sales plummeted to $2 million per year, Wieboldt's closed its once-flagship store in 1975. Sears followed a year later, citing declining sales, the costs of maintaining a 41–year-old facility, and the presence of another Sears outlet five miles away.[9] Walgreen's closed two of its Englewood drug stores between 1965 and 1975. Again, Englewood's decline reflected broader trends within the city. The 1970s witnessed an exodus of 77 chain retailers from west- and south-side Chicago neighborhoods. By the early 1980s, Englewood had only one major store selling groceries: a Jewel supermarket near the 63rd and Halsted intersection.[10]

The decline in Englewood's commercial vitality, in concert with the rapidly changing population demographics, the growing residential abandonment, and the waning attractiveness of the area to potential home buyers, caused banks and insurance companies to restrict their activities in the area. Allstate Insurance Company canceled 171 policies in the neighborhood between April and September 1977. Sharply criticized within Englewood and by public interest organizations throughout the city, Allstate responded, "We are in the insurance business, not in the metropolitan zoning or rehabilitation business." The company simply could not afford to underwrite policies for homes with low values and high risks of fire and arson.[11] The Chicago City Bank and Trust Company, the only bank physically located in Englewood, had $15 in deposits from local residents for every $1 of deposits from suburbanites in 1979. Yet that year it lent only $50,000 in Englewood and West Englewood combined, compared to $2.2 million elsewhere in the city and in the suburbs. A study by the *Chicago Tribune* in 1980 found that the predominantly black area bordered by 55th and 107th Streets, Western Avenue, and the Expressway had less than 9 percent of the residential loans made in a largely white area of similar size and population on the other side of Western.[12] A number of finance companies were routinely accused of violating foreclosure regulations by not accepting late payments on mortgages. The companies assumed (not without some justification) that the likelihood of repayment was small.

The redlining of Englewood extended to black-owned banks as well. The south-side Highland Community Bank made no loans in Englewood or Greater Grand Crossing from 1984 through 1986, a fact that attracted the criticism of bank regulators. The bank was prevented from acquiring the south-side-based United Savings of America until it improved its community lending record; Highland addressed the problem by redrawing its lending area to exclude Englewood and Greater Grand Crossing. Like its white-owned counterparts, Highland viewed the neighborhoods as areas of high risk. Although it strived to be more sensitive to the needs of minorities, the bank was handicapped by the predominance of small, struggling businesses in the communities. Furthermore, as a small community bank laboring to make a profit and satisfy its shareholders, it could not afford to make the below-market loans affordable to Englewood borrowers.[13] The redlining effectively pushed potential home buyers such as Aurie Pennick, a young lawyer who had grown up in Englewood, out of the neighborhood. Trying to buy a home in 1977, she was approved for a mortgage on a house in West Pullman and denied for a less expensive home in Englewood.[14]

Disinvestment from Englewood extended to the nonprofit sector as well. The Hospital of Englewood (THE), one of the neighborhood's largest employers, shut its doors in 1988 as a result of a severe cash shortage. THE had long been operating in an inadequate facility, one that lacked such basic modern features as air conditioning in all of the rooms. The Board of Directors had worked for nearly a decade to expand the existing building and/or construct a new one, but had repeatedly encountered difficulty securing the necessary financing for the project. The neighborhood's declining population raised questions among the members of the Illinois Health Facility Planning Board (the relevant public certifying agency) about the medical need for the hospital. Still, THE's ultimate demise resulted primarily from broader economic and political forces. By the mid-1980s, over half of the hospital's patients were supported by either Medicaid or Medicare, two public insurance programs that fixed the amount that they would reimburse a hospital for services. The State of Illinois was perpetually in arrears in its reimbursement payments, as the rising health costs for the poor and aged continually drew political fire in Springfield. By 1988, the State owed $58 million to hospitals. Since Medicaid and Medicare comprised 70 percent of THE's budget, the hospital's cash flow problems became overwhelming.[15]

The changing demographics in Englewood also led to considerable changes within the local Catholic Church. The predominance of European ethnics in Englewood in the 1930s and 1940s had made the neighborhood one of Chicago's most Catholic. At the height of Englewood's position as a white working-class area, the population was roughly 90 percent Catholic. With the influx of blacks in the 1950s through 1970s—individuals who generally were from the American South and were not Catholic—the Catholic population plummeted to about 4 percent of the community as a whole.

The Church's response in Englewood resembled its response in a number of other changing urban areas previously populated by European ethnics.[16] Community members often described their neighborhood in terms of their parish affiliation; being a part of St. Benedict's, for instance, represented a central component of many individuals' lives. Preserving the character of the parish therefore became increasingly important, and the presence of blacks was seen as fundamentally altering that character. Thus many Englewood churches steadfastly refused to welcome incoming blacks into the community. Pastors were often no different from their congregants, having grown up in the same neighborhood and developed similar views of the world.

This insularity fed into a broader view about the role of the Church. Particularly in the pre-Vatican II era, Catholics often viewed their faith as the only legitimate one and saw the Church's primary mission as one of evangelization. Outsiders had to "act Catholic" by participating in mandatory religious education classes and attending Mass in order to take part in Church-run activities. Those who seemed reluctant to accept such an approach—individuals who attended other church services, for example—were often denied enrollment in Catholic schools and/or participation in Church-sponsored recreational activities.[17] In Englewood such a position guaranteed that the Church remained detached from the growing black community.

The Church's position gradually began to change in the 1960s. Vatican II helped liberalize the Church by encouraging a greater awareness of and participation in ecumenical activities. The process of black consciousness-raising as part of the Civil Rights Movement and the Black Power movement increasingly resulted in direct challenges to the Church's policies among urban congregants. Furthermore, a growing number of liberal priests saw civil rights and anti-poverty work as an integral part of their faith experience. Within Englewood, the Church's ministry slowly moved from a focus solely on serving the Eucharistic community (regular churchgoers) to one that also involved service to both the educational community (those attending parochial schools, including non-Catholics) and the "environmental" community (the individuals, most of whom were not Catholic, who lived in the neighborhood). In 1969, a group of priests joined to form the Catholic Commission of Englewood to develop

an appropriate Church response for the growing needs of the neighborhood. Among other things, the Commission recommended the consolidation of certain parishes and the restructuring of certain schools; the
Archdiocese of Chicago largely ignored the plan and unilaterally closed
two schools in 1975.[18]

The school closings reflected deeper financial problems within the
Englewood Church. Even though the area's Catholic population had declined considerably in the previous few decades (dropping from 10,000
to 300 in a few parishes), the Church continued to operate its 12 greater
Englewood parishes and parochial schools into the 1970s. The closing of
a few schools helped alleviate the financial strain, but the reality remained that Englewood's churches were "on welfare." According to Rev.
Dave Baldwin, the head of the Archdiocesan Department of Planning,
Englewood's churches were receiving a $1.4 million annual subsidy
from the Archdiocese alone in the early 1980s. Fiscal considerations
mandated that the Archdiocese consolidate its 12 Englewood-area
parishes into three by the end of the decade. While creating more viable
bases of parishioners and resources, the consolidation generated some
well-publicized opposition within the affected institutions. The closings
also earned Baldwin the moniker of Father Kevorkian.[19]

Attempted Redevelopment (1965–1990)

Englewood's decline persisted despite a number of attempts to arrest it.
The massive racial turnover had first sparked official concern for the
neighborhood's future in the mid-1950s. The City of Chicago designated
Englewood a conservation area in 1956, giving it access to public funds
for infrastructure improvements and other redevelopment activities. In
particular, the City targeted the 63rd and Halsted area as well as the region surrounding the intersection of 69th and Wentworth. The latter area
ultimately became the site of Kennedy-King College, part of the city's
community college system.

The shopping mall at 63rd and Halsted has always been the focal
point of efforts to redevelop Englewood. The mall's declining sales in the
1960s—caused primarily by the development of the suburban malls described earlier—prompted city officials to submit a redevelopment plan
to the federal Office of Economic Opportunity. OEO provided the City
with $17 million to redevelop the mall, a grant representing the largest
single urban renewal program ever undertaken for business develop-

ment. The redevelopment involved closing 63rd and Halsted to automobile traffic, creating a pedestrian mall amidst the stores, and building large parking lots around the outside of the shopping center. Not only would consumers be able to find parking, but it was assumed that the pedestrian-friendly approach would create a general aura of safety around the mall. Yet the creation of the parking lots necessitated the demolition of 250 generally stable homes and the displacement of a number of middle-class residents, issues that generated widespread opposition and caused Martin Luther King, Jr. to lead a protest march. While the project was successfully completed, the redevelopment backfired. The principal problem was that the parking lots surrounded the back of the mall, away from store signs and display windows. Since people could not easily see what stores were in the mall, shopping continued to decline.

The closing of the Sears and Wieboldt's stores, coupled with the continuing struggles of many of the other mall tenants, convinced developers of the failure of the OEO-sponsored project. In the mid-1970s the Chicago South Development Corporation embarked on a $3 million project to redevelop the area, only to abandon the effort in mid-project and leave the contractor with $800,000 in unpaid bills. Local developers continued to work with city officials to attract large anchor retailers to the site. Both K-Mart and Zayre expressed serious interest in 1987, contingent on the re-opening of 63rd and Halsted Streets to automobile traffic. Their interest, coupled with Mayor Harold Washington's commitment to the project, sparked another redevelopment effort in the late 1980s. Working closely with the City, the nonprofit Greater Englewood Local Development Corporation (GELDCO) succeeded in designating the area both a Special Service Area (SSA) and a Tax Increment Financing (TIF) district, qualifying the mall for a variety of City funds. The redevelopment plan called for a series of improvements, including a renovated el stop, more visible store signage, the creation of safe pedestrian crossing between the mall and the surrounding residences, and new sewers in the area.

A devastating chain of events eliminated the project's initial promise and doomed it to failure. Washington died, and the resulting mayoral battle engendered considerable turnover and delay within the City's Department of Planning and Development, the lead public agency for the project. The mall's location at the intersection of multiple aldermanic wards involved a number of additional politicians, many of whom wanted particular benefits from the project. The alderwoman responsible for the greatest portion of the project, Shirley Coleman, was dealing with serious personal problems which limited her ability to help with the re-development. The private developer involved in the project had to pull out because he encountered severe financial difficulties related to the national savings and loan scandal. At the same time, the national retail market "went into the toilet," in the words of Ted Wysocki, the Executive Director of the Chicago Association of Neighborhood Development Organizations; Zayre was bought out by Ames, which subsequently folded. Jewel was interested in locating a grocery store in the mall, but did not want to compete with Cub Foods or Aldi, two other grocers interested in the area. When Aldi opened a store down the street, Jewel pulled out of the project. Cub remained interested until the Chicago Bulls won their first NBA title, at which point some Englewood residents celebrated by rioting and looting some of the mall stores. (Then GELDCO Executive Director Jim Soens quipped that Cub's decision stemmed from their being based in Whitewater, Wisconsin, and simply not understanding Chicago sports traditions.) The Chicago Transit Authority's decision to close the green el line (including the Halsted station) for repairs in 1993 drove the final nail into the project's coffin by sharply reducing access to the area via public transportation.[20]

Similar false starts characterized efforts to redevelop the neighborhood's residential areas. A 1980 plan called for the rehabilitation of all structurally sound buildings, the demolition of all other residential buildings, and the construction of new townhouses, apartment buildings, small shops, and a day care center in a 223–acre site stretching east and south of 63rd and Halsted. A joint venture among the nonprofit Southtown Planning Association, the Chicago City Bank, and private developer Joel Hillman, the project was going to use private, city, and federal money to create 600 construction jobs and 300 full-time positions associated with the development. By 1982 the project was dead. The Reagan Administration's cutbacks in federal urban funds eroded much of the project's financial base. Community residents protested against what they saw as grand displacement schemes hatched by outsiders. Perhaps most importantly, the project never obtained the strong support of City officials. Without solid political backing, the project slowly died.[21]

Other residential development projects had somewhat more success. In the late 1970s and early 1980s a computerized arson prevention system succeeded in reducing the number of fires set in Englewood. In 1981, Mayor Byrne specified Englewood as a demonstration site for a new program in which the City would sell vacant lots for $1 to owners of adjacent property so that they could use the areas as gardens and/or play areas for their children. Local nonprofit organizations succeeded in building hundreds of new housing units. Two groups joined with the City's Department of Housing to construct 38 townhouses at 61st and Halsted Streets, the first time the City had ever participated in a non-public housing project. Bethel Lutheran Church oversaw the construction of 123 apartments for seniors, and Antioch Baptist Church built a few hundred affordable apartment units around 63rd Street in East Englewood; the latter's Antioch Haven Apartments was lauded as a model development by individuals throughout the city. Although they benefited small portions of the community, these developments had little impact on Englewood as a whole. By 1989 almost 19 percent of the neighborhood's housing stock was in poor condition, and residential abandonment was again on the rise.[22]

A "Neighborhood Under Siege" (1987–present)

Similar to William Julius Wilson's findings in other impoverished urban neighborhoods, the gradual exodus of businesses and middle-class individuals accelerated the increase of drug and gang activity in Englewood.[23] Gangs had been active in the neighborhood as early as the 1960s, when the Englewood-based Gangster Disciples battled with the Woodlawn-based Blackstone Rangers. For the most part, though, such conflicts were limited to gang members. War cries preceded gang battles, alerting non-participants to clear the streets and remain out of trouble. Aurie Pennick claims that the gangs were genuinely concerned about protecting innocent bystanders. They did not coerce people who did not want to join the gangs. Englewood experienced violence, but it was relatively controlled. Much of the violence was self-policed, with law enforcement officials generally looking the other way.[24]

Conditions began to worsen considerably in the mid-1980s with the emergence of crack cocaine and other drugs in the Chicago market. Once people realized the potential money to be made in the drug trade, the nature of the gang activity changed radically. What had initially been battles between bands of youths over physical territory became full-fledged competition over market share among organized crime factions. With fewer and fewer legal job opportunities available to local residents as more and more businesses closed and/or moved away, drug dealing became an increasingly attractive option. The Gangster Disciples became the primary job training and placement center in the neighborhood.

Still, the level of violence in Englewood remained relatively constant until about 1987, when one major dealer was murdered and another kingpin died. After an extended, extremely violent power struggle, Larry (The Assassin) Hoover assumed leadership of the area's drug trade.[25] Englewood witnessed 418 shootings in the first four months of 1990.[26] The area from 67th Street to 69th Street along Halsted became known as Little Beirut. In 1991, the *Tribune* ran a two-page article depicting Englewood as a "neighborhood under siege." Homicides in the area had nearly tripled since 1985, and the first 11 months of the year had seen 1,456 shootings, 729 stabbings, and 1,421 serious beatings. The homicide rate for young males in Englewood was 162 per 100,000, fully 18 times the national average. Some gangs mandated that new recruits commit a random killing in order to become full-fledged members of the group.[27]

While Englewood represented the extreme case, drug-related homicides skyrocketed throughout the city. The number of gang-related killings in Chicago had been less than 80 during most of the 1980s, then rose to 132 in 1991, 166 in 1993, and 240 in 1994. Gang homicides were only 7 percent of all murders in 1987, but 26 percent in 1994. Much of the increase stemmed from the growing use of semi-automatic weapons, which enabled individuals to use more bullets and cause more damage.[28]

Not surprisingly, the increased violence accelerated the exodus from the already-devastated community. The neighborhood's population plummeted, as anyone with the means to get out of Englewood did so. Banks drastically reduced the number of loans they made in the area, from 657 in 1983–1984 to only 367 in 1991–1992.[29] Landlords, seeing little chance of an increase in local property values,[30] reduced the amount of money they spent on building repairs. As tax reforms in the late 1980s phased out some of the loopholes encouraging investment in low-income housing, equity skimming became increasingly commonplace. In a number of cases landlords pocketed money they received from the tenants' FHA mortgages instead of using it to maintain the facility and/or pay off their own mortgages on the properties.[31]

The prevalence of crime and the continuing population decline further worsened Englewood's business climate. Retailers in the area had to pay higher business loss insurance premiums than companies located elsewhere in the city. They typically had higher proportions of uninsured inventory and higher security costs than their counterparts in other areas. In many cases, the retailers simply passed along the higher costs to their customers. Englewood mark-ups on goods such as wholesale jewelry could be as much as 25 percent higher than mark-ups on similar goods sold outside the community. Local residents suffered from higher prices and a lower quality and quantity of goods.[32]

Englewood lost over half of its jobs between 1975 and 1990. The neighborhood's high schools have been hotbeds of gang activity and their students have routinely had some of the lowest average standardized test scores in the city. Both schools were recently singled out for radical restructuring by the Chicago Board of Education. Crime remains high, and quality goods are scarce. Above all, a general feeling of hopelessness pervades much of the community. A local minister lamented to a *Tribune* reporter that people would like to do something about the neighborhood, but the current "generation believes that nobody—God, Mom, politicians, teachers, preachers, neighbors—really cares."[33] Many teenagers believe that they will never obtain a well-paying job and see basketball as "the only ticket out of" the community.[34]

NORTH LAWNDALE

Like Englewood, North Lawndale was a relatively stable, middle-class neighborhood in the 1940s and 1950s. North Lawndale historically was the most Jewish neighborhood in Chicago. In 1930, Russian Jews comprised 46 percent of the community's 112,000 residents. The community was 64 percent Jewish immediately after World War II and 42 percent Jewish as late as 1950.[35] North Lawndale also had one of the highest concentrations of industry on Chicago's west side, with companies such as Campbell Soup, Continental Can, Coca-Cola, and Copenhagen all operating plants in the area. These factories provided thousands of jobs for the city's immigrants, many of whom had relatively low skill levels. Residents remembered post-war North Lawndale as a thriving area, one with good transportation, parks, and schools, and few, if any, vacant lots. The bustling retail and cultural activity of the area surrounding Roosevelt and Homan Avenues reminded longtime resident Danny Davis of Harlem.[36]

At the same time, North Lawndale was Chicago's most densely populated neighborhood, with over twice as many people per square mile as the city as a whole. Overcrowding strained the neighborhood's housing stock and plumbing infrastructure. With the post-war economic boom and the development of the west side expressway (subsequently I-290, or the Eisenhower), more and more of North Lawndale's residents left the crowded neighborhood for the suburbs, where they could afford their own home in a more open setting.

Racial and Demographic Transition (1950–1960)

The decision by North Lawndale's Jews to move out of the community precipitated a rapid racial turnover that surpassed even Englewood's in its speed and comprehensiveness. Between 1950 and 1960 North Lawndale's white population dropped from 87,000 to 11,000, while its black population rose from 13,000 to 113,000. In 1960 the community hit an all-time population high, imposing an even greater demand for housing. Landlords converted single-family apartments into smaller kitchenettes in order to squeeze more tenants into the same space. Fully 35 percent of North Lawndale's occupied housing units had more than one person per room. The density overwhelmed the local public schools. Principals had to resort to double shifting students (having one set of classes in the morning/early afternoon and one from mid-afternoon to the evening) and using mobile classrooms to accommodate all of the youths. In September of 1961 roughly one-third of the students were on double shift, and the average classroom held 56 students.[37]

As in Englewood, blacks moving into North Lawndale struggled to obtain financing for their new homes. Banks were loathe to lend in such a clearly transitional area. Contract buying therefore became the primary means of purchasing homes. Sellers served as their own lenders to the incoming blacks, charging as much as a $20,000 premium on the price of the house as well as high interest rates on the mortgage. Like the Englewood contracts, the North Lawndale agreements contained onerous terms for the purchaser. Buyers received neither the deed nor any equity in their properties until they made the final payment. All improvements a buyer made to a house prior to that final payment were the property of the seller, and a buyer was prohibited from taking out a mechanic's lien (a general requirement of contractors) for any home improvement work. Buyers were routinely evicted from the homes exactly 30 days after missing a single payment, regardless of their stake in the property.[38]

The black immigrants, many of whom had recently moved to Chicago from the fields of rural Mississippi, tended to be poorer than the laborers and artisans that they were replacing. While many of these immigrants found jobs in the local factories, others were not so lucky. North Lawndale had the highest unemployment rate in the city. The lower purchasing power of the new residents depressed the neighborhood's commercial market. Between 1954 and 1958 the number of stores in the area declined from 774 to 685, primarily due to the closing of a number of food stores. The community's struggling economy caused local merchants to delay making repairs to their buildings, hastening the deterioration of the commercial area. Limited incomes, coupled with the realities of contract buying, dissuaded residents from investing the money necessary to maintain their homes. By 1960 city officials classified nearly one-quarter of all of the neighborhood's units as dilapidated or deteriorating. Furthermore, changing patterns of manufacturing were rendering many of North Lawndale's industrial plants increasingly obsolete. The urban renewal report of 1964 found that over 53 percent of the community's industrial structures were generally undesirable because of their ceiling heights, loading areas, and so forth.[39]

External and Internal Response (1960s)

Mirroring Englewood's experience, North Lawndale's decline sparked concern among a number of individuals both within and outside the neighborhood. In 1958 the City declared North Lawndale a Conservation Area, formal recognition that over half of the neighborhood's residential area was in danger of becoming blighted and slum-like. The 1964 Urban Renewal Report, the 1967 Mid West Development Area planning report, and the City's 1968 conservation plan all emphasized a wide range of needs to be addressed. The community lacked adequate recreational space for its citizens, an increasing percentage of whom were of school age. The schools needed to be upgraded and expanded to serve the existing population. North Lawndale's outdated transportation infrastructure—the community had relatively narrow streets and few major thoroughfares—hindered local businesses in their attempts to move goods into and out of the community. The area's housing badly needed rehabilitating, and the neighborhood lacked a regional- or community-level shopping center. The planners warned that unless these issues were addressed, economic and social conditions in the area would continue to decline.[40]

The federal War on Poverty (1964–68) provided an infusion of public resources for neighborhoods such as North Lawndale. For example, the federal Model Cities program provided a mixture of special education, community relations, and public health monies to selected cities. City officials, in conjunction with local leaders, then chose specific neighborhoods for targeted attention. North Lawndale was one of the four designated Chicago neighborhoods, and the resulting programs had distinct benefits for many community residents. Individuals who were employed by the federally-sponsored agencies often made enough

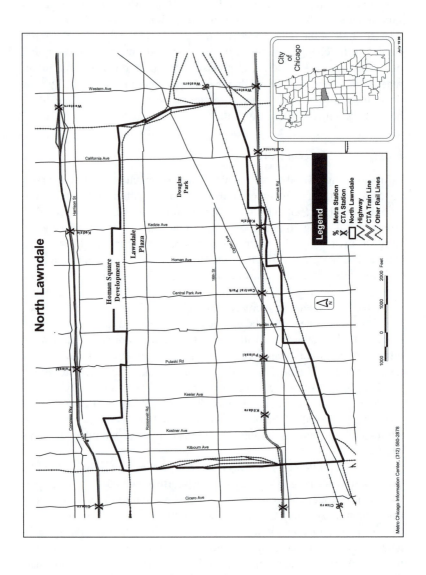

North Lawndale

money to move out of the community into a more desirable area.[41] Yet Lawndale as a whole realized little substantive change.

North Lawndale residents viewed the War on Poverty programs primarily as efforts on the part of Mayor Richard J. Daley and others to pacify a potentially unruly area. As described in Chapter 3, Daley's appointment of his own deputies to run the program ensured that local residents would never attain the "maximum feasible participation" in the decision-making process that the anti-poverty legislation encouraged. While arguably improving the program's administration and helping to preserve social order in the neighborhood, the approach generated considerable local resentment. Over thirty years after the fact, Danny Davis still decries the anti-poverty initiative as a "patronage program," one in which outsiders controlled resource distribution and essentially "neo-colonialized" North Lawndale.[42] Reverend Mike Ivers, the pastor at St. Agatha's Church, contends that Daley and Congressman Dan Rostenkowski diverted money away from the neighborhood in order to promote development of the medical complex on the Near West Side.[43]

Resentment toward outside officials' perceived lack of concern for North Lawndale's plight helped galvanize community leaders to take action. Along with the other predominantly minority neighborhoods on the city's west side, North Lawndale had routinely turned out large majorities for Chicago's Democratic Machine without seeming to receive any substantial benefits in return. A number of the area's clergymen believed that a strong community organization would help improve conditions by giving the neighborhoods a political voice independent of the Machine. In the process, it would help instill meaning in resident's lives by giving them a greater sense of control over their destinies. Thus in 1965 the religious leaders established the West Side Federation.

Whereas the Catholic Church had taken a largely reactionary position in Englewood, it was a major proponent of change in North Lawndale. Part of the difference lay in the larger number of religious denominations in the multi-ethnic Lawndale community; the Church was not as dominant an institution in Lawndale as it was in Englewood and consequently never suffered from as great a loss of power. Perhaps more importantly, the Lawndale Church contained some of the city's most socially active, liberal priests. Reverend Jack Egan at Presentation and Reverend Dan Mallette at St. Agatha's were two of the individuals primarily responsible for the establishment and guidance of the West Side Federation. Both had been involved in the city's civil rights campaign for a number of years and saw the Church's mission as one of crusading for social justice. Mallette opined that if the Church was "perhaps the number one force in the lives of so many citizens, how did it happen that so little progress has been made in making real the brotherhood of all men, in housing and employment and education and legal justice?" To him the Church had a distinct choice: either its parishes became "morgues" as the cities' populations became more heavily minority-dominated, or it "came alive because of interested Christians." Opting for the latter approach, he emphasized the need for "a crash program in involvement. . . . It is a good and Christian thing to do, to apply band-aids to gaping wounds, but one is criminally negligent if he does not at the same time cry out with all his might for an ambulance and the things necessary to heal the wound efficiently."[44]

Mallette's and Egan's public stance, one that they defended in nationally published articles, generated considerable controversy within the local and national Catholic community. Their actions nevertheless drew attention to the conditions in North Lawndale. The work of the West Side Federation convinced Martin Luther King, Jr. to rent an apartment in the neighborhood during his 1966 Chicago campaign. It also attracted roughly 60 local seminarians, who responded to Egan's call to bring the Church to the inner city.

The Federation's organizing efforts had highlighted the gross inequities of the contract buying process and had convinced local leaders of the need to confront the problem. Under Egan's guidance, the seminarians canvassed the neighborhood each Saturday, obtaining copies of the contracts from local home buyers and helping them understand the nature of their exploitation. The process led to the establishment of the Contract Buyers League, a group of local residents who staged rent strikes and filed class action lawsuits against the sellers of the properties. By 1970 the League had succeeded in getting such contracts outlawed, thereby saving an estimated $6 to $7 million for area home buyers.[45] Perhaps more importantly, the League provided a means for local residents to unite against a common enemy for a common goal. Community members realized that many of the poor conditions in the neighborhood were not a result of freaks of nature, but rather the conscious decisions of specific individuals. Specific realtors had manipulated the real estate market to take advantage of changing local dynamics. Yet these actions could be confronted and conceivably overcome given adequate resources and mobilization.

The hope generated by the Contract Buyers League could not overcome the growing despair in the neighborhood, however. Following King's assassination on April 4, 1968, North Lawndale exploded. Angry youths fanned out from Garfield Park, looting and burning massive tracts of land throughout the west side. Rioters triggered 600 alarms in the first 24 hours alone. Nine people were killed, 500 were injured, and 225 major fires were set. Roosevelt Avenue and 16th Street, North Lawndale's primary commercial areas, were almost completely devastated. Some of the businesses that had initially been spared were subsequently torched, often at the request of owners who sought to collect on their insurance and leave the neighborhood.[46]

Disinvestment and Attempted Redevelopment (1968–1980)

The effects of the riots devastated North Lawndale. The riots hastened the middle-class exodus that overcrowding and poverty had begun. Between 1960 and 1970 North Lawndale's population declined by 30,000 residents, a large proportion of whom left after 1968. Insurance companies refused to write policies in the neighborhood. Faced with skyrocketing security costs, high city taxes, and an aging local physical infrastructure, numerous businesses abandoned the neighborhood for safer, more spacious outlying suburbs. Fully seventy-five percent of North Lawndale's commercial establishments in 1960 had left by 1970. An additional 45 companies left North Lawndale for the suburbs in 1971–1972.[47] Changes in the national economy also affected the neighborhood. Reduced demand for manufacturing, coupled with technological improvements that reduced the cost of production, caused International Harvester to close its nearby South Lawndale plant in 1969 and eliminate 3,400 jobs.[48]

The biggest blow came in 1973, when Sears, Roebuck, & Co. decided to move the 10,000 jobs at its world headquarters in North Lawndale to the newly constructed Sears Tower downtown. The move stunned the neighborhood, especially since Sears had long expressed interest in obtaining and developing large tracts of land in the area. A Sears-influenced 1966 plan called for the development of a "New Town in Town" with federal money: buildings on 190 blocks would be demolished to make room for 12,500 units of middle- and upper-income housing and a 45–acre golf course.[49] Following the riots—during which Sears's 200–man private police force had kept the company largely unscathed—the company sought to obtain the land bordered by the expressway, Roosevelt, Kedzie, and Independence.[50] The proposal would have enabled the company to build a corporate empire within the neighborhood, but also would have involved the demolition of hundreds of sturdy homes and the accompanying displacement of relatively affluent residents. Fearing further unrest in the community, the Daley Administration rejected the proposal and inadvertently paved the way for the company's exodus. With only the catalog distribution center remaining in use at the Homan Square site, many of the surrounding retailers moved or went out of business.

The cataclysm of the riots inspired action on the part of both city officials and local leaders. In 1968 the Mayor established the Lawndale Industrial Council to retain local businesses. Yet the more long-lasting response came from the community. Again with the substantial involvement of the Presentation Church, the West Side Federation generated a community-based plan for the development of the neighborhood. The plan emphasized the need for a multi-service shopping center, the concentration of different types of affordable housing, and improvements in North Lawndale's cultural and educational amenities. Unlike previous plans for the neighborhood, the Federation's proposal also established two organizations to carry out the process: the Lawndale Peoples Planning and Action Conference (LPPAC), a nonprofit group to promote community-wide consensus, and the North Lawndale Economic Development Corporation (NLEDC) to coordinate the rebuilding of the neighborhood.

NLEDC, later renamed Pyramidwest Development Corporation, was established as a for-profit entity, with community members and a federally-supported trust among its shareholders. As a profit-seeking organization, it differed from the typical nonprofit urban development group. Community activist Lew Kreinberg explained that such incorporation better reflected the desires of the neighborhood. "Poor people don't want not-for-profit. It's close to *indecent* to be not-for-profit. It's *un-American*."[51] Pyramidwest President Cecil Butler concurred. "We don't live in a not-for-profit society. A community-owned entity could be a force for change and education."[52] The for-profit status also forced a certain degree of accountability on the organization.

Butler and the other LPPAC members believed that industry would relocate in the neighborhood only after the community had stabilized, an outcome which depended on the improvement of North Lawndale's housing stock. By 1979 Pyramidwest had constructed new townhouses, rehabilitated 1,400 rental units, had begun construction on two new housing developments (all with financial assistance from the federal Department of Housing and Urban Development), and had built a nursing home in South Lawndale. Pyramidwest Realty and Management Company (a for-profit subsidiary) oversaw 870 rental units along Douglas Boulevard. In 1980 Pyramidwest began construction on the $7 million, 150–unit Lawndale Terrace project, a mixture of rental units and for-sale townhouses at the southeast corner of Roosevelt and Kedzie. Two years later it started work on the nearby Lawndale Towers, continuing its quest to develop 2,000 housing units in the community. Pyramidwest's efforts earned it considerable local and national attention; it was one of the original 27 recipients of low-interest loans from the newly formed, New York-based Local Initiatives Support Corporation (LISC).

Housing represented only part of Pyramidwest's broader vision for the development of the neighborhood. Revitalizing North Lawndale required access to capital in both the short and long terms. The neighborhood had long suffered from limited commercial and residential lending, a problem that only promised to get worse with the move downtown of the Sears Bank and Trust Company in 1974. In 1977, Pyramidwest opened the Community Bank of Lawndale (CBL), a financial institution "chartered for the purpose of redeveloping this community and for providing a nucleus for the kind of financial services needed in this area."[53] The institution represented a radical new venture and involved complicated legal machinations. The bank was owned in part by local residents (who bought shares) and in part by public sector investors. Pyramidwest served as the bank's holding company under a law permitting agencies doing community revitalization activities to oversee banking entities.[54]

The Bank's first few years were profitable. It was the only bank in the area, and its market encompassed North Lawndale, West Garfield Park, and part of Pilsen. Yet the initial momentum did not last. In 1985 it was still one of the smallest banks in the city, with only $20 million in assets. The tenuous financial base limited what it could do. According to David Doig, then with the Lawndale Christian Development Corporation, the bank "just didn't have deep pockets to support it. It was really woeful in its ability to address the needs of the community."[55] By 1989 the bank's share of the neighborhood's conventional and home lending markets was quite low in comparison to Citicorp, Talman, and Second Federal Bank, financial institutions with neither branches nor expressed interest in the Lawndale market.[56]Although the Bank consistently worked to lend within the neighborhood, it struggled to find many good loan opportunities. Its low level of assets caused federal regulators to examine its transactions much more strictly; CBL's financial condition prevented it from making higher-risk loans that larger banks would have been allowed to make. For example, CBL could not afford to lend to churches unless they had bonded contracts for their projects. The neighborhood's declining economy, coupled with some poor decisions on the part of the bank, caused CBL to write off a number of its loans in the late 1980s. With the Bank's future in jeopardy, the Federal Deposit Insurance Corporation imposed a cease and desist order in 1991 and demanded that CBL be restructured.

Cecil Butler, the head of Pyramidwest, contended that CBL was a victim of outside circumstances. Responding to the charge that the Bank did not lend enough in the community, he contended that the Bank's loan portfolio was routinely 45 to 50 percent of its assets, a much higher proportion than the black-owned Independence and Seaway Banks on the city's south side. He claimed that CBL was limited by neighborhood and regulatory conditions from being more active and more successful.[57] Community residents read a different story. While acknowledging the bank's lack of capital, they lambasted the Bank's management practices. Richard Townsell, now the Executive Director at the Lawndale Christian Development Corporation, saw no apparent desire on the part of the Bank to obtain additional capital. CBL officials did not actively solicit ideas on growing the Bank, did not market effectively, and tolerated "horrendous" customer service. Townsell and others "hated going in and dealing with the tellers—it was a total nightmare. . . . People weren't trained, sophisticated, [or] courteous. They gave you such cold treatment."[58] The Bank itself was physically unwelcoming. Samuel Flowers described it as "the most unattractive bank you ever saw. It was like a boxcar in somebody's yard."[59] Some local residents did not trust Butler's handling of the Bank and questioned the amount of capital it provided for Pyramidwest projects. Yet despite their misgivings, almost all of the residents maintained accounts with CBL; the Bank constituted a neighborhood institution, and there were no other viable options.

Pyramidwest's other economic development activities were even less successful. The organization sought to develop the former International Harvester site in South Lawndale for use as an industrial park. None of the desired corporate tenants ever committed to the project, however. The alternatives that did arise—an industrial laundry company, warehouses, and a county jail—failed to satisfy Butler and his LPPAC compatriots. The possibilities either offered only low-wage, dead-end jobs, too few jobs, or had little to do with industry. Butler adamantly refused to build on speculation or write down land prices to lure companies to the site, stands that earned him a reputation as intransigent, stubborn, inflexible, and arrogant.[60] Nothing ever materialized on the site, the State's Attorney moved to seize the land for unpaid back taxes, and the neighborhood's employment opportunities remained unchanged.

Perhaps the greatest symbol of North Lawndale's plight lay in the vacant area along Roosevelt Avenue between Kedzie and Homan. Like Englewood's 63rd and Halsted shopping center, the Roosevelt strip had once been a vibrant retail area. The riots had wiped it out, and its redevelopment became a central component of every strategy to revitalize North Lawndale. LPPAC and Pyramidwest collectively received $18 million in loans and grants from the federal Office of Economic Opportunity and the Community Services Administration between 1969 and 1977 to develop Lawndale Plaza on the site. The monies included a $1.867 million Economic Development Administration grant in 1972 to build a retail center for 50 businesses employing 800 people and generating $19 million in annual sales. The project never went forward, causing the EDA to take back $1.167 million of the grant in 1985. The private Matanky Realty Group sought to obtain the land from Pyramidwest in 1987, taking advantage of the group's $800,000 property tax delinquency. Again nothing happened. Some financial maneuverings on Butler's part, coupled with aldermanic opposition to Matanky's proposal, kept the vacant land in Pyramidwest's control. In the early 1990s ex-NBA player Mickey Johnson put together a group to develop a shopping center. Walgreen's, Trak Auto, and a McCrory Store expressed interest in being retail anchors for the project, and the City approved a special tax district to speed development. Yet Johnson's group had difficulty purchasing a gutted former health center which sat on a corner of the site. McCrory's joined Zayre and Ames as another victim of the faltering national retail economy. And like Englewood, North Lawndale was the site of rioting after the Chicago Bulls won their first NBA title. The investors pulled out, and the project collapsed.[61]

What prevented Lawndale Plaza from being developed, especially in light of the general interest in making the project happen? Part of the explanation lay in the persona of Cecil Butler. The first black graduate of Northwestern Law School, Butler had obtained a job with the Community Legal Council and had become involved with the West Side Federation. His expertise and commitment to the neighborhood made him an attractive choice to head the implementation of the Federation's 1968 redevelopment plan. Universally seen as a shrewd businessman, he had an uncanny knack for being able to assemble, package, and finance a wide range of projects with public money. He was instrumental in enabling

North Lawndale to obtain a large infusion of funds. At the same time, Butler was widely perceived as aloof, power-hungry, and bullying. He remained inflexible in many of his demands of potential investors, which often hurt the community. Most of the interested parties grew tired of his uncompromising stance and simply left the bargaining table.[62]

A more important reason for the lack of development concerned the realities of the North Lawndale market. Simply put, private sector interest in the site was weak at best. The area's growing poverty, limited buying power, and public safety concerns dissuaded most investors. Developing the Plaza site involved somewhat complicated land assembly and infrastructure issues: a few key parcels were owned by parties reluctant to sell (such as the health center), and sewer and gas lines cut through the heart of the property. Making any project work therefore required a considerable expenditure of human and financial capital, costs which consistently outweighed the site's perceived potential benefits.

"The American Millstone" (1975–1990)

Despite its problems, Pyramidwest was the most successful actor working to combat North Lawndale's decline. In the late 1970s, a group of companies with interests in North Lawndale (businesses such as Sears, Ryerson Steel, and Commonwealth Edison, the area's major utility company) jointly sponsored a study to try to get the neighborhood designated as an official disaster area. Known as Project 80, the effort raised $150,000 and successfully campaigned for the state of Illinois's first urban enterprise zone, an area encompassing both the North and South Lawndale community areas. The collaborative was unable to raise monies to implement its redevelopment proposal, however, and the initiative gradually faded from view.

One of Project 80's recommendations was to encourage the development of small minority-owned businesses in the area. Promoting small business incubators seemed to be an appealing strategy. The incubators provided budding entrepreneurs with office space, secretarial services, technical assistance on issues such as marketing, accounting, and business plan development, and access to low-interest start-up loans. All of these services were factored into the rent. With the encouragement and financial support of the Project 80 corporate participants, local foundations, and some of Chicago's banks, the nonprofit Chicago Economic Development Corporation (CEDCO) began development of a $1.7 million Business Enterprise Center in the decaying industrial area on North

Lawndale's western border. Both the City and the State provided grants for the project, and the corporate supporters implicitly agreed to do business with the start-up ventures. Yet the project imploded in spectacular fashion. CEDCO, the city's oldest organization designed to help minority businesses, squandered over $1 million dollars allocated to the endeavor. The organization's president acknowledged a crippling drug addiction, the board provided little (if any) financial oversight, and the general contractor hired for the project (at the request of the local alderman) was indicted for tax fraud midway through the process.[63] The *Tribune* outlined the sordid story in late 1987 in an article that cast considerable doubt on not only the future of North Lawndale redevelopment efforts but also the trustworthiness of the nonprofit sector.[64]

North Lawndale continued its rapid decline. Roughly 80 percent of the neighborhood's manufacturing jobs left between the early 1970s and the mid-1980s, a result of the community's decline, the pull of suburbanization, and the changing regional and national economy. Copenhagen, Sunbeam, Zenith, Valspar Paint, Dell Farm, Alden's, and a major Post Office center all closed their doors. Western Electric shut its Hawthorne plant in Cicero (the community due west of North Lawndale) in 1984, a move that eliminated 43,000 jobs.

Not surprisingly, the decline carried over into other commercial ventures. The first-ever Sears store, located amid the company's headquarters at the corner of Homan and Arthington, went out of business in 1984. The store had been losing money for seven years, with the size of the losses continually accelerating, and Sears decided that the neighborhood's future retail prospects offered little real hope for change. By 1985, the area had only three major commercial establishments: Ryerson Steel on the east end of the community; Mt. Sinai Hospital, located adjacent to Ryerson; and the Sears Catalog distribution center, whose 3,000 employees included only about 750 local residents.

In 1987 the number of major establishments dropped to two, as Sears decided to close its distribution center. The tightening of the national retail industry had increased the competitive pressures on the company. Sears had been relying on an outdated distribution system, one whose costs were three to four times higher than those of its chief competitors. Introducing a new ordering system would save the company up to $150 million per year once it was fully installed. While some of Sears's distribution centers could be re-fitted to take advantage of the new system, the costs of changing others (such as the one in North Lawndale) were prohibitively expensive. The move made sense for the company's balance sheets, but it generated enormous resentment within North Lawndale. The closing of the center resulted in 1,800 workers being laid off. (The remainder were transferred elsewhere within the company.) It left three million square feet of unused commercial space in the neighborhood. Yet the real animosity toward the company resulted from Sears's failure (or unwillingness) to notify the city in advance of the closing. The Washington administration never had an opportunity to see if it could work out an alternative arrangement to save the jobs. The editorial board of *Crains Chicago Business* lambasted Sears Chairman Edward Brennan for an "appalling lack of awareness of the political ramifications of his decision." The handling of the situation highlighted the "deplorable state of social corporate consciousness in Chicago. . . . There's more to being a good corporate citizen than lending executives [for local functions] and giving money," both of which Sears had historically been quite good at doing.[65]

The corporate exodus had devastating ramifications for the community's residents. Between 1975 and 1990 the 60623 zip code area (encompassing North Lawndale and part of South Lawndale) lost nearly 46 percent of its manufacturing jobs.[66] The total number of jobs on the west side fell from 60,000 in 1972 to less than 36,000 in 1990. The jobs that remained tended to be primarily low-paying, entry-level opportunities: janitors and cleaners, nurses' aids, orderlies, attendants, assemblers, truck drivers, secretaries, laborers, cooks, and machine operators.[67] What had been an area of stable, well-paying industrial jobs became an urban wasteland. From 1975 to 1985 the community experienced a 45 percent increase in the number of its residents receiving public assistance. By 1985, over half of North Lawndale's residents over age 16 were out of the labor pool. Unemployment in the area was more than two and one-half times the city average.[68]

The loss of jobs both triggered and exacerbated other social pathologies within the neighborhood. Without jobs, people struggled to keep and maintain their homes. The neighborhood lost nearly half of its housing units to deterioration and demolition between 1960 and 1985; by the late 1970s, only 8 percent of North Lawndale's units were in good condition.[69] Longtime local resident Sam Flowers bemoaned the loss of role models in the community. Roughly three-fifths of the population lacked a high school diploma, and the vast majority of them were unemployed. Their actions therefore did not instill in children the importance of diligence, study, and hard work. Instead, they inadvertently promoted "chaos," with "kids running wild."[70]

Like Englewood, North Lawndale suffered from virtually every urban ill. For example, the neighborhood had no major grocers. The few stores that did exist typically charged higher prices than stores elsewhere in the city (as a result both of their higher costs and monopolistic situation) and had a disproportionate number of health violations. The fact that the store owners were primarily Arabs fostered ongoing ethnic tensions, with periodic boycotts and vandalism further souring relations.

Problems begat more problems. Drugs infiltrated the community in the early 1980s, so that by 1985 the neighborhood was home to 100 drug houses and a $1.5 million annual cocaine and heroin industry. The drug trade sparked gang battles. By 1991 shootings were a "regular weekend event," and the area's rate of murder and assault were among the highest in Chicago (along with Englewood). Not surprisingly, the social conditions drove even more people out of the neighborhood. Fewer than 48,000 people remained in North Lawndale in 1990. Residential loans in the neighborhood fell by 29.9 percent between 1983–1984 and 1991–1992, the same time in which loans went up 57.3 percent across the city. The Sears YMCA, one of the neighborhood's principal social institutions, closed in 1989. The Y had a budget surplus and served 6,000 people (despite a membership of less than 300), yet was seen by officials in the Y's metropolitan headquarters as outdated and too expensive to maintain.[71]

The neighborhood's political situation offered no real hope for change. If anything, North Lawndale's politics guaranteed that the aldermen would not be at the forefront of efforts to promote radical change. In 1960 Ben Lewis was elected the city's first black alderman in an election that generated considerable enthusiasm and optimism among members of the increasingly black ward. Yet the next day Lewis was found dead, with his hands shackled behind his back. The murderers were never found, Daley appointed a new alderman, and politics in the ward returned to normal.

Politics remained nondescript until the late 1970s, when Bill Henry became the 24th Ward Alderman. The former chauffeur of one of his predecessors, Henry was generally seen as a quintessential Machine politician. A black alderman representing a virtually all-black ward, Henry nonetheless campaigned actively for incumbent Jane Byrne against popular Harold Washington in the city's 1983 mayoral primary. (Henry did support Washington in the general election against Republican Bernie Epton.) Following Washington's death in 1987, Henry actively supported Eugene Sawyer, the choice of the old-line Machine politicians, over Tim Evans, the choice of many of Chicago's black residents.

Yet Henry was more than just a Machine hack. His exploits were legendary, even by Chicago standards. David Doig, now the Deputy Director of the City Department of Housing, described him as "the most corrupt politician I've ever seen. He was just awful. Corrupt, unbelievably self-serving." He routinely provided special City Hall parking benefits to his son and licenses to his friends. He arranged city contracts for his contributors, many of whom had questionable business practices (see the earlier discussion of Allen & Sons); when questioned about his dealings, he replied that there was "no such thing as not rewarding your friends." He worked to obtain a Department of Economic Development loan for the only grocer in the city selling Henry's Soul Cola, the alderman's own soft drink. When that failed, Henry attempted to pass a resolution in City Council making the cola the official soft drink of the annual Taste of Chicago, a two-week public event that attracts millions of people. When queried as to how this would benefit his constituents, he shrugged and replied something to the effect of "They like cola."[72]

The development of the ward was clearly not Henry's primary concern. While he did not hamper the efforts of some local organizations, he actively undermined groups such as LPPAC, whose director regularly criticized Henry's actions. Henry diverted City funds away from LPPAC to some of his designated organizations, short-lived nonprofits set up by the alderman and his supporters. Personal benefit seemed to take precedence over all other interests. For $5,000 a month, Henry allowed waste haulers to dump 700,000 tons of rubble, jagged metal, broken bottles, warped spatulas, waffle irons, and assorted other trash in a vacant lot near the intersection of Roosevelt and Kostner. It came as little surprise to many when he was eventually indicted and convicted in 1990 for accepting kickbacks from Chicago Housing Authority contractors and putting ghost payrollers on the City Council licensing committee.

Taken together, the political, economic, and social conditions in North Lawndale qualified it as one of the most troubled neighborhoods in the entire nation. While similar to Englewood in its level of suffering, North Lawndale received considerably more national publicity. In 1985 the *Tribune* used it as the focus of a series of articles depicting the seemingly intractable state of the urban underclass. The articles ultimately were collected in a book titled *The American Millstone* that publicly defined North Lawndale as an albatross around Chicago's neck. In addition to its employment and crime problems, the neighborhood suffered from "an almost eerie lack of a core," according to the *Tribune*.[73] Laurie Kaye Abraham, Jonathan Kozol, Nicholas Lemann, and William Julius Wilson used North Lawndale as a primary example of the crises confronting urban health care, public education, economic development policy, and job development, respectively.[74] In short, North Lawndale was a well-publicized example of everything that was wrong with the nation's impoverished inner-city neighborhoods.

A Gradual Turnaround (1990–present)

Amid all of the negativity affecting North Lawndale were some small positive trends. Although greatly overshadowed by the pathologies that received so much attention, a number of individuals and organizations sowed seeds for the neighborhood's gradual revitalization. These efforts distinguished North Lawndale from Englewood. Whereas Englewood has continued to decline, North Lawndale has recently begun to turn around.

With most of the businesses in North Lawndale leaving the community between 1965 and 1985, the once-vibrant industrial and commercial center transformed into a community virtually ignored by the market. Yet some corporations and institutions decided to stay and commit to the neighborhood's long-term development. On the eastern border of the neighborhood, Ryerson Steel maintained the largest steel service center in the world, in large part because of the overwhelming expense associated with moving. It worked closely with the nonprofit Neighborhood Housing Services to develop and rehabilitate single-family housing in the area surrounding the site. The Roscoe Company, an industrial laundry business employing 140 people and generating $8 million in annual sales, also decided to stay. Unlike many businesses, Roscoe had been largely unscathed by the 1968 riots. It was located between the expressway and a generally stable residential community, and it enjoyed a good reputation among community residents because of its long-time participation in neighborhood activities. Even Sears kept some presence in the neighborhood after it moved downtown. Sears continued to employ a full-time janitor and gardener throughout the 1980s to maintain its abandoned headquarters building and nearby flower garden.

Mt. Sinai Hospital, a neighbor of Ryerson's on the community's eastern edge, assumed institutional leadership in North Lawndale. Mt. Sinai had served the area's Jewish community since 1911. As the Jews left North Lawndale, the hospital struggled to define its mission and identity. Because of its location on the city's predominantly black west side, it found itself serving a larger and larger percentage of non-Jewish, increasingly poor local residents. The new clientele created severe financial strains for the hospital, as Medicaid and various government grants did not match the monies previously generated by middle-class insurance payments. The fiscal crisis of the early 1970s provoked serious debate about the future of the hospital. Many affiliated with the institution advocated that the hospital move into the northern suburbs, closer to its original patient base, while others pushed for it to become a more secular institution and address the needs of its surrounding community. Due largely to the arguments and efforts of Executive Director Ruth Rothstein, a former union organizer, the board of directors decided to keep Mt. Sinai in Lawndale.

Rothstein believed that the hospital had to become an integral part of the community, partly for altruistic reasons and partly out of basic survival concerns. More specifically, she and others realized that the hospital had to make its surrounding neighborhood safe if it had any hope of attracting a diverse group of patients and visitors. Making the area safe entailed building the local community, both by improving its physical appearance and by enhancing the skills and prospects of the local residents. On behalf of the hospital, she hired a local housing developer to help devise a plan for the area's residential rehabilitation. The hospital pressured city government to tear down certain abandoned buildings in the area and joined with Ryerson to support the local development efforts of Neighborhood Housing Services. At Rothstein's urging, the hospital also reached out to partner with existing Lawndale churches, nonprofit organizations, and schools to help build the community's human capital.[75]

The emergence of stable and effective nonprofit institutions in North Lawndale both allowed for and encouraged Mt. Sinai's approach. Joe Kellman, the President of the Lawndale-based Globe Glass and Mirror Company, had established the Better Boys Foundation in the late 1950s. By the mid-1980s it had grown to include girls and had expanded its recreational activities to include a wide range of educational and other youth development programs. Kellman had also been instrumental in setting up a corporate community school, an alternative educational center that sought to employ business principles in its teaching of students. Funded primarily through corporate contributions, the school initially outperformed its public school counterparts.

As it had in the 1960s, North Lawndale's religious community continued to push for substantive change. Again the Catholic Church played a lead role. Mirroring Englewood, North Lawndale's racial transition decreased the number of ethnic Catholics in the community. Attendance at weekly Mass was down in the late 1970s, and the Archdiocese began contemplating a restructuring of the parishes in North Lawndale. Cardinal Cody had serious doubts about the ability of the neighborhood to sustain multiple churches. He also questioned the willingness of blacks to be solid, long-term Church supporters.[76] Closing St. Agatha's, a low-income, predominantly black parish with an aging church facility, was a distinct option. Rumors of St. Agatha's potential closing triggered widespread opposition within the community, however. A wide variety of local interests—pastors, congregants, businessmen, school principals, doctors, Mt. Sinai administrators, and the like—pressured the Archdiocese not only to keep St. Agatha's open, but also to invest resources in its upgrading. The lobbying worked; in 1982 the Archdiocese invested $1 million for a new church at St. Agatha's, the first new Catholic church built on the west side in nearly half a century.

The community also received a boost with the emergence of the Lawndale Community Church on the neighborhood's south side. The outgrowth of Wayne Gordon's vision and commitment, the Church committed itself to the spiritual, physical, economic, and social rebirth of its surrounding area. Gordon had come to Chicago in the mid-1970s from Iowa as a deeply spiritual man whose sense of faith compelled him to live and work in the inner city. Teaching and coaching at North Lawndale's Farragut High School earned him the friendship and respect of many local residents. Regular Bible study sessions gradually developed into somewhat more organized worship meetings at which participants discussed their day-to-day needs and concerns and brainstormed ways of applying the message of the Gospels to those conditions.

Another primary concern of the Lawndale Community Church was the physical health of the community. North Lawndale had one of the highest infant mortality rates in the city, and many of its residents suffered from diseases such as diabetes, hypertension, and syphilis. With the financial assistance of suburban parishes, the Chicago Community Trust, and other private donors, the Church established the Lawndale Christian Health Center in 1983. Located across Ogden Street from the Church, the health center was serving 1,000 patients each week within its first year. Within the same building, the Church created a gymnasium with a full-length basketball court. Again, support came from a series of private donations, including a fund-raiser hosted by the then-Super Bowl champion Chicago Bears.

Realizing the importance of quality housing to a neighborhood, the

Church in 1987 established the Lawndale Christian Development Corporation (LCDC), a nonprofit entity charged with bettering residential and economic conditions in the area. LCDC initially focused on creating home ownership opportunities for local residents, specifically through the rehabilitation of local two-flats (two-family homes). Starting with the most difficult projects, the organization bought its first two buildings from drug dealers on the 2200 block of S. Avers Street. The block's drug activity had earned it a reputation as one of the worst on Chicago's west side; *Tribune* writers had dubbed it "Easy Street" because of the ease with which dealers could peddle their wares. Yet LCDC successfully rehabbed the homes and found individuals courageous enough to buy. The development helped arrest the drug trade and catalyzed subsequent housing activity on the block, outcomes which attracted the attention (and money) of numerous local philanthropies.[77]

LCDC has become one of Chicago's more successful nonprofit development organizations, having built and/or rehabilitated 104 units of low-income housing in the past ten years. (Another 65 are presently under development.) Yet while the group has received the most attention for its housing efforts, it has also worked to address other neighborhood needs. In 1990 LCDC started a college opportunity program. The group begins working with students in eighth grade and provides them with ongoing counseling and an educational enrichment program throughout the remainder of their time in school. Those who are able to go on to college receive $3,000 scholarships for each of their four years in school. Twenty students have attended college thus far, and an additional 80 are in the program.

The organization attempted to operate a few small businesses in the late 1980s as a means of providing on-the-job training to local residents, but was never able to sustain them; nevertheless, two employees were able to find full-time jobs elsewhere. More recently, LCDC and the Church successfully enticed the regional Lou Malnati's pizza chain to open a restaurant in the neighborhood. The Church put up half of the money for the store in exchange for any profits that the store realized. Although the restaurant is struggling, it is the only place in the neighborhood with the capacity to seat as many as 90 for dinner. LCDC's efforts have generated generally positive feelings throughout North Lawndale. Individuals respect the group for doing what it can to revitalize its section of the community and praise it for its clearly evident successes in housing and health care.

The activities of local institutions such as Mt. Sinai and LCDC represented positive trends in North Lawndale, yet the development of Homan Square has been the principal turning point for the neighborhood.[78] As mentioned earlier, Sears's move downtown left a huge void in North Lawndale. Sears continued to own 55 acres of land in the community, property that included the still-maintained headquarters site and the abandoned catalog distribution center. The company had been trying to sell the site ever since it pulled out, yet its marketing efforts had ultimately failed. In 1989 the effort took on additional urgency. Two of Sears's senior executives, Ed Brennan and Charlie Moran, were approaching retirement. Brennan had been born and raised in the adjacent Austin neighborhood, and both he and Moran had spent much of their careers working for Sears in North Lawndale. Finding a suitable and beneficial use for the site would help enable them to make a positive impact on the community.

At the same time, Sears was under considerable public pressure to do something with its North Lawndale property. The company had found that the office space in the Sears Tower did not adequately serve its needs, and had been looking for an alternative site for its headquarters. Taking advantage of the ongoing competition among states and municipalities to attract major corporations, Sears threatened to move 10,000 jobs out of Illinois if the State did not help it obtain an acceptable new location. In response, state officials arranged a deal in which Sears obtained roughly $90 million of undeveloped land at the outskirts of Cook County for considerably less than its market value. *Crains Chicago Business* estimated that the value of the Hoffman Estates site would approach $1 billion when it was fully built out to Sears's specifications. The arrangement generated significant controversy within the Illinois State Assembly, where Chicago-based representatives challenged the perceived corporate giveaway. A number of the Assemblymen, especially Lawndale resident Art Turner, decided to extract a promise from Sears to do something with its Homan Square site in exchange for their votes on the Hoffman Estates deal.[79]

Still, the pressure on Sears to deal with its former site did not immediately generate long-nonexistent market interest. What enabled something to go forward was ultimately Brennan's friendship with Charlie Shaw, a well-established national developer. Shaw had built a track record of a series of successful, high-profile residential developments, including Lake Point Tower, Garibaldi Square, the restoration of the Hilton (all in Chicago), as well as Museum Towers on top of the Museum of Modern Art in New York. Shaw had long-standing interests in creating mixed-income housing and in re-shaping the urban environment. After a series of conversations, Brennan and Shaw agreed on a plan to create 600 units of mixed-income housing, community services, and institutional and commercial space on the Sears site. The catalog distribution building would be demolished, but the administrative building would be converted into office space for local businesses, nonprofit organizations, and city agencies.

Construction on phase I of the project (a mix of single-family townhouses and rental apartments) began in 1992. The City provided assistance in the form of new sewers, water mains, and local roads. It also committed to locate a new police station in the rehabbed administration building. Shaw obtained federal low income housing tax credits for the rental units, enabling them to be rented for at least $150 per month less than comparable units elsewhere on the west side. He also obtained support for the moderate-income townhouses (those selling for less than $120,000) through the city's New Homes for Chicago program, which provided a $20,000 loan to low- and moderate-income individuals purchasing such homes. If the homebuyers remained in their homes for a certain number of years, the city's loan would become a grant. Sears paid for the area's environmental cleanup, provided additional subsidies on each of the homes, and established an endowment for a local park. The project provided a significant economic infusion to the community. The Shaw Company leased all of the initial rental units and sold all 24 Phase I townhouses. Nine of the units were purchased by North Lawndale residents, and three by people living outside of the city; the median income of home buyers was $43,300, indicating considerable interest in the area on the part of the middle class. Phases II, III and IV exhibited similar success.[80]

The Homan Square development has universally been cited as a significant catalyst for new investment in the neighborhood. While any development in an area signifies investor commitment, the construction of new homes has a particularly strong psychological impact because of its inherent long-term focus. The effect in North Lawndale has been notable. In the past few years, Color Communications has expressed interest in building a new printing plant adjacent to its existing facility on Fillmore Street. The historically star-crossed Lawndale Plaza has finally been developed. The Toronto-based Cineplex Odeon committed $38 million for the construction of a 10–screen movie theater on the site. The First National Bank of Chicago committed to opening a new branch in the plaza, which is anchored by a 40,000 square foot Dominick's supermarket (one of the Chicago region's two biggest grocery chains). Michael Scott,

the President of Prime Cable and a longtime Lawndale resident, has purchased 37 properties near Douglas Park for current and future development. Walgreen's, a company noted for making decisions purely on market
trends, opened a new drug store at the intersection of Roosevelt and
Homan.

Shaw's development has paralleled a restructuring of the Community Bank of Lawndale. Michael Brown joined the Bank's board of directors in 1989, before CBL was told by federal regulators to reorganize.
Convinced that a local bank could tailor its programs to serve the needs
of the local market better than the major downtown banks, Brown and
other investors established Sable Bancshares and purchased the shares
held by Cecil Butler and Pyramidwest. Having satisfied the federal regulators, the newly structured CBL attracted investment from the Steans
Family Foundation, the Northern Trust Company, and a number of other
downtown interests. CBL has actively sought to change its perception in
the neighborhood, both by intensifying its marketing efforts and improving its community relations. Sable has committed to develop the community and in January 1997 was awarded status as a Community
Development Financial Institution by the federal Department of the
Treasury.

Taken together, these changes have encouraged revitalization in a
neighborhood only recently described as one of the country's most devastated. North Lawndale's real property values have increased. The total
number of residential loans made in the community jumped 137 percent
from 1991–1992 to 1994–1995, compared to a 24 percent increase for
the city as a whole. The increase in conventional mortgages was even
more startling. While Chicago experienced a 16 percent increase during
the period, North Lawndale's conventional loans went up a whopping
233 percent.[81]

Perhaps most importantly, the perception of North Lawndale has
improved dramatically. A 1995 survey of 13 local businesses found that
12 intended to expand and/or improve their property within the next five
to ten years. The companies believed that the neighborhood definitely
would not worsen and was at least somewhat likely to improve.[82]
Michael Scott explained his investment as a result of "life-giving elements coming back" to North Lawndale. The strengthening of the Community Bank of Lawndale, in conjunction with Mayor Richard M.
Daley's commitment to public school reform and neighborhood renewal,
the upgrading of local parks, and the development of the United Center
on the Near West Side have all boded well for the neighborhood's future.
Scott sees increasing numbers of property owners willing to invest,

especially in the area surrounding the Lawndale Community Church. For him and others, the neighborhood is now "an area of real opportunity."[83]

NOTES

[1]Chicago Fact Book Consortium, *Local Community Fact Book—Chicago Metropolitan Area 1990* (Chicago: University of Illinois, 1995), p. 194.

[2]"City's Solution for Dying S. Side Mall: Auto Traffic," *Crains Chicago Business* (Jul. 27, 1987), p. 1.

[3]Interview with Pennick in Chicago, May 5, 1997.

[4]Much of the following discussion on the effects of FHA policies in Englewood is derived from Gregory Gordon and Albert Swanson's *Chicago: Evolution of a Ghetto* (Chicago: Home Investment Fund, 1977).

[5]Realtors also made profits by serving as intermediate owners of properties. A realtor would often purchase a home from a white eager to sell and then would quickly sell the property to a black buyer.

[6]"Sellers' Farewell Gift?" *Chicago Sun-Times* (Aug. 12, 1976), p. 54. Harvey Molotch discusses the nature of the dual housing market in Chicago's South Shore neighborhood in the late 1960s in *Managed Integration* (Berkeley: University of California Press, 1972).

[7]"Do VA Loan Policies Contribute to Panic Peddling, White Flight, and Resegregation?" *Chicago Reader* (Apr. 4, 1986), Sec. 1, pp. 3, 25.

[8]Interview with Coleman, 18th Ward Alderman, Chicago, May 20, 1997.

[9]"City's Solution."

[10]Jennifer Robles, "Captive Grocery Market Pits Blacks against Arabs," *Chicago Reporter* (Nov. 1989): 1–11.

[11]"Allstate Redlines 13 Areas: MAHA," *Chicago Tribune* (Feb. 27, 1978), Sec. 1, p. 1.

[12]"Blacks' Savings Piped into White Suburbs," *Chicago Tribune* (June 24, 1980), Sec. 1, p. 1.

[13]Walter M. Perkins, "Chicago's Black-Owned Banks Face Community Challenges," *Chicago Reporter* (Mar. 1989): 3.

[14]Pennick interview.

[15]Englewood Hospital Board minutes, May 1977–Feb. 1988, Chicago Historical Society, Chicago. After the hospital closed, Chicago Bear Richard Dent attempted to buy it and turn it into a homeless shelter. Although Dent was able to raise a fair amount of money, the project ultimately failed due to a mix of poor project implementation and oversight as well as local opposition. Community organizer Chris Brown described the whole endeavor as "just another shitty thing to happen to the neighborhood." (Interview, Apr. 9, 1997.)

[16]See, for example, J. Anthony Lukas's discussion of the Catholic Church's struggle in certain Boston neighborhoods in *Common Ground* (New York: Vintage Books, 1985).

[17]Interview with Rev. Jack Farry, St. Thomas the Apostle, Chicago, June 12, 1997. Farry was previously the pastor at St. Bernard's in Englewood.

[18]Ibid.

[19]Interview with Baldwin in Chicago, May 29, 1997. Baldwin also serves as the pastor of St. Benedict's the African (East) in Englewood.

[20]Interviews with Jim Soens, Ravenswood Industrial Council, Chicago, Apr. 28, 1997 and with Wysocki in Chicago, June 13, 1997.

[21]Interview with Squire Lance, North Washington Park Community Development Corporation, Chicago, Apr. 30, 1997; see also "South Side Renewal Plan Told," *Chicago Tribune* (Aug. 21, 1980), Sec. 1, p. 1.

[22]Karen Snelling, "Low-Income Renters Suffer While City Hunts for Landlords," *Chicago Reporter* (June 1989): 4. Englewood also suffered from a number of colorful residential development failures. The Englewood Community Development Corporation, one of the groups involved in the Department of Housing project, proposed to build a series of additional units in the late 1980s and early 1990s. None of the proposals ever went anywhere. Another group, Basic Economic Neighborhood Development (BEND), proposed to expand its youth training activities and build 80 townhouses in the early 1990s. The organization never survived. Its founder was fired from his city government job for taking bribes, the private developer involved in the proposed project was sentenced for defrauding tenants in some of his buildings, and BEND's Executive Director was indicted for asking for kickbacks from other potential developers. (Brown interview of April 17, 1997.)

[23]See Wilson, *When Work Disappears,* especially Chapters 3 and 4.

[24]Pennick interview.

[25]Widely considered to be one of the most ruthless gang leaders in the country, Hoover is presently serving an extended sentence in a federal penitentiary for assorted drug- and gang-related crimes.

[26]"Shootings Feed Englewood Despair," *Chicago Tribune* (June 3, 1990), Sec. 2C, p.1; interview with John Paul Jones, Neighborhood Capital Budget Group, Chicago, May 5, 1997.

[27]"Englewood Longs for the Safe Old Days," *Chicago Tribune* (Dec. 29, 1991), Sec. 2C, p.1.

[28]"The Violence of Street Gangs," pp. 4–6.

[29]Immergluck, pp. 50–51.

[30]The number of sales of single-family homes in Englewood declined from 74 in 1987–1988 to 19 in 1993–1994 (Sources: Immergluck and the Chicago Association of Realtors).

[31]"U.S. Targets Rent Skimming," *Chicago Tribune* (Feb. 18, 1997), Sec. 2, p.1.

[32]See Edward J. Ollarvia, "The Sustainable Economic Development of the Village," report prepared for the New Englewood Village Governance Corporation (Chicago), May 1997, pp. 17–21.

[33]"Englewood Longs for the Safe Old Days."

[34]"It Is the Only Ticket Out of Here," *Chicago Tribune* (June 9, 1997), Sec. 1, p. 21.

[35]Chicago Fact Book Consortium (1995), p. 107; *American Millstone,* p. 206.

[36]Interview with Danny K. Davis, Member of the U.S. House of Representatives, Chicago, June 13, 1997.

[37]Chicago Department of Urban Renewal, "Lawndale: Background for Planning," 1964.

[38]See Margery Frisbie, *An Alley in Chicago* (Kansas City: Sheed & Ward, 1991), p. 201, and Carlyle C. Douglas, "The Curse of Contract Buying," *Ebony* (June 1970): 43–52.

[39]Chicago Dept of Urban Renewal, "Lawndale: Background for Planning."

[40]See Ibid. and Chicago Department of Urban Renewal, *Lawndale Conservation Plan,* March 1968.

[41]Davis interview and Lemann, *Promised Land,* pp. 250–251.

[42]Davis interview.

[43]Interview with Ivers in Chicago, Apr. 29, 1997.

[44]Daniel Mallette Papers (1965–1966). Chicago Historical Society, Chicago.

[45]Interview with Egan, DePaul University, Chicago, Apr. 16, 1997.

[46]See "The Night Chicago Burned," *Chicago Reader* (Aug. 26, 1988), Sec.1.

[47]"Lawndale Fights to Halt Industry's Flight." *Chicago Tribune* (May 9, 1972), Sec. 1, p. 2. The riots had strong negative repercussions throughout Chicago. Roughly half a million white Chicagoans moved out of the city between 1970 and 1975 ("The Night Chicago Burned"). Between 1969 and 1971, the city lost 85 factories employing 7,040 people (Prue Brown, Lisa Marie Pickens, and William Mollard, "The Steans Family Foundation: History of North Lawndale" (Chicago: Chapin Hall Center for Children, 1996), p. 4).

[48]Wilson, *When Work Disappears,* p. 35.

[49]Charles Bowden and Lew Kreinberg, *Street Signs Chicago* (Chicago: Chicago Review Press, 1981), p. 175.

[50]Interview with Abraham Morgan, R.E.G. Development Corporation, Chicago, May 22, 1997.

[51]Interview with Kreinberg, Jewish Council on Urban Affairs, Chicago, Apr. 24, 1997.

[52]Interview with Butler in Chicago, May 15, 1997. Capitalizing the new corporation was tricky, though. North Lawndale's residents did not have enough money to finance NLEDC/PDC, so the organization applied for federal funds through OEO and other War on Poverty agencies. Since the government would not directly fund a for-profit corporation, LPPAC was designated the holding company for NLEDC/PDC. Federal grants were placed in a special trust fund whose proceeds went to LPPAC.

[53]"Bank Finds Returns Justify Risk," *Chicago Sun-Times* (Feb. 1, 1979), p. 88.

[54]This law subsequently helped foster the creation of community development financial institutions, entities that will be discussed in more detail in Chapter 7. Pyramidwest's status as a bank holding company gave it control over CBL's activities, but also subjected its investment decisions to the review of the Federal Reserve Board. The latter process introduced an additional barrier to development.

[55]Interview with Doig, Chicago Department of Housing, Chicago, Apr. 22, 1997.

[56]Michael F. Schubert, "A Housing Strategy for North Lawndale: Achieving the Dual Vision of Neighborhood and Family Stability," report prepared for the John D. & Catherine T. MacArthur Foundation, Sep. 21, 1993, p. 21a.

[57]Butler interview.

[58]Interview with Townsell in Chicago, Apr. 29, 1997.

[59]Interview with Flowers, HICA of North Lawndale, Chicago, May 1, 1997.

[60]*American Millstone*, pp. 182–185.

[61]"Speed Wash: A West-Side Business Story," *Chicago Reader* (June 11, 1993), Sec. 1, pp. 1, 12–23.

[62]See, for instance, pp. 182–185 of *The American Millstone*. Many of the individuals that I interviewed believed that Butler's unwillingness to compromise on community-related issues dissuaded potential investors.

[63]The contractor, Allen & Sons, was a major campaign contributor to Alderman William Henry. It had been regularly accused of shoddy work, particularly in work at O'Hare International Airport, yet nonetheless received the highest recommendation from the alderman.

[64]"Did Dream Have to Die?" *Chicago Tribune* (Nov. 15, 1987), Sec.7, p. 1.

[65]"Ambush in North Lawndale," *Crains Chicago Business* (Mar. 9, 1987): 10.

[66]Immergluck, pp. 78–79.

[67]See Virginia Carlson and Nikolas Theodore, "Labor Market Profile of Westside Communities" (Chicago: Chicago Urban League, 1995).

[68]*American Millstone*, p. 28.

[69]Ibid., pp. 257–258.

[70]Flowers interview.

[71]*American Millstone,* p. 72; Immergluck, pp. 50–51; interview with Rutherford Maynard, Bobby E. Wright Comprehensive Mental Health Center, Chicago, May 22, 1997.

[72]Interviews with Doig and with Timothy Wright, Urban Fishing Community Development Corporation, Chicago, Apr. 14, 1997. Wright was formerly an assistant to Harold Washington. See also David Doig, "The Split among Black Politicians" (master's thesis, University of Chicago, 1988) pp. 34–38.

[73]*American Millstone,* p. 180.

[74]Abraham, *Mama Might Be Better Off Dead* (Chicago: University of Chicago Press, 1993); Kozol, *Savage Inequalities* (New York: Harper Perennial, 1991); Lemann, *The Promised Land;* Wilson, *When Work Disappears.*

[75]Interview with Rothstein, Cook County Hospital, Chicago, May 29, 1997. See also Abraham, Chapter 7.

[76]Despite coming to Chicago from New Orleans, Cody had an uneasy relationship with the black community. Many current and former priests in the Archdiocese of Chicago were puzzled at Cody's attitude toward inner-city churches. Some found him to be racially prejudiced, while others suggested that he was struggling with some deeper issues that they simply did not understand. The reaction to Cody stands in sharp contrast to that surrounding his successor, Joseph Bernardin, a man almost universally revered for his openness and willingness to listen to others.

[77] Doig interview.

[78]The Homan Square development is located outside of the official North Lawndale community area, as it is on the north side of Arthington Street. Yet virtually everyone considers it to be within the neighborhood, as North Lawndale's boundaries are assumed to stretch as far north as the Eisenhower Expressway (a few blocks north of Arthington). Although the statistics for the neighborhood use the official community area boundaries, the case study considers the assumed territory as well.

[79]Interviews with Doig and with Wayne Gordon, Pastor of Lawndale Community Church, Chicago, June 3, 1997.

[80]U.S. Department of Housing and Urban Development, "North Lawndale Homeownership Zone Application," fall 1996, p. 6.

[81]Immergluck; Woodstock, *1994 Community Lending Fact Book.*

[82]Trkla, Pettigrew, Allen, & Payne, "Summary of Businesses/Employers Survey—North Lawndale Strategic Alliance," preliminary report prepared for the Steans Family Foundation, Chicago, Oct. 1995, p. 1.

[83]Interview with Scott, Prime Cable Co., Chicago, June 19, 1997.

CHAPTER 6

Explaining Revitalization:
A Comparative Case Analysis

The previous chapter outlined the recent history of both Englewood and North Lawndale. It presented a story of two neighborhoods that had been relatively stable middle-class communities during the 1930s but had experienced radical racial change, disinvestment, and decline in the years following World War II. By the late 1980s, the two neighborhoods had become some of the most economically and socially troubled urban communities in the country. Well over two-fifths of their residents lived in poverty. Their rates of violent crime were among the highest in Chicago. The private sector routinely shunned the areas as potential sites for investment capital. The *Chicago Tribune* used North Lawndale as a case study for its "American Millstone" series, but it just as easily could have used Englewood.

On one level, conditions are not noticeably different in the mid-1990s. Both of these neighborhoods remain deeply troubled. Neither area's 1995 per capita income was more than 43 percent of the city average. The neighborhoods' 1994 homicide rates were more than double those for Chicago as a whole. The quality of public health in both North Lawndale and Englewood is among the worst in the city. For example, the 1992–1994 tuberculosis rate in Englewood was 1.6 times that of the city, and the North Lawndale rate was twice as high as Chicago's. The median 11th grade reading scores place the communities in about the 25th percentile nationally; in other words, 75 percent of the nation's high school juniors read at a higher level than Englewood and North Lawndale's students. Over 40 percent of Englewood's entering freshmen, and almost 57 percent of North Lawndale's, never graduate from high school.[1]

The neighborhoods continue to suffer from low levels of private investment. Residential loan rates remain less than 60 percent of the city-wide average. Median property values in North Lawndale are only half of the city median, while Englewood's are an abysmal 26 percent of the city figure.[2] The communities' once-vibrant commercial areas are mere shadows of their former selves, with an abundance of boarded-up stores and vacant lots. In short, a snapshot view of the two neighborhoods shows little real difference. Both remain symbols of urban blight, areas of high poverty, unemployment, and crime.

Nevertheless, a more long-term view of the communities indicates some variation. North Lawndale has experienced positive economic change in the last 20 years, while Englewood has shown little improvement. North Lawndale's economic index score (see Chapter 4) increased by nearly 11 points from 1979 to 1995, while Englewood's dropped by roughly 5 points in the same period. Relative to the city median, North Lawndale's property values rose by over 24 percentage points while Englewood's fell by over 24 points.

More subjectively, many public, private, and nonprofit officials in Chicago believe that North Lawndale is beginning to revitalize. Nikki Stein, the Executive Director of the Polk Bros. Foundation, has a sense that "something's about to pop" in the neighborhood.[3] There exists a feeling of anticipation among community residents and local investors that the neighborhood finally has real potential for improvement. Wilson Daniels, the Pastor at North Lawndale's United Baptist Church, describes the community as "all of a sudden prime property," with a number of resources available for investment.[4]

In contrast, there is little optimism about Englewood's economic future. The mention of Englewood typically provokes head-shaking, sighs of resignation, and general feelings of helplessness among these same officials. The neighborhood connotes hopelessness and even death. Chris Brown, the Housing Director at the United Way/Crusade of Mercy, describes the area as "a black hole," while others use the term "pit."[5] The image of failure is indelibly marked in people's heads:

> "Englewood," so they say, is drowning in "runaway drug use and drug dealing"; Englewood has "the highest crime rate in Chicago"; there is "nothing in Englewood" but abandoned buildings and burnt-out stores; the "street gangs run Englewood"; gang bangers and gang banger wannabes "harass and threaten business people" and they are even so bold as to demand "street taxes" from the few businesses that dare re-

main; everybody in Englewood is "a high school dropout," "on drugs," "on welfare," "in a gang" or all of the above.[6]

The negative perception of Englewood relative to Lawndale persists despite certain facts to the contrary. While the two neighborhoods are roughly similar in population, Englewood had an average of almost 1,600 *fewer* crimes per year from 1992 to 1995. North Lawndale's rates of gonorrhea, AIDS, tuberculosis, and elevated lead screenings were all higher than Englewood's from 1992 through 1994. To the media, however, Englewood has been the metropolitan area's center of crime and decay. The majority of the *Tribune*'s coverage of Englewood in the past five years has had to do with the area's violence. In the summer of 1991 it ran a series of articles on the "neighborhood under siege," including one titled "Violence Never Far Away in Bloody Englewood." Similarly, a number of *Sun-Times* articles have led off with a variation of "another shooting in Englewood." The overwhelmingly negative perception of Englewood has dissuaded private investment. Jack Swenson, the Deputy Commissioner of the City's Department of Planning and Development, described the difficulty in trying to interest retailers and housing developers in the area surrounding 63rd and Halsted Streets. At various times the City tried to entice businesses such as Dominick's, Cub Foods, Walgreen's, and McDonald's to the neighborhood, but never had any luck.[7] Numerous people have bemoaned the lack of any local attractions. There is no apparent reason why individuals would want to move into the neighborhood. What assets the neighborhood might have are overwhelmed by its liabilities. Investment in the community is seen as an unacceptably high risk.

A number of factors explain the relative improvement of North Lawndale vis-à-vis Englewood. The development at Homan Square represents the most obvious difference between the two neighborhoods. Construction activity on the site of the old Sears headquarters has sparked considerable additional investment in North Lawndale. In contrast, Englewood has not had any such catalytic project. Lawndale has benefited from the presence and commitment of both large corporate institutions and capable community organizations, while Englewood lacks a large institutional base and has never developed a strong nonprofit sector to spearhead revitalization. Perhaps the most fundamental difference between the two neighborhoods lies in their levels of social capital. Lawndale has a better-developed network of social relationships, which has enabled it to access and employ more internal and external resources.

Englewood's limited social capital has hampered efforts to attract and mobilize the resources necessary for economic improvement. The remainder of this chapter describes and analyzes these differences in more detail.

CHARLIE SHAW AND HOMAN SQUARE

As discussed in the previous chapter, the primary spark for Lawndale's resurgence has been the development of the former Sears headquarters site by the Shaw Company. The creation of new, mixed-income housing, coupled with the rehabilitation of the headquarters building for various commercial and nonprofit uses, has helped catalyze other investment in the area while creating a general sense of possibility for the community. Yet why did Shaw become involved, considering the perception of North Lawndale in the late 1980s and the lack of interest that had been exhibited in the Homan Square site?

Part of the answer lies in the personality of Charlie Shaw. A spiritual man, Shaw feels a moral and ethical obligation to promote social justice in the urban environment. He believes in the fundamental importance of affordable housing and mixed-income areas to the long-term health of cities and their metropolitan areas. The vibrancy of the economy depends on upper-, middle-, and lower-class workers being able to get to their places of work easily. Furthermore, being exposed to people with different incomes, experiences, and lifestyles breeds greater tolerance (and thus greater civility) among members of the community. "From a moral and a long-term perspective," he asserts, Homan Square "is a very important piece of property."[8]

Shaw also emphasizes the role of enlightened self-interest. As a trustee of Rush Presbyterian Hospital on Chicago's west side, he argued that the institution had to take some responsibility for the surrounding neighborhood. For his part, he developed the moderate-income Garibaldi Square housing complex. Homan Square represented a way of expanding upon the Garibaldi model in a much more unstable, high-risk (yet potentially high-reward) environment.[9] Shaw's commitment to addressing immediate local needs while simultaneously creating a broader public good has led to such innovative projects as the development of Museum Towers above the Museum of Modern Art in New York. The project simultaneously provided luxury housing and an endowment for the museum (based on its "air rights"). Such a concern for community welfare has met with some scorn from other, more financially successful developers: Donald Trump, for one, called Shaw a "chump" for his MOMA deal.[10]

While lauding Shaw's willingness to be a pioneer, individuals associated with the Homan Square development emphasize the relatively low risk that the project entailed for him. Already financially secure, he did not need to seek out a large money-making deal. "It's a great role for him," opined Jack Markowski, the City's Deputy Director of Housing. "He's not making a profit, but there's no risk, and he gets a fee for everything, including property management."[11] Much of Shaw's involvement undoubtedly stems from the mix of timing and commitment. "He was at a point in his life where he really wanted to do something" for the community, stated Kristin Faust, the head of community lending at LaSalle National Bank.[12]

Shaw's personal vision and commitment to urban improvement made him receptive to the entreaties of his friend Ed Brennan. Retiring from Sears, Brennan sought Shaw's advice about how best to deal with the company's vacant former headquarters. After almost two years of discussion, the two men agreed on the mixed-income development. For Shaw, Sears's long-term commitment to the project was crucial. Not only did he receive a large tract of vacant land free (thus avoiding acquisition costs and potential conflicts with existing residents), but he also obtained a multi-year financial commitment from Sears. "Sears backing in the early days" was crucial, Shaw attests, because "there's no profit in this [development]."[13] Sears's involvement in the project resulted in part from the personal interest of people such as Brennan, but it also helped address the company's economic and political needs. Continuing to own and maintain the vacant Homan Square site imposed a considerable financial drain on the company; helping Shaw develop it provided a way of phasing out the company's financial responsibility for the property. In addition, it provided a way of ameliorating city opposition to Sears's impending move from downtown to Hoffman Estates.

The Homan Square negotiations took place during the recession of 1990 and 1991, a slowdown that had deadened the metropolitan area's real estate market. With sharp reductions in suburban development, some corporate officers and private developers began to re-consider the largely untapped market potential of neighborhoods such as North Lawndale. While the development of moderate-income urban housing did not promise the profits of more up-scale suburban endeavors—and in many cases was no more than a break-even proposition—it did help developers meet overhead costs and thus forestall cutbacks. Homan Square therefore became a more enticing proposition than it may have been a few years earlier or later.

Another factor in the equation was the perceived commitment of Mayor Richard M. Daley to develop the city's neighborhoods. Extensive downtown development during the Byrne and Washington administrations had effectively sated the Loop real estate market. Devoting resources to community building efforts offered both economic benefits for the city and political benefits for Daley. The Mayor routinely emphasized neighborhood rehabilitation as crucial to the long-term viability of the city as a residential and commercial center. Focusing on the neighborhoods served as a way of distinguishing himself from his father, who had concentrated on the development of major downtown building and infrastructure projects. It also gave Daley an opportunity to make political inroads into a portion of Washington's constituency, individuals who were convinced that their communities routinely suffered at the expense of downtown interests. Consistent with his belief that vacant land provides an opportunity and vacant buildings and abandoned properties constitute problems, Daley quickly endorsed the proposal to redevelop the Sears site.[14]

Shaw's vision and the fortuitous timing of a number of external forces made the Homan Square development viable, but Shaw's track record enabled it to happen. Very few development projects are self-financed; most require a mixture of debt and equity from a number of different sources. The poor economic conditions in North Lawndale had long been sticking points in potential development deals, as banks had been wary to lend money in such a high-risk community. Shaw's past success in real estate enabled him to overcome this barrier to development. He had been a customer of First Chicago's for a number of years, had received loans from the bank, and knew how to allay the bankers' fears. Ed Jacob, a Vice President at First Chicago, believed that the bank would have provided financing for the project even if it had not had the additional pressure of the Community Reinvestment Act to consider. "Shaw's been a good customer, and you do things for good customers." Despite its reservations about the long-term viability of a mixed-income project in North Lawndale, First Chicago joined LaSalle, Talman, Northern Trust, Harris, and others in the project.[15]

Shaw's track record in development therefore helped to legitimize the community in the eyes of other private investors. His standing as a for-profit developer cannot be underestimated. His willingness to undertake the project, coupled with his early success in completing and selling single-family homes, convinced others of the neighborhood's nascent market potential. Homan Square has proven that at least certain parts of North Lawndale can support market-rate housing. The presence of a well-known developer was crucial in attracting Walgreen's, Cineplex Odeon, and Dominick's to the area; few believe that the Lawndale Plaza shopping center would have gone forward without Shaw's involvement in Homan Square.[16]

The Homan Square development has clearly been instrumental to North Lawndale's revitalization. The willingness of a respected, successful private developer to take the first step has catalyzed a series of other investments. Yet individual decision-making does not take place in a vacuum. Shaw was influenced by a number of other factors promoting revitalization: Sears's desire to do something productive with the site and willingness to underwrite a large portion of the development costs, the Mayor's commitment to neighborhood improvement, a sluggish real estate market encouraging re-consideration of urban locations, and so forth. As with any development, the project was in part an issue of judicious timing. As evidenced by the attempted redevelopment of the Englewood Mall, projects with the support of major actors can still fall prey to the vagaries of outside conditions.

As Homan Square has triggered other activity in the neighborhood, numerous factors within the community precipitated the development of Homan Square. Furthermore, while Shaw's project has certainly encouraged revitalization in North Lawndale, it has not been the only force driving it. Shaw selected North Lawndale over neighborhoods such as Englewood because of the presence of other factors within the west side community. These factors have enhanced the impact of the Homan Square development. The lack of such factors in Englewood not only precluded its serious consideration for such a project, but also would have limited its impact on the surrounding community. It is to these other important components of revitalization that we now turn.

NEIGHBORHOOD LOCATION AND PHYSICAL AMENITIES

Geographic location has historically played a major role in the development of cities and their neighborhoods. Boston, New York, and Baltimore benefited from excellent harbors, making them ideal centers of maritime trade. Chicago's location on Lake Michigan enabled it to be reached by land or by water. Its midwestern location made it an ideal railroad and then airline hub, easily accessed from the east or west. As Michael Porter and others have discussed, certain neighborhoods within a city have distinct locational advantages for business. Proximity to other companies encourages the development of economies of scale, access to transportation routes allows for goods to be moved quickly from place to place, and so forth. Realtors continually emphasize the three principles of real estate: location, location, and location. A neighborhood's position vis-à-vis downtown tends to be strongly associated with revitalization, as illustrated in Chapter 4.

When discussing the economic changes in North Lawndale and Englewood, the individuals I interviewed consistently emphasized the neighborhoods' geography. Virtually everyone in North Lawndale focused on the community's prime location. It is easily accessed by the Eisenhower Expressway, which enables commuters to travel from the neighborhood to the Loop in ten minutes. It is serviced by two "el" lines, which enable residents to get to jobs downtown or elsewhere in the city. North Lawndale borders suburban Cicero and is within a few miles of Oak Park, an attractive middle-class suburb just west of the city's Austin neighborhood. The suburbs can be easily reached by the Expressway. Both O'Hare and Midway International Airports are 25 minute drives from the community. North Lawndale has a number of parks and boulevards. Furthermore, basements in the neighborhood do not flood after heavy rains.

Whereas North Lawndale is seen as a great location, people perceive Englewood to be "in the middle of nowhere." Lawndale sits just west of one of the nation's pre-eminent medical complexes, while Englewood is not proximate to any major institution or university. Englewood sits in the heart of the city's south side, surrounded by other low- and moderate-income communities. It does not abut a suburb, Lake Michigan, or any of the city's particularly desirable neighborhoods.

In reality, though, Englewood does not have a bad location. Located just off the Dan Ryan Expressway, it has easy access to downtown or to the southern suburbs. It is only 3.5 miles due east of Midway, the nation's eighth busiest airport. A newly refurbished "el" runs through the heart of the community along 63rd Street. While perhaps not as ideal a location as North Lawndale, Englewood is not noticeably worse off than Chatham, Avalon Park, Auburn Gresham, or other predominantly black, economically better-off neighborhoods on the south side.

The different perceptions of the two communities result in part from their physical boundaries. North Lawndale has easily defined and widely accepted boundaries: the Expressway on the north, the Belt Railroad on the east, the B&O Railroad on the south, and the city limits on the west. Englewood's borders technically are 55th Street on the north, Racine on the west, 75th on the south, and the Dan Ryan Expressway on the east. Of these, only the Dan Ryan serves as a clear boundary; many throughout the city tend to lump West Englewood, Englewood, and the southern New City community areas together as part of "Englewood." Lawndale's mixture of parks, boulevards, and major thoroughfares such as Roosevelt, Pulaski, and Ogden Avenues makes it easier for developers to make a concentrated, delineated impact in the neighborhood, whereas Englewood's relative amorphousness dissuades such development. According to Mark Angelini, North Lawndale "presents itself in digestible bites." Lawndale also has areas with attractive, well-built homes, especially the greystones north of Homan Square; much of Englewood's housing stock features wood frame construction, which is inherently less durable (and thus less appealing to potential investors) than homes built of stone or brick. Taken together, these characteristics help to explain the different levels of interest (and by extension, investment) in the two neighborhoods.[17]

Although the locational and physical characteristics of the neighborhoods have not changed, their perceived value has varied with developments elsewhere in the city. North Lawndale certainly possesses distinct locational advantages, but it has always had those advantages and has only recently begun to revitalize. The neighborhood enjoyed easy access to the Loop and the suburbs in the 1970s and 1980s, the time when its economic meltdown earned it notoriety in *The American Millstone*. Sears has recently promoted the area's ideal location in its work with Homan Square, yet the company made little mention of the neighborhood's amenities either when it moved its headquarters out in 1973 or when it closed its catalog distribution center in 1987.

North Lawndale has benefited from the extensive development taking place on Chicago's Near West Side, activity that has caused numerous investors to "rediscover" Lawndale's inherent locational advantages. As described briefly in Chapter 4, the Near West Side has experienced considerable private investment in the past decade or so, beginning with the development of the luxury high-rise Presidential Towers just west of the Loop. Widespread real estate development has occurred around Rush Presbyterian/St. Luke's Hospital, the University of Illinois Medical Center, and the rest of the area's medical complex.

The University of Illinois at Chicago has expanded. The United Center was built to replace the old Chicago Stadium. In addition to serving as the new home for the Bulls and Blackhawks, the arena hosted the 1996 Democratic National Convention. In preparation for the Convention, the City of Chicago invested millions of dollars in local infrastructure improvements. What had long been one of the city's poorest community areas has now become one of its more desirable regions. Real estate prices have skyrocketed and middle- and upper-income townhouses increasingly dot the landscape. Developers are looking to sell townhouse condominiums near Western Avenue for between $250,000 and $300,000.

Because of its location adjacent to the Near West Side's western edge, many investors see North Lawndale as the "next frontier." They have little doubt that the community will be the next one to experience considerable development and are therefore looking to take advantage of its still-low land values. The neighborhood's current blight makes land reasonably cheap, but its location promises high rewards.

Englewood, whose location once attracted numerous middle-class families, does not sit in the path of any current development. It is far enough from the Loop and the lake not to entice real estate investors and developers, particularly since there are substantial tracts of undeveloped (or underdeveloped) property in neighborhoods such as Douglas, North Kenwood/Oakland, and the Near West Side. Unlike North Lawndale, Englewood does not benefit from adjacent market activity. It also suffers from a generally negative perception of much of the old south-side "Black Belt." Many developers and investors see the south side as "a public housing hole," a series of horrendous Chicago Housing Authority high-rises.[18] Even though the west side has its share of public housing complexes (most notably the Henry Horner and ABLA Homes in the Near West Side), it somehow seems less harsh and foreboding. Kristin Faust describes the Dan Ryan Expressway as "just more depressing" than the Eisenhower, as it runs past the notorious Stateway Gardens and Robert Taylor Homes.[19]

Yet while location matters, it alone does not drive revitalization. The development in the Near West Side has had some positive spillover effect on North Lawndale by changing the neighborhood's perception in the eyes of potential investors. The development still has at least a mile to go before it hits the heart of North Lawndale, however; parts of Western Avenue are clearly showing signs of improvement, but much of the area essentially remains "no-man's-land." If location were the only factor, investor interest in East and West Garfield Park should be similar to that in Lawndale. All three communities sit just west of the Near West Side. The Garfields lie on the other side of the Eisenhower Expressway to Lawndale's north. They are also served by two "el" lines. Although the Garfields have shown real improvement on their economic indices (see Chapter 4), they have not generated the same sort of excitement among investors and public officials that North Lawndale has.

Englewood's location is not bad: lying adjacent to the Dan Ryan and served by the refurbished green line, it enjoys more locational amenities than neighboring communities such as Auburn Gresham, West Englewood, or Greater Grand Crossing. Nevertheless, it has fared much worse economically than any of its neighbors. Neither Englewood nor its surrounding region presently has the appeal of Lawndale or the Near West Side, but in the late 1980s Englewood's prospects seemed brighter than its west side counterpart's. The failed redevelopment of the Englewood Mall had devastating consequences for the community; some contend that its rejuvenation would have made Englewood the success story instead of Lawndale. The different trends in the two communities therefore result more from non-locational factors than locational ones. The presence and commitment of major local institutions has played a major role in shaping economic conditions in each neighborhood.

THE IMPORTANCE OF LOCAL INSTITUTIONS

In their 1984 study of eight Chicago communities, *Paths of Neighborhood Change,* Richard Taub, Garth Taylor, and Jan Dunham emphasized the central role that major institutional actors play in encouraging local investment. A decision by a large corporation or hospital to remain in a neighborhood sends a signal to others that the community would have at least a base level of activity. A large institution's ability to buy surrounding property (as the University of Chicago did in Hyde Park in the 1940s and 1950s) can effectively create and/or maintain a desired level of local market activity.

The experiences of North Lawndale and Englewood largely reinforce many of Taub et al.'s findings. Many of North Lawndale's institutional actors have made a commitment to the community's improvement, while most of Englewood's institutions have historically tried to operate independently of their neighborhood. The variation in institutional involvement and commitment has been a major factor behind the communities' different economic experiences.

Financial Institutions

All neighborhoods need access to capital. Companies need money to develop and expand, and individuals need funds to buy, maintain, and improve their homes. Since relatively few people and organizations have the internal monies necessary to carry out their desired projects, they rely on loans from banks and other financial institutions. These private institutions weigh the likelihood of repayment in their decisions to invest in individuals and businesses. The poor economic conditions of inner-city neighborhoods and many of their residents often cause lenders to avoid the areas, thus limiting the flow of capital into the communities.

Despite its checkered financial past, the Community Bank of Lawndale has always been committed to the redevelopment of North Lawndale. Because of that underlying mission, it has always received at least lukewarm support from the neighborhood residents. From the beginning CBL was seen as an institution "of the neighborhood." It had emerged in response to the decision to move the Sears Bank downtown to the Sears Tower in 1974. The state Commissioner of Banking refused to let Sears abandon the community entirely and insisted that it maintain the financial institution in some form. Sears claimed that the Bank was an independent entity and that the company therefore had no responsibility for its activities. Following on the heels of the company's move, the claim incensed many local residents. The Bank had never enjoyed much local support—mainly because less than one percent of its deposits were used for loans in the neighborhood—yet it was still North Lawndale's financial institution.[20] A group of community members successfully mobilized to prove that the Bank was owned principally by Sears employees and that Sears therefore had to adhere to the Commissioner's mandate.

Sears dealt with the situation by trying to sell the bank. A group of local investors associated with Pyramidwest sought to buy it for $2 million, but were refused a meeting. A lawsuit ultimately forced Sears to accept the offer but led to a protracted legal struggle as to the legality of a development corporation serving as a bank holding company. Unsure of the ramifications and unwilling to confront the politics of the situation, the Federal Reserve Board simply never ruled on Pyramidwest's claim. A district judge subsequently ruled in favor of Pyramidwest, citing the Board's failure to deny the application in the time allotted by law.

The opening of the Community Bank of Lawndale was therefore a major source of pride for local residents. Many of them owned shares in a bank whose mere existence represented a victory over Sears, the corporate behemoth that had recently forsaken the neighborhood for greener downtown pastures. The fact that CBL has remained in business represents a significant psychological victory for the community. "People said [North Lawndale] was an unbankable community, but the Bank survived," explains Cecil Butler. "Lots of other banks have failed during [the past 20 years]. It was one of six or seven minority-owned banks in the city at the time. Now it's one of three."[21] Congressman Danny Davis still uses CBL for all of his personal accounts, and even has his paycheck deposited directly in the bank from Washington. "The bank and community development are all part of the struggle, the idea, the sense of 'yes, we can.' It's about being able to say that's something's been accomplished, something's being done" in the neighborhood.[22] More than anything else, the Bank has given local residents a sense of hope for the community. Wayne Gordon remains a "huge supporter of the Bank" despite the problems it has had lending in the neighborhood. "It's the smallest, maybe the most unsuccessful bank in Chicago, but it's here."[23]

CBL also represented a whole new approach to inner-city banking. In concert with Pyramidwest, it was designed as a mixture of a bank holding company, a community organizing group, a small business developer, and a housing rehabilitator and manager. In David Doig's analysis, it "tried the South Shore Bank model before South Shore Bank." Whereas the Shorebank Corporation was owned entirely by institutional investors, CBL was established as a community-owned bank addressing local needs. South Shore Bank operated principally in moderate-income neighborhoods on Chicago's south side, while CBL focused on the more impoverished communities of Lawndale, Garfield Park, Pilsen, and South Austin.[24]

CBL's commitment to the development of North Lawndale has remained strong throughout its existence. "People are often surprised that the bank wants to be so involved in neighborhood activities," explains CBL President Diane Glenn. Yet most of the surprise comes from individuals and institutions located outside the community, many of the same people and groups that have historically given CBL "no respect as a small, African-American bank on the west side." The Bank has maintained a very loyal local customer base, including almost all of the Lawndale area's churches and nonprofit organizations. Its deposits and loans grew by 10 and 16 percent respectively in 1996, even with the increased competition from First Chicago and Harris Bank, both of which have demonstrated growing interest in North Lawndale. CBL's holding company, Sable Bancshares, received a $1 million equity award in 1997 from the federal CDFI Fund for its efforts in the community. Sable also established a community advisory board and a for-profit community development corporation to help it realize its neighborhood development mission.[25]

Whereas CBL has consistently worked to spur change in North Lawndale, the Chicago City Bank has been notable for its lack of involvement in Englewood. The bank invested only $125,000 in the community in 1995, including four conventional mortgage loans for a total of $81,000.[26] The bank has historically had a difficult time meeting the lending requirements of the Community Reinvestment Act. It has a reputation for charging heavily for checking accounts and cashing individuals' welfare checks only if they have a passbook account. Despite its location within the 63rd & Halsted shopping area, the bank has never taken an active role in the various proposed developments of the Mall. It did express interest in the project spearheaded by Squire Lance in 1980, then bailed out once the deal became problematic. The bank's stance has earned it an almost unanimously negative reaction among local residents and organizations. Reactions to the bank among those interviewed (who will remain nameless) ranged from "extremely ultra-conservative," to "a glorified currency exchange" for local residents, to "the biggest bunch of fucking assholes," particularly in the way bank representatives treated customers coming in from the street.

Why has City Bank not become more invested in Englewood? For the most part, there is no compelling financial reason for it to do so. It is a conventional bank out to maximize profits, not a development bank combining a focus on neighborhood rejuvenation with its need to make money. City Bank has been able to make money outside of the community, and there is little apparent economic activity within Englewood. Bank president Gavin Weir has always had a reputation as a hard-nosed business person focused on running the bank and meeting the bottom line. According to Lance, Weir felt that "caring about the neighborhood was somebody else's problem . . . which really made him no different from any other bank or financial institution."[27] Chris Brown and Ted Wysocki were each rebuffed in their efforts to obtain the bank's support for local development efforts, leaving them convinced that the bank "literally didn't get the concept of community investment."[28] As the only bank in Englewood, City Bank has not had any significant competition for the local market. People suspect that its officers would like to move it out of the neighborhood, but have decided to remain because of the expenses associated with such a relocation.

The contrast between the two banks cannot be more stark. The Community Bank of Lawndale has consistently tried (with varying degrees of success) to improve the conditions in its neighborhood; it was chartered for that very purpose. Chicago City Bank, a relatively small, family-owned institution, has been in Englewood for years without taking an active role in the neighborhood's economy. Its unwillingness to become involved has deprived Englewood of a potential anchor for revitalization.

Hospitals

Both North Lawndale and Englewood benefit from the presence of local hospitals Mt. Sinai and St. Bernard's, each of which is the largest employer in its respective neighborhood. Both hospitals suffered through significant financial crises in the 1970s and 1980s yet committed to stay in the communities. As outlined in Chapter 5, Mt. Sinai decided to reorient its mission to serve residents of the surrounding community and to pursue the range of public and philanthropic money available for treating low-income individuals. It entered into partnership with Ryerson Steel and Neighborhood Housing Services to rebuild the area surrounding the hospital and worked with local public and nonprofit agencies to improve North Lawndale's educational and social conditions.

St. Bernard's is owned and operated by the Religious Hospilers of St. Joseph, an order of nuns based in Canada. Like Mt. Sinai's board, the order agreed to keep the hospital open when business interests suggested that it should be closed; the nuns viewed the hospital as necessary to fulfill their mission to serve the needy. The hospital opened a $1.7 million addition to the emergency room in 1983, spent $800,000 to expand and maintain its outpatient service programs, added a 219–bed wing, and purchased adjacent abandoned lots to increase the amount of parking.[29] More recently, it has developed some affordable housing units for local elderly residents.

While both institutions have catalyzed some local activity, only Mt. Sinai is perceived as a real agent of local change. Residents of North Lawndale generally praise the hospital as a good corporate citizen. The American Hospital Association and the Baxter Foundation recognized Mt. Sinai's efforts in 1992 with the Foster G. McGaw Prize, an annual award given to a hospital in the United States demonstrating outstanding community service.[30] In contrast, St. Bernard's continues to receive criticism from many individuals within Englewood. "It has done all of the right things for a large institution—inviting people to meetings, some outreach, health fairs, also some subtle activities (the addition to the hospital, housing for seniors, new housing)—but they haven't really changed the hospital's image," explains Dave Baldwin.[31] The hospital is still seen as aloof and unwilling to become involved in issues pertaining to the neighborhood.

What distinguishes the two hospitals most is their leadership. Ruth Rothstein, the longtime Executive Director of Mt. Sinai, was a former labor organizer who felt comfortable working with community groups and fighting for change within and outside the hospital. Her skills and passion enabled her to rally people around the importance of integrating the hospital within the North Lawndale community. Her vision of neighborhood development translated into a campaign to create jobs for local residents and encourage outside medical staff members to consider both working and living in the community. Rothstein's legacy has survived her departure from Mt. Sinai; the hospital continues to be a major institutional player in North Lawndale.

St. Bernard's, in contrast, has suffered from more fragmented, less community-oriented leadership. The hospital went through multiple presidents within a few years before the nuns took over its management. Relationships between the current leadership and community members remain strained, and neither group has actively sought to improve those ties. The hospital leadership's discomfort with the community (caused in part by the absence of clearly defined community representatives) has limited St. Bernard's willingness to work with local organizations on broader revitalization projects. The hospital's own development efforts have been done primarily with Catholic Charities (a metropolitan area-wide social service organization), which has isolated it in the eyes of Englewood residents.

St. Bernard's internal management practices have also antagonized many community members. The neighborhood's massive racial change precipitated considerable staff turnover, as many of the white doctors and nurses felt increasingly endangered working in a predominantly black and poor area. The hospital's salaries have remained low in order to minimize costs and keep the institution afloat. The management has continually fought staff members' efforts to unionize, a move that has not been well-received on Chicago's largely blue-collar south side. The hospital has had to rely on an increasing percentage of foreign-born doctors, individuals who are willing to take lower pay but who tend to encounter language and cultural barriers with the majority of their patients. The emphasis on cutting costs also led to the closing of the hospital's obstetrics section, a particularly unpopular move in a neighborhood with a large proportion of young residents and single parents. Although St. Bernard's mere presence provides Englewood with valuable health and social services, the hospital has not provided anywhere near the same degree of community leadership as Mt. Sinai has provided North Lawndale.

The Corporate Community

Another factor behind North Lawndale's revitalization has been the support and commitment of many of its large corporate institutions. Sears has historically maintained a presence in the neighborhood despite pulling out its corporate headquarters. In the 1970s and 1980s it provided grants and some staff time for revitalization efforts such as Project 80. It regularly supported minority business development initiatives such as those coordinated by the Chicago Economic Development Corporation. The company gave Mt. Sinai $125,000 to assist with the housing rehabilitation project it undertook with Neighborhood Housing Services.[32] Most notably, Sears has recently provided extensive financial support for the Homan Square development.

Other companies have taken an active role in promoting the neighborhood's recovery. Globe Glass under the leadership of Joe Kellman has been a primary benefactor of both the Better Boys Foundation and the Corporate Community School. The Roscoe Company (industrial laundry) regularly sponsors numerous community events and activities. It also participates in the state's voluntary Earnfare program, which encourages corporations to hire welfare recipients. The individuals work half-time at the outset, with the state paying half of their salary (generally minimum wage or a bit higher). If the workers exhibit an appropriate level of skills and responsibility, the company hires them full-time and pays the full salary.[33]

The companies' community involvement stems from a mixture of altruism and material benefits. For example, Roscoe has been in the neighborhood since 1921. Although it has periodically considered moving elsewhere, financial considerations keep it where it is. Its location on the Eisenhower Expressway gives it easy access to the suburban routes that constitute over half of its business. The company requires 100,000 gallons of water each day for its industrial laundry activities, and only Chicago (drawing its water from Lake Michigan) can guarantee consistent access to that amount. Furthermore, the hot and physically demanding nature of laundry work lends itself to low-skilled, entry-level workers. Chicago has a higher supply of such individuals than do the suburbs. Prevented from moving by inherently high capital costs, Roscoe has made a genuine commitment to the neighborhood's improvement: among other things, it is one of the major investors in Sable Bancshares.[34]

In contrast, Englewood lacks large corporate institutions, and its small businesses have not participated in efforts to revitalize the neighborhood. The bulk of commercial activity in the neighborhood is centered around the intersection of 63rd and Halsted Streets. As mentioned earlier, virtually every significant attempt at development has involved that shopping center. As plan after plan have failed, local businesses have developed a general sense of apathy toward additional initiatives. Although the Englewood Businessman's Association has tried to promote a collective corporate response to the area's needs, it has proven generally ineffective.

Many of these smaller firms have not had the resources to commit to neighborhood improvement, yet other factors have contributed to their relative lack of community involvement. Englewood's racial and economic changes, in concert with its increasing crime rate, have caused many of the older retailers to leave the neighborhood. They have been replaced by a number of immigrants, principally Korean merchants willing to deal with the risks of the inner city. In the process, the community has experienced a demoralizing cultural tension. Conflict arose in the late 1980s when local consumers were rebuffed in their efforts to return what they considered to be shoddy goods. The merchants acknowledged that the goods were cheap, but essentially claimed a "buyer beware" policy; underlying the disagreement was the rarity of return policies in Korea. The merchants' unwillingness to accommodate the consumers, coupled with the frustration already prevalent in the neighborhood, led to a spate of vandalism. In response, the merchants increased security. Not surprisingly, the issue further weakened the relationships between the two groups. The increased security convinced residents that the merchants perceived them only as criminals, and not as potential customers. The residents therefore reduced their patronage of the stores. Residents did not believe that the merchants would hire anyone except fellow Koreans, while the merchants did not think the residents would work with or for them. Conditions worsened to the point that then–U.S. Senator Carol Moseley-Braun's office was called in 1993 to help mediate the dispute.[35]

More than anything else, the cultural conflict has poisoned any possibility of concerted small business involvement in the revitalization of Englewood. Neither side believes that the other is seriously committed to creating a mutually beneficial situation. Residents view the merchants as only interested in taking money out of the community, while the merchants do not believe that they, as outsiders, would ever see any return on investment in the neighborhood.

The Catholic Church

As the principal religious institution in the city of Chicago, the Catholic Church has historically been a major social and political actor in almost all of the city's neighborhoods. It has not, however, taken similar approaches or experienced similar results throughout the city. Its different responses to change in North Lawndale and Englewood help explain the former's revitalization and the latter's stagnation.

The Church's history of community activism is perhaps richer in North Lawndale than in any other Chicago neighborhood. Church leaders have continually made public commitments to serving North Lawndale's existing residents, whomever they may be. People still talk favorably about a Sunday in the late 1940s or early 1950s when the pastor of St. Agatha's stated from the pulpit that the neighborhood was changing and that St. Agatha's would support the newcomers. St. Agatha's and Presentation, under the leadership of priests such as Dan Mallette, Mike Ivers, Jim Martin, and Jack Egan, have consistently engaged in a variety of neighborhood anti-poverty initiatives. Presentation was the chief sponsor of the Contract Buyer's League and is currently organizing Community in Action, a group involved in the development of affordable housing. Ivers chairs the Lawndale Conservation Committee and has helped spearhead the emerging Bethesda Waters affordable housing project.

On one level, the Church's response in North Lawndale has been the logical outgrowth of the Catholic commitment to serving the poor. Ivers describes his (and by extension St. Agatha's) role as "meeting the needs of individuals, getting to know folks, realizing you're there for them." Most importantly, a priest should "get to know them in all aspects of their lives" and then work to address their various needs.[36] The Church in North Lawndale has also been quite willing to challenge the Archdiocese when necessary to achieve the desired local change. Egan routinely sparred with Cardinal Cody about Egan's public stances against contract buying and in favor of civil rights; he was ultimately transferred out of

Presentation in large part because of these disagreements. Rev. Jim Martin mobilized widespread local support in the early 1980s to force the Archdiocese to commit resources for a new facility at St. Agatha's.

The Church has been markedly less involved in Englewood in the past 30 years. As described in Chapter 5, the neighborhood's racial and religious transition initially prompted a retrenchment on the part of the Church; many congregations and pastors shunned incoming black residents in their desire to maintain the traditional parish communities. The reactionary mentality took a long time to dissipate. A group of progressive priests and other church members formed the Catholic Commission of Englewood in the late 1960s to restructure the Church's approach to the community. They presented a series of recommendations to the Archdiocese in the early 1970s encouraging it to keep a few of the more troubled parishes open and viable. Yet their efforts were undermined when the pastors of the churches in question wrote the Archdiocese independently to request their closure.[37]

Whereas the Catholic churches in North Lawndale have remained open despite their relatively poor congregations, three-fourths of the churches in Englewood and West Englewood have closed in the past few decades. Those that remain have suffered from limited financial and human resources. Martin, now the pastor at St. Benedict's the African in West Englewood, explains that the Englewood Church's "survival mode" has precluded it from doing more than "periodic band-aid attempts to deal with poverty."[38] Baldwin, the pastor at St. Benedict's in Englewood, would like the Church to do more about the neighborhood's economic conditions. He emphasizes, though, what the Church has quietly done for the community: it is the "biggest social service provider, educator, and investor," having spent $2 million on the development of St. Benedict's School. The Church (including St. Bernard's Hospital) provides health care and a variety of elderly ministries and basic needs programs.[39] Still, it enjoys neither the widespread respect nor the acknowledged position of local leadership that it has in North Lawndale. As a result, it has not been an effective catalyst of revitalization.

COMMUNITY DEVELOPMENT ORGANIZATIONS

Both Englewood and North Lawndale have suffered principally from the absence of an active market. Until the past few years (and then only in North Lawndale), private investors have basically shunned these neighborhoods. What little development occurred took place as the result of small community development groups being willing and able to cobble together a variety of resources to carry out designated real estate projects. In North Lawndale, the success of these endeavors helped convince outside investors of the presence—or at least the possibility—of nascent market forces. In contrast, the failure or the relatively limited impact of Englewood's development organizations has further reinforced the perception of the community as economically dead.

Any discussion of community development efforts in North Lawndale must begin with Pyramidwest. On one hand, the organization has had little apparent positive impact. It controlled the majority of the proposed Lawndale Plaza site for years without making anything happen. Each effort to develop a shopping center fizzled, no new jobs were created, and local residents' access to quality goods and services remained poor. There exists a widespread belief in North Lawndale that Cecil Butler's intransigence cost the neighborhood numerous redevelopment opportunities. Companies that would have attracted other investment simply refused to deal with Butler and took their money elsewhere. Individuals within and outside the community question the maintenance of some of the properties that Pyramidwest manages. They suspect that in some ways the group has hampered efforts to improve the neighborhood.

On the other hand, Pyramidwest has been an important catalyst of revitalization. The organization has been around for almost 30 years, making it one of the oldest community development corporations in the country. If nothing else, Pyramidwest earns respect from other North Lawndale actors for its ability to survive and continue pursuing its original development mission. The organization has stuck it out while refusing to bow to political pressure or buy people off; Butler's intransigence results from his unwillingness to cut a deal that does not maximize the benefit for the organization and the neighborhood. Alderman Michael Chandler contends that Pyramidwest has probably rehabilitated more housing units than any other organization on Chicago's west side. It has created 1,300 units of affordable housing under the federal Section 8 program, developed a senior center, established the Community Bank of Lawndale, and helped attract Cineplex Odeon to the neighborhood.

Perhaps Pyramidwest's greatest contribution has been less tangible. The organization has indirectly helped instill in many neighborhood residents the belief that something can be done to change the community. The fact that Pyramidwest was able to obtain monies for development indicated that resources were available to North Lawndale. Its controversial use of those resources helped mobilize other attempts at revitalization. In short, its efforts convinced others both that they could do something to improve the neighborhood, and that they could do it better than Butler and Pyramidwest had done.

The Lawndale Christian Development Corporation (LCDC) was one response to Pyramidwest. Like Pyramidwest, LCDC's efforts helped seed the market for subsequent investment. LCDC's impact has been more direct, however. Kristin Dean, the Senior Vice President at the Shaw Company, believes that LCDC's success in beginning to stabilize the southern portion of North Lawndale was one of the reasons Charlie Shaw undertook the Homan Square project.[40] Others emphasize LCDC's critical catalytic role in sparking neighborhood change. "You really have to give [Wayne] Gordon and [David] Doig credit for laying the groundwork and providing the framework" for revitalization to take place, attests Tom Lenz, the former Program Director of the Chicago Local Initiatives Support Corporation.[41]

As outlined in Chapter 5, LCDC has pursued a variety of revitalization strategies. It has focused on creating home ownership opportunities for local residents, convinced that such an approach will foster both internal and external investment in the neighborhood. Its success in rehabilitating single-family homes on "Easy Street" and a multi-family apartment building at 19th and Pulaski convinced people both within and outside of the community not only of LCDC's own capacity, but also of the possibilities for improvement in North Lawndale. Its college opportunity program has helped over 150 students receive higher education, and its economic development efforts succeeded in attracting Lou Malnati's to the neighborhood.

LCDC has not single-handedly revitalized North Lawndale. It has had its share of problems, including ill-fated attempts to operate small businesses in the late 1980s and early 1990s and its current conflict with the alderman over the proposed redevelopment of Ogden Avenue.[42] Nevertheless, it has certainly improved economic conditions in the southern section of the community, and its health care and educational efforts have undoubtedly made an impact in the lives of residents in a much broader area. Most importantly, though, LCDC has catalyzed other investment. The City's Department of Housing has given it grants because department officials perceive LCDC as "strong, solid, realistic, effective, and committed."[43] Both LaSalle National Bank and First Chicago have provided the group with grants and loans for its community projects. Kristin Faust lauds LCDC's financial stability, organizational capacity, and holistic approach; Ed Jacob at First Chicago emphasizes that the group "passes the gut test" and is a good local partner. Both bankers emphasized that LCDC has helped make North Lawndale a more viable community for lending.[44]

The Lawndale experience contrasts sharply with Englewood. Although neither LCDC nor Pyramidwest would qualify as the most effective community development corporation in Chicago, they have collectively sparked and maintained a base level of market interest in North Lawndale. Englewood has no such community anchor. It simply has not had any organization with the breadth of vision and the internal capacity necessary to generate any noticeable market activity.

Englewood's version of Pyramidwest was the Greater Englewood Local Development Corporation (GELDCO), founded in 1972 to promote local business development. Originally a loan packaging organization, GELDCO within a few years focused on community redevelopment, especially on the revitalization of the Englewood Mall. Like the star-crossed Lawndale Plaza, the 63rd and Halsted shopping center promised considerable economic benefits for the neighborhood. GELDCO and others contended that infrastructure and other improvements to the mall, as well as increased economic opportunities through the retention of small factories and the development of light industry, would bring an infusion of needed capital to the community.[45] GELDCO devoted virtually all of its efforts to the mall's redevelopment, with some success. It created a marketing brochure for the area in partnership with advertising giant Leo Burnett. It obtained public financing for mall improvements by having the area designated as both a blighted commercial district and a Special Service Area. GELDCO itself received public funding as a delegate agency for the Department of Economic Development. It received financial assistance from the nonprofit Local Initiatives Support Corporation and technical planning help from LISC and the Chicago Association of Neighborhood Development Organizations (CANDO).

GELDCO never succeeded in redeveloping the mall, however, and the organization disbanded in 1993. Part of its plight could be attributed to outside factors (see Chapter 5), but much resulted from its own structure and approach. Tom Lenz asked, "Where to start? The organization was just really bad. The exec was weak, the board was lousy, there were real politics," and so forth.[46] Executive Director Jim Soens never earned the respect of many individuals within Englewood. Some people simply did not trust him, a white man in an almost entirely black area. They routinely accused him of talking down to others, alienating members of the community and GELDCO's board of directors, and failing to appreciate the community's goals. One woman lamented, "I wish he were dead so I could talk really bad [sic] about him."

Perhaps more importantly, GELDCO could not and/or would not broaden its focus beyond commercial development. Virtually everyone associated with neighborhood revitalization considers commercial development to be inherently more difficult than housing development. Commercial projects typically involve more actors and are more subject to the whims of the economy. Their success depends on the continued presence of a strong local market. GELDCO viewed the mall not only as the key to revitalizing Englewood, but also as a source of organizational stability. The mix of an equity share in the project, a percentage of the developer's fee, and potential management fees would ideally have generated enough money to enable GELDCO to do other projects. When the proposed redevelopment failed, GELDCO had nothing on which to fall back.

The absence of any other potential market catalysts magnified GELDCO's failure. Despite various attempts, Englewood has never really had a strong local institution that could catalyze change. BEND and the Englewood Community Development Corporation were "jokes," in Tom Lenz's words. The Boulevard Arts Center, a group that has periodically attempted to spur economic activity through the development of arts- and fashion-related businesses, has never successfully implemented any projects of scale. As mentioned earlier, Englewood's schools have been especially troubled. Less than nine percent of high school students recently scored at or above national norms on standardized reading and math tests.[47] What credibility the schools may have had in the neighborhood largely disappeared when Englewood High School honored gang members in a public assembly and regularly provided meeting space for 21st Century Vote, the political arm of the Gangster Disciples.

The lack of stable, effective development organizations has precluded outside investors from considering Englewood. Jack Markowski emphasizes the general desire on the part of the City's Department of Housing to become more engaged in the neighborhood. "Englewood has good housing stock, but the institutions just aren't there."[48] Similarly, the Polk Bros. Foundation has expressed interest in becoming active in the community, but has struggled to find a worthy grantee. Executive Director Nikki Stein continues to search for "an organization with an audit," a group that she senses "will still be functioning within a year." Yet she has not been satisfied with Englewood's existing institutions. "Englewood doesn't have a LCDC. . . . The energy [LCDC] brings to Lawndale is very impressive."[49]

One bright spot on Englewood's institutional horizon is Antioch Baptist Church. Under the leadership of Rev. Wilbur Daniel, the church has developed 849 units of affordable housing in Englewood, Roseland, and Fort Wayne, Indiana. The developments, particularly Antioch Haven on 63rd Street, have elicited almost universal praise. Chris Brown considers them a "fine example of how revitalization could be done."[50] Markowski and others applaud their maintenance and general management. Daniel is perhaps the only individual in Englewood widely respected both within and outside the community. Local residents have "nothing but praise for him and what he's done." The City renamed part of 63rd Street in his honor, and the *Tribune* ran a feature story commemorating his fortieth anniversary at Antioch.[51]

Antioch's efforts have had a very limited effect on Englewood, however. The church's development activities have focused on the production of low-income housing; the projects have met the shelter needs of local residents but have not sparked market activity. For the most part, Antioch does not want to develop Englewood. It is "not the Fund [for Community Redevelopment and Revitalization] and Bishop [Arthur] Brazier," explains Markowski. Antioch has "smaller goals, lesser qualifications, lesser aspirations, and more immediate goals."[52] "Rev. Daniel is a pastor first and a developer second," attests his son. Antioch would like to create more housing but has been stymied by cutbacks in public funds. Reductions in federal housing monies, coupled with the tightening of the Illinois Housing Development Authority's budget, have forced the organization to identify and arrange multiple sources of funds for each project. The time and energy required to package such deals has severely taxed Antioch's limited staff.[53] Perhaps most importantly, Antioch has been unwilling to partner with other organizations to promote the revitalization of Englewood. Part of the reason lies in Daniel's desire to use housing development as a way of meeting the needs of his church. The other component is the lack of qualified, capable local partners. For him, the costs of collaboration far outweigh any benefits.

SOCIAL CAPITAL

The presence of stable local institutions helps attract private investment in two ways. The groups themselves often engage in development activities designed to meet local needs and spur market activity, as Pyramidwest and LCDC have done in North Lawndale. More intangibly, the institutions represent a certain degree of social organization within a given community. St. Agatha's and Presentation, for example, are reasonably stable congregations of local residents committed to the improvement of their lives and the lives of those around them. Although difficult to quantify, this collective commitment to a place has significant ramifications for its economic well-being. It creates a sense of order and continuity within a neighborhood. Individuals believe that they can and will continue to work with each other. They therefore develop a sense of inter-personal and intra-community trust, faith that can help them persevere through the inevitable setbacks associated with neighborhood development efforts. Scholars such as James Coleman and Robert Putnam have highlighted the importance of this "social capital" for a community. They posit that areas with higher amounts of this resource will fare better socially, economically, and politically.[54]

Much of North Lawndale's comparative success results from a base level of social organization. That structure does not manifest itself in political mobilization—Englewood's rate of voter turnout in the 1995 mayoral election was six points higher than North Lawndale's (28% v. 22%)—but rather in a general sense of stability and opportunity for change.[55] The greater amount of social capital in North Lawndale has helped attract outside investment. Banks such as First Chicago, the Northern Trust, Bank of America, and LaSalle have either made loans in the neighborhood or invested in community institutions because they sensed that they could trust and work with members of the community. They also felt that the relationships that these individuals enjoyed with other local residents and institutions would help lead to additional business opportunities. The Steans Family Foundation, having decided to target one low-income Chicago neighborhood for concentrated investment, considered North Lawndale and Englewood among five possible communities. It ultimately selected North Lawndale largely because of its social capital. Executive Director Greg Darnieder knew and trusted a number of people in the area and believed in their commitment to stay in the community and work for its improvement. North Lawndale also possessed a number of individual and institutional anchors that would help ensure a base level of social organization while supporting and enhancing efforts at revitalization.

In contrast, Englewood has suffered from an ongoing lack of social structure and stability. Virtually everyone associated with the community considers its lack of organization to be its biggest problem. Squire Lance described numerous failed attempts to form umbrella-like coalitions of residents and institutions, none of which could overcome the community's "little fiefdoms" of power and social control.[56] Dave Baldwin lamented the absence of inter-denominational interaction. "There's cordiality, but no unity."[57] The community has remained factionalized, with little sense of trust or collective support for change.

Four factors explain the differing amounts of social capital in the two communities. First, North Lawndale residents have rallied around a number of distinct events within the community; Englewood has not. Second, black residents of Chicago's west side have historically had different socioeconomic backgrounds and different views of their communities than blacks on the south side; different mind-sets have helped bring about different responses to change. Third, North Lawndale has historically had a much greater appreciation of the need for community organizing than Englewood. Finally, North Lawndale has benefited from respected and capable local leadership. Englewood's leadership has generally been factionalized, unwilling to work with outsiders, and unable to mobilize local residents. The remainder of this section addresses the first three components. The next section takes up the discussion of local leadership.

Distinct Rallying Points

As outlined in Chapter 5, a series of well-publicized, distinctly negative incidents have affected North Lawndale in the past 30 years. These events caused the neighborhood to become one of the most devastated in the country. At the same time, they provided local residents and institutions with clearly defined "enemies" against which they could mobilize. The practice of contract buying in the 1960s angered hundreds of residents and led to the establishment of the Contract Buyers League. The riots of 1968 helped spawn Pyramidwest and instilled a steely determination in the minds of certain individuals to stay in the community and restore it to its former condition. Sears's decision to move downtown in 1973 provoked local resentment which ultimately led to the founding of the Community Bank of Lawndale. In the early 1990s, a proposal by the C&S Recycling Company to build a waste transfer station in the neighborhood sparked a successful campaign by local churches, block clubs, and community organizations to block the project. The mountain of trash generated by Bill Henry's illegal deals with campaign contributors helped galvanize support for Alderman Michael Chandler and his redevelopment plans.

The event with the greatest impact was arguably the Tribune's publishing of *The American Millstone* in 1986. North Lawndale residents derided the book as "terrible," one that focused only on the negatives within the community. The book was "accurate but not true," according to Wayne Gordon, in that it ignored the underlying sense of hope and commitment in the community.[58] Michael Scott concurred. "It never told the real story of people holding on, fighting with nothing but holding on" nonetheless.[59] To them and others the book demanded a community response, one that would prove to outsiders that Lawndale was and could be a viable community. Richard Townsell was "really awakened" by the Millstone series. It was a "clarion call" to stand up against "African-American communities being destroyed by the mainstream media."[60]

These various incidents both spawned and sustained individual and collective commitments to revitalization. Each further deepened the resolve of a core group of residents to see the neighborhood improve. Sometimes the events generated clear by-products, as in the establishment of the Contract Buyers League and Pyramidwest. More often, they increased the willingness of individuals to support some of the community's existing block clubs and small organizations: the Lawndale Civic and Education League, the Greater Lawndale Conservation Committee, the Marcy Newberry Center, and so forth. These grassroots organizations did not generate much fanfare, but they did promote a certain level of social interaction and thus create social capital.

Englewood suffered not from easily recognizable calamities, but rather from a slow, steady, often imperceptible decline. The riots of 1968 had nowhere near the devastating effect they had on North Lawndale. Both Sears and Wieboldt's closed their Englewood stores, yet neither had the overwhelming employment or social presence that Sears and International Harvester had in North Lawndale. Rev. Jim Martin moved from St. Agatha's to St. Benedict's in the early 1980s and initially did not realize the extent of Englewood's economic problems. Like others, he did not recognize Englewood's worsening decay. "People thought everything was fine [in the neighborhood] until the mid-80s," at which point they started to comprehend the nature of the situation. What triggered the realization was the closing of some Catholic churches. Martin explained that the parishioners "thought they were making it on their own. They never thought they were being subsidized" by the Archdiocese.[61] Because residents did not experience any drastic deteriorations in their lifestyle, they never developed a passion for real change. Englewood was "not an awful place to live," explained Aurie Pennick, and it was "not trying to withstand adversity like some other neighborhoods."[62]

Clearly Englewood was encountering adversity with the changes in the city's racial, demographic, and employment composition. Englewood's position as a predominantly residential area masked some of the more public indicators of these changes, however. People lost their jobs, but generally not as a result of an Englewood-based company shutting its doors. The mall remained, even though its retail tenants changed. Churches closed because downtown officials deemed them too expensive to keep open. The result of a complex series of primarily external factors, Englewood's decline could not be easily understood by its residents. Unlike in North Lawndale, there were few definable "enemies" against which to organize.

Englewood residents increasingly saw themselves as victims of largely unknown external circumstances. Unsure of how to respond and accustomed to having well-publicized development efforts fizzle, most simply did nothing. Subsequent attempts to change the situation, such as Richard Dent's proposal to renovate the vacant Hospital of Englewood as housing for the homeless, were met with suspicion and little enthusiasm. In Baldwin's view, residents were "too used to getting burned" by seemingly attractive opportunities to risk becoming involved in new projects. What essentially emerged in the community was a type of victim or welfare mentality. Instead of developing and/or supporting potential solutions to the neighborhood's decline, individuals tended to bemoan their neighborhood's or organization's condition relative to others. Conversations and meetings focused more on how and why Englewood was being unfairly treated instead of on how it could be improved.[63]

Different Resident Mind-sets

These different responses to external events stemmed in part from the historical characteristics of individuals in the two neighborhoods. Understanding the differences between Englewood and North Lawndale requires an appreciation of the differences between Chicago's west and south sides. As outlined in Chapter 3, blacks migrating to Chicago from the American South initially settled on the city's south side. Overcrowding and the easing of segregationist practices subsequently led to the growth of a large black community in the area extending west from the Loop. Like the neighborhoods in the rest of the city, these communities quickly took on their own particular characteristics, prejudices, and rivalries. West-side blacks tended to view their south-side counterparts as snooty and aloof, whereas the south siders often considered the west siders to be raffish and uncouth. Part of the rivalry stemmed from regional and cultural differences. The west siders typically came from Mississippi, while south siders usually hailed from Alabama, Tennessee, and Arkansas. Among other things, the two groups of people had distinct dance styles. "There's a west-side bop," insists Aurie Pennick," and don't let anybody tell you differently."[64]

The stereotypes did have some root in reality. South side blacks tended to be more affluent than the west side counterparts. Bronzeville (the area surrounding 35th Street and King Avenue) was historically the heart of the city's black middle class. The area contained numerous poor residents, but it also housed most of the city's black doctors, dentists, and entrepreneurs. Its residents tended to have more education and greater economic mobility. They were more likely to move out of their communities and integrate more desirable areas such as Englewood, Chatham, and the southern suburbs. Englewood, which was once a coveted location, gradually developed many of the same problems that had caused its residents to leave other south-side communities. More affluent residents of the neighborhood responded by moving to better locations further south and west, as their parents had done before. The individuals that remained tended to be disproportionately poor and uneducated, people most likely to be negatively affected by changing economic conditions.

The original black residents of the west side tended to be poorer than their south-side counterparts. Many were manual laborers who came to North Lawndale together from rural Mississippi, where they regularly returned to help with the cotton harvest.[65] This history of communal activity, coupled with their limited mobility options within the Chicago metropolitan area, helped create a greater commitment to the health of North Lawndale. While many residents did leave the neighborhood, enough stayed so as to create a mutually reinforcing support system. Numerous individuals associated with the community speak of the strong, positive spirit and determination of the Lawndale citizens. Danny Davis explains that there are "lots of people with lots of will in Lawndale."[66]

The presence of this informal support system in North Lawndale constitutes social capital that has leveraged both internal and external resources. It has reinforced the efforts of unsung heros such as Sam Flowers, who along with his wife has taken in 16 foster children. The willingness of such people to take risks and cling to a hope for a better future for the community has helped convince people such as Mike Ivers, Michael Chandler, and Richard Townsell to remain in the neighborhood. Shaw Company Vice President Mark Angelini emphasizes that these people "could all have gone elsewhere and didn't." Their involvement in and commitment to the neighborhood "created the underlying foundation for Homan Square to work . . . [it's been] more [important] than you think."[67]

Embracing of Community Organizing

The vast majority of economically distressed urban neighborhoods suffer from considerable social disorder. Drug activity, crime, political apathy, and a feeling of victimization all result in large part from the community's inability to mobilize for the collective good. Interpersonal ties tend to be weaker in these areas than in more affluent communities. People often have less time to socialize because they are working multiple jobs to make ends meet. The fear of crime keeps many residents indoors and makes them suspicious of strangers. The scarcity of jobs often promotes considerable transiency, with people leaving the neighborhood for better opportunities elsewhere. Such turnover can easily weaken local institutions that have been reliant on certain groups of people for their success and/or survival. The disruption of these more traditional forms of social interaction in low-income neighborhoods reduces their social capital and thus limits their ability to leverage internal and external resources.

Slowing and/or reversing the trend toward individual isolation and social disorder generally requires some form of concerted action. People need to make a conscious effort to promote interaction among the members of the community. The task takes on heightened importance when there is a collective problem to be addressed. In many low-income neighborhoods the only real local power lies in some form of political mobilization: high voter turnout to support or oppose a candidate or proposal, protest marches, boycotts, and so forth. Community organizing consequently becomes crucial for the development and enhancement of social capital in distressed neighborhoods. A major difference between Englewood and North Lawndale has been their approach to such organizing. Influential individuals in North Lawndale have generally embraced the process as a neighborhood necessity, while Englewood has consistently rejected the idea of community organizing.

An effective community organizer is able to piece together the various interests of local individuals into a workable plan of action. At the most basic level, residents must trust the organizer to do what is in their best interest. The organizer must be seen as legitimate, aware of and sensitive to the community's culture, history, and needs and principally concerned with the neighborhood's well-being. To a certain extent successful organizing requires a leap of faith on the part of local residents. At the same time, it needs to be coordinated with tangible product development. The degree to which the organizer can translate the community's goals into concrete changes ultimately determines the process's success. The community therefore needs "both tree-shakers and applesauce makers," according to David Doig.[68] The former gather information, set goals, and advocate on the community's behalf, while the latter work to implement those goals.

North Lawndale has a history of effective organizing efforts, mobilization strategies that have produced tangible outcomes. The West Side Federation spawned the Contract Buyers League and eliminated the usurious practice of buying on contract. It also indirectly sparked the residential integration of the metropolitan area that stemmed from the *Gautreaux* case; at the Federation's insistence, a number of west-side public housing residents wrote letters that became the basis for the lawsuit. St. Agatha's successfully mobilized community members in the late 1970s and early 1980s not just to save its church but to compel the Archdiocese to build a new one. Thanks to the efforts of longtime west-side political activist Richard Barnett and others, the community's residents ousted Aldermen Bill Henry and Jesse Miller. To a certain extent, the continued application of pressure on Sears forced it to remain involved in North Lawndale.

Rev. Mike Ivers, the pastor at St. Agatha's and the individual generally credited with being one of North Lawndale's most effective organizers, credits much of the recent success to the involvement of the Industrial Areas Foundation. Founded by Saul Alinsky and consistently supported by the Catholic Church, the IAF has worked to organize low- and moderate-income individuals in urban areas throughout the country. Ivers invited it to St. Agatha's in the early 1990s to train him, interested parishioners, and other residents in the Alinsky model of organizing. Armed with the IAF's confrontational approach, participants mobilized local residents in protest against the Chicago Housing Authority and forced CHA and HUD to tear down and replace deteriorated public housing units along Douglas Boulevard.[69]

Whereas North Lawndale has a history of community organizing, Englewood is notable for its lack of effective mobilization efforts. The good intentions have certainly been there; Rev. Jack Farry, former pastor at the now-closed St. Bernard's Church, recalls numerous meetings at which "we were organizing Englewood ... again ... to create the United Whatever of Englewood."[70] Yet inevitably these attempts failed. The personal and institutional "fiefdoms" that Squire Lance discussed ultimately refused to subordinate their perceived power to a collective effort. Other actors lacked the necessary long-term commitment to the organizing process. Not having experienced the success that such efforts could produce, they were unwilling to become involved and risk worsening their existing condition.

Saul Alinsky once explored the possibility of organizing Englewood with the IAF, and the group subsequently offered its services to the neighborhood. Each time the IAF's overtures have been rejected. Individuals with ACORN, a national organization based in Arkansas, have tried to mobilize Englewood residents around affordable housing issues. The efforts contributed to the development of a few single-family homes, but never blossomed into a stronger movement for change. None of those interviewed in the neighborhood mentioned ACORN as a force in Englewood.

Englewood residents have typically been wary of any outsiders coming in to help them because they question the motives of the helpers. The neighborhood as a whole tends to have an "us versus them" mind-set. Many residents feel as though the neighborhood has routinely been exploited and/or willfully ignored by businesses, city government, developers, and purported revitalizers. This "victim mentality," coupled with a lack of knowledge and experience of the benefits of community organizing, has led to an ongoing repudiation of the mobilization approach. With its history of involvement with the IAF, the Catholic Church could theoretically invite the group into the community, as St. Agatha's has done in North Lawndale. Yet the Church in Englewood does not have a tradition or a real understanding of community organizing. Its legitimacy among neighborhood residents remains questionable, and its resources are already strained. Furthermore, the instability and lack of cohesion within the community has given organizers themselves pause. Multiple organizers have shied away from Englewood because it has few of the ingredients necessary for successful resident mobilization: clearly defined leaders, strong local institutions, a general sense of social stability, and so forth.

LOCAL LEADERSHIP

The organization and mobilization of a community is a product of numerous individual decisions. People weigh the benefits of participating in efforts to change their surroundings; if the benefits outweigh the costs, they are more likely to participate. The costs of involvement tend to be high, however. Participation requires time and energy. It carries with it the distinct risk of failure, as individuals and institutions usually resist attempts at change. Residents of particularly crime-ridden neighborhoods may fear that violent retaliation will accompany confrontation of drug dealers. Some members of especially low-income communities have become resigned to the drudgery of poverty and have little reason to expect that anything could change their situation.

The organization and improvement of a low-income neighborhood at some level represents a classic collective action problem. Individuals typically lack the resources to develop and sustain a public benefit such as a community bank or a drug-free area on their own. Only when a large group of local residents act together in a concerted manner can such benefits be achieved. Citizens have to work closely and consistently with the police to identify and eradicate drug and crime problems in an area. Electing desirable politicians and/or pressuring current officials for allocations of public resources demands a certain amount of popular organization. A certain critical mass of local investment is necessary to attract and sustain a local bank. Yet many people are wary of committing their personal resources to such inherently uncertain projects. They would generally prefer to have others bear the risk of getting the project underway, and join the effort only when it seems likely to succeed. In short, they would like to reap the benefits of others' work: the classic "free rider" problem. Unfortunately, this lack of widespread commitment and participation generally dooms the effort almost before it begins.[71]

Overcoming the collective action problem involves either increasing the potential benefits and/or reducing the costs of participation. Potential activists need to believe that their involvement will result in an improved quality of life for themselves and their community. Outside events can occasionally redefine the benefit-cost calculus (as the historic *Brown v. Board of Education* decision encouraged blacks to integrate Southern public schools), but usually the redefinition depends on the actions of local individuals. Influential people within a community somehow convince others of both the need to work for change and the likelihood that such change can be achieved.

The process of galvanizing local action varies according to the issue in question, the method of promoting social change, and the personalities of the individuals involved. Yet amid situational and stylistic differences are some general characteristics of successful local leadership. First, such individuals can clearly identify, formulate, and articulate a community's common ideas and values. They have the ability to pull together the seemingly inchoate sentiments of local residents and present them as a widely accepted set of goals and aspirations. Second, they use these goals as the basis for envisioning and defining an improved set of conditions. They present a vision of a better community, a vision that resonates with other local residents and with outsiders who have an interest in the area.

While crucial, vision alone does not make a successful leader. An effective leader must be able to develop a plausible plan for realizing the vision and be able to market the plan to potential supporters. The marketing components also vary across situations, but some similarities exist. The leader must convince others of his or her trustworthiness and commitment to the process, often by publicly taking responsibility for the implementation of the plan. The ability to generate and use favorable public relations—regarding both the community in general and the plan itself—helps considerably. Leaders who can identify and emphasize the assets present within an area (location, entrepreneurial spirit of residents, and so forth) can help skeptical individuals view the area and its future prospects in a more positive light. Perhaps most importantly, the leader needs to be able to relate to a variety of individuals on their terms, convincing them of the particular reasons why they should buy into the vision and participate in the process.[72]

Taken together, these characteristics and actions of local leaders help to address the collective action problem. The leaders can highlight potential benefits of a collective effort, de-emphasize or reduce the accompanying costs, and potentially generate a solidarity of purpose that effectively constitutes an extra intangible benefit. In building local support for their program, they build personal legitimacy among residents of the area. Such local legitimacy also leads to legitimacy with outsiders interested in the well-being of the community, at least at the outset. Philanthropists seeking to improve conditions in the neighborhood tend to provide seed monies to community groups whose leaders have a clearly delineated, widely supported vision and plan for change.

Much of the difference between North Lawndale and Englewood results from the quality of leadership in the two neighborhoods. Even though many of the individuals and organizations in North Lawndale continue to fight with each other, the community has had and currently has a number of generally respected leaders. Jack Egan earned widespread praise for his leadership of the campaign against contract buying in the 1960s. Ruth Rothstein continues to receive plaudits for her work in convincing Mt. Sinai Hospital to stay in the neighborhood and participate in community-building activities. Local residents and activists speak highly of Wayne Gordon for his work establishing and maintaining the Lawndale Community Church and LCDC programs. Mike Ivers earns praise for his commitment to mobilizing the St. Agatha's community. Even his detractors admit that Cecil Butler has been influential in establishing the Community Bank of Lawndale and obtaining resources for the neighborhood. Similarly, many residents laud Alderman Michael Chandler for his commitment to community improvement; even his critics emphasize his accessibility to his constituents.

In contrast, Englewood has only one widely accepted leader, and his influence is decidedly limited. Rev. Wilbur Daniel, the pastor at Antioch Baptist Church, is the one person who consistently receives praise from others associated with the neighborhood. People describe him as a "dynamo" and a model for other ministers. Yet as described earlier, Daniel's vision and focus have not been on Englewood as a whole, but rather on selected areas surrounding Antioch and its interests. The church has had essentially no involvement with other local organizations in matters of development, a position which has bred a certain amount of jealousy and resentment within the community. People admire Daniel for what he has done, but they do not look to him as a catalyst of revitalization.

No one else in the neighborhood appears to have widespread local legitimacy. Individuals have failed to identify and elucidate a clear goal for the area. Doris Wilson, a former lender at First Chicago, explains that "nobody's ever come up with a vision for the community. What makes it a compelling place to be?"[73] The neighborhood certainly has its share of visionaries, but the visions have neither the comprehensiveness nor the structure to attract significant support. Perhaps most importantly, the individuals behind the visions seem to have relatively little credibility either within or outside the neighborhood. Whereas certain people have earned widespread respect in Lawndale, almost all of Englewood's leaders are largely self-defined. Longtime community activist James Stampley has described himself as the "spokesman for all of Englewood,"[74] a claim that causes others to roll their eyes, shake their heads, and chuckle. Alderwoman Shirley Coleman believes she is a well-respected agent of change, but few in the private or nonprofit sectors consider her a player in the economic development of the area. People routinely discredit all of the usual leadership suspects except for Daniel. Often when asked who they consider to be the major player in the neighborhood, they respond "me."

The prevalence of self-appointed, competing leaders, none of whom seems able to coordinate efforts for change, has hampered Englewood's ability to attract significant outside resources. Consider the application process for the federal empowerment zone in Chicago. As low-income areas, both Lawndale and Englewood were eligible for inclusion. Community coalitions in each neighborhood submitted applications to the public officials charged with designating the zone boundaries. When finally drawn, the empowerment zone encompassed part of North Lawndale while excluding Englewood entirely. Much of the decision stemmed from a focus on job and business development, with the presence of industrial property and significant amounts of contiguous vacant land in Lawndale working in its favor. (Englewood's largely residential character made it less appealing in that regard.) Yet part of the decision also stemmed from the lack of a single influential individual or group of individuals working on Englewood's behalf. U.S. Representative Cardiss Collins, among others, worked extensively to ensure that Lawndale reaped some of the zone's potential benefits. Valerie Jarrett, the then-Commissioner of the City's Department of Planning and Development, contrasted the opportunities and resources already present in Lawndale to the lack of any activity in Englewood. "Englewood had no potential, to be blunt."[75]

The lack of well-defined leadership has also caused investors to shy away from Englewood. Tom Lenz, the former Program Director of the Local Initiatives Support Corporation in Chicago, explains the difference between the two communities by quoting Paul Grogan, LISC's former President: private investors are attracted to "a single, unified voice within a community." Lenz believes that "there are maybe four voices in Lawndale, but twenty in Englewood. You just get lost down there."[76] Even nonprofit organizations with vested interests in inner-city development (such as LISC and the MacArthur Foundation) have not become involved in Englewood because of their lack of confidence in the local leadership.

Maintaining Legitimacy

The presence of a well-defined vision, a plan for carrying it out, and credible public relations can help a leader generate some legitimacy within and outside his or her community. Legitimacy is a form of political capital, one that waxes and wanes as situations change. Leaders must work to maintain and build their legitimacy lest it erode. The most important factor in the process is the extent to which the leader can deliver on his or her promises. If a leader can successfully implement projects that contribute to the betterment of the community, the leader's credibility rises among local residents and outside investors. People believe that the leader can get things done and therefore are more likely to support his or her projects. The collective action problem diminishes, and the flow of resources into the community increases. The opposite also holds. If projects do not go forward, the leader loses credibility and support.

Successfully implementing revitalization programs requires the mobilization of a variety of resources: not just money, but meeting places, technical assistance, volunteer labor, and so forth. All neighborhoods— even the most economically distressed—have a latent supply of some of these resources. The remainder need to be accessed from outside the community, with poorer neighborhoods requiring a greater infusion of external human and financial capital. A local leader must consequently be aware of and able to tap these outside resources in order to carry out his or her plan for community betterment. A leader has to be an effective networker and coalition-builder both within and outside his or her neighborhood. "Leaders [who are] unwilling to seek mutually workable arrangements with systems external to their own are not serving the long-term interests of their constituents."[77]

North Lawndale's leaders have been able to attract and coordinate outside resources effectively. Wayne Gordon's friendship with a member of the Urban Land Institute helped convince ULI to select North Lawndale as the site of a neighborhood planning study it conducted as part of its 1986 convention in Chicago. ULI's study helped establish a framework for the subsequent LCDC, Homan Square, and Lawndale Plaza developments. LCDC and the Lawndale Christian Health Center have routinely benefited from contributions of money and volunteers from suburban and national churches because of Gordon's involvement in the national Christian Community Development Association. LCDC has obtained financing from the Chicago Department of Housing in part because David Doig (one of LCDC's founders) was the Deputy Commissioner for a number of years. North Lawndale's history as a Jewish neighborhood has enabled it to access another set of resources. Lew Kreinberg and the Jewish Council on Urban Affairs have devoted considerable organizing and research time to the improvement of the community. Mt. Sinai officials have been successful in tapping Jewish donors for the hospital.

North Lawndale leaders' connections with external actors have helped attract outside attention and resources. Nationally known scholars and journalists such as William Julius Wilson, Jonathan Kozol, and Nicholas Lemann have used the neighborhood as a case study for their books. The *Tribune* featured Lawndale in its "American Millstone" series, a decision that gave the area considerable publicity throughout the newspaper's midwestern market. Such coverage has not only increased outside awareness of the community's dynamics, but also exposed some Lawndale residents to the broader regional environment. The neighborhood's leaders have become increasingly willing to challenge influential individuals and institutions to help change the community. Gordon, Richard Townsell and others berated *Tribune* editors for their failure to portray the positive things occurring in the neighborhood; more recent articles have tended to focus on various redevelopment efforts taking place. Protests against Sears helped convince it first to continue maintaining its headquarters and garden and then to underwrite much of the Homan Square redevelopment. Pastors Jim Martin and Mike Ivers, along with many members of the St. Agatha congregation, successfully fought the Chicago Archdiocese's plans to close the parish.

In contrast, Englewood's leaders have generally taken a more isolated, insular, and territorial approach. Instead of soliciting and embracing outside resources, they have historically been distrustful, if not downright paranoid, about the motivations of external actors. Community residents kicked Saul Alinsky and the IAF out of the area when they attempted to organize individuals for change in the 1960s and early 1970s.[78] Subsequent organizing attempts faltered in the face of the community's multiple competing factions. Mayor Richard J. Daley came to the neighborhood for a meeting in the early 1970s and was publicly excoriated in front of local news cameras, an event which eliminated much of the sympathy he may have had for the neighborhood's plight. Much of James Stampley's 1979 book about Englewood lauds the formation of block clubs as a way of uniting against outsiders and telling them what residents wanted and what they did not. He and others derided former Commissioner of Housing Marina Carrott as a racist for rejecting an application for public support of a proposed local housing development. (Deputy Commissioners Markowski and Doig cited the project's shaky financial and organizational structure as reasons for turning it down.) Many Englewood residents believe that city officials have designated the neighborhood as the dumping ground for poor people, especially those evicted from public housing complexes. As mentioned earlier, this deep-seated distrust of outsiders results in part from the neighborhood's historical sense of being acted upon by complex, difficult-to-define external forces. With no clearly identifiable "villains," people have tended to view everyone with suspicion.

The Emergence of Local Leadership

In analyzing leadership, scholars typically take one of two approaches. The first takes a "great man" perspective, arguing that the particular characteristics and personality traits of an individual largely shape the person's ascent to power and subsequent performance. The second approach focuses more on the environmental context in which the individual operates. Proponents of this view contend that an individual's effectiveness depends primarily on forces largely outside his or her control: economic conditions, the general public mood, organizational stability, and so forth. Individuals who could have accomplished great things at one time may be ineffective in another, and vice versa.[79]

Studies of less public figures have naturally focused more on the contextual factors of leadership, if for no other reason than there is less information available about such people. Mark Granovetter, for example, has emphasized the "social embeddedness" of local economic leaders.[80] Such individuals are intrinsically tied to others through a series of interpersonal networks; the breadth and strength of those networks largely determines the character and effectiveness of their leadership.

What most studies fail to address is the actual emergence of leaders. Leaders are not necessarily public figures. In many cases they are unknown outside their communities, and their influence may well be limited to a certain aspect of local life. Most neighborhoods have a group of identifiable individuals who shape the future of the area. They have a certain degree of clout in different economic, political, and social arenas. One would assume that neighborhoods of roughly similar size, population, and economic condition would produce a similar number of capable leaders. Yet the disparate leadership histories of North Lawndale and Englewood suggest that emergence and effectiveness depend largely on particular neighborhood characteristics.

Leaders tend to develop more readily in neighborhoods with more supportive social networks and institutions. Communities that have and exhibit an orientation toward inclusiveness better allow for the release of individual energies and talents. People's creativity can more easily emerge and develop in environments that respect and embrace a diversity of perspectives and cultures. Established local institutions (churches, businesses, and so forth) can play a critical role in creating and maintaining such tolerant environments. The social capital within a community helps shape the area's culture and provides sustenance to emerging leaders. Networks of interpersonal relationships help prospective leaders generate ideas and access resources. They also provide the individuals with a valuable social support system.[81]

Leaders should be more likely to emerge in areas with built-in mechanisms for helping to overcome collective action problems. Mark Schneider and Paul Teske found that the presence of strong business groups increased the likelihood of political entrepreneurs being active in suburban governments. Business organizations and neighborhood groups—regularly cited as the most important entities in the entrepreneurs' careers—proved effective in mobilizing individuals and companies around specific goals. Such mechanisms made it easier for potential leaders to promote collective action.[82]

Aspiring leaders need models of effective leadership. They need a frame of reference to guide their actions; having the opportunity to see and emulate a respected community member helps them develop and refine their own leadership talents. Budding leaders also need opportunities to exert leadership. In the corporate world, individuals who find their potential for job growth limited will often leave their current employer for a more promising position elsewhere. Similarly, budding public and/or community leaders may choose to move to areas with more opportunities. Schneider and Teske found that constitutional rules, incumbency benefits, and resource availability could effectively limit the possibilities for public entrepreneurship in a given municipality.[83] Similar barriers could exist in neighborhoods. If, for example, the only available outlet for widespread public influence is a particular local institution, the neighborhood could have a smaller number of leaders relative to its counterparts.

These criteria help to explain the presence of more legitimate, established leadership in North Lawndale. Lawndale has historically had a more diverse, tolerant social environment than Englewood. Many of its residents have made a long-term commitment to improving the neighborhood, and its churches have openly welcomed newcomers. In contrast, Englewood historically served as more of a way station, with many of its more sophisticated residents moving on to better areas when the neighborhood began to decline. As described earlier, many of its churches resisted the immigration of blacks.

North Lawndale's social capital has nourished existing and emerging leaders. Robert Steele, the head of the nonprofit Lawndale Business and Local Development Corporation, emphasizes the importance of the regular meetings he has with LCDC Director Richard Townsell and Steeve Kidd, the Director of Agency Metropolitan Program Services. In discussing their personal and professional experiences, they challenge and reinforce each other's commitment to change the neighborhood. The community has had a number of role models for aspiring leaders. Townsell returned to North Lawndale because of his relationship with Wayne Gordon and the Lawndale Community Church. He personally felt a need to reconnect with the community after feeling isolated and uncomfortable in college at Northwestern University, and he knew that the neighborhood offered a support system. Ivers has drawn upon Egan's experiences at Presentation Church for his own work at St. Agatha's. In contrast, emerging leaders in Englewood have relatively few opportunities for positive reinforcement because of the continual backbiting and self-promotion. Aurie Pennick asserts that the community used to be much more supportive in the early 1970s, but time and personal frustration eliminated the neighborhood's leaders. "Everybody I'll tell you [to talk to] is dead. . . . Either you die or you go crazy" in Englewood.[84] The neighborhood's ongoing decline, coupled with the increasing scarcity of public and private resources, has led to growing desperation. Taking credit for every small improvement has become a key to economic survival. "There are few enough victories in Englewood without having to share them," explains Rev. Jack Farry, the former pastor at St. Bernard's.[85]

Lawndale benefits from a much stronger, more community-oriented set of institutions, making it easier for motivated individuals to promote collective action. The Community Bank of Lawndale, the Roscoe Company, and St. Agatha's have no real counterparts in Englewood. Lawndale's network of institutions and social relationships has created numerous opportunities for the development and exercise of leadership. Entities such as the Lawndale Peoples Planning and Action Committee, LCDC, and Presentation have served as alternatives to the corruption that long characterized 24th Ward politics. In contrast, the lack of a social and/or institutional base in Englewood has left ward politics as the only real venue from which to exercise power. Unfortunately, Englewood's political winners have been generally ineffective leaders of revitalization.

For many years Englewood was represented by 16th Ward Alderman

Jim Taylor, a stalwart of the city's old Democratic Machine. Taylor had succeeded William Dawson as the chief black Machine politician on the south side. He wielded considerable clout within City Council because of his ability to deliver votes from Englewood and its environs. Taylor's hold on his ward did not translate into local popularity, however. He was widely derided (largely after the fact) as dictatorial, clownish, a "buffoon," and an "embarrassment to be representing the community." Like most Machine politicians, neighborhood revitalization did not resonate strongly with Taylor. He did not fully grasp the nuances of the process, and he was loathe to "knock down any building that house[d] people; you los[t] votes that way."[86]

Local resentment finally led to the election of Anna Langford in 1971. A criminal defender who was staunchly anti-Machine, Langford was the first black alderwoman elected in Chicago.[87] She concentrated on promoting civil rights issues—her area of expertise—within City Council and spent little time or energy on issues of local economic development. Such a stance satisfied many of her constituents. "The game in town is race, not neighborhood development," attests Squire Lance, an acquaintance of Langford's. "On the black side, it's always race. You expend energy on civil rights stuff. You march, not research—maybe some stuff against redlining, but that's about it. . . . People just were not focusing on getting resources for housing or the creation of economically viable areas. Neighborhood redevelopment was seen in very negative terms in the black community; it was too much like urban renewal."[88] As Langford's tenure in the Council grew, her limited focus on Englewood's economic development tended to dissipate even more. A desire to run for Congress caused her to concentrate on more national and regional issues, which compromised some of her support in the 16th Ward. She also continued to serve as a criminal defender, working with gang members and training some of them to be poll watchers. Such actions reduced her credibility among Englewood's residents and did little for the community's economic condition.

Langford's successor, Shirley Coleman, was a manager at the Chicago Department of Human Services before becoming Alderwoman. Some question her legitimacy in the neighborhood (especially since the mayor's political supporters nominally endorsed her campaign) and few outside Englewood even know that she's an Alderwoman. While she truly seems to care about conditions in the community, she has neither the understanding of revitalization nor the capacity at this point to catalyze meaningful change.

Some of the weakness of Englewood's political leadership stems from the political fragmentation of the community. The community area of Englewood is part of three different wards; when West Englewood is included, six wards come into play. The boundaries resulted in part from the 1992 redistricting, in which many black wards were restructured to accommodate the city's growing Hispanic population, and partly from historic trends. The division of the neighborhood has effectively weakened political accountability for the area. Since it constitutes no more than a portion of any one alderman's ward, Englewood tends not to be (and realistically cannot become) a politician's chief concern. The neighborhood consequently has no consistent advocate in the City Council. Furthermore, programs to benefit the whole neighborhood need the political blessing of three separate people, a much more problematic scenario than one involving a single alderman. In contrast, North Lawndale is almost entirely contained in the 24th Ward, which makes it more likely for its politicians to address its needs.

The lack of favorable social and institutional conditions in Englewood has not necessarily precluded the development of strong leadership, but it has certainly had a retarding influence. The relative strengths of Lawndale have not by themselves produced the community's leaders; strong-willed, entrepreneurial individuals have had to take the risks required to create and sustain local institutions. The comparative analysis of the two communities illustrates the local factors that are instrumental in encouraging neighborhood leadership. Lawndale's experience indicates the latent potential for individual development in even those areas ignored and abandoned by the middle class. It shows that the seeds of renewal can still grow in seemingly fallow communities.

NOTES

[1]Claritas/NPDC estimates; Chicago Department of Public Health, *Community Area Health Inventory, 1992–1994,* Vol.1 (1996); Chicago Board of Education data.

[2]See Table 4-1.

[3]Interview with Stein in Chicago, Apr. 10, 1997.

[4]Interview with Daniels in Chicago, June 18, 1997.

[5]Brown interview (Apr. 9, 1997).

[6]Ollarvia, p. 5.

[7]Interview with Jack Swenson, Chicago Department of Planning and Development, Chicago, Apr. 30, 1997.

[8]Interview with Shaw in Chicago, Oct. 22, 1997. A number of other individuals, including Erika Poethig at the Civic Committee of the Commercial Club of Chicago and Dave Silverman at S.B. Friedman & Company, have said similar things about Shaw. Shaw was featured briefly by Thomas J. Paprocki in "Option for the Poor: Preference or Platitude?" *America* (Apr. 22, 1995): 11–14.

[9]Shaw interview.

[10]Interview with Mark Angelini, The Shaw Company, Chicago, May 8, 1997.

[11]Interview with Markowski in Chicago, Apr. 17, 1997.

[12]Interview with Faust in Chicago, May 21, 1997.

[13]Shaw interview.

[14]Markowski and Butler interviews.

[15]Interviews with Ed Jacob, First National Bank of Chicago, Chicago, Apr. 9, 1997, and with Angelini.

[16]Gordon interview. The presence of a mixed-income market in the neighborhood surprised many people, including Cecil Butler. He had assumed that only lower-income individuals would be interested in living in the neighborhood, not the moderate- and middle-income people who purchased some of the Homan Square homes.

[17]Ollarvia, pp. 5–6; Angelini interview; and Brown interview (4/9/97).

[18]Angelini interview.

[19]Faust interview.

[20]Scott interview.

[21]Butler interview.

[22]Davis interview.

[23]Gordon interview.

[24]Doig interview. South Shore Bank represented one of the first attempts to use a local bank for community development purposes. The bank's success in maintaining a "double bottom line" (financial profitability as well as improved social and economic conditions in Chicago's South Shore community) earned the praises of Presidential candidate Bill Clinton in 1992 and indirectly led to the establishment of the federal Community Development Financial Institutions (CDFI) Fund in 1994. Shorebank (South Shore Bank's holding company) was actually formed in 1973, a few years before CBL. While the two banks each set out to promote investment in their respective communities, CBL retained a much more conscious emphasis on community ownership of and participation in the process. For a discussion of Shorebank's early years, see Richard P. Taub's *Community Capitalism* (Boston: Harvard Business School Press, 1988).

[25]Interview with Glenn in Chicago, May 22, 1997.

[26]Woodstock, *1995 Community Lending Fact Book.*

[27]Lance interview.

[28]Brown interview (4/17/99). Weir and others at the bank repeatedly denied my requests for interviews.

[29]"Englewood Hospital Spends on Growth as Rx for Its Area," *Crains Chicago Business* (Sep. 19, 1983): 44.

[30]"Healing a Community: Health Care Just the Start for Mt. Sinai," *Chicago Tribune* (Jul. 28, 1992), Sec. 2C, p. 1.

[31]Baldwin interview.

[32]"Lawndale Tries to Shrug Off Sears' Warehouse Defection," *Crains Chicago Business* (Mar. 9, 1987): 2.

[33]Interview with Dave Silverman, S. B. Freedman & Company, Chicago, Mar. 5, 1997. He conducted an extensive market analysis of North Lawndale for S. B. Freedman.

[34]Interview with Don and Jim Buik, Roscoe Company, Chicago, May 29, 1997.

[35]See Ollarvia, pp. 14–15 and "Koreans Sell, Blacks Buy: A Clash of Cultures at the 63rd Street Mall," *Chicago Reader* (Feb. 13, 1987): 3.

[36]Ivers interview.

[37]Farry interview.

[38]Interview with Martin, St. Benedict the African (West), Chicago, May 19, 1997.

[39]Baldwin interview.

[40]Interview with Dean in Chicago, July 23, 1997.

[41]Interview with Lenz, University of Illinois-Chicago Great Cities Institute, Chicago, June 9, 1997.

[42]Alderman Michael Chandler disagrees with LCDC's proposed plan for Ogden's redevelopment. He also feels that the organization does not adequately represent the community's interests; it acts on what is good for LCDC, not necessarily what it good for Lawndale (interview in Chicago, June 11, 1997). Some community members (including Chandler) resent LCDC's ability to access funds from the Department of Housing, where former LCDC staffer David Doig has been Deputy Commissioner.

[43]Markowski interview.

[44]Faust and Jacob interviews.

[45]Ted Wysocki, whose Chicago Association of Neighborhood Development Organizations worked closely with GELDCO in the mall's redevelopment, believed that the mall was the key to Englewood's future. "If [the redevelopment] went forward, the question would be why Englewood turned around and Lawndale didn't." (Interview, June 13, 1997)

[46]Lenz interview.

[47]"Ultimate School Reform: Start Over," *Chicago Tribune* (June 10, 1997), Sec. 1, p. 1.

[48]Markowski interview.

[49]Stein interview.

[50]Brown interview (4/9/97).

[51]See "7–Days-a-Week Minister Marks 40 Years of Care," *Chicago Tribune* (Apr. 18, 1997), Sec. 2, p.1.

[52]Markowski interview. Bishop Brazier is the Pastor of the Apostolic Church of God (on 63rd Street in Woodlawn) and is one of the most influential individuals on the south side of Chicago. He serves as President of the Fund, a well-endowed nonprofit coordinating the revitalization of the Woodlawn and North Kenwood/Oakland communities.

[53]Interview with Rick Daniel, Antioch Foundation, Chicago, May 7, 1997.

[54]See Coleman, pp. 300–321; Putnam, *Making Democracy Work* and "Bowling Alone: America's Declining Social Capital," *Journal of Democracy* 6: 65–78; and Michael Schubert, "Community Development and Social Capital," paper prepared for the Community Development Work Group, Chicago, 1996.

[55]Unpublished tabulations by Wesley Skogan, Northwestern University.

[56]Lance interview.

[57]Baldwin interview.

[58]Gordon interview.

[59]Scott interview.

[60]Townsell interview.

[61]Martin interview.

[62]Pennick interview.

[63]Baldwin interview. Tom Lenz expressed similar sentiments. Almost everyone that I interviewed in the community emphasized how Englewood had been "screwed" by various officials and organizations throughout the city. Very few offered any sort of vision for the neighborhood's future.

[64]Pennick interview.

[65]Martin interview.

[66]Davis interview.

[67]Angelini interview.

[68]Doig interview.

[69]While individuals within North Lawndale have been supportive of Ivers and the IAF tactics, the approach has caused hesitation among outsiders sympathetic to the community's future. Dave Baldwin, for one, expresses concern that the embracing of IAF's confrontational approach precludes other, potentially more effective forms of organizing and advocacy.

[70]Farry interview.

[71]The classic discussion of the collective action and free rider issues is Mancur Olson's *The Logic of Collective Action* (Cambridge: Harvard University Press, 1965).

[72]See, among other discussions of leadership characteristics, Chapter 1 of John W. Gardner's *On Leadership* (New York: Free Press, 1990) and Chapter 1 of Mark Schneider, Paul Teske, and Michael Mintrom's *Public Entrepreneurs* (Princeton: Princeton University Press, 1995).

[73]Interview with Wilson, Fund for Community Redevelopment and Revitalization, Chicago, May 19, 1997.

[74]James O. Stampley, *Challenges with Changes: A Documentary of Englewood* (Chicago: By the Author, 1979), p. 74.

[75]Interview with Jarrett, The Habitat Company, Chicago, Dec. 11, 1997. Abraham Morgan, Cecil Davis, John Paul Jones, and Henry Wilson—all of whom were involved in the EZ application process—also offered their reactions.

[76]Lenz interview.

[77]Gardner, p. 99.

[78]Pennick interview.

[79]Regarding Presidential leadership, an example of the former is James David Barber and his iterations of *The Presidential Character*. David Skowronek (*The Politics Presidents Make*) takes the latter view.

[80]See Granovetter, "Economic Action and Social Structure: The Problem of Embeddedness," *American Journal of Sociology* 91 (1985): 481–510.

[81]See Cornelia Butler Flora and Jan L. Flora, "Entrepreneurial Social Infrastructure: A Necessary Ingredient," *Annals of American Association of Political and Social Sciences* 529 (Sep. 1993): 48–58.

[82]See Schneider, Teske, and Mintrom, especially pp. 96–110.

[83]Schneider and Teske, "Toward a Theory of the Political Entrepreneur: Evidence from Local Government," *American Political Science Review* 86 (Sep. 1992): 737–747.

[84]Pennick interview.

[85]Farry interview.

[86]Lance interview.

[87]To win election she had to overcome (among other things) the best efforts of her husband, who actively campaigned for Jim Taylor. Apparently the influence of the Machine superseded that of marriage, at least in the 16th Ward.

[88]Lance interview.

CHAPTER 7

The Role of Institutional Actors in Revitalizing Neighborhoods

The previous chapter outlined the components of revitalization in two Chicago neighborhoods. Comparing the improving North Lawndale community with its less successful Englewood counterpart enabled us to identify the institutional, social, and personal factors that contribute to effective attempts at inner-city development. The chapter's scope was necessarily broad, emphasizing the interplay among various economic, historical, political, and social forces. It reiterated the findings in Chapter 4 that there is no single overarching cause of revitalization, and that the process is best understood through a qualitative analysis of local decisions and interactions.

This chapter takes a more focused look at the process of revitalization by concentrating on the contributions (and non-contributions) of six distinct urban actors: banks, community development corporations (CDCs), churches, social service agencies, foundations, and city government. Drawing upon the existing literature, interviews with various agency and organizational representatives, and the case studies of North Lawndale and Englewood, the chapter explores the roles that each of these actors plays in turning around inner-city neighborhoods.

The findings of this chapter are meant to be suggestive, not definitive. Unlike most studies, this one has selected case studies based on the dependent variable (revitalization) rather than on independent variables such as CDCs or churches. The analysis therefore has focused primarily on what causes revitalization, and secondarily on how and to what extent particular entities affect the process. In addition, the observations of individual actors' roles are based on a small sample of communities within a single city. North Lawndale and Englewood are certainly representative of economically distressed urban neighborhoods, and Chicago's experience is similar to that of other old industrial cities, yet there may well be some differences across neighborhoods and municipalities.

While recognizing the importance of schools to the life and health of a community, this chapter deliberately does not focus on their role in revitalization. The quality of public education largely determines the fortunes of a community. Neighborhoods with good schools tend to attract stable families, as individuals seek to ensure a quality education for their children. Parents who place a high value on education are typically well-educated themselves, with decent jobs paying them livable wages. They generally have good labor skills and benefit from a range of interpersonal relationships within the workplace, characteristics that help build both the community's human and social capital. In contrast, the presence of poor schools in a neighborhood dissuades families with school-age children from living there. The low quality of urban public school systems has been a leading cause of the middle class's exodus from the nation's central cities to the surrounding suburbs. Mayor Richard M. Daley's primary focus for improving conditions in Chicago has thus been to improve the city's historically abysmal public school system. He rightly contends that only by enhancing public education can the city hope to retain large proportions of its middle-class residents.

Daley's efforts build on a local school reform movement that began in the late 1980s. Although some involved in the process contend that real improvements have taken place, many schools and their surrounding neighborhoods remain deeply troubled. Englewood's schools continue to be among the worst in the city, as evidenced by a recent decision to overhaul the schools' management. North Lawndale's public education system is not much better. Both communities have average parochial elementary schools: they are generally seen as more effective than the public schools but are nothing special in comparison to other parochial schools throughout the city. In short, while excellent local schools can be building blocks for neighborhood revitalization, the schools in North Lawndale and Englewood have not and are not serving that purpose. Neither their conventional educational efforts nor their external, "community-related" activities have played any substantial role in the economic rejuvenation or stagnation of their neighborhoods. How they could become more central players in the process involves much broader issues of educational reform, managerial and bureaucratic restructuring, family stabilization, improved health care, and so forth, topics which lie outside the scope of this study. The following sections examine the role of some of the other major actors in inner-city neighborhoods.

BANKS

Capital is crucial for the development of any community. People need money to make long-term investments in their homes and businesses. Decisions to reroof, add another room, or re-stabilize the foundation of a house represent a commitment to the physical maintenance and improvement of the house and, by extension, the broader community. Similarly, decisions to modernize a business, start a company, and/or upgrade to a larger location indicate faith in the area and a willingness to enhance the local economy.

All of these investment decisions require access to a reasonable amount of capital, monies that most individuals (and most small businesses) generally do not have on hand. Investors therefore choose to incur debt to finance their projects. As the most accessible source of debt financing, banks become essential to the economic future of a neighborhood. They offer a safe place in which to keep money, and they provide mortgages, small business loans, and home improvement funds. With fewer available public funds for housing and small business development, local developers and investors have had to rely increasingly on private sources of capital to improve conditions in the communities.

Banks and inner-city neighborhoods have long viewed each other with suspicion, however. The Federal Housing Authority's rating of minority neighborhoods as poor lending risks caused numerous financial institutions to redline the communities, effectively shutting them off from access to credit (see Chapter 3). Banks closed most of their inner-city branches and opened additional offices in more stable suburban communities. Without access to conventional loans, residents of neighborhoods such as North Lawndale and Englewood had to resort to contract buying and other usurious forms of borrowing.

Although banks have become more active in these communities, they are still not a major presence. Check cashing facilities outnumber bank branches by a ratio of 12 to 1 in North Lawndale and 7 to 1 in Englewood. Check cashers provide valuable services to local residents, particularly in enabling them to access cash quickly, but they do not offer the broader lending, deposit, and other financial services of a mainstream bank. The check cashers' fees typically exceed those of a bank, placing local residents at a financial disadvantage.[1]

One solution to the problem of limited capital access has been the establishment of community- and development-oriented banks. Institutions such as the Community Bank of Lawndale and South Shore Bank tend to be owned at least in part by individuals with a vested local interest, many of whom are minorities. The banks focus on providing a set of services to a traditionally under-served community, assuming that they can create a market niche for themselves by tapping into the unmet demand for financial services. At the same time, they hope to spur reinvestment in the neighborhood by providing seed capital to local real estate and small business concerns. The loan portfolios of these banks tend to constitute a much larger proportion of their assets than do the loans of more mainstream banks. Yet the higher risk associated with many of these loans leads to higher rates of default. The banks' continued solvency results in part from the willingness of their investors to receive a lower return on their money; for example, officials at South Shore Bank actively solicited depositors who were willing to forsake a higher financial return in exchange for promoting the social good of redeveloping the South Shore community.

These locally oriented banks have had mixed results. Minority-owned banks have historically struggled both to lend within their targeted neighborhoods and to remain financially viable entities. Their record of lending in low-income minority communities is not markedly better than that of their white-owned counterparts; many have received relatively poor ratings from Community Reinvestment Act regulators.[2] For example, as mentioned in Chapter 5, the black-owned Highland Community Bank on Chicago's south side faced considerable local opposition to its proposed purchase of a white-owned bank because of Highland's poor lending record in Englewood, West Englewood, and Greater Grand Crossing.[3] Much of the community banks' difficulty results from their relatively low levels of available loan capital. Operating in low- and moderate-income neighborhoods, they do not generate a particularly large base of local deposits. Their location, minority ownership, and limited marketing generate limited investment from whites, many of whom are wary of (and/or prejudiced against) supporting institutions in poor inner-city areas. Because of the banks' limited asset base, their loans tend to be more closely scrutinized by federal regulators concerned about the banks' ongoing financial viability. The banks hesitate to make higher-risk loans lest they be censured or restructured by the regulators.

Inner-city development banks have fared somewhat better. Unlike traditional banks, development banks focus principally on the comprehensive revitalization of a community or communities, not on the provision of credit and financial services. They see the provision of capital as merely one component of the broader revitalization process and often have affiliated organizations that provide other community-building activities.[4] The Chicago based Shorebank Corporation, for example, manages development banks in Chicago, Cleveland, and Detroit, and has contemplated opening another bank in Washington, DC. Other development banks have emerged in cities as diverse as Kansas City, Louisville, Milwaukee, and Oakland.

South Shore Bank, one of Shorebank's subsidiaries, has regularly been profitable for its shareholders (although not as profitable as other, non-development-oriented banks) while remaining true to its mission of helping to redevelop the South Shore community. Yet the bank's impact on its community is difficult to quantify. South Shore has declined noticeably in the past few decades. Poverty and unemployment are up, and both per capita incomes and property values have fallen relative to the city average. Clearly the neighborhood's decline has stemmed from a variety of the social, economic, and political factors described in Chapter 3. The bank may well have succeeded in slowing the decline and/or moderating its effects.[5] The fact nevertheless remains that it alone could not staunch the economic deterioration of its community. The Community Bank of Lawndale has played a major role in the revitalization of North Lawndale, yet its influence has been as much psychological as financial. Like other minority institutions, it struggled to earn the respect of regulators and investors. It has been limited in its ability to promote and support local economic activity. In short, it has not single-handedly sparked change in the community.

Although development banks such as CBL and South Shore Bank can promote change, the long-term viability of a neighborhood depends more on the involvement of larger financial institutions that have historically been leery of inner-city communities. As mentioned in Chapter 3, banks have become increasingly active in low-income neighborhoods in response to the Community Reinvestment Act. Banks are regularly evaluated on their performance in their designated service areas and the assessments are made public. Banks must also submit to public scrutiny when they apply for a new "deposit facility" (a new branch or an off-site ATM facility, for example). Although the CRA carries with it no particular sanctions, regulators can deny a bank's application if they find the bank's local lending practices wanting. Bankers consequently have two primary reasons for complying with the CRA. They want to avoid the negative public relations sure to accompany a "needs to improve" or "substantial noncompliance" CRA evaluation. They also want to preclude time-consuming CRA challenges from community groups when they are looking to merge with another bank and/or substantially expand their activities. The Act has helped promote inner-city lending. CBL President Diane Glenn claims that "CRA has helped poor communities get attention and respect" from the banking community.[6] One tangible example has been The Northern Trust's opening of a new branch in the south side Chicago neighborhood of Chatham as a result of pressure from the Department of Justice to address the bank's previous discrimination against minority mortgage applicants.

CRA considerations constitute the primary reason for banks' investment in neighborhoods such as North Lawndale. Kristin Faust, the Senior Vice President at LaSalle National Bank, explains that "CRA is why we're there [in low-income neighborhoods]. There's intense CRA pressure to be active" in these areas.[7] Ed Jacob, a Vice President at First Chicago, concurs with Faust. "We need loans in Lawndale because of CRA." The regulations have caused the bank to provide numerous loans and grants to the Lawndale Christian Development Corporation and to establish a direct deposit program with the Lawndale Health Center. Would First Chicago support LCDC without the pressures of CRA? "I don't know," he replied.[8] CRA considerations, not the involvement of established developer Charlie Shaw, drove the initial financing of the Homan Square project.[9] The success of that development, coupled with the improvements in other sections of the community, have made North Lawndale a prime target for banks' neighborhood lending programs. First Chicago regularly competes with Northern, LaSalle, and (to a lesser extent) Harris for loans in the area, especially with the new CRA emphasis on small business lending.

Bankers are also realizing the increasing profitability of loans in these neighborhoods. Chris Brown, the Housing Director at Chicago's United Way, remembers only a few years ago having "to drag bankers in and tell them they're making a loan" in low-income neighborhoods. "That's changed with the realization that profits are possible."[10] Banks such as First Chicago, LaSalle, and Bank of America have become involved in these communities to a much greater extent than CRA requires. Bottom-line considerations drive their actions. Mary White, a Vice President at Bank of America-Illinois, emphasizes that the bank looks for tangible returns on its inner-city investments. Its profitability in these markets has committed it to additional lending, with or without the

CRA.[11] The *American Banker* reported that all of the city's banks are making money from their neighborhood lending programs.[12] Bankers no longer view CRA-inspired investment as simply a cost of doing business, but as a way of increasing the bank's assets. A Bank One representative explains that inner-city lending "is good business, you don't lose money doing CRA, [and] it's the right thing to do."[13] Bank of America President William Goodyear has repeatedly stated that investment in the inner-city is in the bank's economic and personal self-interest. In the early 1990s the Shaw Company scrambled to attract financial support for the Homan Square project; now First Chicago, The Northern Trust, Harris Bank, Chase Manhattan Bank, American National Bank, and PMC Bank are all involved.[14]

In fulfilling CRA regulations and maximizing their local profits, bankers still favor certain low-income neighborhoods over others. For example, First Chicago recently opened a branch in North Lawndale; it has not considered opening one in Englewood. Local demographic and economic factors still dominate bankers' decision-making processes, particularly for the significant capital commitments involved in opening new branches. Kristin Faust explains that LaSalle looks first to moderate-income neighborhoods such as Chatham and Roseland for new branches. Englewood, as one of the poorest neighborhoods in the city, simply does not have the capital base that could support a branch.[15]

Banks have sought to maximize their potential for profits and local impact by targeting a few neighborhoods for concentrated investment. First Chicago focused on Grand Boulevard and South Lawndale (Little Village) in the late 1980s and has recently added North Lawndale. As part of the bank's commitment to a community, bank officials establish a consumer outreach and education division, help potential home buyers understand the responsibilities associated with owning a home, and work with local organizations to encourage small business development.

Deciding to invest in a neighborhood depends in large part on the relationships bankers have and can build with local individuals and organizations. First Chicago selected its target communities because its lenders knew community leaders and believed in their ability to help create and maintain a reasonably stable financial environment. Bankers certainly conduct extensive market research, but a considerable part of the neighborhood investment process is much less scientific. It is a "matter of turning a big corporate bank into a small town, community bank. . . . The corporation is risk-averse and the community is risky. You have to make a lot of gut decisions," explains former First Chicago lender Susan

Plasmeier.[16] Ultimately a bank's decision to lend depends on the trust between the banker and the potential borrower. Particularly with loans to small businesses (most of which have not been around long enough to have demonstrated financial stability, even to the point of creating financial statements), the bank is essentially financing the owner. "If the owner has good credit, we assume the business will be the same," explains Ed Jacob, who emphasized that Charlie Shaw's presence enabled the bank to become involved in Homan Square.[17]

Relationships with individuals ultimately determine the extent of a bank's involvement in a particular neighborhood, yet building those relationships remains a tricky process. Banks looking to move into a community rarely have a wide array of local contacts. Bankers may know a few influential people in the neighborhood, but those individuals by themselves are seldom able to support a broader lending strategy. Bankers therefore rely on local institutions to help them develop a local market. In exchange for financing, the institutions can help the bankers become more familiar with the local environment and identify other potential borrowers. Good working partnerships with stable and respected local institutions are therefore crucial for successful investment in inner-city markets.

COMMUNITY DEVELOPMENT CORPORATIONS (CDCS)

Community development corporations, or CDCs, help banks create such partnerships. Generally nonprofit organizations governed by boards of local residents, CDCs pursue a variety of strategies designed to improve conditions in their neighborhoods. An outgrowth of both the settlement house and community organizing movements, CDCs formally came into being in the mid-1960s, when then-Senator Robert Kennedy helped establish the Bedford-Stuyvesant Restoration Corporation in Brooklyn. Kennedy envisioned that the groups would create employment opportunities for community residents through a mixture of education and training efforts, small business development, and grass-roots advocacy. Above all, they would serve as intermediaries among public, private, and nonprofit agencies, helping to galvanize the support and participation of each sector for the revitalization of the inner city.[18]

By the mid-1990s there were a few thousand CDCs in operation throughout the country, including over 75 in Chicago. The groups had earned a reputation as some of the leading actors in the neighborhood revitalization industry, capable of bringing a variety of people together around common goals and successfully leveraging public and private monies for specific development projects. California Congressman Matthew Martinez lauded the groups for achieving a $4 return for every federal dollar they received.[19] Both former Treasury Secretary Robert Rubin and former HUD Secretary Henry Cisneros praised the groups' efforts on numerous occasions. In Chicago alone the groups have developed over 10,500 units of affordable housing and over 1.5 million square feet of commercial real estate in low- and moderate-income neighborhoods since 1980.[20] As detailed in Chapter 4, the presence of a CDC or similar community organization in a neighborhood is positively correlated (.52) with improvements in the community's economic conditions.

Although initially designed to improve local economic conditions using a wide range of methodologies, CDCs have focused principally on real estate development. Andrew Ditton, a private developer in Chicago who was formerly the Vice President at LISC, has described CDCs as "nonprofit real estate companies." The groups are best known for their development of affordable housing. With the cutbacks in HUD's budget and the boom in suburban real estate in the 1980s, CDCs for a few years were producing more units of low-income housing than either the federal government or the private sector.[21] The organizations have taken advantage of housing monies made available through multiple sources: federal Community Development Block Grants and homeless programs, the federal Low Income Housing Tax Credit, city and state grants and low-interest loans, foundations, corporate donations, and banks seeking to meet CRA requirements, to name a few. Developing housing has enabled the groups to meet a distinct local need and create a clearly visible product, one that could show individuals within and outside the neighborhood that physical improvements were taking place. According to Bill Jones, a long-time CDC director who also served as a LISC Vice President, housing is the "one tangible thing that adds value and has a use. It can't fail as quickly or as readily as a commercial strip."[22]

The CDCs' positive track record in developing residential and commercial real estate has made them particularly attractive to banks interested in investing in inner-city neighborhoods. An internal study by LaSalle National Bank found a strong positive correlation between bank lending and the presence of CDCs in low-income Chicago neighborhoods.[23] Chapter 4 of this study found similar relationships: the presence of CDCs and similar community organizations was correlated .31 with increased residential loan activity in all low- and moderate-income communities, and .43 with increased loan activity in the poor neighborhoods of the old "Black Belt." Accomplished and active CDCs—those with strong local leadership, professional organization and discipline, and demonstrated sustainability—tend to be highly sought-after commodities for area bankers. Ed Jacob contends that Lawndale Christian Development Corporation is routinely courted by the five major Chicago banks and a number of smaller financial institutions. The group has the demonstrated ability to carry out real estate projects, and bankers have confidence in Executive Director Richard Townsell.[24] LCDC's effectiveness, along with that of groups such as The Resurrection Project in Pilsen, the Woodlawn Preservation and Investment Corporation, and Lakefront SRO in Uptown has convinced bankers of the relative security of CDC loans. Officials at First Chicago, the largest bank in the city, do not "see the lending to CDCs as any different than lending to a for-profit developer, in terms of the default rate."[25]

CDCs not only provide loan opportunities for the banking community but also help banks develop their business within the neighborhood. First Chicago Vice President Therese Mierswa considered CDCs one of the best ways of increasing the accessibility of credit for consumers and small businesses. Individuals wishing to buy single-family homes developed by a CDC must first submit to the group's own screening process, an assessment that banks rely on when considering a subsequent mortgage application. Similarly, a number of CDCs are working to promote the development of small businesses by helping budding entrepreneurs with business plans, start-up capital, and other "incubating" services. With the increased CRA emphasis on small business loans, groups such as the Lawndale Business and Local Development Corporation have become increasingly important to banks. Bankers simply do not have the knowledge about the assets, liabilities, cash flow, and potential returns of small companies in communities such as North Lawndale, and they have neither the time nor the resources to obtain the necessary information. CDCs such as LBLDC can help them identify viable business entities and develop appropriate financial packages.

Not surprisingly, the presence and quality of CDCs in a neighborhood often determine the level of outside investment in the area. Both LaSalle and First Chicago have tried to become more involved in Englewood but have been stymied by the lack of established, effective local organizations. Englewood simply does not have an organized CDC, claims Kristin Faust; there are "rumblings," but little significant local activity. "Even without Sears, Lawndale is a little ahead of Englewood because of LCDC."[26] Lenders at First Chicago have generally not found individuals or agencies in Englewood with whom they feel comfortable. The bank really had to stretch its lending guidelines to write mortgages for ACORN's single-family homes.[27]

The impact of CDCs extends beyond banks to other private-sector investors. The groups' real estate efforts help to establish and maintain a base level of market activity in even the most economically distressed communities. Their ability to carry out projects convinces people inside and outside the area that some change is possible. Cecil Butler, one of the largest individual investors in Lawndale, views such organizations as important catalysts for revitalization. "Everything LCDC does helps us. . . . All development in an area is good, even that which fails. It brings in resources, attracts attention, and lays the groundwork" for future projects.[28]

CDCs and their supporters have consistently claimed that they are more than real estate developers, that their range of organizing, job development, and advocacy efforts makes them catalysts of a comprehensive approach to neighborhood development. In a 1992 survey of 130 of the country's more advanced CDCs, Avis Vidal found that over 70 percent engaged in some form of advocacy, 52 percent offered job training and/or placement services, and 41 percent were involved in some sort of social service provision.[29] In the past few years a number of groups have broadened their range of activities. There has been an increased emphasis on influencing local politics through voter registration drives and CDC-sponsored protests. CDCs in Chicago have undertaken projects such as health clinics, day care facilities, charter high schools, and alternative elementary schools.

Yet, as mentioned earlier, the major contribution of CDCs remains real estate development. Affordable housing continues to be the primary activity of the vast majority of these groups, and it is easily their most visible product. New and/or rehabilitated buildings clearly indicate improvement in a distressed area. The number of housing units and the amount of commercial square footage constitute "hard," quantifiable measures of production, whereas determining the impact of "softer" programs such as advocacy, organizing, job preparation, and crime prevention proves much more difficult.[30] Some believe, however, that CDCs have become too focused on packaging deals and carrying out specific projects and have moved away from their overall mission of revitalizing the neighborhood. Bill Jones, for one, contends that CDCs have to be social and political leaders as well as developers. Real estate projects provide tangible, deliverable benefits to an area but need to be supported by efforts to improve community safety, education, and employment prospects. One of the groups for which he has the highest regard is LCDC: "It's not the best-run or most productive group in the city, but it's really about leadership-building." Not only does the group operate a college opportunity program, but it has consistently striven to encourage local individuals to take positions of responsibility. David Doig phased himself out of the organization so that Lawndale resident Richard Townsell could become Executive Director; Townsell has mandated that his staff members live in the neighborhood.

The extent to which the CDCs' non-real estate activities contribute to the economic revitalization of their neighborhoods remains unclear. Xavier de Souza Briggs and Elizabeth Mueller's recent case studies of three of the country's most comprehensive CDCs suggest that the groups have limited effects. The CDCs's anti-crime efforts have helped produce real and perceived improvements in neighborhood safety, but there otherwise has been no noticeable enhancement in the communities' level of social capital.[31] LCDC's real estate efforts (including the development of its health center) are seen as its primary contributions to North Lawndale's revitalization; relatively little mention is made of its youth programs and community organizing efforts. Undoubtedly these efforts (and similar ones of other CDCs) have an indirect effect on revitalization by adding to the neighborhood's social capital, but the CDCs' more direct contribution still lies in their real estate activity.

CHURCHES

The development of social capital nonetheless remains a critical part of effective inner-city revitalization efforts. In the fall of 1996, LaSalle National Bank sponsored two public forums on "Lessons Learned" from its experience lending in Chicago's low- and moderate-income neighborhoods. Two general themes emerged from the sessions. First, effective investment resulted from partnerships between banks and local institutions. Second, a certain amount of community organization and stability were essential for attracting investors. It was much easier for banks to lend in neighborhoods in which strong institutions promoted and maintained a sense of order and social cohesion. Among other things, such organizing efforts helped create the stability necessary for physical development projects to go forward. The success of residential complexes and retail facilities was much less likely in areas with high levels of crime and social disorder.

Although CDCs and other local organizations have tried in various ways to develop this form of social capital, they have not had as much apparent success as local churches. Long viewed as institutional anchors in a community, churches have recently attracted increased attention from urban policy makers. There is a growing sense that the outreach efforts of many local churches have begun to stabilize communities previously wracked by crime and drugs.[32] Churches have often provided needy congregants and area residents with meals, clothing, counseling, and occasional shelter. These activities, coupled with regular worship services, have helped to bring people together for a common purpose. The churches can therefore mobilize people for change, especially if the preacher uses the pulpit to encourage congregants to action.

The quantifiable effect of church activity on neighborhood development remains unclear. This study found no correlation ($-.01$) between the number of churches in a community and its degree of revitalization.[33] A recent examination of church activity in inner-city neighborhoods found little effect of church attendance on increased education levels. Both predominantly black and predominantly white churches offer a range of social service activities, yet little is known about their impact on a neighborhood.[34] The qualitative and historical evidence of churches' importance in promoting social change is indisputable, however. Southern Baptist churches played a crucial role in spawning and sustaining the Civil Rights Movement.

Churches have clearly been active in addressing the needs of Chicago's low-income neighborhoods. United Baptist operates a number of social service programs, including a food pantry and a drug prevention program, for needy residents of North Lawndale. Both the Lawndale-based Union Hill and Greater Open Door Baptist churches provide a range of counseling services and basic sustenance to community members. St. Agatha's runs an after-school program. Antioch Baptist has developed hundreds of housing units in Englewood, and a group of churches have formed the Bethesda Waters consortium to develop affordable housing in Lawndale. Churches throughout the west and south sides have held prayer vigils and have sponsored neighborhood watch efforts to address local problems of drugs and violence. The Catholic Church continues to operate a number of elementary schools in both North Lawndale and Englewood. Including St. Bernard's Hospital and the social agencies operated out of former church facilities, the Church is the largest human needs provider in Englewood.

Although they have been active in each community, churches have had a greater impact on revitalization in North Lawndale than in Engle-wood. As described in Chapters 5 and 6, Presentation, St. Agatha's, and the Lawndale Community Church have promoted community organiza-tion and stimulated local economic development. Each has worked to re-duce some of the systemic barriers to neighborhood change. For the most part, the activities of the Englewood churches have focused on meeting the immediate needs of individual residents, but not the broader develop-ment needs of the community as a whole.

Within North Lawndale, the Catholic churches have been noticeably more active than the Baptist churches in promoting revitalization. Part of the difference results from the personalities involved. Wayne Gordon contends that "Mike Ivers and [Presentation pastor] Tom Walsh dream dreams of revitalization every night," while other clergymen in the neighborhood do not. Yet the churches' activism typifies a broader trend throughout Chicago. With a few exceptions (most notably Arthur Bra-zier's Apostolic Church of God in Woodlawn and the Episcopal St. Ed-mund's in Washington Park), the Catholic Church tends to be the religious institution most involved in mobilizing local residents and pro-moting revitalization in the city's low-income neighborhoods.[35] The Resurrection Project, arguably the most successful CDC in the city, emerged from the organizing efforts of Pilsen's Catholic churches.

Catholics have historically constituted the largest single religious community in Chicago, a result of the city's considerable Irish, Polish, Italian, and Mexican populations. The majority of the city's twentieth-century mayors have been Catholic, most notably the Daleys, as have a significant proportion of their aides and appointees. The regularity with which ethnic Catholics have supported the two Daleys has given the in-stitutional Church a certain degree of political clout within the city. St. Thomas Pastor Jack Farry views the Church as an "arrival institution," one that has traditionally given a Catholic new to Chicago a slight leg up over his or her non-Catholic counterparts.

As part of the larger Archdiocese, each local Catholic church is as-sociated with a substantial pool of human and financial resources. The Archdiocese has the resources to build a new church in North Lawndale and/or a new school in Englewood should it choose to do so. It regularly transfers resources from more affluent parishes to poorer ones. It has a long-standing relationship with the Industrial Areas Foundation, the community organizing legacy of Saul Alinsky. The Cardinal (or Arch-bishop) routinely receives widespread coverage in the local media. These built-in structural characteristics contrast with the largely self-sufficient, independently chartered Baptist churches that predominate in low-income areas such as Lawndale and Englewood. Whereas individual Catholic churches are part of a regional and global institutional hierarchy, Baptist churches are accountable only to their members. "Nobody can tell the pastor how to run the church" in the Baptist community, asserts Leonard DeVille, the pastor of Englewood's Alpha Temple Missionary Baptist Church.[36] Because individual Baptist churches tend not to be as institutionally and politically connected as their Catholic counterparts, they tend to have a more difficult time accessing resources. Lawndale Alderman Michael Chandler, a Catholic, explains that the City "doesn't see black churches as positively [as CDCs or other churches] in terms of lending money for economic development. A number of [church] groups have been turned down for CDBG money."[37]

Difficulty securing resources partly explains the relatively limited involvement of black Protestant churches in neighborhood development. Numerous churches in the city's low-income neighborhoods can barely afford to maintain a storefront location, let alone embark on a campaign to change their surrounding neighborhood. The preeminent role of the pastor in most black denominations tends to reduce the number of lay leaders in inner-city religious communities. In his efforts to mobilize interdenominational support for IAF organizing, Tom Lenz has found members of many black Protestant churches much less receptive than the Catholics, Lutherans, and Jews with whom he has met.[38] In the black churches, the decision to become involved in community development activities tends to rest almost entirely with the individual minister. While many ministers try to improve conditions in their neighborhoods, others prefer to remain outside the economic and political arenas. According to United Baptist pastor Wilson Daniels, there is a certain wariness among many black ministers of becoming involved in Chicago politics. Without the backing of a broader church consortium or federation (a daunting task considering the vagaries of church politics), individual ministers tend to be perceived by the media as greedy or self-interested. They run the risk of being seen within their communities as either selling out to the establishment or doing nothing if their actions do not quickly lead to tangible improvements.[39] Furthermore, there are simply "lots of ministers without a commitment to doing anything outside of saving souls in church. That's fine," acknowledges Rick Daniel, the son of Antioch pastor Wilbur Daniel, "but [places like Englewood] really need help."[40]

The lack of strong leadership from the pulpit has combined with other forces to limit the involvement of many inner-city black churches in activities geared to promoting social change. Many regular worshipers now live in the suburbs and come back to their original neighborhood only to attend church. The focus of their lives is much different from that of individuals still living in North Lawndale or Englewood; they are more likely to have jobs, live in safer neighborhoods, and have access to a wider range of economic and social opportunities. In short, they are not as personally vested in issues of neighborhood revitalization. (Wilson Daniels contends that too many people within the black community have become "at ease in Zion," content with the opportunities they have and somewhat oblivious to the distinct problems of their inner-city neighbors. Because they have access to some of the region's best jobs, many young blacks "don't see the need for things like Operation PUSH," Jesse Jackson's organization for promoting minority hiring.[41]) Without a strong, unified commitment to change on the part of their members, the churches are unlikely to become major players in local revitalization efforts.

Many people question if churches should be at all concerned with such activities. Neighborhood revitalization is not the primary mission of churches, regardless of their denomination. The churches are primarily places of worship, and the priests and ministers' chief responsibility is to be spiritual leaders. At the same time, many clergymen and lay people believe that effective ministry must somehow address individuals' economic, social, emotional, and political needs, not just their spiritual needs. The churches' moral and institutional position both within neighborhoods and in the city as a whole makes the churches potentially strong forces for economic and social change. Whether or not that potential is actualized depends on a mixture of personal and political factors.

SOCIAL SERVICE AGENCIES

Although they have not always been catalysts of social change, churches have historically played a leading role in providing basic human services. The Biblical tenet of providing alms to the poor has manifested itself in the operation of soup kitchens and homeless shelters, the establishment of orphanages, the counseling of battered women, and so forth. The churches' activities spawned a number of organizations specifically geared toward addressing particular human needs. The settlement houses of the late 1800s sought to improve conditions for the urban poor through a mixture of education, emergency food and shelter assistance, exposure to the arts, and community-building. Their success led to the emergence of schools of social work and the professionalization of human services. By 1990 there were over 2,000 human service agencies in Chicago alone, many of whose staff members held advanced degrees in social work. The United Way identified 25 such agencies in both North Lawndale and Englewood in 1994.[42]

The most successful settlement houses—Jane Addams's Hull House, for example—effectively blended individual service provision with more social, community-oriented programs. Few organizations today successfully combine the two approaches; nevertheless, their efforts help to promote social capital within a neighborhood. Community centers foster interpersonal networks by providing educational, recreational, and social opportunities for local residents. The centers' programs enable people to meet and get to know and trust each other. For example, the Ada B. Wells senior agency in Englewood offers a place where the community's elderly residents can meet, share friendship, and obtain needed basic services. The loss of such organizations can negatively affect a neighborhood. Local residents viewed both the Sears YMCA in North Lawndale and the Englewood YMCA as integral parts of their respective communities and feel that the areas have not been the same since their closing.

The vast majority of social service agencies, though, focus on addressing the needs of particular individuals. The range of groups is staggering: food pantries, homeless shelters, AIDS hospices, health clinics, after-school programs, and counseling centers, to name only a few. The Marcy Newberry Association in North Lawndale encourages local youths to stay out of gangs. The National Committee to Prevent Child Abuse, located in the former Sears administration building at Homan Square, works with local mothers giving birth at Mt. Sinai Hospital. Case workers visit the new mothers in their homes to help them care for their new babies. Many of the mothers are teenagers and their babies have low birth weights. Early intervention and regular monitoring of health and nutrition are crucial to the infants' well-being. These and other nonprofit service providers promote revitalization in a community indirectly, by increasing individuals' capacities. Educational groups, health agencies, and other human service organizations are strongly correlated with increases in neighborhood per capita incomes, and less strongly associated with local increases in private investment.[43] Meeting basic human needs and building academic, emotional, and interpersonal skills presumably help enhance people's earning potential.

Staff members at these agencies often view themselves as some of the few stable, concerned individuals in the lives of the needy people with whom they work. Building interpersonal relationships and specific skills therefore take on primary importance. Rutherford Maynard, a social worker at the Bobby E. Wright Comprehensive Mental Health Center on Chicago's west side, believes that the groups are "important in helping individuals find alternatives" to their present situations. By "exposing people to something else," social service agencies "create an appetite [for improvement], counteract despair, and promote social involvement."[44] Wilson Daniels contends that such groups "keep the neighborhood afloat. . . . Lots of people are helped by the food and other things they provide. The little [the groups] do makes a big difference."[45] They both provide a safety net for disadvantaged individuals and help people interact better with each other.

At the same time, the vast majority of these agencies have little involvement in broader issues of neighborhood economic development. They rarely develop real estate, they do not interact with potential investors, and they do not organize community residents around particular political or economic goals. Almost nobody identifies them as catalysts of change in their neighborhoods; they are seen principally as helping to create and maintain a social safety net for area residents.

The groups do not directly engage in revitalization efforts partly because of limited resources. Agencies such as the Chicago Youth Centers (CYC) are trying to work with thousands of poor children suffering from inadequate education, unstable and/or abusive family situations, few supervised recreational opportunities, and other similar problems. They are attempting to provide increased educational, recreational, and counseling services at a time when federal, state, and city monies for antipoverty efforts and social service provision are declining. In effect, they have been given more responsibilities with fewer resources to carry them out. CYC Executive Director Del Arsenault feels that it is unrealistic to expect social service organizations to do much more than they currently are doing. For example, CYC no longer has the funds it used to have to work with young teenagers, individuals whose emerging strength, energy level, need to establish themselves socially, and general insecurity make them potentially some of the the most physically and sexually dangerous members of society. Arsenault would like to expand CYC into Austin and Englewood to address some of those communities' problems but simply cannot afford to do so. He and others remain leery of addressing broader issues of neighborhood revitalization because of the experience of Ben Kendrick at Marcy Newberry in North Lawndale. Kendrick expanded the organization's focus to include affordable housing development and ended up in chapter 11 bankruptcy.[46]

Although funding for education and social services may currently be tight, it has traditionally been more available than monies for development. Agencies such as CYC and the Better Boys Foundation have a wide range of potential donors because of the non-controversial nature of their services. Supporting programs that educate disadvantaged children or counsel battered women is much more appealing to many individual and corporate donors than contributing to affordable housing or economic development initiatives.

The contentions of social service workers notwithstanding, many actively engaged in neighborhood revitalization believe that social service agencies can and should be more involved in the process. As community institutions, the groups do not induce the type of respect that churches do, particularly in North Lawndale. LCDC Executive Director Richard Townsell does not hide his antipathy for the groups. "The agencies tend to have a client relationship with people; they advocate for them and for money for them, but they don't advocate with them. . . . They only advocate around money-related issues. It's just a hustle. . . . They're not mission-driven. It's all straight financial transactions. . . . The staff don't live here. They treat people like crap. . . . The whole thing sickens me."[47] Michael Chandler characterizes them as "grant hustlers."[48] Rev. Mike Ivers believes that the groups are more concerned about their own survival than anything else. Their activities look great on paper, but they have a questionable impact on the problems they are trying to address.[49]

Even though some of the agencies (such as the Better Boys Foundation) have been in North Lawndale for years, they have never taken a leadership role in the community's revitalization. While grudgingly admitting that the organizations have provided some opportunities for area youths, many people associated with the community do not feel as though the groups have made a demonstrable local impact. Longtime Lawndale resident Sam Flowers sees the groups as too narrowly focused in their activities and thus unable to see the broader needs of the neighborhood.[50] Rebecca Riley, the Vice President at the Chicago-based MacArthur Foundation, sees the agencies as too self-absorbed to take an active role in promoting change. "They're primarily concerned with their client base and maintaining their funds." The primary focus of a recent social service consortium that she attended was how the groups could obtain more money and avoid being cut back in their United Way allocations, not how to respond better to community needs.[51]

The competing perspectives stem from fundamentally different approaches social service agencies and more development-oriented groups have toward neighborhood improvement. Development groups tend to focus on promoting investment in the community, whereas social service organizations focus on building the capacity of individual residents. Social service workers generally operate from the premise that if the problems of particular people can be addressed, the neighborhood as a whole will become a better place to live. The specific objectives of social service programs all have a very personal bent: helping people learn to set goals for themselves, developing individuals' self-esteem, building social skills, enhancing participants' ability to think critically, enabling people to become self-sufficient, providing realistic alternatives to gang membership, and so forth. If successfully met, each of these objectives improves conditions for community members, yet the outcomes are much less visible and tangible than a new apartment complex.

Effective social service agencies promote neighborhood revitalization indirectly by strengthening individuals' skills and generally enhancing local social capital. Because the impacts of their activities are not readily apparent, difficult to measure, and often slow in materializing, the groups tend to be seen as non-contributors to the revitalization process. Asking these organizations to take on more of a development, organizing, and/or advocacy focus may simply be unrealistic. "Our first role is to deliver programs for kids, then to become part of the community," explains Arsenault. "We have to make a real decision between public policy and service provision. How many things can we do and do well?"[52] Abraham Morgan, the current head of the Community Bank of Lawndale's development corporation, argues that local agencies such as Family Focus, Marcy Newberry, WACA, and the Duncan YMCA "haven't done a lot, but what do people expect? They're always there to provide services."[53]

There is evidence that some social service groups are trying to become more involved in economic development, however. Meeting the basic needs of disadvantaged individuals and enhancing their skills ideally helps them become better able to function and succeed in society. Yet the individuals' ability to succeed depends in large part on the opportunities available to them; without jobs, they likely cannot make enough money to support themselves and their families. Some agencies have therefore begun to combine job training and job creation. Certain child care centers and food providers have trained members of their target populations for positions within the organizations. Service recipients have become paid service providers. Similarly, some groups providing home-based health care have trained and hired local residents as paraprofessional workers. The programs effectively combine social service provision and economic development.[54]

FOUNDATIONS

Many CDCs and social service agencies owe their continuing existence to the largess of the philanthropic community. Foundations have become increasingly important for nonprofit organizations as the public sector has reduced its financial support for urban development and social welfare programs. Foundations ratcheted up their support of low-income housing efforts in the 1980s. They have continued to be primary supporters of groups and programs that target youths and families, especially in the areas of education and health. The vast majority of foundations and corporate giving programs in Chicago count youth development as a primary area of interest. For example, the Chicago Community Trust in 1996 made grants totaling $6.7 million for health-related programs and $4.2 million for its Children, Youth, and Families Initiative.[55]

Foundations are implicitly involved in local revitalization efforts because of their financial support of local nonprofits, yet their direct support of economic development initiatives has traditionally been limited. Within Chicago, the MacArthur Foundation and the Amoco Foundations have been the only major philanthropies to fund specific neighborhood revitalization efforts on a substantial, consistent basis. Other large, independent foundations such as the Polk Bros. Foundation, the Chicago Community Trust, and the Fry Foundation have concentrated their giving in more traditional arts, education, and social service arenas. Although CDCs and other neighborhood development groups have received some foundation monies, their donations have come principally from banks and other corporations with a vested interest in real estate.

Part of foundation officers' reluctance to support broader revitalization strategies stems from the complexity of the process. Most program officers understand that poverty has multiple components (poor housing, a dearth of good jobs, inadequate education, and the like) but realize that their foundation cannot effectively address all of them. They consequently choose to focus on components that can directly benefit from a relatively small infusion of money. Grants to hire a teacher, buy books for a library, establish an after-school program, hire a counselor, and/or purchase a defibrillator for a hospital offer relatively quick, distinct benefits for a potentially large number of people. In contrast, projects such as housing and commercial development require more money and have immediate benefits for only a few individuals. A grant of $100,000, for example, would typically pay annual salaries of three domestic abuse counselors. The same money would fund the construction of no more than two housing units or a portion of a shopping center.[56] The latter projects might well spur additional investment in the neighborhood, which could ultimately improve conditions for a much larger group of people, but the effects would become evident only after a few years. The revitalization of a neighborhood does not happen overnight, just as its decline takes many years.

Relatively few organizations take such a long-term view, however. Nonprofits need to show results in order to convince their funders (or investors, in the corporate world) of their viability and effectiveness. Foundations are no different. They prefer to fund organizations that can produce quick, definable, and measurable outcomes, "products" that demonstrate that both the grant recipients and, by extension, the foundations have had a positive impact on the designated problem. As a result, foundations tend to fund specific programs instead of providing general organizational support. They hesitate to support ongoing activities and may encourage applicants to structure grant requests around a new initiative.[57]

Those associated with foundations like to perceive themselves as social innovators and the foundations as experimental institutions that can use their monies to test and promote new solutions to social problems. Many foundation officers continually look to fund new groups offering a different approach to a particular problem; some foundations even have moratoriums against funding an organization for more than a few consecutive years. The emphasis on funding new programs encourages creative thinking among potential grant recipients. A number of past foundation initiatives have reshaped the design and implementation of national social policy. For example, the Ford Foundation's Gray Areas program in the early 1960s, one that bypassed existing governmental bureaucracies and directly funded nonprofits to undertake preventive antipoverty measures, served as the blueprint for the federal Community Action Program. More recently, the New York-based Surdna Foundation's Comprehensive Community Revitalization program in the South Bronx has served as a model for similar neighborhood development projects in Chicago.

At the same time, the quest for innovation can prevent organizations from concentrating the bulk of their energies on developing, enhancing, and maintaining existing programs that are successful. Too often nonprofits must try to add new wrinkles to their programs in an effort to satisfy foundation officers of their ability to develop innovative solutions. The foundations' focus on programs and aversion to providing general support has provoked widespread criticism from both donees and scholars of philanthropy.[58] Staff members in the recipient groups find themselves so busy scrambling to keep programs operational from one year to the next that they cannot devote sufficient time to broader concerns of organizational development and stability.

Foundation-driven innovations such as the Gray Areas Program and the Comprehensive Community Revitalization initiative are notable in large part because they are so rare. In general, foundations tend to be remarkably similar in their grantmaking, funding most of the same organizations and types of programs in cities throughout the country. Critics have routinely chided foundations for their lack of imagination in designing and implementing grant programs.[59] Most foundations approach grantmaking with a conservative orientation toward problem-solving. Issues of service delivery, not power and politics, typically constitute their primary concern. For all of their rhetoric about innovation, foundations tend to be unwilling to challenge the social and economic status quo. Few foundations support community organizing activities, efforts on the part of local groups to mobilize residents to push for economic, political, and/or social change. In Chicago, the birthplace of modern community organizing, only the Woods Fund and the Wieboldt Foundation have consistently funded such efforts. Foundation officers tend to think in terms of specific programs that address specific individual needs, not more complicated endeavors targeting broader neighborhood and/or systemic deficiencies. The most active foundations in terms of promoting broader structural change currently tend to be conservative in their political outlook.[60]

The foundations' propensity to pursue more traditional approaches to social problem-solving has affected their choice of neighborhoods in which to target grant monies. In Chicago, Grand Boulevard has received a considerable amount of foundation monies because of its large number of social service agencies working with poor public housing residents. Similarly, the Near West Side has received millions of dollars because of the presence of agencies such as Hull House and the hospitals associated with the area's medical complex. North Lawndale has received a fair amount of philanthropic dollars because of its base of established social organizations. In contrast, Englewood and Washington Park, two of the city's poorest and least organized communities, have received relatively little foundation assistance. To Rebecca Riley, the geographic disparities are to be expected. "Foundations are basically conservative entities. . . . They follow others and go where it's seemingly safer."[61] Aurie Pennick, a former Program Officer at MacArthur, considers foundations to be "like everyone else in making calculated risks": Englewood is essentially a dead area, one with little chance of generating a positive return on a foundation's investment.[62]

With a few exceptions, foundations respond to local concerns as expressed through grant proposals, but do not actively start new endeavors in especially troubled areas. Here again local leadership plays an important role. Individuals within the needy community must convincingly call attention to a problem and propose a reasonable solution for it. More organized communities tend to have better, more competent local leaders. Riley and other MacArthur staff members do not see anybody in Englewood with the capacity to implement a meaningful neighborhood improvement program. Certain individuals have repeatedly applied for grants, but they are "simply not the answer." One person so regularly badgered and harassed Foundation staff members that he became the only person in MacArthur's history to be given a moratorium against future involvement with the Foundation.[63]

It would be a mistake to portray foundations as entirely reactive, however. In the late 1980s, MacArthur devoted $11 million to the multiyear Fund for Community Development, a program jointly operated with the Chicago LISC office to build the organizational capacity of the city's CDCs. The Boston-based Riley Foundation has been particularly active in promoting local change. It essentially adopted the Dudley Street Neighborhood Initiative (DSNI), a grassroots organization seeking to revitalize the severely disinvested Dudley section of south Boston. In addition to providing seed money for staff salaries, community planning, and tenant organizing, the Foundation helped coordinate and facilitate meetings among local residents, among outside public, private, and nonprofit institutions, and between community members and these external groups. The Riley Foundation has remained integrally involved in the revitalization process while steadfastly refusing to guide it, choosing instead to have DSNI and Dudley residents design and carry out the organizing and development strategy.[64]

The Riley Foundation's approach has served as a model for the

Steans Family Foundation. A relatively small Chicago philanthropy established by the Steans family in the early 1990s, the Foundation has actively promoted the revitalization of North Lawndale. Like most other foundations, Steans initially focused on youth education. The Foundation sponsored an "I Have a Dream" program to provide higher education opportunities to selected poor elementary school students in the city. Convinced of the importance of family- and community-based programs, the trustees decided in 1995 to expand and restructure the Foundation's activities to concentrate on improving conditions in one disadvantaged Chicago neighborhood; Steans's funds could achieve the greatest impact if they were concentrated in a relatively small area. Executive Director Greg Darnieder and the trustees identified five of Chicago's most distressed areas (including North Lawndale and Englewood), and Darnieder met with individuals associated with each community. Based on these meetings, he and the Steanses decided to target at least 70 percent of the Foundation's annual giving (between $600,000 and $1 million) to North Lawndale. The community had the greatest number of individuals and organizations in whom Darnieder had confidence, and Charlie Shaw's involvement in Homan Square indicated renewed market interest in the neighborhood.

Having committed the bulk of its resources to the neighborhood, the Foundation did not wait for locally generated proposals. Instead, Darnieder and Steans family members consulted extensively with individuals associated with North Lawndale to develop a strategy that would maximize the impact of the Foundation's money. The resulting plan— one that continues to evolve—called for a multi-pronged approach to neighborhood improvement. The Foundation has provided grants to Manley High School to help it establish school-to-work programs for its students, including a year-round student builders initiative that focuses on housing rehabilitation. It has funded the opening of a Neighborhood Housing Services office in the community and has established a loan fund to finance the acquisition and construction of single- and multi-family housing. The Foundation has supported the expansion of local child care facilities and paid CANDO to conduct a feasibility study for commercial development at the intersection of Roosevelt and Pulaski Avenues. It has promoted the development of local leadership by funding LCDC's Lawndale Leadership Initiative, a nascent community organizing effort seeking to enhance and create local block clubs, increase voter registration, and potentially establish a community newspaper.

In contrast to the typical philanthropic orientation toward social services, the Steans Family Foundation has sought to catalyze invest-ment in North Lawndale. In seeking to leverage an additional $2 for each of its grant dollars, the Foundation has taken a role similar to that of the Riley Foundation in Boston. Darnieder and the Steanses regularly pro-mote North Lawndale's physical, locational, organizational, and human as-sets. The Foundation is one of the largest investors in Sable Bancshares, and staff members meet regularly with the bankers to explore lending and development opportunities in the neighborhood. Darnieder and the Steanses routinely serve as brokers and facilitators among organizations within North Lawndale and between Lawndale groups and outside insti-tutions, helping to build inter-agency relationships and mobilize extra fi-nancial and human resources for the neighborhood.

The Foundation's efforts have earned it widespread praise both within and outside the community. LCDC Executive Director Richard Townsell lauds it for being "really good." Steans has not come in with its own particular agenda, but has been willing to listen, work closely with members of the community, and approach revitalization in a very strate-gic manner.[65] Deputy Housing Commissioner David Doig has a "real re-spect for the way [the Foundation has] done this." It looks at the community strategically to see where it can add the most value and em-phasizes a grassroots, bottom-up methodology. For example, the Foun-dation has designated a small pool of money (roughly $50,000) for a committee of local residents to allocate annually as the committee sees fit. Although Steans has obviously not eliminated North Lawndale's problems, it is slowly making a noticeable impact in the community.[66]

CITY GOVERNMENT

As the philanthropic community has justly received mixed reactions to its involvement in neighborhood revitalization activities, so too have the vast majority of city governments. Mayors and city council members across the country have routinely come under fire for neglecting the needs of low-income neighborhoods while devoting considerable public resources to projects in the central business district and more affluent communities. Community activists in Chicago have consistently lam-basted City Hall for seeming to ignore poorer neighborhoods. The Neighborhood Capital Budget Group, for one, has accused the City of fa-voring particular wards in the allocation of resources for public infra-structure improvements. Both the Chicago 21 plan (a proposal to redevelop the communities surrounding the Loop) in the early 1970s and the City's application to host the World's Fair in the early 1990s generated widespread opposition among residents of low- and moderate-income neighborhoods. Local activists viewed the plans as inequitable concentrations of scarce resources: each proposal would principally benefit corporate interests at the expense of needy neighborhoods. Lawndale residents have historically doubted the City's commitment to the community's well-being, and many Englewood activists believe that the City considers their neighborhood to be a dumping ground for its more vexing problems.

City officials by themselves simply cannot address the problems of poor neighborhoods. The physical and economic regeneration of certain communities requires a significant infusion of resources, and municipal governments have a limited pool of funds from which to draw. Those monies must support the provision of basic city-wide public services such as fire prevention, policing, education, and garbage pickup, services that maintain both a city's economic activity and its general quality of life. Obtaining the monies to meet other needs proves problematic. Cities already tend to have higher property tax rates than their surrounding suburbs, in part because of the broader range of services they provide and because of the proportionally higher concentration of tax-exempt non-profit and governmental property in the downtown area. If public officials raise taxes much more, they risk driving individual and corporate residents out of the municipality, thereby reducing many sources of revenue (property taxes, sales taxes, income taxes, user fees, and so forth). The reduction in federal revenue-sharing programs in the past few decades has further hampered cities' ability to provide "non-essential" services.[67]

Cities still have a number of tools with which to facilitate revitalization, however. Zoning regulations help determine the types of land uses in particular neighborhoods. Local governments can designate areas to receive special funding and/or other breaks such as waived regulations. In Chicago, Tax Increment Financing (TIF) districts, Model Industrial Corridors, empowerment zones, and Strategic Neighborhood Action Planning (SNAP) districts all constitute means of promoting the redevelopment of particular areas. City governments allocate federal low-income housing tax credits to qualifying developers, who then sell them to project investors. They often allow developers to purchase city-owned lots for either $1 or the difference between the lots' assessed value and a set price in order to spur new construction. The City of Chicago provides a $20,000 subsidy for each moderate-income home built under the New

Homes for Chicago program and offers a number of financial incentives for first-time home buyers.

City governments also promote revitalization through the improvement and maintenance of the public infrastructure. Opening, closing, and/or repaving streets can have significant effects on the economic and social condition of a neighborhood. Improved lighting and sewerage similarly enhance local conditions. Locating city agencies in particular areas—a new police station in Homan Square, Chicago's 911 center in the Near West Side, and so forth—is another way of increasing activity in an area.

The longtime dominance of the Democratic Machine in Chicago has convinced many local activists of the overwhelming importance of political considerations in the allocation of public resources. More specifically, individuals have regularly claimed that lower-income areas have suffered relative to their more affluent counterparts in the provision of public services. In many ways such accusations are overblown. Kenneth Mladenka studied public resource allocation from 1967 to 1977, a time when critics considered the Daley machine to be especially discriminating in the distribution of public goods. He found that the allocation of parks, park services, fire protection, educational resources, and trash collection was based not on Machine-driven political considerations, but on historical, technical, and demographic considerations. For example, communities with larger populations received more services.[68] A recent study of the city's planned capital expenditures by the Neighborhood Capital Budget Group found that wards surrounding the downtown Loop received more monies than other wards, but that the non-Loop wards received a roughly equal amount of resources.[69] Such an allocation seems reasonable considering the high volume of traffic in the downtown area and the increased strains consequently placed on roads, highways, and other parts of the infrastructure.

Political considerations play a greater role in the distribution of more discretionary, "non-essential" goods and services. Most of the aldermen that Mladenka interviewed believed that votes were important for service delivery. Communities that provided strong electoral support for a particularly influential politician (such as Bridgeport has for both Mayor Daleys) might well receive better public services, prompter responses to local concerns, and so forth. Harold Washington's strong base of support in the city's low- and moderate-income, predominantly minority neighborhoods led him and his administration to allocate a greater portion of Community Development Block Grant funds to these areas.

For example, the Washington Administration devoted considerable energies to the redevelopment of the Englewood Mall, in contrast to the preceding Daley, Bilandic, and Byrne Administrations. The increased attention paid to such previously less influential neighborhoods (and the reduced attention paid to others) was a chief cause of the polarizing Council Wars between Washington and many aldermen.[70]

Although political interests certainly influence the City's actions, the allocation of resources for neighborhood revitalization efforts depends in large part on economic factors. Individuals within Chicago's Department of Planning and Development use public incentives to try to attract business to the city. Every tool at DPD's disposal is designed to encourage market forces by streamlining the regulatory process, reducing the costs of development, and ensuring that all potential developers have similar opportunities to carry out their projects. The Department and its tools prove most useful when existing informational, financial, and/or other barriers limit market activity in a community.

Resource constraints prevent agencies such as DPD from targeting all of Chicago's needy neighborhoods for development. They therefore must be strategic in the communities they do target, concentrating on areas whose inherent regional and locational advantages and existing social and institutional base offers the greatest potential return on the City's monies. For example, certain neighborhoods within Chicago are more suitable for retail development than others because of their higher population densities, existing commercial activity, land availability, and so forth. Staff members for DPD's Retail Chicago initiative have concentrated on locations in the Near West Side and South Chicago (community area 46) while not focusing as much on Grand Boulevard (CA 38) and Greater Grand Crossing (CA 69).

The experiences of Englewood and North Lawndale illustrate the importance of economic considerations. Both communities are among Mayor Richard M. Daley's six redevelopment priorities,[71] and each has at least one specially designated city resource area. Yet the City has thus far done little in Englewood besides draft different plans for the redevelopment of the Englewood Mall, none of which has begun to be implemented. In contrast, it has coordinated the improvement of streets and sewers in the area surrounding Homan Square. The Department of Housing has funded every viable residential proposal emerging from North Lawndale.[72] City officials drew the federal empowerment zone boundaries so as to include a significant portion of the neighborhood; the lack of a viable commercial base caused Englewood to be left out of the zone.

Again, the difference in outlook toward the two communities stems from the growing economic vitality of North Lawndale. The Homan Square development in particular has changed the character of (and thus the interest in) the neighborhood. Its size and early success have affected surrounding market values, generating positive economic spillover and increasing demand for new police and other services. The community's location relative to the Loop and its institutional strength offer a greater potential return on both public and private investment.

While various city agencies take responsibility for the implementation of such revitalization strategies, aldermen often serve as the conduit between city government and local individuals and corporations. Chicago is divided into 50 wards, each of which is represented by an alderman (or alderwoman). Aldermen have historically wielded considerable local influence. Overwhelmingly Democratic, they determined much of the allocation of Machine-generated goods and services. They have traditionally held veto power over public projects planned for their wards as well as over sales of city-owned land. They have engaged in a certain amount of patronage, devoting somewhat more attention and benefits to friends and contributors than to the common constituent. While patronage can lead to graft and corruption in any environment, Chicago has developed a notorious reputation for political favoritism. The recent Silver Shovel probe, in which numerous aldermen have been indicted for taking bribes from waste haulers, is merely the latest in a series of incidents resulting in criminal indictments and convictions. Those who have to work closely with members of City Council accept a certain amount of aldermanic self-promotion and pocket-lining as an inherent part of the political process.

Relatively few Chicago aldermen have actively pursued social and economic reform, even those representing the city's poorer wards. Many black aldermen historically focused on strengthening their position and influence within their neighborhoods and within the Machine, not on revitalizing the communities in their wards. Former Washington aide Tim Wright, who is black, derided the "plantation politics" of the black wards. "A guy'd sell out for a bag of hot licks," trading votes for control over particular jobs or resources. Trying to mobilize the electorate into a thinking, acting, more organized body carried the distinct risk of creating a more independent constituency and thus jeopardizing the alderman's influence. Wright contends that the quest for reelection causes aldermen to shy away from activities such as economic development that could create political (and thus electoral) controversy.[73]

Aldermen in Chicago can facilitate revitalization by supporting particular projects and working within City Council to obtain public resources for them. Michael Chandler, for example, has been instrumental in arranging for the removal of the mountain of trash deposited in the middle of North Lawndale. He helped facilitate Cineplex Odeon's entrance into Lawndale Plaza by meeting regularly with Cineplex representatives, developers, and the mayor. He has pressured members of the local police district to increase their presence within the community. Mark Angelini, the Vice President of the Shaw Company, believes that Chandler has been "an articulate advocate for the good things happening in Lawndale," providing political leadership that the community had lacked for many years.[74] Chandler has earned the respect of many Lawndale residents for his efforts to be accessible to and active on behalf of the neighborhood.

At the same time, neither Chandler nor aldermen in general tend to take a leading role in developing or implementing revitalization strategies. Change, no matter what its long-term benefits might be, inevitably upsets certain individuals and institutions who have profited from existing conditions. Politicians who embrace change antagonize certain individuals and invite opposition. Kristin Faust, whose lending activities with LaSalle have brought her into contact with numerous aldermen, contends that Council members "are usually just facilitators. . . . An alderman who likes a project can make a big difference . . . [but they] generally are not movers and shakers."[75]

The political structure of Chicago militates against attempts to promote substantial neighborhood change. With limited city resources, new endeavors implicitly involve trade-offs and reductions in other programs; targeting additional resources to a community requires the diversion of funds from another locale and/or the expansion of the revenue base, both of which prove highly problematic ventures. The city's inter-ethnic and inter-neighborhood tensions have hampered attempts to establish and maintain the broad coalitions necessary for inter-neighborhood projects, to say nothing about initiatives tailored to a single community. The continued dominance of the mayor in the development of city-wide policies has caused more policy-oriented aldermen to opt for positions in the State Senate, the State Assembly, or the United States House of Representatives. The prevailing acceptance of the status quo, a legacy of the Machine and a product of American politics in general, has effectively marginalized reformers. According to Wilson Daniels, a longtime pastor on the city's west side, some of the newer aldermen initially "want to change, but they get into office and seem to accept what is. . . . Everyone seems to fall into the same set of traps and trends, despite their promises."[76]

Aldermen can ultimately do only a limited amount to revitalize distressed neighborhoods. They can veto undesirable land transactions and help funnel monies and properties to individuals and organizations able to carry out particular development projects. Influence with the mayor and/or within City Council can lead to the passage of policies and establishment of programs that will benefit the alderman's ward. Yet an alderman controls few political resources. He or she has marginal influence over the decisions of individuals and institutions to invest in his or her ward. Ward boundaries sometimes do not match neighborhood and/or commercial boundaries, as exemplified by the intersection of wards at 63rd and Halsted Streets; the needs and interests of the entire ward may not match those of individual component communities. Above all, an alderman has little ability to ease the resource constraints within city government. With limited resources and numerous political factors militating against substantial economic and social change, the public sector rarely plays a leading role in revitalization.

CONCLUSION

This chapter has briefly examined the role that major urban actors can and do play in the revitalization of economically distressed neighborhoods. Each of these institutions contributes in some way to community development, although banks and CDCs typically make much more concrete and direct contributions than social service agencies and churches. No one actor alone can revitalize a neighborhood. Banks provide critical investment capital, but they do not commit to a neighborhood over the long term unless they can obtain profitable returns on their investments. These returns depend on the establishment of a local market. Through their real estate activities, CDCs help to stimulate such market activity. They also help bankers and investors identify potential investment opportunities. CDCs in turn rely on banks and foundations for operating capital and on city government for housing-related tax credits and zoning waivers. These tools are some of the financial and technical resources city governments can provide for neighborhood plans and development projects. Yet the impact of these resources depends on the presence of other economic and social factors both internal and external to the community in question. The extent of social capital in a community helps determine the level of investment. More than any other institutions, human service agencies and churches help build social capital by developing and strengthening individual skills and interpersonal networks. Foundations can encourage both the enhancement of social capital and the economic development of a neighborhood by funding organizations involved in the process. They can also help facilitate inter-agency relationships and strategic planning.

The process of revitalization thus clearly involves numerous inter-related and interdependent institutions and agencies. Each has a unique role to play. The extent to which participants can recognize and fulfill these roles largely determines whether or not conditions in an economically distressed neighborhood improve.

NOTES

[1]Woodstock Institute, "Currency Exchanges Add to Poverty Surcharge for Low-Income Residents," Reinvestment Alert #10 (March 1997). The difference in fees charged by banks and currency exchanges increases with income; Woodstock estimates that a family of 3 on public aid would pay about $17 more annually to a currency exchange, while a family making $25,000 would pay an annual surcharge of roughly $300. Currency exchanges and pawn shops are notorious for charging high fees and high interest rates, practices which have caused many to accuse them of willingly perpetrating poverty in the inner cities. Although high, their fees tend to result primarily from the high-risk nature of the business and the monopolistic conditions they enjoy in the neighborhoods. The absence of a viable banking presence in these communities probably has a more profound effect on local economic conditions than do the currency exchanges. For a discussion of the alternative financial industry, see John P. Caskey, *Fringe Banking* (New York: Russell Sage Foundation, 1994).

[2]Douglas Evanoff and Lewis Segal, "CRA and Fair Lending Regulations: Resulting Trends in Mortgage Lending," *Economic Perspectives* 20 (Nov./Dec. 1996): 28.

[3]Perkins, pp. 3–5.

[4]Kathryn Tholin, *Banking on Communities: Community Development Banks in the United States* (Chicago: Woodstock Institute, 1995), pp. 5–7.

[5]Benjamin C. Esty, "South Shore Bank: Is It the Model of Success for Community Development Banks?" *Proceedings of a Conference on Bank Structure and Competition* (Chicago: Federal Reserve Bank of Chicago, May 1995), pp. 192–217. Recent Shorebank figures suggest that its investments are having a distinctly positive effect in the west-side Austin neighborhood, however. Austin's

median value for attached housing units rose by over 19 percent between 1994 and 1996. The number of lending institutions in the community increased by 97 percent from 1984 to 1995, and the dollar volume of bank loans in the neighborhood increased by 170 percent between 1987 and 1995. Again, the extent to which Shorebank's investments have caused these changes remains unclear.

[6]Glenn interview.

[7]Faust interview.

[8]Jacob interview.

[9]Angelini interview.

[10]Brown interview, Apr. 9, 1997.

[11]Interview with White in Chicago, Oct. 1, 1997. She believes that the CDFI legislation has helped to highlight inner-city investment opportunities in Chicago.

[12]"Chicago Banks Seek, Find Profits in the Inner City," *American Banker* (July 23, 1997): 1.

[13]Cited in Squires, "Community Reinvestment," p. 23.

[14]Angelini interview.

[15]Faust interview.

[16]Phone interview with Plasmeier, University of Chicago, May 13, 1997.

[17]Jacob interview.

[18]U.S. Congress, Senate, *The Federal Role in Urban Affairs. Hearings before the Senate Subcommittee on Executive Reorganization.* 89th Cong., 2d sess., Aug. 15–16, 1966.

[19]U.S. Congress, House, *A Review of Community Development Corporations. Hearing before the House Subcommittee on Human Relations.* 102d Cong., 2d sess., Sep. 16, 1992.

[20]The figures are based on estimates generated by the Chicago LISC office.

[21]Teamworks, *Against All Odds* (Washington: National Congress for Community Economic Development, 1989), pp. 6–7.

[22]Interview with Jones in Chicago, June 7, 1995.

[23]Faust interview.

[24]Jacob interview.

[25]Remarks of First Chicago Vice President Therese Mierswa at the U.S. House Hearing on CDCs, Sep. 16, 1992.

[26]Faust interview.

[27]Jacob interview. ACORN, the Association of Communities Organized for Reform Now, is a nonprofit group focused on resident mobilization around issues of affordable housing. It has developed a limited number of single-family homes of its own on Chicago's southwest side, with mixed success.

[28]Butler interview.

[29]Vidal, p. 64.

[30]Many have struggled with the problem of assessing CDCs' broader impact in their communities. See, for instance, some of the publications of the Community Development Research Center in New York: Taub; *Nuance and Meaning in Community Development* (1989); Mercer Sullivan, *Studying the Effects of Community Development Corporations on Social Control* (1990) and *More than Housing: How Community Development Corporations Go About Changing Lives and Neighborhoods* (1993); George Galster, *Neighborhood Evaluations, Expectations, Mobility, and Housing Reinvestment: Measuring the Social Impacts of Community Development Corporations* (1990); and Xavier de Souza Briggs and Elizabeth Mueller, *From Neighborhood to Community: Evidence on the Social Effects of Community Development* (1996).

[31]See Briggs and Mueller.

[32]See Joe Klein, "In God They Trust," *The New Yorker* (June 16, 1997): 40–48.

[33]Quantifying the effect of churches is inherently problematic because of the difficulty of developing an appropriate variable. The qualities of congregations and ministers are probably much more important than the quantity of churches in an area, but the former characteristic is far more troublesome to measure.

[34]Linda Datcher Loury and Glenn Loury, "Churches and Development in Low-Income Communities," paper presented at the National Community Development Policy Analysis Network conference, Washington, Nov. 1996.

[35]The Catholic Church's activity is notable relative to its counterparts. There is very little Episcopal, Presbyterian, Methodist, or Jewish presence in most of Chicago's low-income neighborhoods due to the city's religious demographics, and many of the African Methodist and other local Protestant churches are not engaged in economic development. At the same time, many predominantly black Protestant churches actively mobilized their communities during Harold Washington's mayoral campaigns, helping to produce remarkably high voter turnout in the city's black neighborhoods and contributing heavily to Washington's election.

[36]Interview with DeVille in Chicago, July 2, 1997.

[37]Chandler interview.

[38]Lenz interview.

[39]W. Daniels interview.

[40]R. Daniel interview.

[41]W. Daniels interview.

[42]United Way, *Human Care Services Directory 1994–95.*

[43]The correlations between the number of agencies and revitalization ranged from .36 to .39. The correlations between the number of agencies and

changes in the neighborhood's per capita income ranged from .55 to .62. (See Chapter 4.)

[44]Maynard interview.

[45]W. Daniels interview.

[46]Interview with Arsenault in Chicago, June 2, 1997.

[47]Townsell interview.

[48]Chandler interview.

[49]Ivers interview.

[50]Flowers interview.

[51]Interview with Riley in Chicago, May 8, 1997.

[52]Arsenault interview.

[53]Morgan interview.

[54]See Malcolm Bush, Sidra Goldwater, and Sean Zielenbach, *Increasing Returns: The Economic Development Potential of Social Service Programs* Vol. 1 (Chicago: Woodstock Institute, 1995).

[55]Chicago Community Trust 1996 Annual Report. The Trust's $32 million in grants also included a number of other youth- and health-related donations that fell within other program areas.

[56]The Chicago Community Trust provided a $150,000 grant in the early 1980s to help with the establishment of the Lawndale Christian Health Center, yet the Trust has been reluctant to provide Lawndale Community Development Corporation with substantial support for its housing and economic development efforts.

[57]Because many nonprofits are dependent on foundation money for survival, they may accede to the foundation's request and develop a range of new programs. The danger in such an approach is that the nonprofit can become so diffuse and overextended in its activities that it can no longer effectively fulfill its initial mission.

[58]See, for example, Pablo Eisenberg, "Allusions of Blandeur," *Foundation News and Commentary* (July/Aug. 1996): 28–32, and Christine W. Letts, William Ryan, and Allen Grossman, "Virtuous Capital: What Foundations Can Learn from Venture Capitalists," *Harvard Business Review* 75 (Mar.-Apr. 1997): 36–44. Many in the CDC and social service fields have lambasted foundations as mercurial, unrealistic, and both unaware of and unwilling to understand the fundamental issues involved in economic development and poverty reduction.

[59]See Peter Frumkin, "Left and Right in American Philanthropy," *Minerva* 22 (winter 1994): 475. Pablo Eisenberg has repeatedly attacked foundations' general lack of vision and creativity in responding to social problems in his speeches and in his articles in the *Chronicle of Philanthropy*.

[60]Interview with Malcolm Bush, Woodstock Institute, Chicago, Sep. 16, 1997. See also "Allusions of Blandeur."

[61]Riley interview. The Washington-based National Committee on Responsive Philanthropy leveled similar charges against the Chicago Community Trust in its 1995 report, "The Chicago Community Trust and the Disenfranchised: Caring, Controlling, and Cautious."

[62]Pennick interview.

[63]Riley interview.

[64]Peter Medoff and Holly Sklar provide an in-depth, first-hand account of the Dudley project in *Streets of Hope*.

[65]Townsell interview.

[66]Doig interview.

[67]See, among other discussions of urban fiscal constraints, Peterson and Fuchs, *City Limits*.

[68]Kenneth R. Mladenka, "The Urban Bureaucracy and the Chicago Political Machine: Who Gets What and the Limits to Political Control," *American Political Science Review* 74 (Dec. 1980): 991–98.

[69]Neighborhood Capital Budget Group, *Moving Beyond the Basics: Building Chicago for the Next Century* (Chicago: NCBG, 1996).

[70]One of Washington's major achievements was numerically equalizing certain expenditures across communities, a move which effectively benefited his black and Hispanic constituents. Residents (and aldermen) of communities that had previously received a greater proportion of the expenditures naturally opposed Washington's policies. See Chapter 3 for more discussion of the issue.

[71]The other four are the ABLA and Cabrini Green public housing projects, the downtown State Street commercial district, and the south-side Bronzeville area (a region comprising part of the Douglas, Grand Boulevard, and Oakland community areas).

[72]According to Deputy Director Jack Markowski, the Department has only turned down projects that either were unfeasible or conflicted with other planned uses for the sites.

[73]Wright interview. Wilson Daniels expressed similar views.

[74]Angelini interview.

[75]Faust interview.

[76]W. Daniels interview.

CHAPTER 8

Conclusion

This study has focused on the kinds and causes of economic change in low- and moderate-income neighborhoods in Chicago. Examining conditions in Chicago may offer insights into the process of inner-city development in numerous other cities. Chicago in many ways resembles old industrial centers such as Cleveland, Milwaukee, Philadelphia, and Pittsburgh. In the last 40 years it has lost much of its manufacturing base and has consequently struggled to re-define itself as a financial service center. Like most northern cities, Chicago experienced a significant population loss, as residents moved from the central city to the surrounding suburbs and/or to the more favorable climate of the South and West. Between 1970 and 1990 Chicago lost over 17 percent of its population.[1]

Chicago has long served as a microcosm of the country's ethnic and racial diversity. The city has been a primary attraction for immigrants from Eastern Europe, Latin America, and Southeast Asia. In the years following World War II, it served as a chief destination for hundreds of thousands of low-income whites from Appalachia and poor blacks from the American South. Blacks currently comprise roughly 40 percent of Chicago's population, a proportion comparable to that of Atlanta, Baltimore, and Boston. As in these and other cities, the growth of Chicago's black population has sparked considerable racial tension. Chicago was among the dozens of cities that experienced race-related riots in the 1960s. Its historical patterns of segregation contributed to prolonged struggles over fair housing, conflicts that mirrored those in Boston and Detroit over the issue of elementary and secondary school busing.

As in other cities, the mixture of changing economic conditions,

suburbanization, and racial discrimination has contributed to a high inci-
dence of poverty in Chicago. Chicago's 1990 poverty rate of 21.6 placed
it 8 points above the national average but within a few points of the rates
of cities such as Baltimore, Boston, Los Angeles, Milwaukee, New York,
Philadelphia, and Pittsburgh.[2] A number of Chicago's neighborhoods
have historically been among the country's most economically devastated. The concentrated poverty and crime within many of the city's public housing high-rises have sparked a national movement to restructure
public housing.

While its problems resemble those of other cities, Chicago has a
number of characteristics especially beneficial for neighborhood revitalization. The city has clearly defined neighborhoods, communities in
which residents strongly identify with place. This local commitment has
historically contributed to strong neighborhood activism and to the development of numerous community-based organizations. Jane Addams
and Saul Alinsky both focused their efforts in Chicago, and the city remains a national leader in the community development field. On a
broader scale, the Chicago metropolitan area has experienced considerable economic growth throughout much of the 1990s, increasing the resources available for local economic improvements.[3] The presence of
numerous Fortune 500 corporations within the region, as well as some of
the nation's top universities, further expands the pool of potential financial and human resources. Chicago's neighborhoods have historically attracted the attention of many scholars and policy makers, making them
some of the most studied and experimented upon places in the country.
In short, Chicago is one of the most promising areas in the country for
successful neighborhood revitalization. If distressed inner-city communities are to improve, Chicago would be one of the most likely places for
that change to occur.

NEIGHBORHOOD REVITALIZATION
AMID URBAN DECLINE

Although the Chicago region has experienced considerable growth in the
past few decades, the city itself has declined. Chicago has lost over
520,000 residents since 1970, and its real per capita income has fallen.
The city's poverty rate increased by roughly 50 percent between 1970
and 1990. The decline has particularly affected the city's low- and moderate-income neighborhoods. Only 12 community areas saw an increase
in their per capita incomes relative to the city average between 1979 and

1995; all but two of those 12 had average incomes above the city mean in 1979. Many middle- and upper-income Chicago neighborhoods have declined in the past 20 years.

Examining trends in all 77 of the city's community areas provided a context for understanding the broader changes affecting Chicago, but the bulk of the study focused on the city's low- and moderate-income communities. I eliminated from consideration the 41 neighborhoods whose per capita incomes exceeded the city mean in 1979. Not only did the process take class differences out of the study, but it also largely excluded the issue of race: whites were a minority in all 36 of the remaining community areas. Within this smaller subset I measured neighborhood economic change relative to the city as a whole. Such an approach controlled for the economic, political, and social changes that have affected Chicago in the past 20 years. It controlled for inflation in property values and per capita incomes, and it alleviated the need for elaborate transformations of the data. But it is important to remember that while many low-income neighborhoods improved relative to the city average, they usually declined in absolute terms. Real per capita incomes continued to fall (as they did in the city as a whole). In most cases neighborhood "revitalization" actually meant slower decline.

This book defines revitalization of a low-income community as both the reintegration of the neighborhood into the market and the improvement of economic conditions for existing residents. Such a focus combines the traditional physical redevelopment and private investment aspects of revitalization with an anti-poverty component. Some may argue that the two are antithetical, in that economic improvements in a neighborhood have little positive effect on the poor. They feel that increases in property values, private investment, and the number of more affluent residents in a community leads to the displacement of low-income incumbent residents of the neighborhood; in short, all revitalization is a form of gentrification. Others believe that the two may go hand-in-hand. They cite examples of incumbent upgrading and adaptive reuse, in which local residents spearhead the physical redevelopment of an area for their own benefit. Inner-city development and poverty alleviation may or may not be synonymous—that is an empirical question—but the improvement of low-income urban neighborhoods is essential for the betterment of their residents. Individual opportunity and achievement depend in large part on environmental factors. People who live in stable, safer, and more affluent neighborhoods typically fare better socially and economically than individuals who live in areas of high crime and high poverty. Communities that are better integrated into the urban and metropolitan markets typically attract more outside resources and therefore increase the opportunities available to their members. The book's focus on the benefits for existing residents not only addresses the issue of poverty reduction but also differentiates revitalization from gentrification. In the latter process, improvements generally benefit more affluent individuals living outside the community and can often lead to the displacement of the neighborhood's present population.

This study found that although they are positively correlated, changes in a neighborhood's level of private investment have generally operated independently of changes in a neighborhood's per capita income. Only two of the 36 communities in the study experienced positive increases relative to the city in both private investment and individual economic opportunity, and gentrification has characterized both of those neighborhoods. To the extent that revitalization has occurred, it has been driven by increased private investment. That additional market activity has not yet translated into improved economic conditions for low-income individuals.

Part of the explanation for the discrepancy between the two components of revitalization may lie in the time period under consideration. Revitalization is fundamentally a measure of change from one time to another. It compares the difference between two snapshots. The various aspects of economic change may not move at the same rates. Private investment may well precede individual economic improvement; another snapshot taken in a few years might indicate more of a reduction in poverty.

More likely, the factors that promote private investment in inner-city neighborhoods are not entirely the same ones that improve individuals' economic well-being. As will be highlighted in more detail in what follows, increased private sector activity in a community largely results from factors characteristic of that particular area. Some of Chicago's low-income neighborhoods have experienced real increases in their property values and residential loan rates, while others have remained constant and/or declined. The vast majority of the city's neighborhoods (including many of its more affluent ones) have experienced real declines in their per capita incomes, which indicates that broader systemic forces are driving economic trends. The characteristics of individual neighborhoods may help moderate these decreases, but they cannot by themselves reverse the trends. The qualities of cities as a whole have only a limited impact on the economic conditions of their low-income residents. Real per capita incomes for low- and moderate-income individuals have fallen nationally since the early 1970s. Even in the Chicago metropolitan region, where an economic boom has created hundreds of thousands of new jobs, low-income individuals have continued to become absolutely and relatively worse off.

REVITALIZATION ACROSS URBAN NEIGHBORHOODS

Using an index comprised of the two previously outlined components of revitalization, the study analyzed economic change in Chicago's 36 low- and moderate-income communities between 1979 and 1995. It considered a number of quantifiable socioeconomic, demographic, and locational variables and correlated them with changes in a neighborhood's index score. The process identified significant relationships between revitalization and certain factors such as proximity to the Loop and presence of nonprofit community organizations, but neither simple correlational analysis nor multivariate regression could account for the tremendous variation among the city's neighborhoods. Part of the difficulty lay in the small number of cases in the study, which made it hard to identify statistically significant relationships among the different variables. The absence of variables that measured more intangible, less quantifiable factors such as leadership and non-monetary resource allocation constituted another limitation.

More importantly, factors interacted with each other in different ways (and therefore had different impacts) in different communities. Neighborhoods changed at different rates, at different times, and for different reasons. Population growth signified economic growth in certain areas and decline in others. Clustering neighborhoods by ethnicity and geography, and then examining change within these clusters, helped to explain local trends. While communities within a single cluster usually experienced similar economic changes for generally similar reasons, neighborhoods in different clusters showed few similarities. Cluster 1 communities experienced gentrification, in large part because of their proximity to either the Loop and/or Lake Michigan. The cluster 2 communities, predominantly moderate-income Hispanic neighborhoods on the northwest side, experienced decline primarily because of a recent influx of poor immigrants. Neighborhoods in cluster 3, moderate-income African-American communities on the city's far south side, declined as a result of the exodus of the middle class in the 1980s and the aging of the remaining residents. Cluster 4 communities, near south and southwest moderate-income areas with a high proportion of ethnic residents, have either stagnated or slowly declined because of decreasing loan rates. Many local residents have low levels of education and hesitate to use traditional financial institutions. The overwhelmingly black neighborhoods of cluster 5, the poorest areas in the city, experienced economic improvement as a result of increasing loan rates and property values. In short, the characteristics and causes of change in a neighborhood such as the Near West Side (cluster 1) differed fundamentally from those of communities such as Albany Park (cluster 2), Roseland (cluster 3), Bridgeport (cluster 4), and Woodlawn (cluster 5). Understanding local mechanisms of revitalization required in-depth analyses of communities within a particular cluster.

REVITALIZATION IN LOW-INCOME
BLACK NEIGHBORHOODS

As a way of understanding the characteristics of revitalization more fully, I selected two neighborhoods within cluster 5 for more detailed ethnographic study. North Lawndale, on the city's west side, experienced positive economic change relative to the city between 1979 and 1995, while the economic fortunes of the south side Englewood community declined. Neither of these neighborhoods has experienced gentrification pressures, and there has not been any threat of local residents being displaced. The communities have similar demographics and relatively similar histories. In short, they allowed for a good comparative analysis of revitalization processes. I focused initially on those local factors identified as important by other researchers and by the quantitative study: neighborhood location and community organizations. Yet the case studies remained flexible enough to examine other potential causes of change that emerged in the course of the research.

The qualitative analysis found that no single factor accounted for economic change in these low-income, overwhelmingly black neighborhoods. Revitalization resulted from the interplay of numerous local individual, institutional, and organizational decisions, in concert with the locational characteristics of the community and the economic and social forces affecting the city and the broader metropolitan region. The skills and motivations of particular individuals (factors that defy easy quantification) played instrumental roles in catalyzing and shaping economic improvement. The social capital within the community greatly affected the decision-making of these individuals and their institutions, as well as the impact of those decisions on the broader community. The remainder of this section briefly summarizes the various components of revitalization.

Location

A community's physical location affects its likelihood of revitalization. For Chicago, proximity to the Loop, the largest employment center in the region, constituted the most statistically significant factor associated with revitalization. Transportational access to the Loop—specifically the concentration of bus lines and elevated train stops—also enhanced a community's chances of improvement. Individuals within and outside of North Lawndale regularly cited the community's location as a chief reason for its economic improvement: the presence of the Eisenhower Expressway and major arterials such as Ogden and Roosevelt Avenues offered residents and businesses easy access to both the Loop and the western suburbs. The bracketing of the community by two elevated train lines further enhanced its desirability. In contrast, many public and private sector officials saw Englewood's location as a liability, using phrases such as "the middle of nowhere" when referring to it.

Location matters, but to a lesser extent than many think. Englewood's location along the Dan Ryan Expressway makes it possible to get to the Loop in under 15 minutes; riding the elevated train to downtown takes a half-hour or less. The neighborhood is located a few miles east of Midway Airport, the country's eighth-busiest air facility. The community clearly has some locational assets, and it has some history of economic vitality. Up through the 1950s, Englewood was one of Chicago's most vibrant communities. It had the second most active shopping center in the city (behind the Loop) and a relatively stable middle class. The neighborhood's locational and physical assets have not changed since then (if anything, they have improved with the redevelopment of the green line "el"), yet Englewood's economic fortunes have declined noticeably. North Lawndale is closer to the Loop and to the suburbs than Englewood is, but it has only recently attracted private investment. North Lawndale's locational advantages did not prevent it from declining precipitously from the mid-1960s through the late 1980s.

While a neighborhood's physical and locational assets generally do not change, the perception of those assets varies with social and economic changes taking place elsewhere in the metropolitan region. Broader economic trends greatly influence the health of a neighborhood.

As the decline of manufacturing and the movement of jobs to the suburbs devastated many of Chicago's neighborhoods, the resurgence of the Loop and the saturation of the suburbs have increased the appeal of those same communities. Many individuals who work downtown have grown frustrated with the congestion and sprawl of the suburbs and have chosen to move back into the city. The relatively cheap housing and proximity of the Near West Side and West Town have generated increasing demand for property in those areas and have helped heightened interest in North Lawndale. Individuals have begun to reconsider investing in the community after ignoring it for years.

Increased economic activity in surrounding communities can enhance the appeal of previously ignored neighborhoods, especially for developers seeking to capitalize on expected future demand in an area. Such external activity cannot explain the different economic experiences of individual neighborhoods, however. Location alone would suggest that North Lawndale, East Garfield Park, and West Garfield Park would have benefited to a similar extent from the economic growth of the Near West Side. Both North Lawndale and the Garfield Parks are situated due west of the Near West Side. The Eisenhower Expressway borders each neighborhood (Lawndale on the north, the Garfields on the south). Each community is served by two elevated train lines. Residents of these neighborhoods can get into the Loop in no more than 15 minutes. Each of the communities has shown economic improvement since 1979; both Garfields have larger changes in their index score than does North Lawndale. Yet Lawndale generates considerable enthusiasm among investors and officials throughout the city, while the Garfields continue to be perceived as deeply troubled, largely unchanging areas.

The region surrounding Englewood has not been the site of renewed economic activity, and all of the neighborhoods have experienced some decline in the past 20 years. Englewood remains markedly worse off than any of its neighborhoods, though, despite the presence of locational advantages. Englewood's 1995 index score was just over half that of Auburn Gresham, even though Auburn Gresham has neither an "el" nor immediate access to the Dan Ryan Expressway. Greater Grand Crossing, also without "el" access, had an index score 22 points higher than Englewood's. Were locational assets the sole factors driving neighborhood economics, there would be much less of a disparity between Englewood and its neighbors.

North Lawndale's somewhat better location relative to Englewood cannot fully explain the different economic fortunes of the two communities. For much of the 1980s, the revitalization of Englewood held more promise than that of Lawndale. The proposed redevelopment of the Englewood Mall generated more interest among city officials and potential investors than the creation of Lawndale Plaza. The Mall's renovation offered real hope for the neighborhood, and it seemed to have the necessary support to go forward. Ted Wysocki, who as director of the Chicago Association of Neighborhood Development Organizations (CANDO) has been involved in economic development projects in both communities, contends that if the redevelopment of the Englewood Mall had taken place, the revitalization of Englewood would now be much further along than that of Lawndale.[4]

Physical Amenities

The physical characteristics of a community, particularly its housing stock, also help determine the extent of revitalization. Developers and investors emphasized the presence of elegant greystones as a plus in Lawndale's favor. Many of the same individuals considered the preponderance of wood frame houses in Englewood to be a drawback for that neighborhood.

Other physical amenities had little apparent effect on a community's likelihood for revitalization. The presence of parks, brownfields, and public housing units had seemingly little impact on economic change. Woodlawn and Grand Boulevard, two communities with high concentrations of public housing, both experienced economic improvement relative to the city. Two other public housing-heavy neighborhoods, the Near West Side and Douglas, have witnessed considerable gentrification. Despite the negative correlations found in the quantitative study, rates of home ownership within a neighborhood had little observable effect on local revitalization.

Local Institutions

Locational and physical amenities contribute to the attractiveness of a particular neighborhood, but the actual revitalization of a community hinges on the decisions of individual investors. People weigh the benefits of devoting resources to an area with the costs of doing so. How strongly the components are weighted often depends as much on intangible feelings as on quantifiable indicators.

Institutional actors within a community play a crucial role in shaping the benefit-cost calculus. Echoing the findings of Richard Taub,

Garth Taylor, and Jan Dunham, this study found that commitments on the part of major institutions largely determine the long-term health of the community. The Community Bank of Lawndale provided investment capital to North Lawndale when virtually every other major financial institution shied away from the area. Mt. Sinai Hospital, Ryerson Steel, and the Roscoe Company all decided to remain in the community, maintaining both a base of jobs and a sense of financial and institutional stability. Their involvement in local development efforts, combined with the Catholic Church's refusal to close any of its North Lawndale parishes, nurtured a sense of hope and commitment to local improvement on the part of local residents. The Steans Family Foundation has selected North Lawndale for an infusion of up to $1 million annually. Most importantly, Sears remained concerned about Lawndale's future and continued to devote resources for that purpose. The development at Homan Square, almost universally acknowledged as the catalyst for the neighborhood's recent improvement, would not have taken place without Sears's extensive subsidies. The activity on the former Sears site has attracted individual investors as well as corporations such as First Chicago, Cineplex Odeon, and Dominick's.

The institutional commitment to North Lawndale contrasts sharply with the experience in Englewood. Chicago City Bank and Trust, the only bank in Englewood, has a long history of ignoring the neighborhood's financial needs and antagonizing most of the local actors. St. Bernard's Hospital decided to remain in the neighborhood and has attempted to contribute to its well-being, but it has never been able to shed its negative reputation within the community. The historical antagonism on the part of the local Catholic churches to the neighborhood's black residents, coupled with the consolidation of parishes within the area, has effectively precluded the Church from being a respected part of the revitalization process. No foundation has adopted the neighborhood; two of the city's larger philanthropies hesitate to give money to Englewood-based groups. Without the financial and psychological commitment of institutions within or outside of the neighborhood, Englewood has continued to decline.

Community Organizations

Although they lack the size and resources of major hospitals and corporations, locally-based nonprofit organizations also serve as important local institutions. Neighborhoods with higher concentrations of community organizations and development corporations typically experience greater relative increases in property values. Effective CDCs such as Pyramidwest and Lawndale Christian Development Corporation were able to generate some market activity through their real estate and small business development efforts. These projects, in concert with the groups' knowledge of local economic actors, helped attract the interest of banks and other investors. No comparable group has developed and sustained itself in Englewood, a failing which has limited the community's prospects for revitalization.

Like CDCs and community organizations, churches and social service agencies can play an important part in promoting local economic change. Their contributions tend to more indirect, however. Whereas CDCs directly promote investment through their real estate activities, churches can help build a community's social capital. They and social service agencies focus principally on the educational, psychological, and spiritual needs of local residents. They promote the development of social networks both by providing community meeting places and by encouraging interpersonal trust and civility. Such contributions are difficult to quantify and therefore tend to escape detection, both by individuals within the community and by outside evaluators.

Local Leadership

Mobilizing and effectively using the resources of various local institutions requires the commitment and leadership of specific individuals. The lack of interest and investment in distressed inner-city neighborhoods militates against the development of effective community organizations and the material involvement of corporate and nonprofit institutions. In many cases bottom-line economic considerations encourage further disinvestment from the community. For example, Sears closed its catalog distribution center in North Lawndale because the center's age hindered the company's national and international competitiveness. Mt. Sinai's board members actively looked for a new suburban location for the hospital, one closer to a more Jewish, more affluent patient base. The Archdiocese strongly considered closing St. Agatha's Church because of Lawndale's shrinking number of Catholics and the accompanying decline in the parish's revenue base. Only strong leadership on the part of individuals personally committed to the neighborhood kept these institutions active in the neighborhood. Ed Brennan's desire to find a socially beneficial use for his company's abandoned former headquarters, coupled with Charlie

Shaw's willingness to develop the property, led to the commitment of Sears monies for the development of Homan Square. Ruth Rothstein's belief in Jewish charity helped convince skeptical board members to keep Mt. Sinai in North Lawndale, and her belief in the mutually beneficial nature of community development led to the hospital's involvement in numerous local partnerships. A profound commitment to social justice inspired the Reverends Jack Egan, Jim Martin, and Mike Ivers to confront the Archdiocesan hierarchy and insist on a strong Catholic presence in North Lawndale.

A strong commitment to change by itself does not make for effective leadership. Individuals must be able to change the internal and external perceptions of a neighborhood. People within the community must view the leaders as legitimate representatives of their needs and interests, as individuals with compelling visions of change. The leaders must also have the ability to translate their visions into reality, a process that requires access to resources inside and outside the neighborhood. North Lawndale has benefited from the presence of respected individuals willing and able to tap into outside financial and human capital. Cecil Butler leveraged millions of dollars in public monies for Pyramidwest's various development projects. Wayne Gordon drew upon the resources of suburban churches and the Chicago Community Trust to build the Lawndale Christian Health Center. Egan enlisted the support of metropolitan-area seminarians in his campaign against contract buying, and Ivers invited the Industrial Areas Foundation into Lawndale to help organize local residents. In contrast, Englewood's leadership has suffered from a more combative and parochial approach. Community representatives have antagonized public officials, resisted the entreaties of outside organizers, and continually bickered among themselves.

Social Capital

The impact of institutional commitments and strong leadership ultimately depends on the social capital present within a neighborhood. Real estate developers may base their initial investment decisions primarily on a community's locational attributes, but the long-term viability of their projects hinges on social factors such as the safety of the community. Bankers emphasize the important role trust plays in their decisions whether or not to invest in a particular community. They typically look much more favorably on neighborhoods with greater social organization and stability. Similarly, foundation officers select communities for investment based on the neighborhoods' capacity to sustain and build on an infusion of resources. The Steans Family Foundation, one of Chicago's most investment-oriented charities, deliberately selected North Lawndale over Englewood in large part because of Lawndale's greater number of capable individuals and effective interpersonal relationships. The lack of such social organization within Englewood has caused other foundations to shy away from the neighborhood, despite the expressed desire of their officers to help address the community's many needs. Englewood simply does not have the established interpersonal networks necessary to leverage outside resources.

The relationship among local institutions, leaders, and social capital is complex. Institutions hesitate to commit resources to an area unless it has enough capable local leaders and social organization for the resources to have an impact. An institutional commitment to a distressed inner-city neighborhood results from the concerted efforts of selected individuals who feel an intense personal and societal responsibility to the community. Such individuals draw their emotional sustenance largely from their relationships with others within the community who share their hope and aspirations for change. Yet the development of these interpersonal relationships—particularly in areas with high crime, fear, and suspicion of others—requires the concerted commitment of time, energy, and other resources on the part of individual and institutional leaders.

The different experiences of Lawndale and Englewood highlight the importance of community organizing to the development of a neighborhood's social capital. Residents need to be mobilized around some sort of common goal in a manner that fosters interpersonal interaction and the development of a shared commitment to change. The process requires both talented organizers and willing organizees, people who sense that they can do something to improve their lives. It benefits from clear, well-defined events that arouse considerable anger among local residents. Lawndale residents have banded together at various times in response to distinctly negative stimuli: the widespread practice of contract buying, the 1968 riots, Sears's decision to move downtown, the *Chicago Tribune*'s selection of the community as the focus of *The American Millstone*, and so forth. Englewood residents have not had as many clearly negative, easily observable and understood events around which to mobilize. They consequently have never developed as strong or as active a commitment to change. The sense of victimization that pervades Englewood, a product of the neighborhood's seemingly unattributable decline, has hampered the development of stable, goal-specific community organizations.

Although neighborhood economic development stems from a number of interactive factors, social capital is the most essential. Revitalization is a product of numerous individual decisions. People make those choices in response to and in conjunction with the decisions of others. Since individuals rarely have all of the information they desire, many of their decisions result from basic gut feelings. They risk their (or their organization's) resources because they believe that a particular neighborhood will improve. They trust in the motives and abilities of people within that community to manage resources effectively and promote positive change. Such trust depends on the presence of strong local networks of interpersonal relationships.

PROMOTING INNER-CITY REVITALIZATION

Building social capital within a neighborhood is a crucial component of any successful revitalization strategy. Individual leaders play a significant role in creating that capital, but their efforts are only part of the process. Local residents need to feel comfortable interacting with others in order to build the trust necessary to pursue collective goals. They have to feel safe, confident that such interaction will not result in physical harm. The residents also need to have a sense that their efforts matter, that they can do things to improve their lives. The "victim mentality" that pervades communities such as Englewood largely precludes the mobilization of residents for collective action. People seem to spend more time railing against existing conditions than devising strategies to improve them. Much of the inability to envision alternatives results from a lack of exposure and sophistication. Residents lack the breadth of experience and the accompanying analytic and problem-solving skills that allow for the development and/or appreciation of creative solutions.

While essential, the presence of social capital alone cannot spark revitalization of distressed inner-city neighborhoods. Significant private investment requires a well-developed local physical infrastructure. Individuals and businesses hesitate to locate in communities with poor roads, antiquated communication lines, and outdated sewer and other basic utilities. Successful neighborhoods have access to transportation lines that allow for the rapid movement of people and products. Particularly in the most distressed communities, private investment also typically requires a catalytic infusion of either public and/or nonprofit resources. Most individuals and businesses are risk-averse and therefore unwilling to be the first investors in a troubled area. They depend on other investors to go in before them and lay some of the groundwork, thereby alleviating some of the investment risk. Because neither government nor the philanthropic community has the profit constraint of the private sector, each can more easily make that initial high-risk resource commitment.

An increase in private investment should ultimately better conditions for a neighborhood's existing residents, but other activities are also crucial to individual well-being. Many residents of low-income urban communities lack access to quality health care. Untreated ailments not only reduce the quality of life but also hamper the residents' ability to find and hold jobs. Part of the health problem typically stems from inadequate housing. A significant percentage of housing units within a distressed urban neighborhood are substandard, and many others become that way as a result of overcrowding. The dearth of adequate, affordable housing has far-reaching implications. Many low-income individuals spend as much as 75 percent of their incomes on housing, leaving little for food or other life essentials.[5] Underlying the economic problems of many inner-city residents is an absence of steady, well-paying jobs. As mentioned earlier in the study, unemployment rates in some low-income urban communities exceed 40 percent. Those individuals who are employed may have to work multiple jobs in order to maintain an acceptable standard of living, as many positions do not pay a sustainable wage. There is also no guarantee that such low-paying jobs will provide any sort of health insurance or other benefits.

Toward an Enhanced Public Sector Role

Addressing these various problems would significantly increase the chances of revitalization within economically distressed urban neighborhoods. Enhanced public safety would help promote greater interpersonal interaction among local residents, building the networks essential to social capital. Improving the quality of education, specifically in the area of analysis and problem-solving, would help individuals better assess conditions in their lives and see alternative possibilities. Greater exposure to ideas and cultures would help foster greater understanding of others' goals and motivations, which could alleviate some of the distrust and other emotional barriers that can hinder the development of social capital. Enhanced academic and technical skills would increase the employability of low-income residents: they would have access to more lucrative and interesting job possibilities, and their greater skills would help attract more companies to the region. Improving access to health care would help residents become more productive, happier, and better able to take advantage of opportunities they encounter. The development of more affordable housing would help alleviate overcrowding (thus improving health conditions) and would enable individuals to devote more of their resources to other concerns.

Some of these issues can be addressed principally by local residents in conjunction with the private sector. Maintaining a safe neighborhood depends in large part on the vigilance of local individuals who refuse to tolerate a wide range of unacceptable conditions. In addition to offering in-house education and training to their employees, companies can provide human, financial, and technical resources to improve the quality of education in local schools. Parents and other community residents can take greater interest in and responsibility for the education of children in a neighborhood, both through informal teaching and by setting high standards for professional educators.

Yet many of the issues require a more active involvement on the part of the public sector. For example, private developers simply cannot afford to build housing that is affordable for very low-income individuals; although the demand is great, the fixed costs of rehabilitation and/or new construction make it impossible to create adequate facilities for a price that fits within a low-income individual's budget and allows the developer to make a profit. Only the public sector has the resources necessary to fill the gap between the two points. Similarly, it is unlikely that private industry would have the resources or the motivation necessary to develop and maintain a community's physical infrastructure.

City governments have certain tools at their disposal to promote revitalization. Public officials can provide some subsidies (in the form of grants and low-interest loans) to nonprofit and private-sector developers. They can commit to the improvement of streets, sewers, and other parts of the urban infrastructure. They can play a brokering role among bankers, developers, community groups, and other actors in the revitalization process. They can target discretionary monies to high-need areas and reorganize public institutions such as police departments and the public schools to make them more responsive to local needs.

Yet city officials are fundamentally limited in what they can do. Because individuals and businesses can choose to locate in any number of municipalities, cities are effectively competing continuously with each other and with the suburbs for a revenue-generating population. Cities simultaneously have to maximize their attractiveness to potential investors and minimize their drawbacks. A low tax rate constitutes a major attraction, but it limits the city's ability to address problems such as decaying infrastructures and inadequate low-income housing. Because they typically have fewer problems than central cities (a result of their relative youth and lower proportions of poor residents), suburbs typically have less serious fiscal constraints.

Although state officials can help compensate the differences between cities and suburbs, much of the inter-municipality competition crosses state lines. Companies regularly threaten to move from one state to another. Even if they choose to remain in the same metropolitan area, they may easily move to a different state. The Chicago metropolitan area encompasses part of Indiana and arguably part of southern Wisconsin. The New York metropolitan area certainly includes northern New Jersey and southern Connecticut. Greater Philadelphia encompasses parts of New Jersey and Delaware, and so forth. In these contexts, the federal government necessarily becomes a crucial actor in increasing the relative attractiveness of the central city.

The history of federal involvement in urban development and inner-city revitalization is mixed. In many ways federal policies have promoted urban decline. The Federal Housing Authority's lending guidelines effectively caused the redlining of racially mixed and predominantly minority city neighborhoods. The establishment of the interstate highway system promoted the development of the suburbs and the depopulation of the central cities. A lack of a coordinated national industrial policy contributed to the decline of the country's manufacturing industry, which disproportionately affected the nation's central cities. Cutbacks in the resources available for public housing have worsened conditions in existing facilities (with devastating effects for the surrounding neighborhoods) and have accentuated the affordable housing crisis. Recent reductions in public welfare monies, including those devoted to education and employment programs, have further limited the opportunities available to many inner-city residents.

At the same time, a number of federal policies have helped to promote inner-city revitalization. Many of the War on Poverty programs improved conditions for existing residents (although many of those residents subsequently left the inner cities). The Low Income Housing Tax Credit has encouraged corporations to invest in affordable housing projects and has directly contributed to the development of tens of thousands of housing units in low-income neighborhoods. The Home Mortgage Disclosure Act has compelled banks to make the geographical distribution of their loan dollars public knowledge. Community groups have used this information to highlight and force changes in discriminatory lending practices, campaigns which have significantly increased the capital available to inner-city neighborhoods. Similarly, the Community Reinvestment Act has forced banks to be more responsive to the credit needs of the communities that they serve. More recently, the Community Development Financial Institution Act has encouraged investment in organizations specifically addressing local economic revitalization.

Although suspicion of federal social policies pervades the current political climate, the long-term revitalization of inner-city neighborhoods requires more concerted federal involvement. Only the federal government has the resources necessary to address the dearth of affordable housing and the decay of the physical urban infrastructure. Certain aspects of a concerted public safety effort (such as a reduction in the availability of handguns) lie in the federal purview. Perhaps most importantly, the federal government has responsibility for shaping the national economy. In addition to using monetary policy to promote and sustain economic growth, federal legislators need to find a way of enabling less-skilled individuals to benefit from this growth. Policy-makers need to figure out how, in an increasingly technological and international economy, the polity can create meaningful and adequately paying jobs for society's less talented individuals. Part of the process entails increasing the individuals' skill base to make them more employable. Part involves the development of new industries and jobs to sustain under-worked segments of the population. Above all, it requires a greater appreciation of the conditions affecting low-income individuals and a commitment to improving them. Only with such a commitment can economically distressed urban neighborhoods become fully revitalized.

NOTES

[1]London and Puntenney, pp. 21–34.
[2]Ibid., p. 20.
[3]The Chicago area gained more than 360,000 jobs from 1992 to 1996 ("Midwest Briefs," *Chicago Tribune* (May 5, 1997), Sec. 4, p. 1).
[4]Wysocki interview.
[5]See De Parle, pp. 52–102.

Sources Consulted

BOOKS/ARTICLES

Abraham, Laurie Kaye. *Mama Might Be Better Off Dead.* Chicago: University of Chicago Press, 1993.

Anderson, Alan B., and George W. Pickering. *Confronting the Color Line.* Athens, GA: University of Georgia Press, 1986.

Anderson, Elijah. *Streetwise.* Chicago: University of Chicago Press, 1990.

———. "The Code of the Streets." *Atlantic Monthly* (May 1994): 81–94.

Bailey, Robert Jr. *Radicals in Urban Politics: The Alinsky Approach.* Chicago: University of Chicago Press, 1974.

Barber, James David. *The Presidential Character.* Englewood Cliffs, NJ: Prentice-Hall, Inc. 1972 (1st of numerous editions).

Baron, Harold M. *Building Babylon: A Case of Racial Controls in Public Housing.* Evanston, IL: Northwestern University Center for Urban Affairs, 1971.

Bartik, Timothy J. "Neighborhood Revitalization's Effects on Tenants and the Benefit-Cost Analysis of Government Neighborhood Programs." *Journal of Urban Economics* 19 (1986): 234–248.

Bennett, Susan. "Community Organizations and Crime." *Annals of American Association of Political and Social Sciences* 539 (May 1995): 72–84.

Biles, Roger. *Richard J. Daley: Politics, Race, and the Governing of Chicago.* DeKalb, IL: Northern Illinois University Press, 1995.

Blank, Rebecca. "The Employment Strategy: Public Policies to Increase Work and Earnings." In *Confronting Poverty,* pp. 168–204. Edited by Sheldon Danziger, Gary Sandefur, and Daniel Weinberg. Cambridge: Harvard University Press, 1994.

Bolton, Roger. "'Place Prosperity vs. People Prosperity' Revisited: An Old Issue with a New Angle." *Urban Studies* 29 (1992): 185–203.

Bond, Philip, and Robert Townsend. "Formal and Informal Financing in a Chicago Ethnic Neighborhood." *Economic Perspectives* 20 (Jul./Aug. 1996): 3–27.

Bowden, Charles, and Lew Kreinberg. *Street Signs Chicago*. Chicago: Chicago Review Press, 1981.

Briggs, Xavier de Souza, and Elizabeth Mueller. *From Neighborhood to Community: Evidence on the Social Effects of Community Development*. New York: Community Development Research Center, 1996.

Burgess, Ernest W. "The Growth of the City: An Introduction to a Research Project." In *The City*, pp. 47–62. Edited by Robert E. Park, Burgess, and Roderick D. McKenzie. Chicago: University of Chicago Press, 1925.

Bush, Malcolm; Sidra Goldwater; and Sean Zielenbach. *Increasing Returns: The Economic Development Potential of Social Service Programs*. Vol. 1. Chicago: Woodstock Institute, 1995.

Caine, Paul. "The Dream That Died." *Chicago Reporter* (Jan. 1993): 3–15.

———. "Mortgage Lending in Chicago: Separate, Unequal." *Chicago Reporter* (May 1993): 11–15.

Camacho, Eduardo, and Ben Joravsky. *Against the Tide*. Chicago: Community Renewal Society, 1989.

Caskey, John P. *Fringe Banking*. New York: Russell Sage Foundation, 1994.

Chapralis, Sally. "Laboratory for Inner-City Development, Chicago." *Urban Land* (Nov. 1993): 15–20.

Chicago Community Organizations Directory. Chicago: Community Renewal Society, 1990. Reprint.

Chicago Comprehensive Needs Assessment, Vol. II. Chicago: Melaniphy & Associates, 1982.

Chicago Fact Book Consortium. *Local Community Fact Book—Chicago Metropolitan Area*. Chicago: Chicago Review Press, 1984.

———. *Local Community Fact Book—Chicago Metropolitan Area 1990*. Chicago: University of Illinois, 1995.

Chicago Tribune, *The American Millstone*. Chicago: Contemporary Books, 1986.

Clay, Phillip L. *Neighborhood Renewal*. Lexington, MA: D.C. Heath & Co., 1979.

Cloward, Richard, and Lloyd Ohlin. *Delinquency and Opportunity*. New York: Free Press, 1960.

Coleman, James S. *Foundations of Social Theory*. Cambridge, MA: Belknap Press, 1990.

Coulton, Claudia; Jill Korbin; et al. "Community Level Factors and Child Maltreatment Rates." Cleveland: Case Western Reserve University, 1994.

Crane, Jonathan. "Effects of Neighborhoods in Dropping Out of School and Teenage Childbearing." In *The Urban Underclass,* pp. 299–320. Edited by Christopher Jencks and Paul E. Peterson. Washington: Brookings Institution, 1991.

Crenson, Matthew A. *Neighborhood Politics.* Cambridge: Harvard University Press, 1983.

De Parle, Jason. "The Year That Housing Died." *New York Times Magazine* (Oct. 20, 1996): 52–105.

Directory of Community Organizations in Chicago. Chicago: Loyola University Institute of Urban Life, 1992. Updated in 1996.

Doig, David. "The Split among Black Politicians." Master's thesis. University of Chicago, 1988.

Donovan, John. *The Politics of Poverty.* 2d ed. Indianapolis: Bobbs-Merrill Company, 1973.

Douglas, Carlyle C. "The Curse of Contract Buying." *Ebony* (June 1970): 43–52.

Downs, Anthony. *Neighborhoods and Urban Development.* Washington: Brookings Institution, 1981.

Ehrenhalt, Alan. *The Lost City.* New York: Basic Books, 1995.

Eisenberg, Pablo. "Foundations Should React to GOP Policies." *The Chronicle of Philanthropy* (Nov. 30, 1995): 37–38.

———. "Allusions of Blandeur." *Foundation News and Commentary* (July/Aug. 1996): 28–32.

Elwood, David. *Poor Support.* New York: Basic Books, 1988.

Esty, Benjamin C. "South Shore Bank: Is It the Model of Success for Community Development Banks?" In *Proceedings of a Conference on Bank Structure and Competition,* pp. 192–217. Chicago: Federal Reserve Bank of Chicago, May 1995.

Evanoff, Douglas, and Lewis Segal. "CRA and Fair Lending Regulations: Resulting Trends in Mortgage Lending." *Economic Perspectives* 20 (Nov./Dec. 1996): 19–46.

Fainstein, Susan S.; Norman I. Fainstein; Richard Child Hill; Dennis R. Judd; and Michael Peter Smith. *Restructuring the City.* Rev ed. White Plains, NY: Longman, 1986.

Flora, Cornelia Butler, and Jan L. Flora. "Entrepreneurial Social Infrastructure: A Necessary Ingredient." *Annals of American Association of Political and Social Sciences* 529 (Sep. 1993): 48–58.

Freeman, Richard. "Employment and Earnings of Disadvantaged Young Men in a Labor Shortage Economy," In *The Urban Underclass,* pp. 103–121.

Edited by Christopher Jencks and Paul E. Peterson. Washington: Brookings Institution, 1991.

Frisbie, Margery. *An Alley in Chicago.* Kansas City: Sheed & Ward, 1991.

Frumkin, Peter. "Left and Right in American Philanthropy." *Minerva* 22 (winter 1994): 469–475.

Fuchs, Ester R. *Mayors and Money.* Chicago: University of Chicago Press, 1992.

Fukuyama, Francis. *Trust.* New York: Free Press, 1995.

Gale, Dennis E. *Neighborhood Revitalization and the Postindustrial City.* Lexington, MA: D.C. Heath & Co., 1984.

Galster, George. *Homeowners and Neighborhood Reinvestment.* Durham: Duke University Press, 1987.

————. *Neighborhood Evaluations, Expectations, Mobility, and Housing Reinvestment: Measuring the Social Impacts of Community Development Corporations.* New York: Community Development Research Center, 1990.

Gardner, John W. *On Leadership.* New York: Free Press, 1990.

Garreau, Joel. *Edge City.* New York: Doubleday, 1991.

Garrow, David J. *Bearing the Cross.* New York: Vintage Books, 1986.

Gills, Doug. "Chicago Politics and Community Development: A Social Movement Perspective," in *Harold Washington and the Neighborhoods,* pp. 51–75. Edited by Pierre Clavel and Wim Wiewel. New Brunswick, NJ: Rutgers University Press, 1991.

Giloth, Robert. "National Trends Shatter Local Economy." *The Neighborhood Works* 10 (June 1987): 16.

————. "Community Building on Chicago's West Side: North Lawndale 1960–1997." In *Rebuilding Urban Neighborhoods.* Edited by W. Dennis Keating and Norman Krumholz. Newbury Park, CA: Sage Publications, forthcoming.

Gittell, Ross J. *Renewing Cities.* Princeton: Princeton University Press, 1992.

Gordon, Gregory, and Albert Swanson. *Chicago: Evolution of a Ghetto.* Chicago: Home Investment Fund, 1977.

Gordon, Wayne L. *Real Hope in Chicago.* Grand Rapids: Zondervan Publishing House, 1995.

Granovetter, Mark. "Economic Action and Social Structure: The Problem of Embeddedness." *American Journal of Sociology* 91 (1985): 481–510.

Greenstone, J. David, and Paul E. Peterson. *Race and Authority in Urban Politics.* New York: Russell Sage Foundation, 1973.

Grimshaw, William. *Bitter Fruit: Black Politics and the Chicago Machine, 1931–1991.* Chicago: University of Chicago Press, 1992.

Gurwitt, Rob. "The Projects Come Down." *Governing* (Aug. 1995): 16–25.

Halperin, Jennifer. "Here Comes the Neighborhood." *Illinois Issues* (Jan. 1996): 12–16.

Halpern, Robert. *Rebuilding the Inner City*. New York: Columbia University Press, 1995.

Henig, Jeffrey R. *Neighborhood Mobilization*. New Brunswick: Rutgers University Press, 1982.

Hirsch, Arnold R. *Making the Second Ghetto*. New York: Cambridge University Press, 1983.

Hofferth, Sandra; Johanne Boisjoly; and Greg J. Duncan. "Does Children's School Attainment Benefit from Parental Access to Social Capital?" Paper presented at annual meeting of the Society for Research in Child Development, Indianapolis, IN, April 1, 1995.

Hunter, Albert. *Symbolic Communities*. Chicago: University of Chicago Press, 1974.

Ihlanfeldt, Keith. "The Importance of the Central City to the Regional and National Economy." *Cityscape* 1 (June 1995): 125–150.

Immergluck, Daniel. *Focusing In: Indicators of Economic Change in Chicago's Neighborhoods*. Chicago: Woodstock Institute, 1994.

Jacob, Steven G., and Fern K. Willits. "Objective and Subjective Indicators of Community Evaluation: A Pennsylvania Assessment." *Social Indicators Research* 32 (June 1994): 161–177.

Jacobs, Jane. *The Death and Life of Great American Cities*. New York: Random House, 1961.

———. *The Economy of Cities*. New York: Random House, 1969.

Jackson, Kenneth T. *Crabgrass Frontier*. New York: Oxford University Press, 1995.

Jargowsky, Paul A. *Poverty and Place*. New York: Russell Sage Foundation, 1997.

Judd, Dennis R. *The Politics of American Cities* 3d ed. Glenview, IL: Scott, Foresman and Co., 1988.

Kasarda, John D. "Urban Industrial Transition and the Underclass." *Annals of the American Association of Political and Social Sciences* 501 (Jan. 1989): 26–47.

Katz, Michael. *The Undeserving Poor*. New York: Pantheon Books, 1989.

Kirshenman, Joleen, and Kathryn Neckerman. "'We'd Love to Hire Them, But . . .': The Meaning of Race for Employers." In *The Urban Underclass*, pp. 203–232. Edited by Christopher Jencks and Paul E. Peterson. Washington: Brookings Institution, 1991.

Klein, Joe. "In God They Trust," *The New Yorker* (June 16, 1997): 40–48.

Kleppner, Paul. *Chicago Divided: The Making of a Black Mayor*. DeKalb, IL: Northern Illinois University Press, 1985.

Kozol, Jonathan. *Savage Inequalities*. New York: Harper Perennial, 1991.

Kretzmann, John, and John McKnight. *Building Communities from the Inside Out*. Evanston: Northwestern University Center for Urban Affairs, 1993.

Ladd, Everett Carll. *The American Ideology*. Storrs, CT: Roper Center for Public Opinion Research, 1994.

Lee, Wilma. "Taxing Minority Communities." *The Neighborhood Works* 3 (Aug. 15, 1980): 1–5.

LeGates, Richard T., and Hartman, Chester. "The Anatomy of Displacement in the United States." In *Gentrification of the City*, pp. 178–200. Edited by Neil Smith and Peter Williams. Boston: Allen & Unwin, 1986.

Lemann, Nicholas. *The Promised Land*. New York: Vintage Books, 1991.

————. "The Myth of Community Development." *New York Times Magazine* (Jan. 9, 1994): 26–60.

Letts, Christine W.; William Ryan; and Allen Grossman. "Virtuous Capital: What Foundations Can Learn from Venture Capitalists." *Harvard Business Review* 75 (Mar.-Apr. 1997): 36–44.

Logan, John R. and Harvey L. Molotch. *Urban Fortunes*. Berkeley: University of California Press, 1987.

London, Rebecca and Deborah Puntenney. *A Profile of Chicago's Poverty and Related Conditions*. Evanston, IL: Northwestern University Center for Urban Affairs and Policy Research, 1993.

Loury, Linda Datcher, and Glenn Loury. "Churches and Development in Low-Income Communities." Paper presented at the National Community Development Policy Analysis Network conference, Washington, Nov. 1996.

Lukas, J. Anthony. *Common Ground*. New York: Vintage Books, 1985.

Lutton, Linda. "There Goes the Neighborhood." *The Neighborhood Works* (Jul./Aug. 1997): 16–23.

Marciniak, Ed. *Reviving an Inner City Community*. Chicago: Loyola Univ. Dept. of Political Science, 1977.

Marcuse, Peter. "Abandonment, Gentrification, and Displacement: The Linkages in New York City." In *Gentrification of the City*, pp. 151–177. Edited by Neil Smith and Peter Williams. Boston: Allen & Unwin, 1986.

Markusen, Ann. "National Policies Cause Local Steel Decline." *The Neighborhood Works* 9 (Mar. 1986), pp. 3–4.

Massey, Douglas S., and Nancy A. Denton. *American Apartheid*. Cambridge: Harvard University Press, 1993.

Maxwell, Ann, and Dan Immergluck. *Liquorlining: Liquor Store Concentration and Community Development in Lower-Income Cook County Neighborhoods*. Chicago: Woodstock Institute, 1997.

Medoff, Peter, and Holly Sklar. *Streets of Hope*. Boston: South End Press, 1994.

Meyerson, Martin, and Edward C. Banfield. *Politics, Planning, and the Public Interest.* New York: Free Press, 1955.

Mladenka, Kenneth R. "The Urban Bureaucracy and the Chicago Political Machine: Who Gets What and the Limits to Political Control." *American Political Science Review* 74 (Dec. 1980): 991–998.

Mollenkopf, John. *The Contested City.* Princeton: Princeton University Press, 1983.

Molotch, Harvey L. *Managed Integration.* Berkeley: University of California Press, 1972.

Moynihan, Daniel Patrick. *Maximum Feasible Misunderstanding.* New York: Free Press, 1969.

Nasar, Jack, and Julian, David A. "The Psychological Sense of Community in the Neighborhood." *Journal of the American Planning Association* 61 (Spring 1995): 178–184.

Nathan, Richard P. *The Methodology for Field Network Evaluation Studies.* Albany, NY: Nelson A. Rockefeller Institute of Government, 1982.

National Committee on Responsive Philanthropy. "The Chicago Community Trust and the Disenfranchised: Caring, Controlling, and Cautious." Washington: NCRP, 1995.

Neighborhood Capital Budget Group. *Moving Beyond the Basics: Building Chicago for the Next Century.* Chicago: NCBG, 1996.

O'Connor, Len. *Clout.* New York: Avon Books, 1975.

Olson, Mancur. *The Logic of Collective Action.* Cambridge: Harvard University Press, 1965.

Osterman, Paul. "Gains from Growth? The Impact of Full Employment on Poverty in Boston," In *The Urban Underclass,* pp. 122–134. Edited by Christopher Jencks and Paul E. Peterson. Washington: Brookings Institution, 1991.

Page, Benjamin I., and Shapiro, Robert Y. *The Rational Public.* Chicago: University of Chicago Press, 1992.

Paprocki, Thomas J. "Option for the Poor: Preference or Platitude?" *America* (Apr. 22, 1995): 11–14.

Parmenter, Trevor R. "Quality of Life as a Concept and Measurable Entity. *Social Indicators Research* 33 (Aug. 1994): 9–46.

Perkins, Walter M. "Chicago's Black-Owned Banks Face Community Challenges," *Chicago Reporter* (Mar. 1989): 3–5.

Peterson, Paul E. *School Politics Chicago Style.* Chicago: University of Chicago Press, 1976.

———. *City Limits.* Chicago: University of Chicago Press, 1981.

Phillips, Kevin. *The Politics of Rich and Poor.* New York: Random House, 1990.

Pogge, Jean; Josh Hoyt; and Elspeth Revere. *Partners in Need: A Four-Year Analysis of Residential Lending in Chicago and Its Suburbs.* Chicago: Woodstock Institute, 1986.

Polikoff, Alexander. *Housing the Poor: The Case for Heroism.* Cambridge, MA: Ballinger Publishing Company, 1978.

Porter, Michael E. "The Competitive Advantage of the Inner City." *Harvard Business Review* 75 (May-June 1995): 55–71.

Preston, Michael B. "The Resurgence of Black Voting in Chicago: 1955–1983." In *The Making of the Mayor: Chicago 1983,* pp. 39–51. Edited by Melvin G. Holli and Paul M. Green. Grand Rapids: William B. Eerdmans Publishing Co., 1984.

Putnam, Robert D. *Making Democracy Work.* Princeton: Princeton University Press, 1993.

———. "The Prosperous Community." *The American Prospect* (Spring 1993): 37–42.

———. "Bowling Alone: America's Declining Social Capital." *Journal of Democracy* 6 (Jan. 1995): 65–78.

Rakove, Milton. *Don't Make No Waves . . . Don't Back No Losers.* Bloomington: Indiana University Press, 1975.

Ralph, James R. Jr. *Northern Protest.* Cambridge: Harvard University Press, 1993.

Reardon, Patrick T. "Biggest and Best." *Chicago Tribune Magazine* (Mar. 9. 1997): 15–27.

Reed, Adolph Jr. "The Black Urban Regime: Structural Origins and Constraints." *Comparative Urban and Community Research* 1 (1988): 138–189.

Rich, Michael J. *Federal Policymaking and the Poor.* Princeton: Princeton University Press, 1993.

Rivlin, Gary. *Fire on the Prairie.* New York: Henry Holt & Co., 1992.

Robin, James. "Poverty in Relation to Macroeconomic Trends, Cycles, and Policies." In *Confronting Poverty,* pp. 147–167. Edited by Sheldon H. Danziger, Gary D. Sandefur, and Daniel H. Weinberg. Cambridge: Harvard University Press, 1994.

Robles, Jennifer. "Captive Grocery Market Pits Blacks against Arabs." *Chicago Reporter* (Nov. 1989): 1–11.

Rose, Don. "How the 1983 Election Was Won: Reform, Racism, and Rebellion." In *The Making of the Mayor: Chicago 1983,* pp. 101–124. Edited by Melvin G. Holli and Paul M. Green. Grand Rapids: William B. Eerdmans Publishing Co., 1984.

Rosenbaum, James, and Susan Popkin. "Employment and Earnings of Low-Income Blacks Who Move to Middle-Class Suburbs." In *The Urban Underclass,* pp. 342–356. Edited by Christopher Jencks and Paul E. Peterson. Washington: Brookings Institution, 1991.

Rossi, Peter H. "Community Social Indicators." In *The Human Meaning of Social Change,* pp. 87–126. Edited by Angus Campbell and Phillip E. Converse. New York: Russell Sage Foundation, 1972.

Royko, Mike. *Boss.* New York: Signet Books, 1971.

Rusk, David. *Cities without Suburbs.* 2d ed. Washington: Woodrow Wilson Center Press, 1995.

Schneider, Mark, and Paul Teske. "Toward a Theory of the Political Entrepreneur: Evidence from Local Government." *American Political Science Review* 86 (Sep. 1992): 737–747.

Schneider, Mark, Paul Teske, and Michael Mintrom. *Public Entrepreneurs.* Princeton: Princeton University Press, 1995.

Skocpol, Theda. *Social Policy in the United States.* Princeton: Princeton University Press, 1995.

Skogan, Wesley G. *Disorder and Decline.* New York: Free Press, 1990.

Skogan, Wesley G., and Susan M. Hartnett. *Community Policing, Chicago Style.* New York: Oxford University Press, 1997.

Skowroneck, Stephen. *The Politics Presidents Make.* Cambridge: Harvard University Press. 1995.

Snelling, Karen. "Low-Income Renters Suffer While City Hunts for Landlords." *Chicago Reporter* (June 1989): 4.

Sööt, Siim, and Ashish Sen. *Analysis of Employment Hubs and Work Trip Patterns in the Chicago Metropolitan Region.* Chicago: University of Illinois-Chicago Urban Transportation Center, Oct. 1994.

Squires, Gregory D. "Community Reinvestment: An Emerging Social Movement." In *From Redlining to Reinvestment,* pp. 1–27. Edited by Squires. Philadelphia: Temple University Press, 1992.

Squires, Gregory D.; Larry Bennett; et al. *Chicago: Race, Class, and the Response to Urban Decline.* Philadelphia: Temple University Press, 1987.

Stampley, James O. *Challenges with Changes: A Documentary of Englewood.* Chicago: By the Author, 1979.

Stone, Clarence N. *Economic Growth and Neighborhood Discontent.* Chapel Hill: University of North Carolina Press, 1976.

———. "Social Stratification, Nondecision-making, and the Study of Community Power." *American Politics Quarterly* 10 (July 1982): 275–302.

————. *Regime Politics*. Lawrence: University Press of Kansas, 1989.

Stone, Clarence N; Robert K. Whelan; and William J. Morin. *Urban Policy and Politics in a Bureaucratic Age*. 2d ed. Englewood Cliffs, NJ: Prentice-Hall, 1986.

Suchman, Diane. "Homan Square: Rebuilding the Inner City." *Urban Land* (Sep.1996): 41–44.

Sullivan, Mercer. *Studying the Effects of Community Development Corporations on Social Control*. New York: Community Development Research Center, 1990.

————. *More than Housing: How Community Development Corporations Go About Changing Lives and Neighborhoods*. New York: Community Development Research Center, 1993.

Sugrue, Thomas J. "Crabgrass-Roots Politics: Race, Rights, and the Reaction Against Liberalism in the Urban North, 1940–1964." *Journal of American History* 82 (Sep. 1995): 551–578.

Suttles, Gerald D. *The Social Order of the Slum*. Chicago: University of Chicago Press, 1968.

————. *The Man-Made City*. Chicago: University of Chicago Press, 1990.

Swanstrom, Todd. *The Crisis of Growth Politics*. Philadelphia: Temple University Press, 1985.

Taub, Richard P. *Community Capitalism*. Boston: Harvard Business School Press, 1988.

————. *Nuance and Meaning in Community Development: Finding Community and Development*. New York: Community Development Research Center, 1989.

Taub, Richard P.; D. Garth Taylor; and Jan D. Dunham. *Paths of Neighborhood Change*. Chicago: University of Chicago Press, 1984.

Taylor, Garth. *Trends for the Nineties: Changes in Quality of Life Indicators in the Chicago Region*. Chicago: Metro Chicago Information Center, 1996.

Teamworks. *Against All Odds*. Washington: National Congress for Community Economic Development, 1989.

Tholin, Kathryn. *Banking on Communities: Community Development Banks in the United States*. Chicago: Woodstock Institute, 1995.

Travis, Dempsey J. *An Autobiography of Black Chicago*. Chicago: Urban Research Institute, 1981.

United Way/Crusade of Mercy. *Social Service Directory 1977–78*. Chicago: United Way, 1978.

————. *Social Service Directory 1980*. Chicago: United Way, 1980.

————. *Human Services Directory 1981*. Chicago: United Way, 1981.

————. *Human Care Services Directory 1986*. Chicago: United Way, 1986.

————. *Human Care Services Directory 1989–90*. Chicago: United Way, 1990.

————. *Human Care Services Directory 1992*. Chicago: United Way, 1992.

————. *Human Care Services Directory of Metropolitan Chicago 1994–95*. Chicago: United Way, 1995.

Varady, David P. *Neighborhood Upgrading*. Albany: SUNY Press, 1986.

Vidal, Avis. *Rebuilding Communities: A National Study of Urban Community Development Corporations*. New York: Community Development Research Center, 1992.

"The Violence of Street Gangs." *The Compiler*. Illinois Criminal Justice Information Authority. (Fall 1996): 4–6.

Washington, Laura. "Cecil Butler: Tough Professional Dominates West Side Rebirth." *Chicago Reporter* (Nov. 1980): 4–5.

Welfeld, Irving. "The Courts and Desegregated Housing: The Meaning (if any) of the Gautreaux Case." *Public Interest* 45 (fall 1976): 123–134.

Wilson, William Julius. *The Truly Disadvantaged*. Chicago: University of Chicago Press, 1987.

————. *When Work Disappears*. New York: Alfred A. Knopf, 1996.

Woodstock Institute, *1993 Community Lending Fact Book*. Chicago: Woodstock, 1995.

————. *1994 Community Lending Fact Book*. Chicago: Woodstock, 1996.

————. *1995 Community Lending Fact Book*. Chicago: Woodstock, 1997.

Yin, Robert K. *Case Study Research: Design and Methods* 2d ed. Thousand Oaks, CA: Sage Publications, 1994.

INTERVIEWS

Englewood

Baldwin, Rev. Dave. St. Benedict's the African (East), Chicago. May 29, 1997.

Beard, Kahm. Boulevard Arts Center, Chicago. June 6, 1997.

Coleman, Shirley. 18th Ward Alderman, Chicago. May 20, 1997.

Daniel, Rick. Antioch Foundation, Chicago. May 7, 1997.

Davis, Cecil. Englewood CDC, Chicago. May 7, 1997.

De Ville, Leonard. Alpha Temple Missionary Baptist Church, Chicago, July 2, 1997.

Devine-Reed, Pat. Boulevard Arts Center, Chicago. June 6, 1997.

Drew, Audrey. Englewood Businessmen's Association, Chicago. May 7, 1997.

Farry, Rev. Jack. St. Thomas the Apostle, Chicago. June 12, 1997.

Holly, Diana. National Equity Fund, Chicago. Mar. 25, 1997.

Jones, John Paul. Neighborhood Capital Budget Group, Chicago. May 5, 1997.

Lance, Squire. North Washington Park Community Development Corporation, Chicago. Apr. 30, 1997.

Martin, Rev. Jim. St. Benedict the African West, Chicago. May 19, 1997.

Miller, Karl. Antioch Foundation, Chicago. May 7, 1997.

Pennick, Aurie. Leadership Council for Metropolitan Open Communities, Chicago. May 5, 1997.

Soens, Jim. Ravenswood Industrial Council, Chicago. Apr. 28, 1997.

Stampley, James. Chicago. May 19, 1997.

Wilson, Henry. Englewood Community Conservation Council, Chicago. May 23, 1997.

General

Arsenault, Del. Chicago Youth Centers, Chicago. June 2, 1997.

Bookman, Joel. Lawrence Avenue Development Corporation, Chicago. Feb. 7, 1997.

Brown, Chris. United Way/Crusade of Mercy, Chicago. Apr. 9 & 17, 1997.

Bush, Malcolm. Woodstock Institute. Sep. 16, 1997.

Capraro, Jim. Greater Southwest Development Corporation, Chicago. Feb. 8, 1997.

Dowell-Cerasoli, Pat, Mid-South Planning and Development Commission, Chicago. Feb. 12, 1997.

Egan, Msgr. John. DePaul University, Chicago. Apr. 16, 1997.

Faust, Kristin. LaSalle National Bank, Chicago. May 21, 1997.

Jacob, Ed. First National Bank of Chicago, Chicago. Apr. 9, 1997.

Jarrett, Valerie. The Habitat Company, Chicago, Dec. 11, 1997.

Jones, Bill. Fund for Community Redevelopment and Revitalization, Chicago. June 7, 1995 and May 19, 1997.

Kretzmann, Jody. Neighborhood Innovations Network, Evanston, IL. Sep. 8, 1997.

Lenz, Tom. Great Cities Institute, University of Illinois-Chicago, Chicago. June 9, 1997.

Levavi, Peter. Chicago Association of Realtors, Chicago. Feb. 2, 1997.

Lukehart, John. Leadership Council on Metropolitan Open Communities, Chicago. Apr. 23, 1997.

Markowski, Jack. Chicago Department of Housing, Chicago. Apr. 17, 1997.

Plasmeier, Susan. University of Chicago, Chicago. May 13, 1997.

Poethig, Erika. Civic Committee of the Commercial Club of Chicago, Chicago. Mar. 21, 1997.

Riley, Rebecca. John D. & Catherine T. MacArthur Foundation, Chicago. May 8, 1997.

Stein, Nikki. Polk Bros. Foundation, Chicago. Apr. 10, 1997.

Swenson, Jack. Chicago Department of Planning and Development, Chicago. Apr. 30, 1997.

White, Mary. Bank of America-Illinois, Chicago. Oct. 1, 1997.

Wilson, Doris. Fund for Community Redevelopment and Revitalization, Chicago. May 19, 1997.

Wright, Tim. Urban Fishing Community Development Corporation, Chicago. Apr. 14, 1997.

Wysocki, Ted. Chicago Association of Neighborhood Development Organizations, Chicago. June 13, 1997.

North Lawndale

Angelini, Mark. The Shaw Company, Chicago. May 8, 1997.

Barnett, Richard. Chicago. June 20, 1997.

Brown, Michael. Schwartz & Freeman, Chicago. Dec. 4, 1996.

Buik, Don. Roscoe Company, Chicago. May 29, 1997.

Buik, Jim. Roscoe Company, Chicago. May 29, 1997

Butler, Cecil. Pyramidwest Development Corporation, Chicago. May 15, 1997.

Chandler, Michael. 24th Ward Alderman, Chicago. June 11, 1997.

Daniels, George. George's Music Store, Chicago. May 15, 1997.

Daniels, Wilson. United Baptist Church, Chicago. June 18, 1997.

Darnieder, Greg. Steans Family Foundation, Chicago. Apr. 3, 1997.

Davis, Danny K. U.S. House of Representatives, Chicago. June 13, 1997.

Dean, Kristin. The Shaw Company, Chicago. July 23, 1997.

Doig, David. Chicago Department of Housing, Chicago. Apr. 22, 1997.

Flowers, Sam. HICA of North Lawndale, Chicago. May 1, 1997.

Glenn, Diane. Community Bank of Lawndale, Chicago. May 22, 1997.

Gordon, Wayne. Lawndale Community Church, Chicago. June 3, 1997.

Ivers, Rev. Mike. St. Agatha's Church, Chicago. Apr. 29 & May 9, 1997.

Kidd, Steeve. Agency Metropolitan Program Services, Chicago. May 6 & 15, 1997.

Kreinberg, Lew. Jewish Council on Urban Affairs, Chicago. Apr. 24, 1997.

Maynard, Rutherford. Bobby E. Wright Comprehensive Mental Health Center, Chicago. May 22, 1997.

Morgan, Abraham. R.E.G. Development Corporation, Chicago. May 22, 1997.

Rothstein, Ruth. Cook County Hospital, Chicago. May 29, 1997.

Scott, Michael. Prime Cable Co., Chicago. June 19, 1997.

Shaw, Charles. The Shaw Company, Chicago. Oct. 22, 1997.

Silverman, Dave. S.B. Freedman & Company, Chicago. Mar. 5, 1997.

Sorrels, Virginia. Chicago Department of Planning & Development, Chicago. May 13, 1997.

Steans, Heather. Steans Family Foundation, Chicago. Apr. 3, 1997.

Steele, Robert. Lawndale Business & Local Development Corporation, Chicago. Apr. 14, 1997.

Townsell, Richard. Lawndale Christian Development Corporation, Chicago. Apr. 29, 1997.

Newspapers

"Allstate Redlines 13 Areas: MAHA." *Chicago Tribune,* Feb. 27, 1978. Sec. 1, p. 1.

"Ambush in North Lawndale." *Crains Chicago Business,* Mar. 9, 1987. p. 10.

"Bank Finds Returns Justify Risk." *Chicago Sun-Times,* Feb. 1, 1979. p. 88.

"Blacks' Savings Piped into White Suburbs." *Chicago Tribune,* June 24, 1980. Sec. 1, p. 1.

"Cash Crunch Shuts Englewood Hospital." *Chicago Tribune,* Feb. 12, 1988. Sec. 2, p. 3.

"Chicago Banks Seek, Find Profits in the Inner City." *American Banker* (July 23, 1997): 1.

"City's Solution for Dying S. Side Mall: Auto Traffic." *Crains Chicago Business* (Jul. 27, 1987), p. 1.

"Developer Revives Hope for N. Lawndale Mall." *Chicago Tribune,* Aug. 6, 1987. Sec. 3, p. 1.

"Did Dream Have to Die?" *Chicago Tribune,* Nov. 15, 1987. Sec.7, p. 1.

"Do VA Loan Policies Contribute to Panic Peddling, White Flight, and Resegregation?" *Chicago Reader,* Apr. 4, 1986. pp. 3, 25.

"Englewood Hospital Spends on Growth as Rx for Its Area." *Crains Chicago Business,* Sep. 19, 1983. p. 44.

"Englewood Longs for the Safe Old Days." *Chicago Tribune,* Dec. 29, 1991. Sec. 2C, p.1.

"EZ Does It." *Chicago Reader,* Mar. 3, 1995. Sec 1, p. 1.

"Healing a Community: Health Care Just the Start for Mt. Sinai." *Chicago Tribune,* Jul. 28, 1992. Sec. 2C, p. 1.

"Hope for the Vacant Land of Lawndale." *Chicago Tribune,* June 2, 1977. Sec. 7, p. 1.

"Hot Air Won't Fill Void in Lawndale." *Chicago Tribune,* Mar. 2, 1988. Sec. 3, p. 3.

"'It Is the Only Ticket Out of Here.'" *Chicago Tribune,* June 9, 1997. Sec 1, p. 21.

"Koreans Sell, Blacks Buy: A Clash of Cultures at the 63rd Street Mall." *Chicago Reader,* Feb. 13, 1987. p. 3.

"Lawndale Fights to Halt Industry's Flight." *Chicago Tribune,* May 9, 1972. Sec. 1, p. 2.

"Lawndale Tries to Shrug Off Sears' Warehouse Defection." *Crains Chicago Business,* Mar. 9, 1987. p. 2.

"Lookin' Up Down South." *Chicago Tribune,* Apr. 13, 1996. Sec. 4, pp. 1–4.

"Midwest Briefs." *Chicago Tribune,* May 5, 1997. Sec. 4, p. 1.

"Movie Theater Plan, Park Rekindle Hope in Lawndale." *Chicago Tribune,* Apr. 16, 1997. Sec. 2, p. 1.

"Moving Out." *Chicago Tribune,* Nov. 28 - Dec. 7, 1993. Sec. 1, p. 1.

"The Night Chicago Burned." *Chicago Reader,* Aug. 26, 1988. Sec. 1.

"On West Side, It's Ald. Henry's Way or No Way." *Chicago Tribune,* Sep. 2, 1988. Sec. 1, p. 1.

"Once a Gangbanger." *Chicago Reader,* June 10, 1994. Sec. 1, pp. 1, 16–24.

"A Piece of the Big-Screen Pie." *Chicago Tribune,* July 5, 1996. Sec. 1, p. 1.

"Program Helps Revive Lawndale." *Chicago Sun-Times,* Feb. 28, 1997. p. S H 5.

"Pros Outweigh Cons in N. Lawndale." *Chicago Tribune,* Aug. 3, 1987. Sec. 2, p. 3.

"7–Days-a-Week Minister Marks 40 Years of Care." *Chicago Tribune,* Apr. 18, 1997. Sec. 2, p.1.

"Sears Jolts North Lawndale." *Chicago Tribune,* Mar. 3, 1987. Sec. 3, p. 1.

"Sellers' Farewell Gift?" *Chicago Sun-Times,* Aug. 12, 1976. p. 54.

"Shootings Feed Englewood Despair." *Chicago Tribune,* June 3, 1990. Sec. 2C, p. 1.

"South Side Renewal Plan Told." *Chicago Tribune,* Aug. 21, 1980. Sec. 1, p. 1.

"Speed Wash: A West-Side Business Story." *Chicago Reader,* June 11, 1993. Sec. 1, pp. 1, 12–23.

"The Squabble at Homan Square." *Chicago Reader,* Jan. 29, 1993. Sec. 1, p. 3.

"Trading Places." *Chicago Sun-Times,* Feb. 7, 9, & 10, 1997.

"U.S. Targets Rent Skimming." *Chicago Tribune,* Feb. 18, 1997. Sec. 2, p. 1.

"Ultimate School Reform: Start Over." *Chicago Tribune,* June 10, 1997. Sec. 1, p. 1.

"Unlikely Partners Join to Upgrade Englewood." *Chicago Tribune,* Sep. 7, 1980. Sec. N14, p. 1.

"West Side Riot Area Still Looking for Its Phoenix Among the Ashes." *Chicago Tribune,* Apr. 18, 1974. Sec. N4A, p. 1.

PUBLIC DOCUMENTS

Chicago Department of Planning. *Chicago Statistical Abstract.* 1983.

Chicago Department of Public Health.*Community Area Health Inventory.* Vol. 1. 1984.

———. *Community Area Health Inventory, 1992–1994.* Vol.1. 1996.

Chicago Department of Urban Renewal. "Lawndale: Background for Planning." 1964.

———. *Lawndale Conservation Plan.* March 1968.

Chicago Department of Economic Development. "Tax Increment Redevelopment Area (TIF): Englewood Mall Area TIF Redevelopment Plan and Project." Aug. 1989.

———. "TIF Designation Report: Englewood Mall Area." Aug. 1989.

Lawndale Business and Local Development Corporation. *Roosevelt/Cicero Model Industrial Corridor Strategic Plan.* Chicago, 1996.

U.S. Congress. House. *A Review of Community Development Corporations. Hearing before a Subcommittee on Human Relations.* 102d Cong, 2d sess, Sep. 16, 1992.

U.S. Congress. Senate. *The Federal Role in Urban Affairs. Hearings before the Subcommittee on Executive Reorganization.* 89th Cong, 2d sess, Aug. 15–16, 1966.

U.S. Department of Commerce, Bureau of the Census. 1970 Census of Population and Housing. Washington: Government Printing Office, 1972.

———. 1980 Census of Population and Housing. Washington: Government Printing Office, 1982.

———. 1990 Census of Population and Housing. Washington: Government Printing Office, 1992.

U.S. Department of Housing and Urban Development. *Building Public-Private Partnerships to Develop Affordable Housing.* Edited by Fredric C. Cooper. Washington: HUD, 1996.

———. *U.S. Department of Housing and Urban Development.* "North Lawndale Homeownership Zone Application." 1996.

———. U.S. Department of Housing and Urban Development. *The State of the Cities.* Washington: HUD. 1997.

REPORTS/OTHER DOCUMENTS

Brown, Prue; Lisa Marie Pickens; and William Mollard. "The Steans Family Foundation: Work to Date." Chicago: Chapin Hall Center for Children, 1996.

————. "The Steans Family Foundation: History of North Lawndale." Chicago: Chapin Hall Center for Children, 1996.

Carlson, Virginia, and Nikolas Theodore. "Labor Market Profile of Westside Communities." Chicago: Chicago Urban League, 1995.

Conquergood, Dwight; Paul Friesema; Al Hunter; et al. "Changing Relations: Newcomers and Established Residents in the Albany Park Area of Chicago." Interim Report. Evanston, IL: Northwestern University Center for Urban Affairs, 1989.

Englewood Hospital Board Minutes, May 1977–Feb. 1988. Chicago Historical Society, Chicago, IL.

Foster-Bey, John. "Removing the Barriers: An Approach to Increasing Economic Opportunity and Reducing Poverty." Paper prepared for the John D. and Catherine T. MacArthur Foundation, Chicago, 1992.

Goodman Williams Group. "Residential Market Analysis: Mid-South Area." Report prepared for the Akhenaton/Omnibus Prospective Project, Chicago, January 1995.

Harrison, Bennett. "Building Bridges: Community Development Corporations and the World of Employment Training." Report prepared for the Ford Foundation, New York, Sep. 1994.

H.I.C.A. of North Lawndale. "West Side Redevelopment Plan." Report prepared for City of Chicago, 1992.

Lovik, Schneider, & Associates. "Eligibility Study of a Proposed Redevelopment Project Area for Tax Increment Financing in the Roosevelt-Homan Commercial/Residential Study Area." Report prepared for City of Chicago, July 1990.

————. "Redevelopment Plan (for Roosevelt-Homan Commercial/Residential Redevelopment Area Tax Increment Finance Program)." Report prepared for City of Chicago, July 1990.

Mallette, Daniel. Unpublished papers, 1965–1966. Chicago Historical Society. Chicago, IL.

Ollarvia, Edward J. "The Sustainable Economic Development of the Village." Report prepared for the New Englewood Village Governance Corporation, Chicago, May 1997.

Partnerships for Reinvestment. Chicago: National Training and Information Center, 1990.

Report of the National Advisory Committee on Civil Disorders. By Otto Kerner, Chairman. New York: Bantam Books, 1968.

Schubert, Michael F. "A Housing Strategy for North Lawndale: Achieving the Dual Vision of Neighborhood and Family Stability." Report prepared for the John D. & Catherine T. MacArthur Foundation, Sep. 21, 1993.

———. "Community Development and Social Capital." Paper prepared for the Community Development Work Group, Chicago, 1996.

Trkla, Pettigrew, Allen, & Payne. "Focus Hope: A Revitalization Strategy for the Lawndale Christian Development Corporation's 'Target Area.'" Report prepared for Lawndale Christian Development Corporation (Chicago), Jan. 1993.

———. "Summary of Businesses/Employers Survey—North Lawndale Strategic Alliance." Preliminary report prepared for Steans Family Foundation, Chicago, Oct. 1995.

Woodstock Institute. "CRA Boosts Multifamily Housing Loans in Chicago." Reinvestment Alert #8. May 1995.

———. "Expanding the American Dream: Home Lending Surges in Modest-Income Neighborhoods." Reinvestment Alert #9. May 1996.

———. "Currency Exchanges Add to Poverty Surcharge for Low-Income Residents." Reinvestment Alert #10. Chicago, March 1997.

Index